COMPUTER-AIDED
ENGINEERING DESIGN
GRAPHICS

SECOND EDITION

COMPUTER-AIDED ENGINEERING DESIGN

GRAPHICS

SECOND EDITION

WALTER E. RODRÍGUEZ
B.S. Engrg., B.A. Design, M. Arch., Ph.D. Engrg., P.E.
Georgia Institute of Technology

PRELIMINARY EDITION

McGraw-Hill Book Company
New York   St. Louis   San Francisco   Auckland   Bogotá   Caracas
Colorado Springs   Hamburg   Lisbon   London   Madrid   Mexico
Milan   Montreal   New Delhi   Oklahoma City   Panama   Paris
San Juan   São Paulo   Singapore   Sydney   Tokyo   Toronto

COMPUTER-AIDED ENGINEERING DESIGN GRAPHICS

1234567890 WHT WHT 89321098

ISBN: 0-07-053396-2

Cataloging Publication Data
Main entry under title:

Computer-aided engineering design graphics.

1. engineering graphics 2. computer graphics 3. CADD
3. creative design 4. sketching

Includes index.

ISBN: 0-07-053396-2

This book was processed by the author on an IBM PC XT using WordPerfect, AutoCAD, CADKEY, LOTUS 123, TK Solver, and ICEM software. It was set in Times Roman and printed on a Hewlett-Packard LaserJet Printer II with 2.5 megabytes of RAM and HP Soft Fonts.

The editors were B.J. Clark and John M. Morriss;
the cover was based on an illustration courtesy of GRAFTEX, Inc.;
the production was supervised by Terry Pace.

Whitlock Press was printer and binder.

CONTENTS

(Courtesy of AUTODESK, Inc.)

PREFACE

Purpose

Computer-Aided Engineering Design Graphics has been designed to support introductory courses in visual communication, engineering design and computer graphics.

Background

This CAED/Graphics book was born out of three years of unrelenting efforts to integrate traditional and computer graphics. The concepts introduced here have been tested by thousands of students who register for the "Introduction to Visual Communication and Engineering Design" (EGR 1170) course at Georgia Tech.

Topics

The book responds to the new trends in engineering graphics and descriptive geometry. It combines, in one text, traditional and modern graphics topics, namely: graphical problem solving and design, perceptually-based and rule-based visualization, spatial analysis and descriptive geometry, multiview orthographic projection, axonometric and oblique projections, computer graphics tools, operating systems, computer-aided geometric construction and solid modeling, computer-aided dimensioning, geometric tolerancing and sectioning.

At the beginning, you will be exposed to fundamental visual communication techniques like creative sketching and projection theory. Then, you will learn to present design ideas and solve graphical design problems using computer graphics tools. In this context, you will learn the **generic** structure of CADD system menus and commands as well as some **specific** geometric construction techniques.

Objectives

The objective is to enhance your constructive imagination and visualization skills. And to present the resources and techniques available for the effective communication of engineering design ideas and research findings. Upon successful completion of this book you should:

*   understand how designers are able to design devices, systems and processes using computer graphics systems.

*   discern the design information required by those who will be manufacturing devices, constructing buildings or supervising processes.

*   utilize graphics standards and fundamentals to represent design ideas and solve technical problems.

*   utilize the computer graphics tools available, e.g., CADD, W.P., A.I., Animation, in the production of design documents.

Approach

The book emphasis is on learning the graphics language of computers without the complicated algebraic and algorithmic structure of computer programming. Although, some fundamental computer topics like graphics programming languages, operating systems, Graphical Kernel System (GKS) and device-independence graphics are introduced, no previous computer experience or programming background is required.

Software

The book supports several of the most popular microcomputer graphics programs (e.g., AutoSketch, AutoCAD and CADKEY) available in the market. The mini and mainframe CADD systems are represented by CDC ICEM. Although, this book contains examples using these software packages, the author recognizes the need for supplementary material that contains log-in procedures and command description for the local computer environment. Please contact the publisher, author or manufacturer for the availability of these materials.

Help!

<u>Be aware that this book is in the process of development</u>. The aim of this edition is to provide interim lecture notes and, also, to request comments from readers like you. This process will assist me in designing, writing, editing, and publishing a book that would better respond to your needs and requirements. Please help by sending me your needs, suggestions and critiques. Your contributions will be fully acknowledged. **Walter E. Rodriguez**, Georgia Tech, Atlanta, Georgia 30332-0355

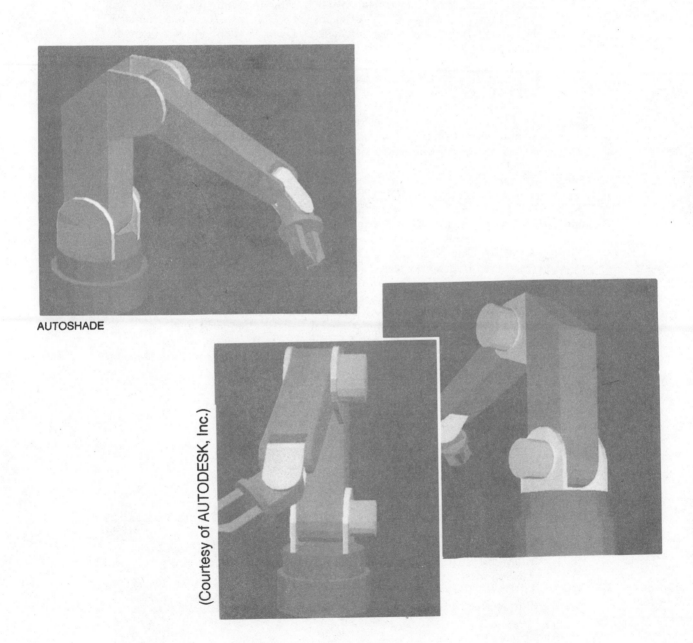

AUTOSHADE

(Courtesy of AUTODESK, Inc.)

Acknowledgements

This book is dedicated to my parents, wife and children in acknowledgement of their love, patience and support.

I am indebted to numerous students who have helped me in writing this book. Special thanks to S. Rowe, S. McWhorter, T. Courtney, S. Otero, B. Wong Shui, W. McCullum, J. Hibbard, C. Merizalde, E. Lynch, D. Dean, W. Petit and B. Murray for their contributions.

My deep appreciation to my colleagues for their support, especially to Drs. Paul Wright, Leland Riggs, Vera Anand and Ronald Barr.

Extended thanks to several anonymous reviewers utilized by McGraw-Hill. This book might have never been written without the energetic leadership of B.J. Clark, Executive Editor of Engineering and Jim Willis, Sales Representative.

Several software developers provided the latest software and gave me permission to reproduce some of the material utilized in this book. Special thanks to the people at: AUTODESK Inc., Micro Control Systems, Inc. and Control Data Corporation. In addition, I should recognize the following products and manufacturers:

* AutoCAD, AutoSketch, AUTOSHADE, CAD/CAMERA and AUTOLISP (registered trademarks of Autodesk, Inc.)
* BASIC (registered trademark of the Trustees of Dartmouth College)
* CADKEY and Solids Synthesis (trademarks of Micro Control Systems, Inc.)
* CADAM and MICROCADAM (trademarks of CADAM Inc.)
* CALMA (trademark of Calma/General Electric Company)
* CATIA (trademark of Dassault Systems)
* COMPUTERVISION (trademark of COMPUTERVISION Corporation)
* dBASE (registered trademark of Ashton-Tate, Inc.)
* Hayes Smartcom II (registered trademark of Hayes Microcomputer Products, Inc.)
* HP (trademark of Hewlett Packard)
* IBM and PC-DOS (registered trademarks of the International Business Machines Corporation)
* ICEM DDN, ICEM Solid Modeler, PLATO, CYBER and NOS VE (trademarks of Control Data Corporation)
* INTERGRAPH (trademark of Intergraph Corporation)
* Lotus 1-2-3 (registered trademark of Lotus Corporation)
* MathSolve, Mechanical Advantage and Sketchpad (trademarks of COGNITION, Inc.)
* MS/DOS (trademark of Microsoft Corporation, Inc.)
* ROMULUS (trademark of Evans and Sutherland Computer Corp.)
* TK!Solver (trademark of Software Arts Products, Inc.)
* UNIX (trademark of AT&T Bell Laboratories)
* Wordperfect (trademark of Wordperfect Corporation)

CHAPTER 1

INTEGRATING CADD AND TRAD/ THE DESIGN PROCESS

Background

The engineering graphics field is currently being revolutionized by the rapid development of electronic computer graphics devices (Fig. 1.1) and Computer-Aided Design Drafting (**CADD**) software tools. University engineering programs are responding by incorporating innovative graphical techniques into their curriculum, while keeping the essential traditional (**TRAD**) engineering graphics concepts. This *Computer-Aided Engineering Design Graphics* book is the author's second attempt to integrate CADD and TRAD. The first attempt was the book entitled *Interactive Engineering Graphics*.

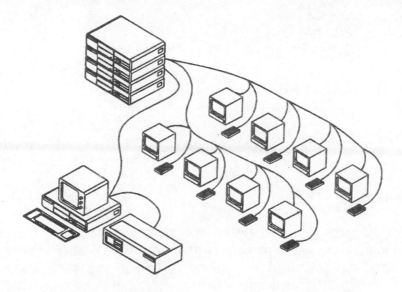

FIG. 1.1 New computer graphics devices

Transformation

Transformation of visual communication from a quasi-empirical field, where certain knowledge-based rules have evolved, into a challenging scientific / artistic field seems unavoidable. We should preserve the valuable aspects of TRAD and at the same time incorporate new technological and graphical modeling tools like CADD, solid modeling,

1

animation and intelligent graphics.

It is vital to ensure that the new tidal wave does not erode centuries of design graphics developments by pioneers like: Gudea (plans), Vitruvius (geometric construction), Gutenberg (printing), Alberti (views), da Vinci (creative design/sketching, see Fig.1.2), Monge (descriptive geometry), and Sutherland (computer graphics). Nor should it dilute the modern engineering graphics concepts presented by contemporary writers and educators. However, the task of preserving the old while merging it with the new is immense.

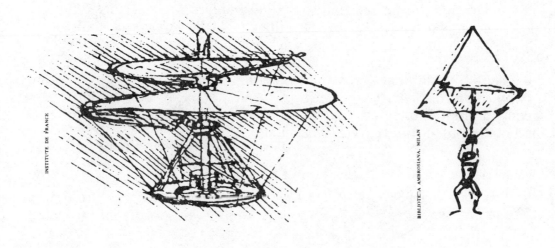

FIG. 1.2 Leonardo da Vinci sketches of "helicopter" and "parachute."

Propositions

In order to provide a direction for new generations of graphics professionals, some basic principles are required. Without them, both present and new generations will be forced to use their instinct or intuition. There is a need not only to preserve the essential aspects of traditional graphics, but also to incorporate the new graphical techniques. Based on this need, four propositions are sketched here to foster a dialogue and provide for the articulation of ideas.

The **axiomatic technique** assists in making resolutions in synthesis and in analyzing the existing engineering graphics approaches. **Axioms** have been defined as un-demonstrated postulates and propositions. They are concerned with an undefined set of relationships but are generally acknowledged to be true. **Propositions** are statements to be offered for discussion. This book is based on the following

2

propositions:

Proposition 1: Maintain the essential aspects of TRAD, namely: spatial visualization, sketching, scaling, projection theory, spatial analysis, descriptive geometry theory, sectioning, dimensioning and geometric tolerancing.

Proposition 2: Incorporate the use of CADD (i.e, and other tools like: AI, solid modeling and animation), without loosing perspective and understanding of the basic graphic principles.

Proposition 3: Minimize the need to learn cumbersome computer programming languages, at the engineering graphics introductory level.

Proposition 4: Maximize design graphics problem solving educational opportunities (i.e., assign open-ended design projects that allow the student to be creative).

These propositions state that we should preserve the traditional aspects essential to the understanding of graphical communications while taking advantage of the new technological tools available. However, curriculum designs that satisfy these axioms are not easily attainable.

One problem is the limited time available to teach and learn all these concepts in the present engineering curriculum. The second problem is the shortage of trained professionals in the area. The constraints are governed by the demands of an overcrowded curriculum, the refusal to expand the engineering program and the scarcity of advanced and graduate level programs in engineering graphics. One alternative solution to the first problem consists of consolidating the new with the old using an integrated graphical approach.

Integrated Graphics

The proposed integrated graphics approach (Figure 1.3) for visual communication is not new. It draws on existing concepts and ideas; however, it has the objective of providing some articulation and perspective to the new variations of the visual communication field.

CADD + TRAD = INTEGRATED APPROACH

FIG. 1.3 Integrated Approach

In the integrated approach, the traditional aspects of engineering design and graphics language are covered in conjunction with interactive graphics and CADD applications. For example, some aspects of descriptive geometry theory (points, lines and planes) are discussed concurrently with geometric entity construction procedures. **ANSI** (American National Standards Institute) standards, dimensioning and tolerancing are presented in conjunction with the CADD software commands and menu operations. Solid Modeling and hidden line removal are taught in conjunction with axonometrics. Traditional descriptive geometry and intersection problems are solved using high-level CADD programming. Both auxiliary-view (reference plane) and computerized rotation (solid modeling) methods are utilized to solve spatial analysis problems.

In this approach, the student utilizes the graphics language to analyze, communicate and reproduce information about design projects using the most productive technological tools available. Traditional aspects are integrated with more recent developments like: Interactive Computer Graphics, Computer Document Composition and electronic transmittal of information.

As mentioned earlier, this book attempts to integrate CADD and TRAD, however much work still remains to be done.

Overview

Computer-Aided Engineering Design Graphics presents state-of-the-art techniques to help you conceptualize, visualize and communicate your design ideas and inventions. The book support three visual communication phases:

Phase I - Visual Perception and Projection Theory

Phase II - CADD and Solid Modeling

Phase III - Detailed Design Documentation and Specification

The **Visual Perception and Projection Theory** phase consists of a series of sketching and visualization exercises to develop your spatial-hemisphere brain functions. You will solve several spatial design problems designed to stimulate your 3-D creative thinking process, enhance your constructive imagination and develop your ability for detailed observation.

Ultimately, the objective of this phase is to show you how to generate pictorial drawings of simple devices.

4

Then, projection theory topics are presented using the "glass box" approach and expanded to cover descriptive geometry and spatial analysis. You will use these concepts to solve visualization, missing-views and missing-lines exercises. You will utilize both logical reasoning (a function of the symbolic-hemisphere) and intuition (a function of the spatial-hemisphere) to solve the given problems. Within this part we will learn spatial analysis and descriptive geometry techniques to determine the true length, angles and shapes of non-orthogonal object components (i.e., oblique planes and lines).

The **CADD and Solid Modeling Software** phase utilizes a graphics packages (e.g., AutoCAD, AutoShade, CADKEY, Solid Synthesis, ICEM) to construct isometric and orthographic projections. One current improvement over the standard CADD approach, presented in the book, is the use of Solid Modeling/Drafting (SM/D) interface arrangements to construct the geometric configuration of the object, device or system created; then, SM files are transferred to a compatible CADD package.

The **Detailed Design Documentation and Specification** phase will demand both your creativity (a function of the spatial-hemisphere) and analytical skills (a function of the symbolic-hemisphere). In this stage you will be required to conceive alternate solutions to several open-ended design projects. Then, we will study examples of detailed-drawings and specifications for production, manufacturing and construction.

Production detail-drawings and working-drawings are completed by using the standard CADD package operations (e.g., hidden-line removal, blanking, auto-dimensioning, tolerancing and attribute management).

Lets get started with the reason for communicating ideas: DESIGN.

Creative Design

Imagine that you have been assigned to design a new spill proof drink holder for automobiles, similar to the one illustrated in Figure 1.4 (Drw. File: CUP HOLDER). Where do you start? In which way do you depict, verbalize or express your thoughts? If the response is to start by defining the problem, then researching similar devices, determining possible improvements and sketching a few ideas... you are correct! Or at least heading in the right direction.

However, engineers usually encounter more intricate problems. No matter how complicated problems may be, engineers follow an approach very similar to the intuitive procedure described above.

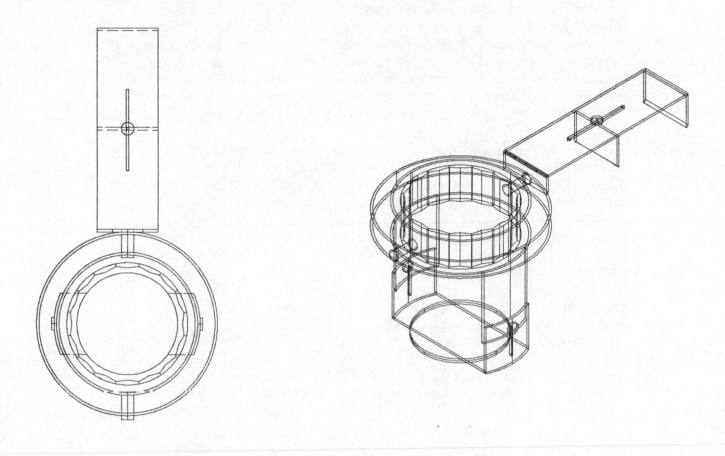

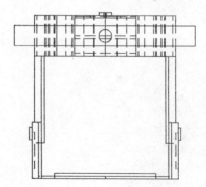
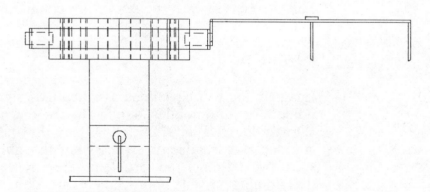

FIG. 1.4 Three-dimensional wire-mesh view of a drink holder; top, front and right side views of the device.

6

Engineers apply scientific and practical knowledge to analyze and develop efficient ways of utilizing resources. The usual byproduct of this ingenious exercise is the design of a device, system or process. Since recorded history engineers, scientists and designers have attempted to approach problems in a methodical fashion. One of such procedures is the design process. The **design process** is basically a methodological avenue to reach a solution to a design problem. It is a way of attaining and evaluating a certain number of alternative solutions to a problem which will finally result in a decision. The procedure is the designer's equivalent of the scientific method. Engineers utilize some form of design process while attempting to respond to society's needs and wants.

The design process is iterative nature. At the risk of appearing contradictory, the design process rarely follows a predetermined set of steps. Nevertheless, it is advantageous to suggest a given set of steps or phases as follows:

1. Selection and/or identification of a need or want.

2. Definition of the problem.

3. Research and analysis of the problem.

4. Proposals or alternative solutions to the problem.

5. Quantitative and qualitative evaluation of the proposed alternatives.

6. Selection, improvement and engineering analysis of the "best" alternative.

7. Graphical modeling (e.g., finite element modeling, solid modeling, working drawings, etc.).

8. Manufacturing, construction or processing.

9. Feedback (i.e., continuous improvement or discard and start all over again).

A simplified way to look at the design process is to think in terms of a broader classification consisting of:

* **NEED**
* **RESEARCH**
* **ALTERNATIVES**
* **MODELING**
* **IMPLEMENTATION**

Figure 1.5 (Display File: HOLDER MODEL), shows a computer generated solid model of the finished car cup holder device. This simple device was designed and modeled by a freshman engineering graphics student. The given problem was to improve existing drink car holders for people who drive erratically or are just clumsy. It was an academic exercise to allow the free-wheeling of ideas without a concern for cost.

FIG. 1.5 Solid model of the proposed car cup holder device.

Preliminary research indicated that the device should be lightweight. It might use some sort of axles, springs or hinges. Several desirable objectives are that it should: fit a wide range of cups and glasses, be capable of swinging without spilling the liquid contents and be small enough to stay out of the way of the driver and be easy to attach. Study the previous illustrations and think of ways to improve this device by applying the design process.

In order to manufacture a similar drink holder device, it is necessary to provide additional drawings and specifications. Design projects similar to this one must be communicated to those who must understand and approve them. Verbal and visual languages provide the engineer with the necessary tools for the effective communication of design ideas. Therefore, engineers are required to become knowledgeable of the basic communication techniques.

Working drawings and construction plans are drafted utilizing standard graphical symbols that provide information to those who must build the engineered devices and systems. An example of the types of detail drawings produced using an interactive graphic system is illustrated in Figure 1.6 (Display File: VALVE ASSEMBLY).

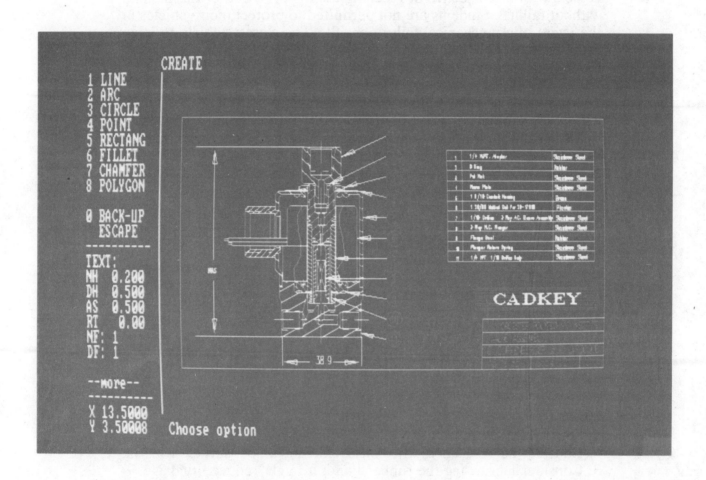

FIG. 1.6 Valve Assembly Drawing. (Courtesy of Micro Control Systems)

Design Term Projects

The following problems might be assigned by your instructor. At this stage your are only requested to research the problem and verbally describe possible alternative solutions. No standard engineering graphics representation is required, at this point, since we haven't cover those concepts yet.

9

PROJECT 1. Rubber-Band Propelled Vehicle Project

Description: Design a small vehicle powered by rubber bands. No high-tech, electromechanical or nuclear means are allowed. The vehicle will be raced on the table that measures 15 feet long. The vehicles will compete against each other. They will be set on one edge of the table. A representative from the design group will release the vehicle with the objective of reaching the opposite end of the table ... without falling! Students are not permitted to protect their vehicles in the event of a mechanical failure or fall. The closest vehicle to edge is the winner. The final presentation will consists of a prototype racing model, written, oral report and working drawings.

Team: This is a team project, consisting of 3 to 5 students per team. The team will consist of students majoring in dissimilar engineering fields. If the students so desire they can each build one vehicle, race it against each other, and select the winner as their representative prototype. Only one entry per group will be allowed on the race date.

Specifications:

Width: Overall width shall not exceed 180 mm.
Length: Overall length shall not exceed 350 mm.
Weight: Weight shall not exceed 285 grams.
Material: Any safe and legal material.
Other: The entire vehicle needs to reach the finish line.
(Equivalents: 1mm = .039 in., 1 gram = 0.035 ounce)

Arbitrator: Conflicts or unpredicted circumstances will be decided by an independent arbitrator, namely: your professor.

Hints:
1. Start fresh! Perform a troubleshooting session.
2. Consider air resistance, wheelbase, axle and wheel surface friction.
3. Consider lubricating the rubber band, it might reduce breakage.
4. Test drive your vehicle well in advance.
5. Consider protection against damage incurred during a possible failure (i.e., fell off the edge of the table).

Important Milestones:
* Begin Project:
* Test Race Time:
* Final Group Presentation (oral & written report) :
* Working Drawings Due Date:

PROJECT 2: Clipboard Design

Students frequently use clipboards to write on while standing, in bed or in the car. There is always the need for direct lighting on the board. The traditional lamps are not easily adjustable to this task. The light is often obscured by the projected shade of an obstacle. Design a clipboard lighting device that is portable and lightweight. It should provide bright and even illumination. Cost should be under $15.

PROJECT 3: Sailboat Rack Design

Due to the lack of space the local Sailing Club needs to have a boat rack that will store two Force-5 sailboats with mast down over a fleet of Coronado-15's. The coronado's are dry dock on trailers, they must be loaded with their mast up standing 25 feet on the air. The rack should be designed so that a Force-5 can be loaded and unloaded between two C-15's. A small (or handicap) person should be able to load and unload the boats with a minimum of effort.

PROJECT 4: Overhead Projector Anti-Glare Shield

Overhead projectors are useful lecturing tools. They are widely used in classrooms to illustrate figures and diagrams conveniently prepared beforehand. This enables the speaker to save time and effort during the conduction of the class or lecture. In spite of all its convenience while the overhead projector is in use, it produces an intense light reflection. This light reflection is so intense that it can irritate the eyes of the person using it. Also, it produces a glare which forces the user to position himself or herself in uncomfortable positions to avoid the glare. A secondary problem is created when the user wants to write on the transparencies while lecturing. The overhead projector stage glass is very hot causing discomfort to the lecturer. Design an overhead projector anti-glare device that will solve this problem. The device should be easy to attach and detach, materials should not cost more that $10. The device should allow the user to be in a comfortable position.

PROJECT 5: Input Device for Computer Graphics

Description: Design a simple, inexpensive device for input in computer graphics. In computer graphics, the user communicates with the computer by responding to a series of prompts. It is convenient to have a peripheral device such as a pointer or mouse to indicate locations on a drawings and select from a menu. Existing devices are to inaccurate, slow and clumsy to do computer sketching. Software packages have to make provisions by requiring you to activate snap and grid options within the system. Devices such as joystick, which operate with two potentiometers in reference to movement of a rod in two dimensions are commercially available are fine to play video games but not for sketching ideas.

Example of a Student Project

Design a mechanical pencil/eraser. The pencil should provide a way to use the lead and eraser refills available in the market.

PROBLEM IDENTIFICATION

1. Project Title:

   Erase 'n' Write Pencil

2. Problem Statement:

   With regular mechanical pencils, the eraser provided is not sufficient for its purpose. Instead, additional erasers must be purchased. In order to eliminate the need to carry two instruments for writing purposes, our design project will incorporate the two into one instrument, thus making it cheaper and convenient.

3. Requirements and Limitations:

   A. Affordable price range ($4 - $8)
   B. Easy to use
   C. Durable and lightweight
   D. Weight and length proportional for easy use
   E. Aesthetically pleasing
   F. Refills available

4. Needed Information / Market Considerations

   A. Price range of other similar pencils and erasers
   B. How many mechanical pencils sold each year
   C. Where mechanical pencils are sold - where is greatest market
   D. How many leads needed per length of eraser
   E. What is a practical length for a mechanical pencil
   F. How does internal mechanism work

PRELIMINARY IDEAS

1. Brainstorming ideas:

   A. Advance for eraser - "clicker"
      1. On end of pencil
      2. On shaft
      3. Fit on eraser track with internal shaft

   B. Length
      1. Lead
         a. Full size (60 mm)
         b. Half size (30 mm)
      2. Eraser
      3. Lead barrel
      4. Overall pencil
         a. Standard mechanical pencil
         b. 18 to 20 cm

   C. Eraser
      1. Eraser and pencil as two separate pieces
         a. Snap on
         b. Screw on
      2. Eraser actually fits into shaft
      3. Have eraser cover

   D. Tip of pencil
      1. Screw on tip
      2. Clip or snap on tip

   E. Weight of pencil
      - should be concentrated in lower or writing end

   F. Overall appearance and materials
      1. Shaft
         a. Clear plastic
         b. Smoked plastic
         c. Opaque, colored plastic
      2. Internal parts
         a. Plastic
         b. Chrome, metal

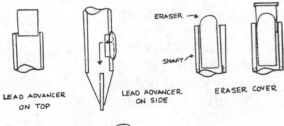

LEAD ADVANCER ON TOP   LEAD ADVANCER ON SIDE   ERASER COVER

ERASER →   SHAFT →

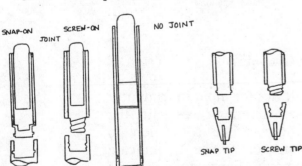

SNAP-ON JOINT   SCREW-ON JOINT   NO JOINT

SNAP TIP   SCREW TIP

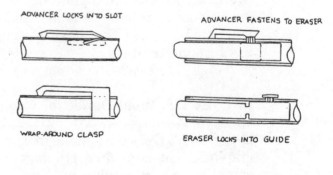

ADVANCER LOCKS INTO SLOT   ADVANCER FASTENS TO ERASER

WRAP-AROUND CLASP   ERASER LOCKS INTO GUIDE

Student Project (see pp. 13-15)

REFINEMENT

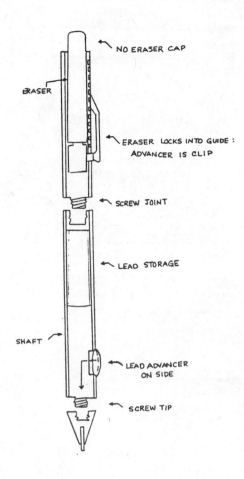

NO ERASER CAP

ERASER

ERASER LOCKS INTO GUIDE:
ADVANCER IS CLIP

SCREW JOINT

LEAD STORAGE

SHAFT

LEAD ADVANCER
ON SIDE

SCREW TIP

Table 1 - Market Survey of Mechanical Pencils

	Cost of Pencil	Cost of Refills
1. Berol Cassette CA5	$3.49	***
2. Kohinoor - Rapidomatic	6.50	12 pcs / .85
3. Pentel - Graph 500	4.49	12 pcs / .90
4. Pentel - Quicker Clicker	3.79	12 pcs / .90
5. Pilot - The Shaker	6.59	***
6. Staedtler Mars Micrograph	5.50	12 pcs / .90

Table 2 - Market Survey of Erasers

	Cost of Eraser	Cost of Refills
1. Faber Castell Jet Eraser	$1.49	$.60
2. Pentel Click Eraser	1.29	.59
3. Staedetler Radelt Eraser	1.29	.58

Table 3 - Erase 'n' Write Pencil Data

Cost of Erase 'n' Write Pencil:	$4.95
Cost of lead refills:	24 pcs / 1.00
Cost of eraser refills:	3 / 1.00

ANALYSIS OF CLICK BUTTON

ANALYSIS

1. Function / Human Engineering
   A. Able to write
   B. Erases easily
   C. Easy to refill - both lead and eraser
   D. Will not "jam" or malfunction

2. Market and Consumer Acceptance (see Tables 1, 2, and 3)
   A. Cost
      1. Keep overall price under $5
      2. Special size eraser refills (3/$1)
      3. Special size lead refills (24/$1)
         - make different lead weights available
   B. Refills easily attained
      1. Leads and erasers sold separately
      2. Leads and erasers sold together
   C. Able to buy complete set: pencil, eraser, lead, and refill

3. Physical Description
   A. Eraser - 50 mm
   B. Lead - 30 mm
   C. Overall pencil - 177 mm
   D. Color - black, blue, clear, red

4. Production Specifications
   A. Materials
      (see WORKING DRAWINGS section for materials specifications)
   B. Costs

Manufacturing	$ 1.50
Overhead	.50
Sales Commission	.50
Manufacturer's Profit	.75
Retail Profit	1.70
Suggested Retail Price	$ 4.95

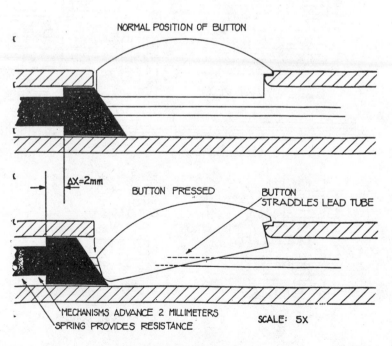

NORMAL POSITION OF BUTTON

ΔX=2mm

BUTTON PRESSED

BUTTON
STRADDLES LEAD TUBE

MECHANISMS ADVANCE 2 MILLIMETERS
SPRING PROVIDES RESISTANCE

SCALE: 5X

(SEE WORKING DRAWINGS FOR DETAILS)

Student Project (cont. from page 12)

13

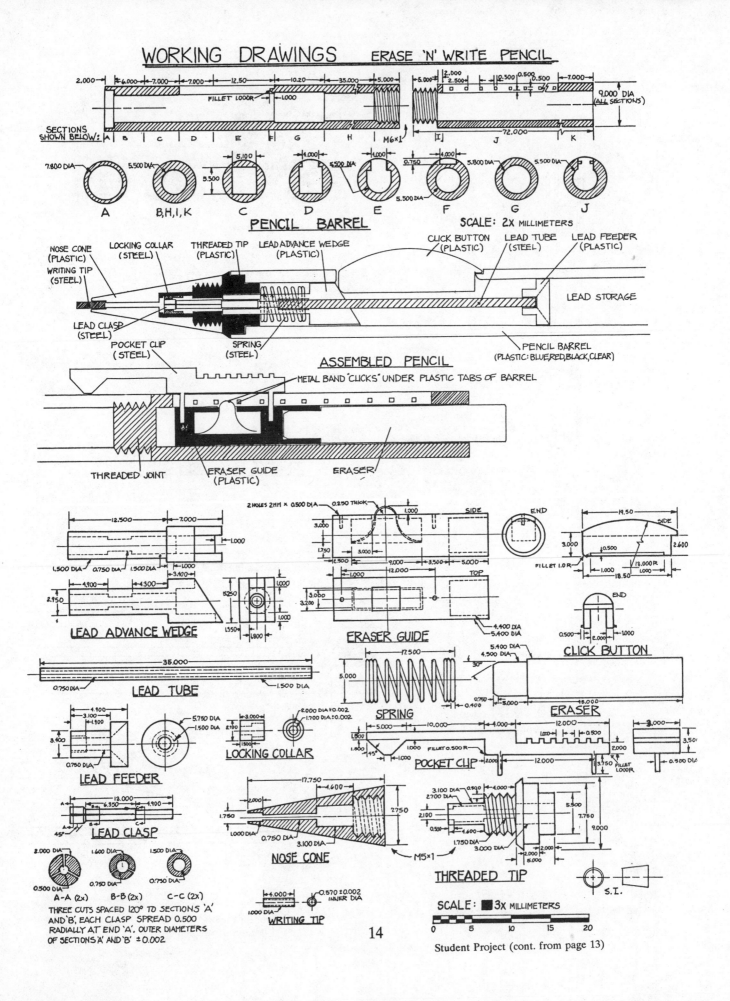

WORKING DRAWINGS   ERASE 'N' WRITE PENCIL

PENCIL BARREL   SCALE: 2x millimeters

ASSEMBLED PENCIL

METAL BAND "CLICKS" UNDER PLASTIC TABS OF BARREL

LEAD ADVANCE WEDGE

ERASER GUIDE

CLICK BUTTON

LEAD TUBE

SPRING   ERASER

LEAD FEEDER

LOCKING COLLAR

POCKET CLIP

LEAD CLASP   NOSE CONE   THREADED TIP

WRITING TIP   SCALE: 3x millimeters

14

Student Project (cont. from page 13)

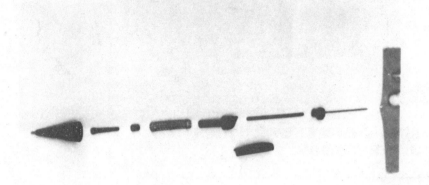

Internal Mechanisms
(unassembled)

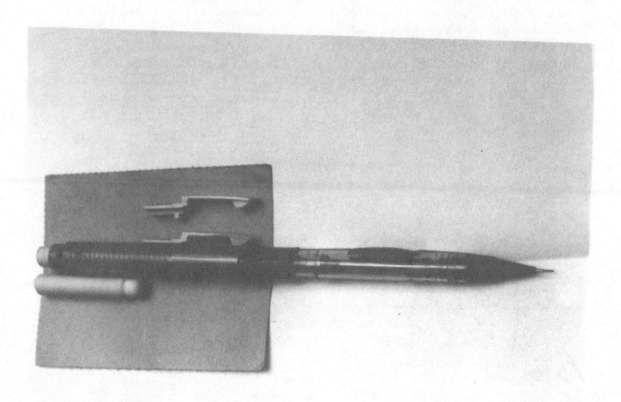

Model of Erase 'n' Write Pencil

Student Project (cont. from page 14)

15

CHAPTER 2

ENGINEERING COMPUTER GRAPHICS
and VISUAL PERCEPTION

What is Engineering Design Graphics?

Engineering Design Graphics is the body of knowledge that comprises visual communication, spatial analysis, and creative design. It consists of a series of graphical methods, rules and standards used in the design and preparation of working drawings. The methods are also used to visualize and analyze spatial geometry. Dr. James H. Earle, Professor at Texas A & M, brilliantly states that "graphics is one of the designer's primary methods of thinking, solving problems, and communicating ideas." In *Engineering Design Graphics, Fifth Edition* (Massachusetts: Addison-Wesley, 1987), Dr. Earle defines engineering graphics as "the total field of graphical problem solving and includes two areas of specialization: descriptive geometry and working drawings."

These two areas of specialization can be defined as follows:

* **Descriptive geometry** or space geometry is the science of solving graphical problems involving true angles, lengths, shapes and other spatial relationships. It provides two-dimensional (2-D) descriptions and information about 3-D objects.

* **Working Drawings** are all the detailed technical-drawings use to specify and/or manufacture a device, system or process.

The engineering design graphics field studies and develops new visual modeling tools to examine and present technical information. Some of the current graphics modeling tools are: CADD, solid modeling, animation, 'intelligent' graphics, 'stereoscopic' and 'holographic' computer graphics. No matter what new technology you use, engineering design graphics provides the conventions necessary to communicate our design ideas to those who will be in charge of approving and manufacturing those ideas.

Historical Landmarks in Engineering Design Graphics

Engineering Graphics Professor Daniel L. Ryan (Clemson University) indicates that "graphics has been a part of man's history since the earliest recorded times. Early man painted on the walls of caves while modern man uses photographs, video tape, or electronic media." (*Engineering Design Graphics Journal*, Vol. 49, No. 3, Autumn 1985).

The historical landmarks of graphics are depicted in Figure 2.1. In the early beginnings, graphics tools were very rudimentary, but useful.

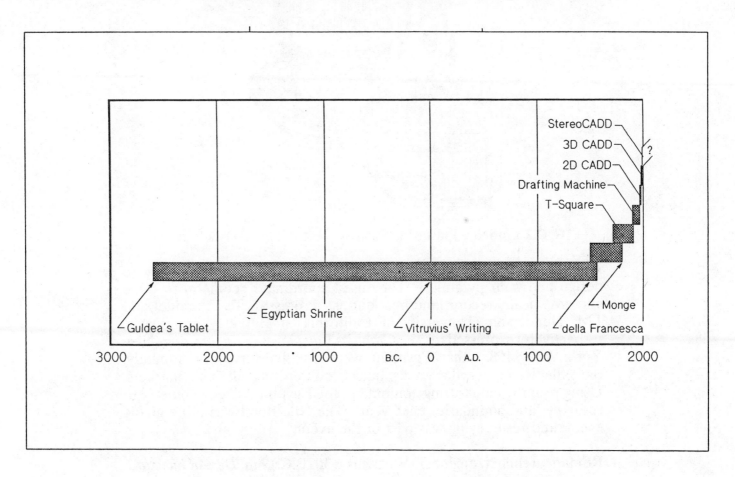

FIG. 2.1 Engineering Graphics Landmarks (Courtesy of Dr. Juricic, U.T. at Austin)

The first known construction drawing is the plan view of a fortress (see Fig. 2.2). It was recorded in a stone tablet by Chaldean engineer Gudea (4000s B.C.). In *Engineering Graphics* (New York: MacMillan, 1985) Giesecke, et al. states that "it is remarkable how similar this plan is to those made by architects today, although 'drawn' thousands of years before paper was invented."

17

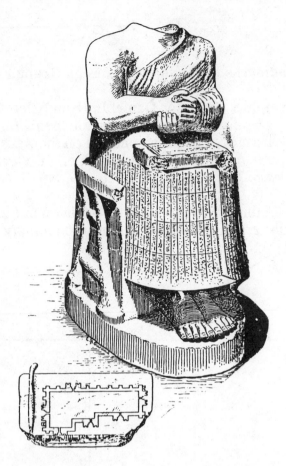

FIG. 2.2 Gudea's Plan of a Fortress (ASCE Transactions (Vol. XXIV, 1891)

As early as 2600-1200 B.C., the Egyptians were using geometry to design and built pyramids. They used coordinate geometry to trace and graphically record land boundaries. Professors R. F. Steidel and J.M. Henderson (University of California at Berkeley and Davis, respectively) expressed in, *The Graphics Languages of Engineering* (New York: Wiley, 1983), that "Egyptians were ... skilled surveyors. Annually, the Nile River overflowed its banks, obliterating all land markets. Using primitive measuring equipment, the Egyptians used geometry to resurvey land boundaries each year. The Nile flood was a life-giving event, and resurveying was part of the event."

Roman architect/engineer Vitruvius (30 B.C.), in *De Architectura*, explains various geometric and construction procedures. His treatise could be consider the first engineering drawing (also, construction/planning) book.

Pierro della Francesca (1500 A.D.) used projections theory (2-D). Drs. Davor Juricic and Ronald Barr, both engineering graphics professors at University of Texas at Austin, confirm that "the first record of what could be called related multiview projections appeared in Renaissance Italy (Pierro della Francesca). The appearance of these related multiview drawings based on principles of orthographic

18

projection could be considered a cornerstone in the attempts to precisely describe a design project." (*Engineering Design Graphics Journal*, ASEE, Vol.51, No. 3, Spring 1987).

Leonardo da Vinci (1452-1519) the famous artist-engineer sketched his ideas using pictorials (3-D). In *The Codex Antlanticus* he sketched several maps and various refrigeration, printing, military and aeronautical machines as shown in Fig. 2.3.

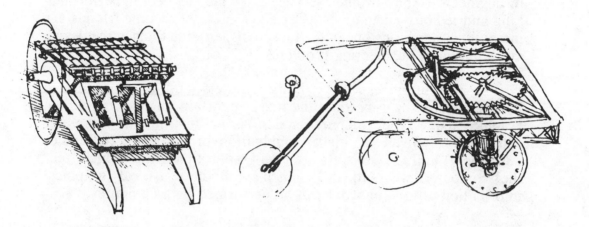

FIG. 2.3 Leonardo's Sketches

Perhaps the most important work in projection theory was conducted by Gaspar Monge (1746-1818), the founder of Descriptive Geometry. He developed spatial analysis techniques to solve military problems. Some of those problems involved the design of fortifications. Monge proposed simple graphical problem-solving techniques to previously complex mathematical methods. Using simple drawing instruments like triangles, compasses and dividers he was able to determine the true shape and angle of oblique surfaces.

What is CAED/Graphics?

The utilization of new computer graphics tools -Computer Sketching, CADD, Solid Modeling, Intelligent Graphics and Animation- is known as **Computer-Aided Engineering Design Graphics** (CAED/Graphics). This is a sub-field of Engineering Design Graphics with overlapping boundaries with Computer-Aided Engineering (CAE) or Computer-Aided Design and Drafting (CADD).

In CAED/Graphics, we still use the drawing standards, developed in the past, to communicate our design ideas. The main difference is in the design/drawing production tools employed to model the geometry of new devices and systems. Namely, we use computers -rather than manual tools- to generate three-dimensional wire-frame images and solid models of the engineered devices and systems.

Digital Computers

Many scientists, engineers, and technologists are discovering the benefits of using the latest technological tools available for the effective communication of their design ideas. Computers are used by engineers to solve problems. They assist the engineer in performing long and tedious calculations. Certainly, these electronic friends are increasingly becoming one of the most indispensable tools in the design and solution of engineering problems.

Digital computers, especially minicomputers and the inexpensive microcomputer, have become the most important engineering design graphics tool. The computer system is an instrument of greater capabilities. Given the right combination of hardware (computer equipment) and CADD software (the graphics programs which "tell" the computer what to do), much of today's typical graphical information processing work can be performed by a computer.

You can now enter your design model directly onto a computer and make on-the-spot-changes, without having to spend several days or weeks of tedious calculations or manual drawings.

Computers are electronic machines that perform high-speed mathematical and logical calculations. They assemble, correlate, process, store and manage information derived from a series of programmed instructions. Computer systems do not manage information -on their own- without some form of human intervention or interaction. As a matter of fact, the term **interactive** computer system denotes this human/machine interrelationship.

The computer user can command the CADD system to (see Fig. 2.4) execute interactive instructions by means of input data. The machine responds to the input, with some output; the user then reacts to the output. This interactive communication continues until certain technological problem is solved, a particular information is processed and/or retrieved.

Engineers and computer programmers develop the **algorithms** (sequence of instructions to solve a problem) and **source code** (computer programming language syntax) necessary for the computer to carry-out instructions. However, in many occasions you will utilize existing computer software programs or "packages", as they are called.

Software packages are named **user-friendly,** if you can access a simple

FIG. 2.4 CADD Timesharing system. (Courtesy of Control Data Corp.)

21

-predefined- standard menu of options or intuitive commands without looking at the program's reference manual. **Menus** are screen displayed lists of options from which you can select an operation to be performed by typing characters or by positioning an indicator on the selection.

Many engineers customize these programs with their own menus and functions. These modified menus provide a specialized interface with the computer.

Historical Overview of CAED/Graphics

The development of the computer had its start four thousand years ago with the invention of the abacus. The **abacus** -a counting device made out of beads and rods- was used by mediterranean merchants for counting, adding and subtracting. As illustrated in Figure 2.5, rods were like arithmetic columns, say beads on the ones rod, worth 1 unit. Those on the tens rods worth 10 units, etc.

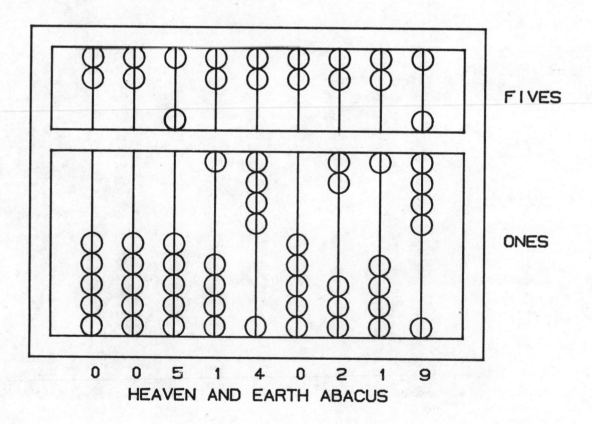

FIG. 2.5 Heaven-and-earth abacus

22

Several advancements -in the nineteenth and twentieth century- namely: Hollerith's design of an electric tabulating device to calculate the 1890 census and Atanasoff's invention of the first electronic digital computer in 1939, led to the current microcomputer systems.

One of the first popular microcomputers was the Apple II, introduced in the late 1970's. The Apple II series has continued to evolve, for example: Apple IIc for the home user, and the Apple IIe for basic computer literacy courses. Both use the same eight-bit chip[1]. In the eighties, the IBM (International Business Machines) entered the microcomputer field with its IBM PC. A year later a model with a hard disk was introduced - the IBM PC/XT. Both are based on the Intel 8088 CPU chip. As manufacturers continued to refine their microprocessors (e.g., 8088 microprocessor into the 80286 and the 80386) computer hardware companies proceeded to come out with updated versions of their products (e.g., IBM came with its 80286-based PC/AT). The major advantage of Intel's 80386 chips was that much of the software for the older CPU chips could be used on the new ones, eliminating the problem of software availability for the new model.

Other manufacturers have introduced microcomputers based on other chips, namely the Motorola 68000 chip and the Hewlett-Packard (HP) superchip. In 1987, Apple Computer Corporation introduced the Macintosh II, that uses a Motorola 68020 CPU running at 16MHz. Because of its large word size (32-bit), the computer can run very quickly and be very user-friendly. Microcomputers featuring this microprocessor are well known for their ease of use and their tremendous graphic capability.

In addition, the 32-bit microprocessors brought a capability shared by few other previous microprocessors which increase the potential of microcomputers: multitasking. This is the ability of a single microprocessor to handle more than one job "at the same time". This allows a user to begin running a very long, very slow program and then switch over to perform some other task while the long program runs in the "background". Since many engineering technology programs tend to be slow to execute, this multitasking capability is one which will definitely be use in microcomputing.

The computer system accepts the information in the form of **electronic signals**. Each character of information needs to be unique (i.e., distinctly different signal). This is accomplished, electronically, by combining two signals: on and off. **On** and **Off** signals are represented by the digits 1 and 0, respectively. For example, the verbal symbol, "a" is translated into computer code as: 01100001.

The technical term **binary digit** (bit) is derived from these two digits. Each graphical symbol is identified by a combination of 8, 16, 32, or 64 bits (word lengths). A **byte** equals 8 bits. **KB** stands for kilobyte or 1024 bytes]

System Classification

Computer graphics systems can be classified by their size, price and capabilities, as: microcomputers, minicomputers, superminis, mainframe and supercomputers. Because of their low cost and relative ease of use, micro and minicomputers are found in many engineering offices. Similarly, since prices have dropped, microcomputers are appearing in homes for use in word processing, finances, budgeting and video games. Several technical colleges and universities require their freshman students to possess their own microcomputers, with a supply of software, namely: operating system (e.g., DOS), word processing (e.g. wordperfect, wordstar), graphics (e.g., AutoCAD, CADKEY), computer languages (e.g., FORTRAN, BASIC, C) and communication packages (e.g., Smartcom). Sometimes the colleges provides the students with free in-house or commercial software, based on previous licencing agreements with software companies.

As technology advances, microcomputers will have the capabilities of the present minicomputers. Minicomputers will become more like large mainframe computers. The microcomputer field has grown by leaps and bounds since the early seventies. Microcomputers and stand-alone minicomputers are popular with engineering offices because of the large amount of user-friendly software packages available for them.

Mini and mainframe computers are preferred by large established engineering companies and manufacturers. These larger systems are composed of a series of interconnected terminals, linked to a supermini computer or mainframe by a communication network.

Shared Computer Environment

Microcomputers -and computer terminals- connected to mainframe computers through advanced communication networks allows the transmission of verbal and visual information from one person to another at a distant location. Lightwave communication technology has overcome the limitations of metallic conductors (e.g., transmission speed, sensitivity to electrical interference and interception of signals).

Figure 2.6 illustrates a partial schematic diagram of a communications network. A similar electronic communications network would allow you to quickly connect, generate and send complex design work via interconnected work stations. In fact, it is now possible to transmit data at more than 20 million pulses of light per second without the need of hard-wired connections.

Availability of this communication technology permits an integrated

24

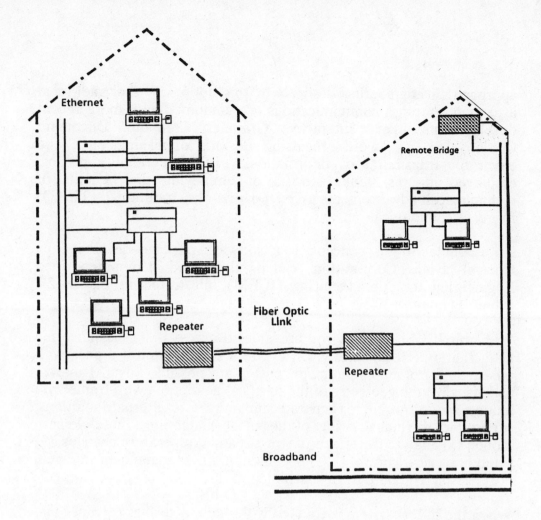

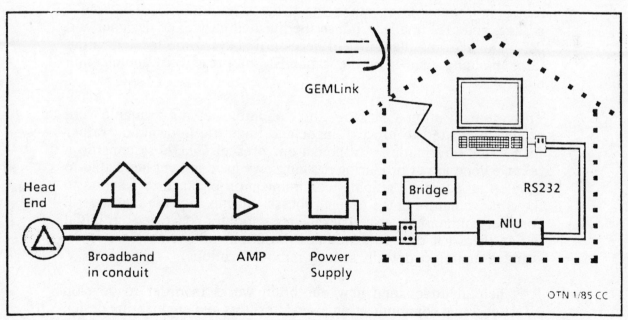

FIG. 2.6 Communications Network

approach to engineering design. In this approach, the traditional aspects of graphics communications are combined with more recent developments, like: Interactive Graphics, Computer Document Composition (e.g., word processing, desktop publishing, etc.), and electronic transmittal of information. The integrated approach, employed in this book, consists of employing the benefits of technological advancements (CADD) and the traditional (TRAD) forms of communication.

An example of this concept, is a software package developed by Control Data Corporation called Integrated Computer-Aided Engineering for Manufacturing (ICEM), illustrated in Figure 2.7 (Photo Sequence: ICEM).

With this ICEM package you are able to access its (1) Engineering Data Library (EDL) facility; (2) create a solid model of a part, with the capability of manipulating the part in any possible way; (3) analyze and visualize the geometry of the part; (4) generate a wire-frame with hidden lines removed; (5) generate similar parts or alternate solutions; (6) produce working drawings of the part; (7) generate a finite-element model; (8) analyze the effects of stresses and temperature changes; (9) setup numerical control (NC) documentation for manufacturing; and, (10) use the NC output for machining.

When the ICEM system is coupled with manufacturing machines and robots it is possible to make the process automatic; (11) namely, milling; and (12) finally, produce the finished part. The designer and the manufacturing plant do not necessarily have to be located in the same building thanks to the capability of present communication networks.

The communication technology and computer software available were originally created to process linear and linguistic information rather than visual information. Although our present CADD systems do a relative good job at producing drawings, we have not yet been able to develop an adequate graphics communication package to respond to the creative nature of the design process. Such is the case that we still consider our handmade sketches the ideal tool for conveying our initial design ideas (of course, sometimes those manual sketches are laser-scanned and electronically sent to remote locations).

It is helpful understand how our brain works in order to develop effective visual communication, user-interfaces and engineering design tools.

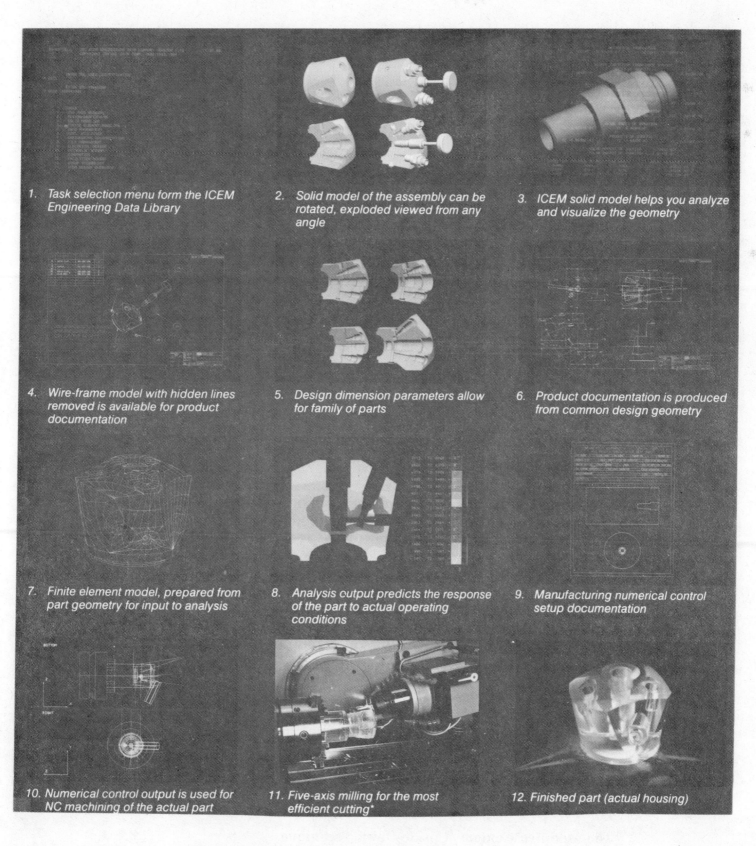

1. Task selection menu form the ICEM Engineering Data Library

2. Solid model of the assembly can be rotated, exploded viewed from any angle

3. ICEM solid model helps you analyze and visualize the geometry

4. Wire-frame model with hidden lines removed is available for product documentation

5. Design dimension parameters allow for family of parts

6. Product documentation is produced from common design geometry

7. Finite element model, prepared from part geometry for input to analysis

8. Analysis output predicts the response of the part to actual operating conditions

9. Manufacturing numerical control setup documentation

10. Numerical control output is used for NC machining of the actual part

11. Five-axis milling for the most efficient cutting*

12. Finished part (actual housing)

FIG. 2.7 From design to manufacturing (Courtesy of Control Data Corp.)

27

Visual Perception and the Spatial Brain-Hemisphere

"The words or the language, as they are written or spoken, do not seem to play any role in the mechanism of thought. The psychical entities which serve as elements in thought are certain signs and more or less clear images which can be 'voluntarily' reproduced and combined." (Albert Einstein).

The brain is divided in two halves called hemispheres. The hemispheres are connected by a "cable" called the **corpus callosum**. This cable provides communications -mainly, transmission of memory messages- between both hemispheres. But each hemisphere has its own independent functions and characteristics.

Roger Sperry, the Nobel prize-winner brain researcher, explains in 'Lateral Specialization of Cerebral Function in the Surgically Separated Hemispheres' that "there appears to be two modes of thinking, verbal and nonverbal, represented rather separately in left and right hemisphere, respectively, and our educational system, as well as science in general, tends to neglect the nonverbal form of intellect. What it comes down to is that modern society discriminates against the right hemisphere. (*Psychophysiology of Thinking*, New York: Academic Press, 1973 - McGuigan and Schoonover Eds.)

It is very possible that if you have been trained in the Western society you think mainly with your brain's **symbolic hemisphere** (left hemisphere) -where the verbal, analytic, digital and logic information processing appears to occur. However, brain characteristics like creativity, drawing talent, intuitive understanding and complex visual and spatial relationships seems to occur in the **spatial hemisphere** (right hemisphere).

Sperry and his colleagues at the California Institute of Technology mapped this brain characteristics by observing the behavior of persons who suffered injuries in to the left and right hemisphere. In the first case, patients experienced problems with speech. In cases where the patients suffered damages to the right hemisphere, they experience visual/perceptual problems.

Betty Edwards in her book *Drawing on the Right Side of the Brain* (Los Angeles: Tarcher, 1979) utilized Sperry's experiences to develop several ingenious drawing exercises. A modification of her **upside-down** technique is reviewed in the following paragraph. The modifications have been made to incorporate the "contour" ideas in *The Natural Way to Draw* by Kimon Nicolaides (Boston: Houghton Miffin, 1941.)

The Modified Contour/Upside-Down Technique
Find a photograph, image, or preferably, a line drawing and turn it

upside down. Then copy (do not trace) the image the way you see the image (upside down). Do not try to identify specific objects in the picture, simply observe and copy the entities that you see. That is, observe and copy the line inclinations, curves, angles and spatial relationships among those entities. The first time you do this exercise go very slowly...imagine that you are actually "touching" the lines and shapes as you draw the image. Nicolaides explains "merely to see ... is not enough. It is necessary to have a fresh vivid, physical contact with the object you draw through as many of the senses as possible." You should visually identify the edges or **contours**, that is, the locations where the different planes of the object intersect. If you can, try to remove your "immediate attention" from the actual drawing - concentrate in perceiving the real image. Finally, do not worry about the final result, this is not a test.

When you are finished turn the drawing right side up. You might be surprised to see that you can really draw!

You should have experienced a "shift" from the symbolic hemisphere way of thinking to the spatial hemisphere way of perceiving. If you had drawn the picture right side up, from the start, your symbolic hemisphere would have probably thought "this is easy to draw" and you would have ended up with a "symbolic" rather than a realistic image of the picture. Also, the fact that you are drawing very slowly -and thinking in terms of contours- helps in making a shift to the spatial hemisphere. The symbolic hemisphere appears to be "bored" by this operation. Lets try the modified upside-down technique on one of da Vinci's sketches, draw Fig. 2.8.

In his article, 'Are your thinking Right?' Stanley L. Englebardt mentions the work of another brain researcher, Ned Herrmann, in which "he found a strong relationship between hemisphere dominance and the way subjects made a living: left-brain-oriented objects were more often lawyers, writers, bookkeepers, doctors, tax experts, etc. - jobs dealing with logical, language related information. Those who favored the right hemisphere turned out to be poets, politicians, musicians, architects, entrepreneurs, dancers and -surprisingly- top executives. Herrmann's studies showed that the most successful people in any occupation are those who use both the left and right brains." He suggest the following exercise to see if you are right or left-brained (Reader's Digest, adapted from *The Tao Jones Averages* by Bennet W. Goodspeed, E.P. Dutton Publishers).

Count the number of f's in this sentence:

**FINISHED FILES ARE THE RESULT OF YEARS
OF SCIENTIFIC STUDY COMBINED WITH
THE EXPERIENCE OF MANY YEARS.**

How many f's did you find?. Englebard states that only 15% of those who took the test found all six f'. He says "you probably missed the f in each 'of.' Since 'of' is pronounced 'ov,' the verbal left hemisphere took the verbal clue and overrode the right, 'seeing' hemisphere, thus forcing the wrong conclusion."

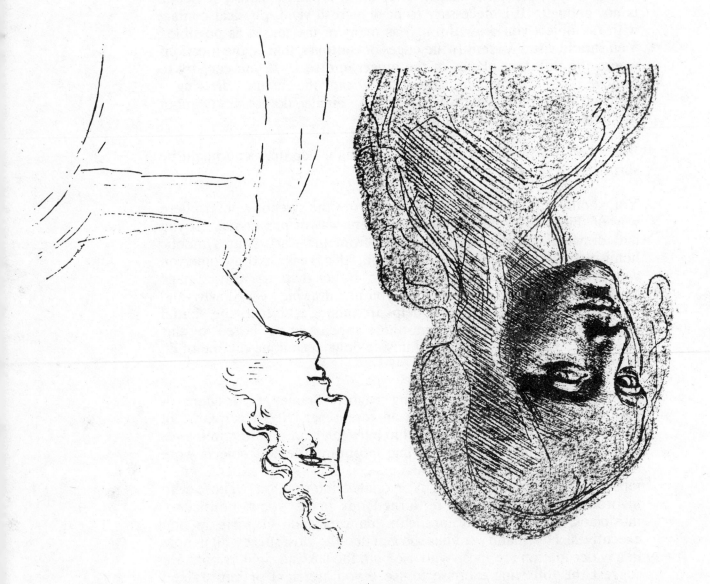

FIG. 2.8 Try this Upside Down Exercise (Leonardo's drawings)

Basic Forms of Communication

The following sections cover the basic forms of communication used in engineering design. The discussion encompasses the basic terminology, resources and tools essential to convey information about design projects and research findings. From the engineer's point of view, the basic forms of communication can be classified in the following categories:

1. Verbal
2. Visual (Graphical)

Both forms are interrelated, as illustrated in Figure 2.9 (Display File: OUTER MAST).

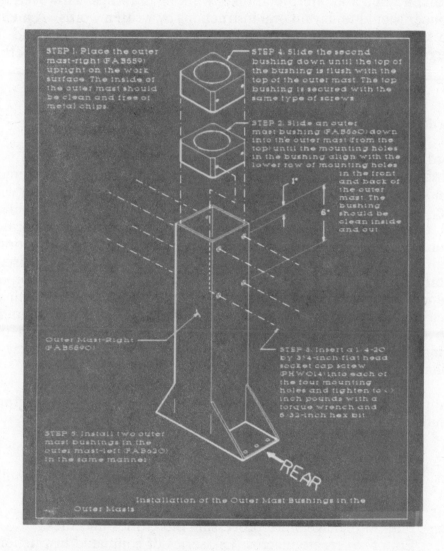

FIG. 2.9 Outermast (Courtesy of Intergraph.)

Verbal Communication

Verbal communication utilizes verbal symbols (words) to convey

31

information. This form of expression, can be further subclassified as follows:

a. Oral (speech)
b. Written (prose)

The engineer devotes a great deal of time to activities that requires the effective oral presentations of ideas to clients and institutions. The oral expression is used by the engineer to convey messages or ask questions about a particular project. Speech is an acceptable form of communication and interpretation of working drawings. However, the engineer should follow up oral instructions by written words. A memo or a letter, with copies to related parties will be reliable evidence in case of legal conflicts. The slang industrial term **"AVO"** -Avoid Verbal Orders-illustrates the point.

Word Processing

Word processors (**WP**), personal computers or terminals linked to a mainframe computer are helpful tools to the technical writer. Memos, letters and technical specifications can be stored in a data base with ease. The written material could be rearranged in any form. Addition and deletion of words, sentences and paragraphs are performed automatically. The user can check the text for spelling corrections. Spelling check and electronic thesaurus are two of the most useful features of software word processing packages. The speller proofs engineering reports on the screen by comparing each word, with an electronic dictionary of more than 100,000 words. Words can be found with an electronic thesaurus. A word processing system with this feature, searches and displays synonymous and words that conveys a similar idea, in a matter of seconds.

Additional functions and operations of sophisticated WP programs includes:

* Shell- to move text from one program to another.
* Calculator- to perform math, trigonometry, statistical, and programming functions.
* Calendar- to keep track of appointments.
* File- to manage word processing directories and files.
* Editor- to create macros (i.e., series of command instructions) and edit text program files.
* Notebook- to keep notes and address information.

The word processing system enables the engineer to save time and production cost associated with the editing and reediting of technical documents. When the system is utilized in conjunction with Computer-

Aided Drafting and Design (CADD) systems, it becomes a powerful and efficient tool. Drawings and text can be transmitted to a designated site in a matter of seconds.

Electronic Mail

Another tool of written communication is electronic mail. Electronic mail is possible through the electronic communication system. The electronic data is transmitted via telephone lines, microwave links, cables or satellites. The messages are displayed on the receiving terminal and/or printed-plotted on an output device. Messages are typed on the terminals keyboard with the company letter head and users signature in a predefined inbox.

A version of an electronic mail system (VMAIL) allows the user to create more than one inbox of messages. It is possible to configure the VMAIL interface to the user's needs. Similar mail linking systems (Mail Link-PROFS) allow the user to send mail and Telex messages to users of other systems around the world.

Database

Drawings of engineering parts and devices can be stored in a **database**. Database is large collection of organized and computerized information required to perform a given task. For example, the drawing files on a disk are stored in a database.

Data Input is the alpha numeric or digitized information transferred into the computer system. The data consist of numbers, letters, facts, and symbols that are stored on the computer.

Computerized drawings may be retrieved for revisions. The efficiency obtained, by being able to re-use and make changes to the database, usually pays for the initial high cost of the system.

Geometric entities, patterns, icons may be created, manipulated and reused endlessly. Most CADD systems are "user-friendly". However, learning the certain systems may take several weeks or even months of frustrating efforts. The reader should expect to encounter some difficulties in learning some of these systems. Despite the unrelenting cussedness of the task, engineers should make every effort to learn CAD systems. Patience and perseverance are the prescription for some of the problems. As more intelligent software is developed, the CAD system will become more and more "user friendly".

The computer graphics system needs the data input from a creative engineering designer. It is usual for the engineer to communicate preliminary ideas and design alternatives using freehand sketches.

The CAE/CAD/CAM system is just another very useful tool that is available for the production of drawings. The systems depend, indirectly, on the traditional theory and principles of descriptive geometry. It is therefore, advisable to become familiar with the traditional methods of engineering graphics while attempting to learn a CAD system.

Visual Perception Problems

Explain the modified contour/upside-down technique and draw the following residential floor framing details:

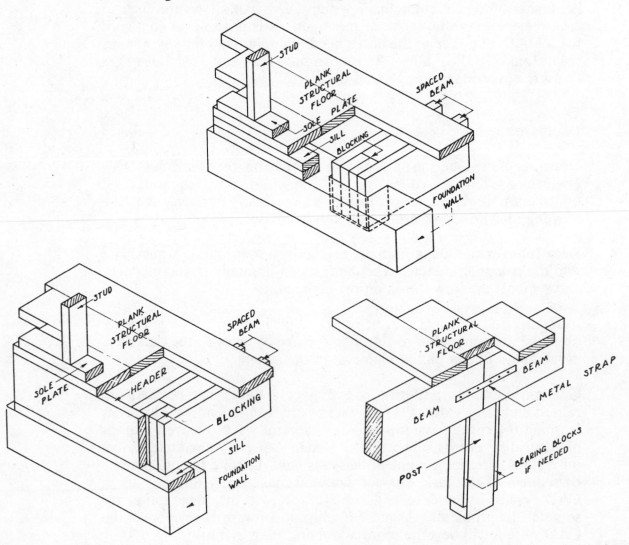

FIG. 2.10 Building Details Exercises (Courtesy of National Forest Product Association)

34

Visual Perception Problems (cont.)

Using the modified contour/upside-down technique draw the following figures:

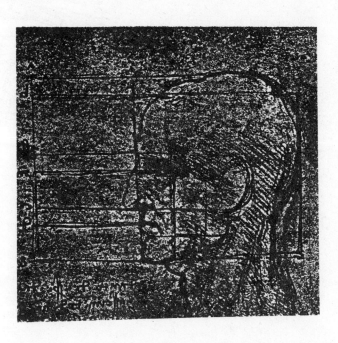
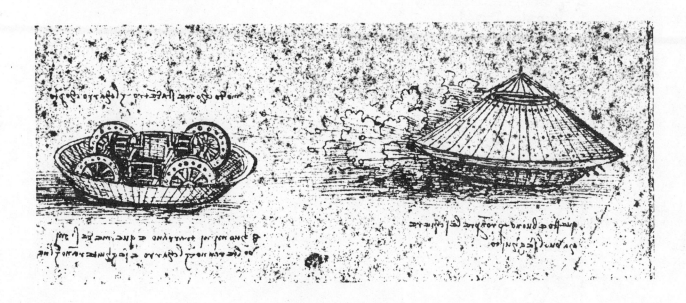

FIG. 2.11 Exercises based on Leonardo da Vinci drawings.

35

Visual Perception Problems (cont.)

Draw the following figure.

FIG. 2.12 Exercise based on Joe Johnson and Nilo Rodis-Jamero book: *The Empire Strikes Back Sketchbook* (Courtesy of Lucasfilm).

Engineering Computer Graphics Exercises

Define and explain the following terms and acronyms:

1. Engineering Graphics
2. Descriptive Geometry
3. Working Drawings
4. CAED/Graphics
4. CADD
5. CAE
6. WP
7. Computer
8. algorithm
9. source code
10. user-friendly
11. menus
12. abacus
13. bit
14. byte
15. kb
16. ICEM
17. NC
18. AVO
19. database
20. input

CHAPTER 3

MULTIVIEW PROJECTION and COMPUTER VIEW-DISPLAY

Projection Theory

This chapter presents some essential projection fundamentals employed in engineering design graphics. The basic projection theory topics, introduced hereinafter are: ANSI linetype standards, perspectives and parallel projections. These basic concepts are utilized by engineers, designers and drafting personnel to prepare and interpret diagrams, production drawings and construction plans.

Additional graphics fundamentals, like: sketching, scales, axonometric projections, spatial visualization, auxiliary views, descriptive geometry, drafting standards (e.g., working drawings, fasteners, sectioning, detailing, dimensioning and tolerancing) are discussed in subsequent chapters and appendices.

One of the most valuable means of communication in engineering graphics is projection theory. Projection Theory is the body of knowledge that comprises the set of rules and principles devised to analyze, draw and display spatial geometry onto two-dimensional surfaces (i.e., sheet of paper, screen monitor, etc.). The aim of projection theory is to describe the shape of objects.

Projection is defined as the visual image produced by mapping a geometric representation of an object onto a viewing surface or plane (see Figure 3.1). Geometric projection involves establishing the relationship among a series of visual variables (e.g., line-of-sight, point-of-sight, picture planes, vanishing-point, horizon, etc.) and the spatial object to be represented or projected. The following discussion will classify the types of projections available and their function. Several important projection theory terms will be defined.

Classification

Projections can be classified into two broad areas:

(I). Perspective Projections and (II). Parallel Projections.

I. Perspective Projection

A <u>Perspective Projection</u> represents objects as perceived by the human

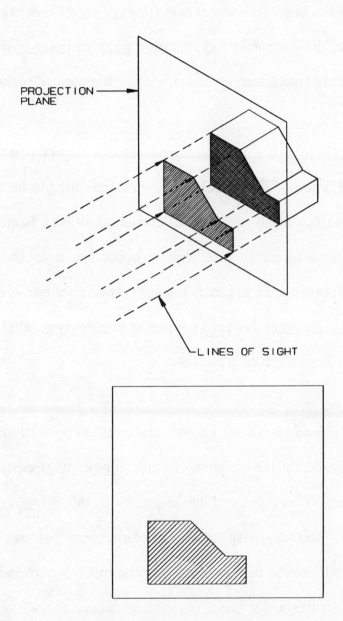

PROJECTION PLANE

LINES OF SIGHT

FIG. 3.1 Projection is the visual image produced by mapping (see dark shaded area) geometric representation of an object onto a viewing surface (see soft shaded area).

eye (i.e., binocular vision). It is a pictorial drawing generated by the intersection of the observer's visual rays (lines-of-sight) converging on a picture plane. The observer's eye (station point or point-of-sight) is located at a finite (measurable) distance from the picture plane.

Photographs taken with a standard lens camara depict perspective images of real objects. Figure 3.2, captures a building photographed as it appears to a camera stationed at certain position. Notice that lines formed by different surface planes -which are supposed to be parallel to each other- tend to vanish toward certain common vanishing points. A vanishing point (VP) is a particular imaginary point at which actual parallel lines seem to converge.

Perspective projections (also known, as central projections) are subclassified based on the number of vanishing-points used to draw them: One-point, Two-point and Three-point. In the One-Point (i.e., also known as, Parallel) perspective, two of the principal axes of the object are parallel to the picture plane and the other is perpendicular. Figure 3.3 illustrates a one-point perspective where the vertical and horizontal axes are parallel to the picture plane and the depth axis is perpendicular to the same. Notice how the depth features of the object tend to vanish towards a single point.

FIG. 3.2 Photograph taken with normal lens camera depicts a perspective visual image of a building. (Courtesy of PR1ME.)

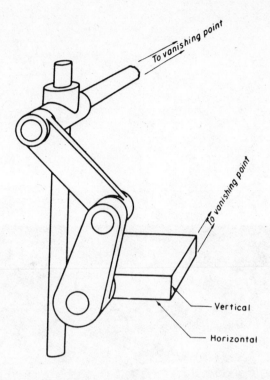

FIG. 3.3 One-point perspective. The vertical and horizontal axes are parallel to the picture plane. (Courtesy of ASME and ANSI.)

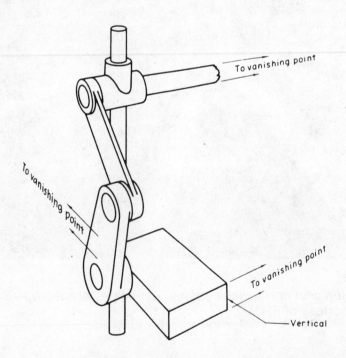

FIG. 3.4 Two-point perspective of a device obtained when two of the axes are inclined and one is parallel to the projection plane. (Courtesy of ASME and ANSI.)

When two of the object's axes are inclined and one is parallel to the picture plane, we obtain a two-point (or angular) perspective. Figure 3.4 illustrates a two-point perspective drawing of a device. Another example of an architectural rendering of a building is shown in Figure 3.5. In the latter drawing, only one of the VPs has been labeled. The other VP is located beyond the drawing limits. Notice that texture lines on the floor and building feature lines tend to converge at these vanishing points. Look once more at Figures 3.4 and 3.5; observe that the vertical axis is parallel to the plane of projection while the horizontal and depth axes will converge towards its respective VP's.

Finally, a three-point (or oblique) perspective is presented in Figure 3.6, by inclining all axes of the object with respect to the picture plane. The American National Standards Institute (ANSI) recommends that the point-of-sight should be placed so that the observer's cone of visual rays, covering the object, should not be greater than 30 degrees (see Figure 3.7). In addition, better results are obtained when the point-of-sight is centralized in the front face; and is located at a convenient height, to expose the horizontal surfaces of the object.

Perspectives are extensively utilized by artists and architects, to realistically depict sculptures, buildings and other structures before they are built. Computer programs able to generate perspectives

43

FIG. 3.5 Architectural employment of a two-point perspective. The image seems to converge at the vanishing points. One of the VP's is located beyond the drawing limits.

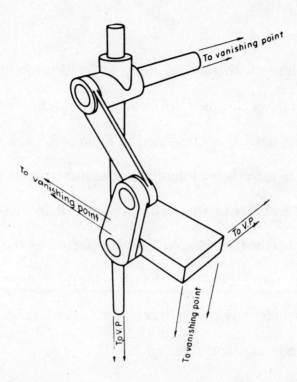

FIG. 3.6 Three-point perspective. Notice that all axes are inclined with respect to the picture plane. (Courtesy of ASME and ANSI.)

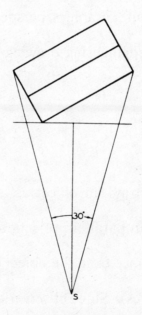

LOCATION OF POINT OF
SIGHT IN PERSPECTIVE

FIG. 3.7 The point-of-sight should be placed so that the observer's cone of visual rays, covering the object, is not greater than 30 degrees. (Courtesy of ASME and ANSI.)

provide the designer with the capability to "walk around" a model. This capability allows the user to inspect the interior and exterior appearance of the design, as illustrated in Figures 3.8 a, b, c, d and e. A great number of the existing interactive graphics systems provide the designer with the ability to rotate the image and to view it from a different point-of-sight (i.e., in CAD this is referred as the <u>view point</u> from which you request to see the drawing). Other interesting applications include: visual checks for interferences, finding intersections, renderings and shading.

Perspectives are not frequently used in engineering practice. However, with the advent of computer graphics, perspective projections are being incorporated in some engineering drawings, as shown in Figures 3.8 and 3.9.

II. Parallel Projection

<u>Parallel Projection</u> portrays an object as a geometric abstraction of human visual reality. In parallel projection, the observer is assumed to be at an infinite distance from the object (i.e., as opposed to a finite distance-like perspectives). Since observer and object are so far apart, the visual rays are parallel to each other. These rays or lines-of-sight are used to project the object onto a standard drawing plane or 2-D display.

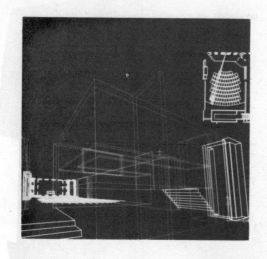
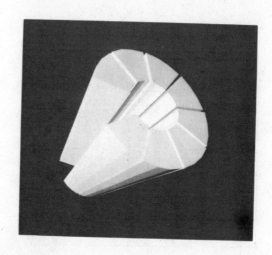
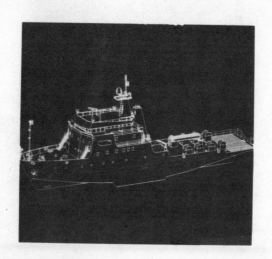
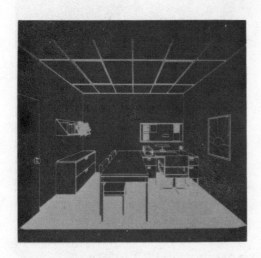
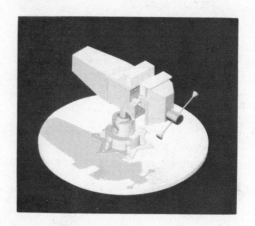

FIG. 3.8 Several computer-generated perspectives views. (Courtesy of CADAM, Inc.)

47

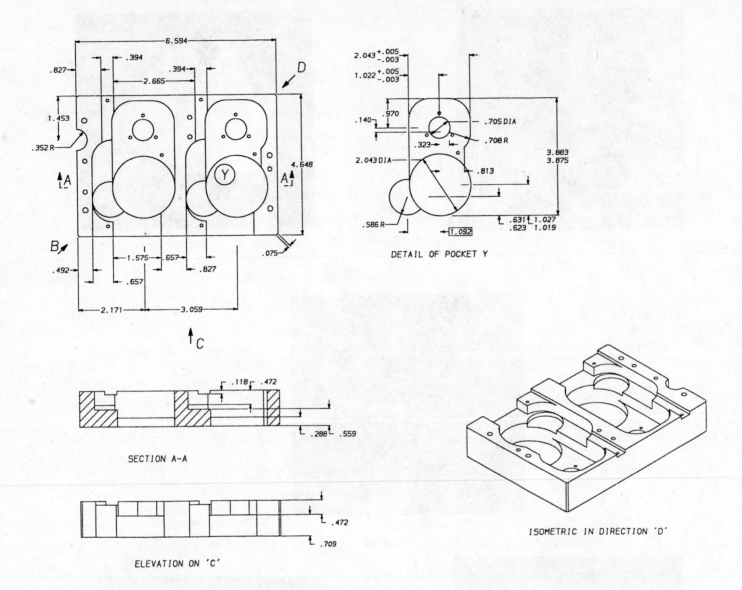

SECTION A-A

ELEVATION ON 'C'

ISOMETRIC IN DIRECTION 'D'

DETAIL OF POCKET Y

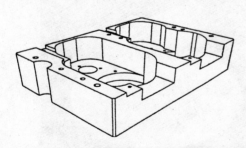

PERSPECTIVE IN DIRECTION 'B'

FIG. 3.9 Working drawings of a valve block, including a perspective! (Courtesy of PR1ME/ MEDUSA.)

Parallel projections are subclassified by the angle formed between projection planes and the observer's line-of-sight. The forthcoming discussion covers the prevailing features of parallel projections. To guide the discussion the following summary is offered (see Table 3.1).

A. Orthographic- visual rays at right-angle with projection plane

    a. Multiview- display of standard 2-D views

        1. First-angle projection- object between observer and plane
        2. Third-angle projection- plane between object and observer

    b. Axonometric- object is rotated to show 3 face

        1. Isometric- equal angles between axes of object
        2. Dimetric- two axes make equal angles

        3. Trimetric- no two axes make equal angles

B. Oblique- visual rays not at right-angle with projection plane

    a. Cavalier- 45 degrees with plane, receding lines in true length

    b. Cabinet- 63 degrees and 26 minutes with plane, receding lines drawn half length

    c. General Oblique- any other angles with plane of projection

C. Standard and special purpose

    a. Sectional- projection plane cuts through solid geometry

        1. Full Section- plane passes fully through an object
        2. Half Section- passes halfway through an object
        3. Offset Section- passes through important features
        4. Other (ribs, revolved, removed, broken-out, phantom)

    b. Auxiliary- not parallel to the principal orthographic planes

        1. Primary- perpendicular to one principal plane
        2. Secondary- inclined to all principal planes

Table 3.1 Summary of Parallel Projections.

Let us now explain these concepts in detail.

Orthographic Projection

A three-dimensional object (i.e., solid geometry) can be represented by projecting its views onto imaginary orthogonal planes, as illustrated in Fig. 3.10. The greek word "orthogonios" -orthogonal- means "composed of right angles". Consequently, the projection method that utilizes parallel lines-of-sight at right angles (90 degrees) to an imaginary plane to represent 3-D objects is named orthographic projection. This standard method allows the engineer to describe a specific device, in every detail, on a 2-D plane.

Although, a solid model generated on the computer will describe the shape of a specific device, it is usually necessary to add some quantitative information like dimensions and specifications. This additional information is conveniently depicted using orthographic projections. Engineering working drawings of a device consists of a series of orthographic views, with enough details to allow its production in a manufacturing plant.

Projection Planes

Projection Planes are imaginary two-dimensional surfaces used to project, draw and/or display the object's views. Figure 3.11 depicts a solid object enclosed by an imaginary "transparent box". The

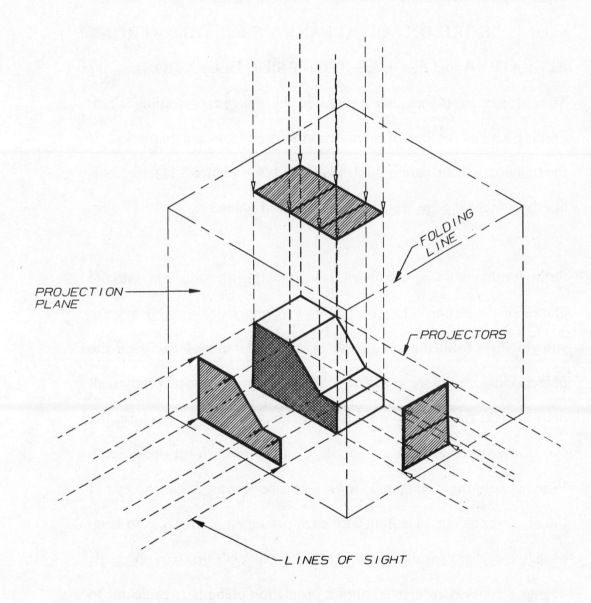

FIG. 3.10 The faces of the imaginary transparent box portrays the projection planes between the object and the observer.

illustrated faces of the box portray the projection planes, between the object and the observer. The projection planes are used to project orthographic views. The three main standard planes of projection are named: HORIZONTAL (PLAN), FRONTAL (FRONT ELEVATION) and PROFILE (RIGHT-SIDE ELEVATION).

The projection planes are separated by imaginary folding lines. Folding-Line is the line of intersection between two image planes. If the imaginary "transparent box" is unfolded (see Figure 3.11), the fold-line becomes an edge view of the projection plane.

Orthographic views are constructed by projecting lines-of-sight onto the planes of projection. Lines-of-Sight, Projectors or Visual Rays are straight lines from the eye of the observer to points located on the object (look once more at Figure 3.10). In orthographic projection, all lines-of-sight are parallel to each other (i.e., as mentioned before, the eye of the observer is at an infinite distance away from the object). When generating orthogonal views, it can be assumed that the eye of the observer changes position with each projected point, so as to keep each line-of-sight parallel to the other. The object's orthographic view or image is always projected onto a projection plane perpendicular to the lines-of-sight. The projection plane can be conveniently located between the observer and the object.

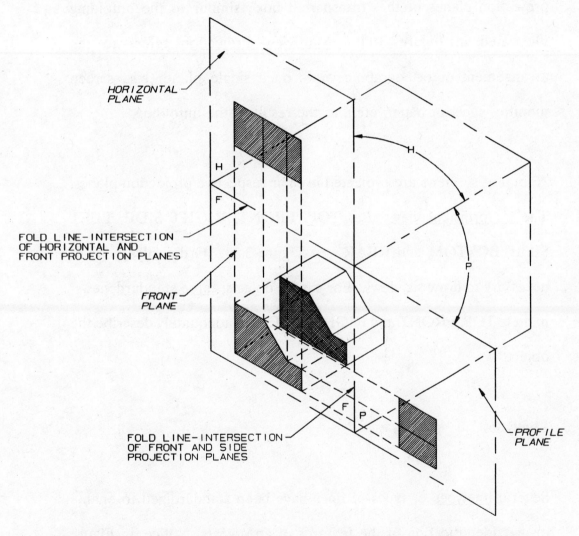

FIG. 3.11 Simulating the unfolding of the profile and horizontal projection planes.

The following labels appear in the figure:

HORIZONTAL PLANE

FOLD LINE-INTERSECTION OF HORIZONTAL AND FRONT PROJECTION PLANES

FRONT PLANE

FOLD LINE-INTERSECTION OF FRONT AND SIDE PROJECTION PLANES

PROFILE PLANE

Multiview Projection

In order to obtain a convenient scaled true-length representation of an object, views are arranged and drawn, as illustrated in Figures 3.12 and 3.13. These views were obtained by an imaginary unfolding of the projection planes of the "transparent box", similar to the unfolding illustrated in Figure 3.11. Multiview Projection refers to the arrangement of orthographic views on a single plane (e.g., screen monitor, sheet of paper, etc.), as the result of the unfolding.

A total of six views are projected in their respective projection planes. The six principal views are: TOP, FRONT, RIGHT SIDE, LEFT SIDE, BOTTOM and REAR, see Figure 3.13. Ordinarily, it is not necessary to draw six views. For simple objects, three standard views- namely TOP, FRONT and RIGHT SIDE- will adequately describe the object.

Linetypes

Several linetypes or types of lines have been standardized to enable proper identification of the features of an object. Notice, in Figure 3.13, several dashed lines (----------). These lines represent lines that are not visible from a specific orthographic view are called hidden lines.

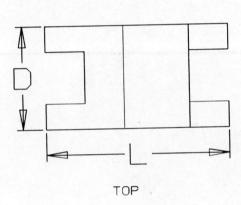

TOP

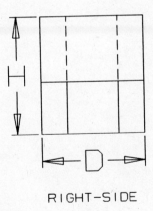

ISOMETRIC

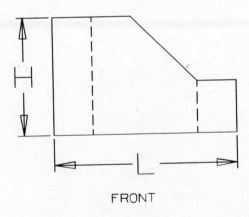

FRONT

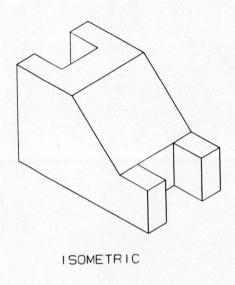

RIGHT-SIDE

FIG. 3.12 Four orthographic projections: top, front, right-side and 3-D display.

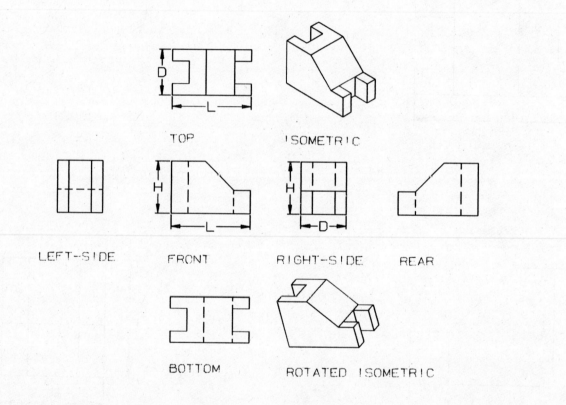

FIG. 3.13 Computer graphics display of six principal multiviews (top, front, right-side, left-side, bottom, rear) and two additional 3-D projections. Notice the use of hidden (dashed) lines.

These hidden lines are shown to clarify details and important features of the object. Ommision of hidden lines might cause important aspects of a device to be neglected or overlooked. Nevertheless, sometimes they have to be ommitted. For example: when they are behind a visible line or when they will confuse, rather than simplify, the drawing. Hidden lines -intersecting other lines- should be drawn so that their end dashes are in contact with the intersecting lines. One exception: when the dash makes a continuation with another linetype. ANSI recommends that features located behind transparent material should also be drawn with hidden lines.

Solid, thick lines delineating the outline or the object's changes in planes (_____) are called <u>visible lines</u>. Visible lines shall be drawn heavier than the hidden line, so that their outline will stand out unobstructed. Adequate contrast between visible lines and all other lines will make the drawing more legible. This has been referred as: "line quality".

<u>Center lines</u> (__ _ __) are drawn in the center of circles and arcs to aid in the view's interpretation. Of course, these alternating long and short dashes are utilized -in all orthographic views- to locate the circular features of the object. Center lines are only ommited when they coincide with hidden or visible lines. However, when ever

possible, their <u>extends</u> (i.e., that portion of the center line that protrudes over the circle) should be drawn. Center lines are also used as an axis of symmetry. For example: to represent the other half of partially drawn views, to indicate the path of a member in motion and to clarify partial sections of symmetrical parts.

<u>Construction lines</u> are used to help in the drawing production process. These lines are erased or deleted once the drawing is finished, as we will see in chapter 4.

Figures 3.14 and 3.15 show several of the standard drafting line conventions and their application. Notice that two width of lines are recommended: thick {.032 inches (.7 mm)} and thin {.016 inches (.35 mm)}. In other words, they should have a recommended ratio of approximately 2:1 between them.

Chain lines, phantom lines, stitch lines, dimension lines, extension lines, leaders, cutting-plane lines, viewing-plane lines, section lines and break lines will be discussed in subsequent chapters.

Projection Standard Systems

There are two projection systems utilized, namely: First-Angle Projection and Third-Angle Projection. The acceptable standard of

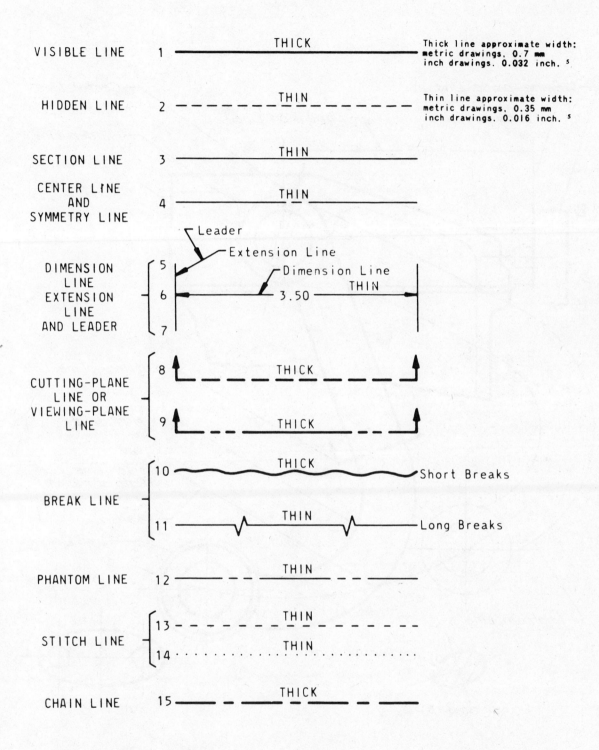

FIG. 3.14 Standard width and type of line conventions. (Courtesy of ASME and ANSI.)

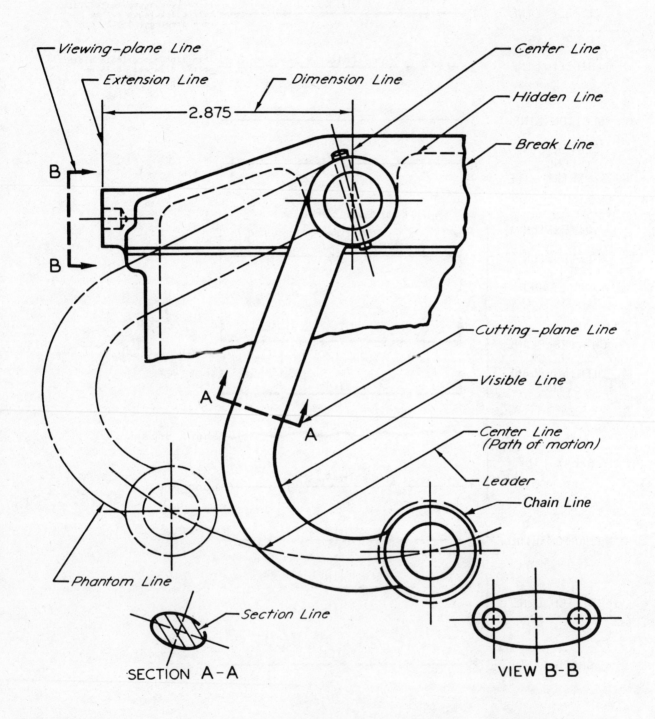

FIG. 3.15 Utilizing the different types of lines. (Courtesy of ASME and ANSI.)

displaying multiviews, in the U.S., is known as third-angle projection. However, many other countries utilize the first-angle projection international standard. In <u>first-angle projection</u>, the object is located between the observer and the plane of projection (see Figure 3.16).

In <u>third-angle projection</u> the plane of projection is positioned between the object and the observer, as shown in Figure 3.17. Since the visibility of lines is obtained from the observer's point-of-view, the orthographic views of the object are the same for both systems. However, the arrangement or relative positioning of the orthographic views is different.

ANSI utilizes a standard graphic symbol to differentiate between First-Angle and Third-Angle projection systems, as portrayed in Figure 3.18. The six principal orthographic views, in the third-angle standard arrangement, are shown in Figure 3.19.

The preceding sections focused on the main types of orthographic projections and their application in engineering graphics. Projection theory is utilized to analyze, draw and display 3-D spatial geometry in two-dimensions. In the next section we will see how we can use projection theory in the solution of an optimization problem.

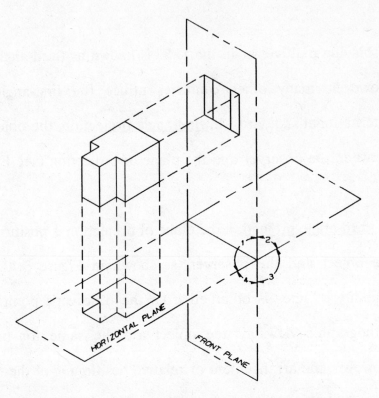

FIG. 3.16 In first-angle projection, the object is placed between the observer and the plane of projection.

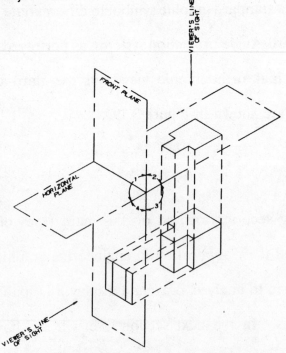

FIG. 3.17 In third-angle projection, the plane of projection is positioned between the object and the observer

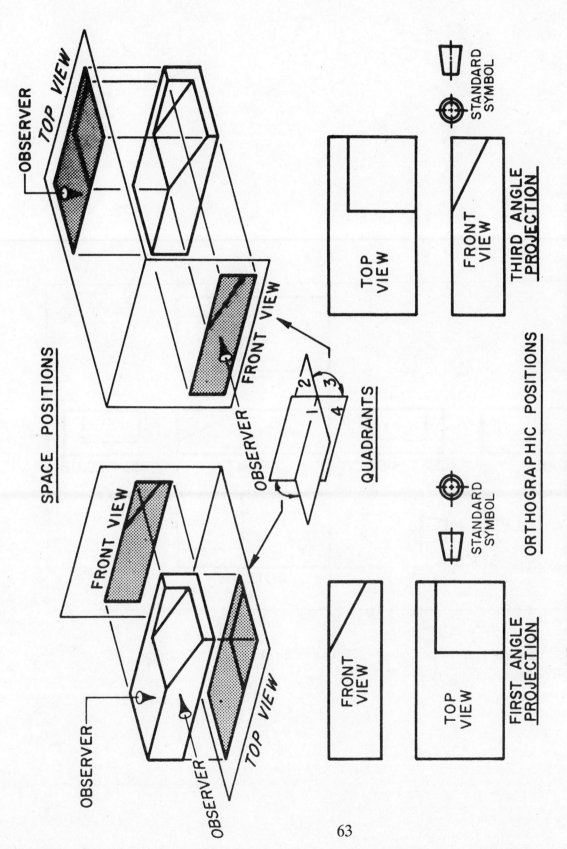

FIG. 3.18 The graphic standard symbols above indicates whether the drawing utilizes first-angle projection or third-angle projection systems. (Courtesy of ASME and ANSI.)

63

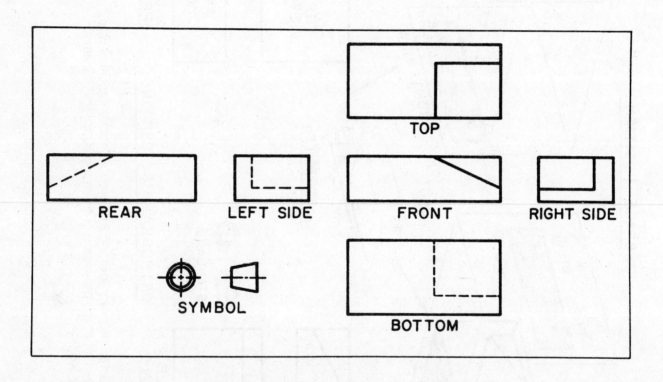

FIG. 3.19 The six principal orthographic views in their standard third-angle arrangement. (Courtesy of ASME and ANSI.)

Graphical Problem Solving

As in the past, engineers use tools -in conjunction to their specialty knowledge-to assess problems and satisfy Society's needs and wants. CAED/Graphics tools facilitate our problem solving and visual communication process.

As an engineering student you are required to solve analytical and design problems.   You usually apply knowledge-based criteria, experience, intelligent deductions and even a little bit of intuition to reach a solution.   You have probably found that your background knowledge -of mathematical and graphical procedures- is extremely useful in attaining a valid solution.

Since engineering is a problem oriented profession, most academic training consists of solving technical puzzles and quandaries.   You discover, very early in your career, that in addition to the technical knowledge it is necessary to graphically record the problem solutions and design alternatives.

The following example will demonstrate the utilization of computer graphics to solve a hypothetical problem. The problem is to find the minimum path traveled by an ant so as to reach a grain of sugar before other ants, located in the same position and traveling at the same velocity, reach the sugar.

Example 1.1: The Ants and the Grain of Sugar Minimum Path Problem.

Once upon a time there were three lonely ants in a plexiglass rectangular box...their names: Bit, Aby and Comp. The ant box measurements are: 60 mm high, 60 mm wide and 150 mm long.

From their observation post they look at the opposite end wall and see a grain of sugar stuck, in the center, 5 mm above the floor of the box, as illustrated in Figure 3.20 (Drw. File: ANT BOX). The ants are located very close to each other on the middle of the opposite wall 5 mm below the ceiling. Each ant will take a different path. Which ant will get the grain of sugar first? Determine the minimum distance traveled. Assume none of the ants will waste time fighting!

CAED/Graphics Solution

A three dimensional box is modeled on an Interactive Computer Graphic System, as shown in Figure 3.20 (Drw. File: ANT BOX). Then a two dimensional representation (partial development) of the

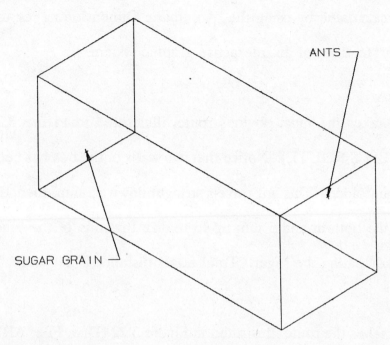

FIG. 3.20 A three-dimensional transparent ant box, showing the relative location of the ants and a grain of sugar.

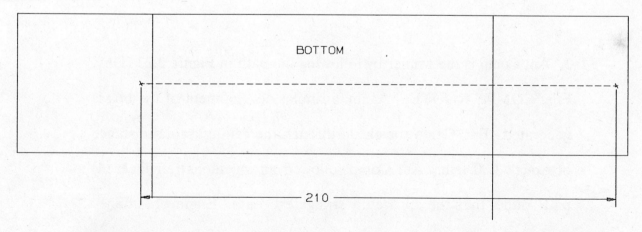

FIG. 3.21 Two-dimensional representation (partial development) of two unfolded walls of the box illustrating Bit's route.

unfolded box is displayed in several ways. The distance traveled by each ant is calculated by using the "Automatic Dimensioning" or the "Data Verify" features of an interactive graphic system.

1. Ant Bit takes the most obvious route, illustrated in Figure 3.21 (Drw. File: BIT'S ROUTE). Notice that two walls of the box has been imaginarily unfolded. This ant travels straight down 55 mm, then 150 mm across the bottom and 5 mm up to realize that one of the other ants is already eating the sugar. Total travel distance is 210 mm.

2. Ant Aby takes the route illustrated in Figure 3.22 (Drw. File: ABY' ROUTE). Notice that the box has been unfolded (development) to mark the path. Aby traveled diagonally down, across the wall, through the side wall and bottom, a total of 203.59 mm ... but Ant Comp was already having a banquet.

3. Ant Comp is the winner by following the path in Figure 3.23 (Drw. File: COMP'S ROUTE). Again, a similar development of the box is generated. But, Comp travels up through the ceiling a total distance of exactly 200 mm. Ant Comp followed an ingenious (engineered) path, rather than the apparently straightest route. Engineers utilize similar graphical optimization techniques to solve real life problems.

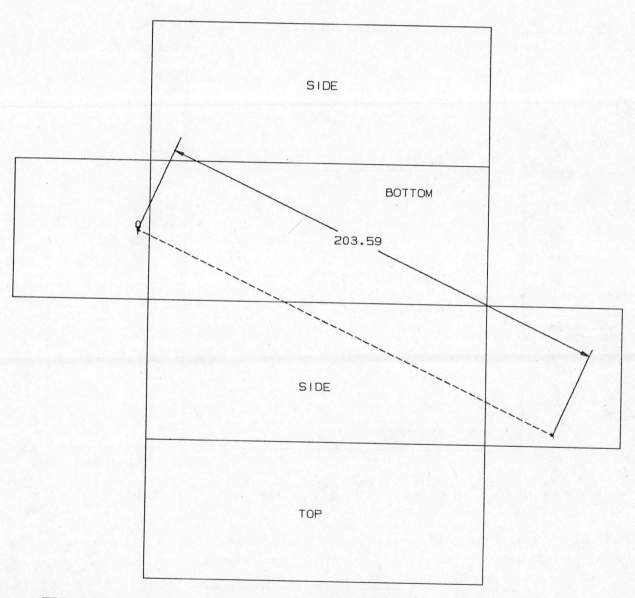

FIG. 3.22 Development of the box marking Aby's path.

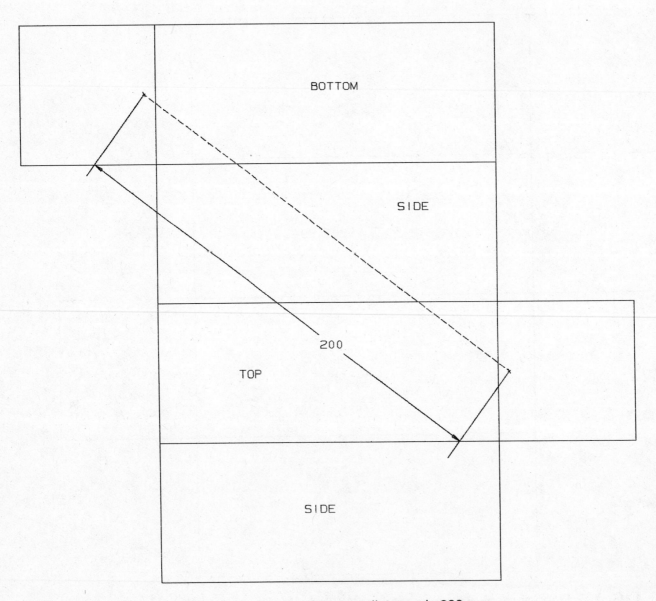

FIG. 3.23 The winner is ant Comp! Shortest distance is 200 mm.

Pages 71 and 72 contain a series of multiview projection problems (A through R). Notice that there is a missing view in each of the problems. Select the correct orthographic view, from the multiple choices in page 73.

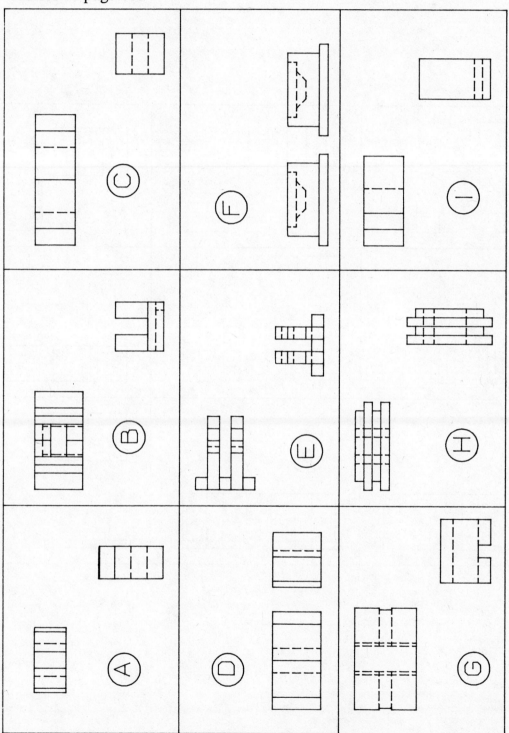

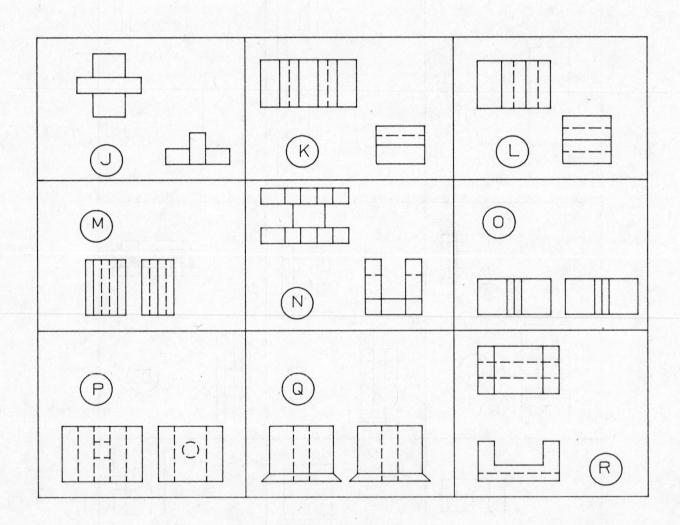

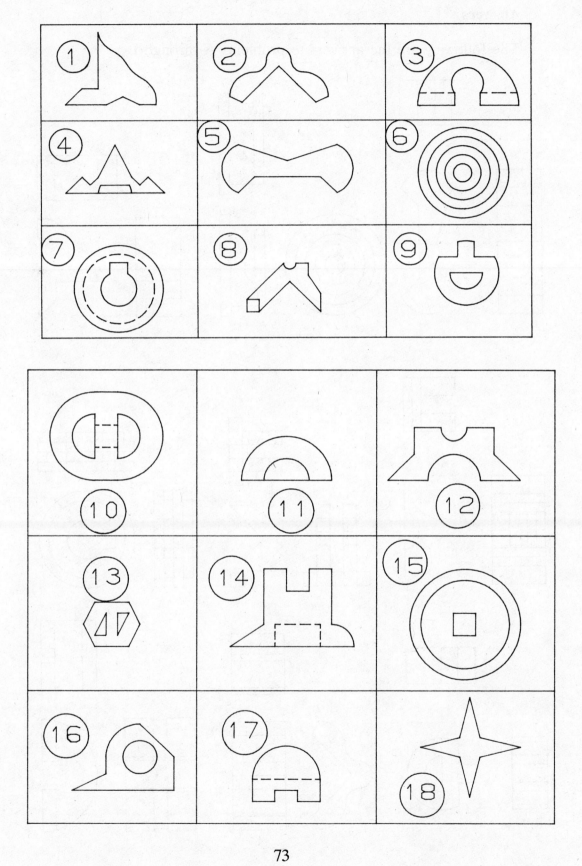

Answers

The following are the answers to problems A through I.

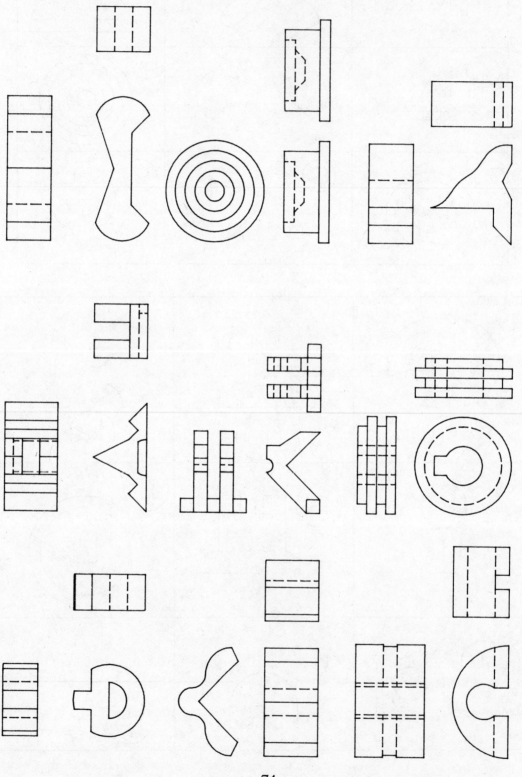

CHAPTER 4

FREEHAND AND COMPUTER SKETCHING

Engineering Sketching

The technique (or skill) to clearly communicate engineering design ideas without the use of traditional mechanical drafting instruments and/or computer graphic systems is called **engineering sketching**.

It is recognized that instrument drawings are more precise than sketches. But, in this age of computers and information, engineering and manufacturing companies are recognizing more than ever the importance of being able to produce proficient freehand and computer-aided sketches to quickly convey design ideas. It is hard to imagine an engineer without freehand or computer sketching talent. This chapter introduces you to freehand-scaled sketching and computer-aided sketching.

Sketching implies technical freehand drawing. As opposed to 'artistic' freehand drawing, engineering sketching is based on the principles of orthographic projection theory as discussed in Chapter 3. In this chapter, we will concentrate our efforts on learning to sketch as a tool for applying the principles of 2-D orthographic projection theory. In

Chapter 5, we will expand our sketching techniques to include 3-D (i.e., axonometrics and oblique projections and drawings) representations.

Sketching orthographic views and three-dimensional pictorial drawings is the engineers' means of generating quick ideas and communicating them to other members of the design team. A sketch on a notebook in the classroom, on a napkin in the restaurant, on a blue-print in the construction site, or on the surface of a workshop table, is far more effective that an verbal explanation.

Engineers-in-Industry know that it is much faster to prepare a manual sketch -than to draw it with mechanical instruments or with computer graphics system- to convey the design ideas to other members of the engineering staff or machine shop. In engineering graphics courses sketching can be a time-saving tool. Dr. Robert Foster co-author, with French and Vierck, of the classic engineering graphics book *Engineering Drawing and Graphics Technology* (New York: McGraw-Hill, 1986) explains "sketching is an excellent method for learning the fundamentals of orthographic projection and can be used by beginners even before they have had much practice with instruments. In training, as in professional work, time can be saved by working freehand instead of with instruments, because with this method more problems can be solved in an allotted amount of time."

How Sketchy are Sketches?

Sketching is not synonym of hastily-, careless- or sketchy-made drawings. As stated by D. Henry Edel, editor of *Introduction to Creative Design* (New Jersey: Prentice-Hall, 1967) and former Project Engineer at GAF Corporation, "the term 'sketch' or 'sketching' is not a license to become sloppy or incomplete, however. Sketches should reflect high quality and a completeness of thought. The term sketch implies freehand; however, straight edges and templates are often used for polishing a sketch in its final form." You do not need to have a complete set of instruments to prepare a neat sketch. If you have the ability, pencil and paper will suffice. Feel free to use a set of 30-60 and 45-degree triangles.

Sketching Skills

Sketching is a simple form of drawing that relies on your ability to construct a clear mental image of the object you are to map onto a projection plane. The best strategy to develop your sketching skills consist in practice, practice and more practice. Careful observation of the physical environment is complementary to the strategy. Refining your visual perception skill is fundamental in freehand drawing. You need to relate to the highlights, textures, characteristics and spatial geometry of the 3-D object you are trying to represent. In *Illustrating for Tomorrow's Production* (New York: McMillan, 1950) Farmer, et al., indicates that sketching "is a means by which the illustrator expresses construction, form, and size."

Sketching as a Design Tool

Although few of Leonardo da Vinci's design ideas were realized, he left us the legacy of amazing works of art and engineering sketches (see Chapter 2). Leonardo, the Renaissance artist/engineer, utilized direct observation of the environment as a means of studying the objects to be drawn. Engineering students can use a similar **visual annotation** technique to keep a record of objects they observe for later retrieval. This annotation technique is similar to the set of notes and records kept by scientists.

The eye and the brain are the most important components in this visual annotation. While observing certain object create a visual hypothesis, constructing an organized mental image and geometry based on your experience and the stimuli reaching your eye. In constructing this visual image you should seize on ingrained physical characteristics of the object at hand. In other words study its main features, form, proportions, orientation, material, color, symmetry, contrast, repetition, etcetera. Then, sketch the general outline of the object imagining that the pencil would actually touch the object as you trace the object on the drawing pad. Always carry a sketching pad with you. Wherever you go take "drawing notes" of what you observe.

Engineering graphics programs are starting to include courses in sketching and visual annotation techniques. As a matter of fact, early engineering programs used to have similar drawing and visualization course but it was abandoned to "make room" for additional technical courses.

Manufacturers and engineering employers usually complain that engineering students are not taught "freehand drawing". They recognize the importance of sketching to generate many alternative solutions to a particular design problem. Sketching is particularly useful in the early brain-storming and formulation stages of the design process. George C. Beakley, Associate Dean at Arizona State University and one of the pioneers in the use of sketching as an educational visual communication tool, states in *Introduction to Engineering Graphics* that "sketching helps to stimulate one's imagination as well as to convey information. For this reason it is ideally suited for the engineer's communication with others <u>and with himself</u>. A sketch frequently serves to clarify an original idea and at the same time suggest additional versions, adaptations, and improvements." He further expands that presenting a concept in a graphical form helps in organizing thoughts, "whether it be a flow chart summarizing the main points of a presentation or a detailed sketch explaining a complicated mechanism." Sketching is also used during the analysis, synthesis, evaluation and even while revising the final working drawings.

Sketching Methodology

Before attempting to sketch the orthographic views of a given part, observe the part carefully. Ask yourself: What are the features that need to be emphasized? Then, decide on the best position and point-of-view to represent the object. Analyze the proportions and determine the outer boundary limits of the object. Based on the dimensions and the drawing paper surface available, determine the scale to use. Measure all height, width and depth features of the object. Picture yourself as looking through a large "glass window" in which the entities of the object are projected. The difference is that instead of tracing "what you see" -as in perspective-drawing (see Chapter 3)- you are to imagine that parallel projection lines are hitting the surface of the "window" (projection plane) at right angles. You are to sketch the image projected onto the surface. Parallel lines in the image should be parallel to each other in the orthogonal sketch. Object surfaces parallel to the projection plane will appear in true shape. However, oblique surfaces to the projection plane will not be in true shape. Truly elliptical features in depth will appear as circles. Parallelograms will be rectangles, etc. Once you are finish make sure you label the title, date and your name. If this is the sketch of a new invention make sure you indicate the date of conception and the inventor's name. This will protect your patent rights.

Sketching Tools

What are the tools required to start your sketch? Normally, the tools needed are a drawing device (e.g., pencil, stylus, joystick), a display surface (e.g., sheet of paper, tablet, monitor). Most sketching beginners prefer to use an 8 1/2" x 11" quadrille sketching pad. Such notebooks are commercially available in several rulings, including: 4, 5, 6, 8 squares to the inch and 5 squares to the centimeter. There are pads with overlaid isometric and orthographic grids. However, the engineer should be capable of sketching a proportional drawing on any paper available. As a matter of fact, one experienced designer claims that some of her greatest ideas have been sketched on a napkin at lunch time! These ideas are later drafted using mechanical instruments or CADD systems.

Getting Ready to Sketch

Although sketching requires some natural ability; it is mostly a technique that can be mastered with practice. The following example illustrates multiview sketching of a given object.

Example 4.1: Drawing Orthographic Views from a Given Object.

Sketch the three standard orthographic views of the object shown in Figure 4.1. Try this problem, manually, without the assistance of instruments or grid paper. Use a medium grade pencil (B, HB, F) and a standard 8 1/2" X 11" sheet of white paper. Utilize the same pencil -throughout the drawing process- but sharpen the pencil, accordingly, to obtain: heavy visible lines, medium hidden lines, thin center lines and light construction lines.

Solution:

1. Visually, estimate the overall measurements and proportions of the object (see Figure 4.1).

2. Block the overall outside boundaries of the part, on the horizontal and frontal faces of an "unfolded transparent box".

3. Indicate the center of circles and label the views.

4. Draw a mitre line (e.i., 45 degree line to extend the right-side view dimensions), as illustrated in Figure 4.2.

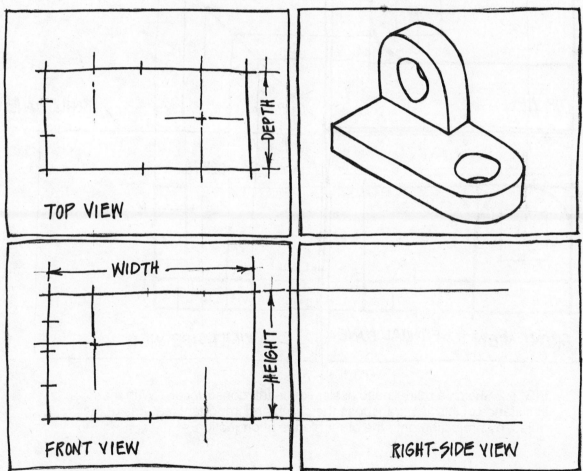

TOP VIEW

DEPTH

WIDTH

HEIGHT

FRONT VIEW

RIGHT-SIDE VIEW

FIG. 4.1 Sketching the orthographic multiviews of an object. Block the overall boundaries of the part.

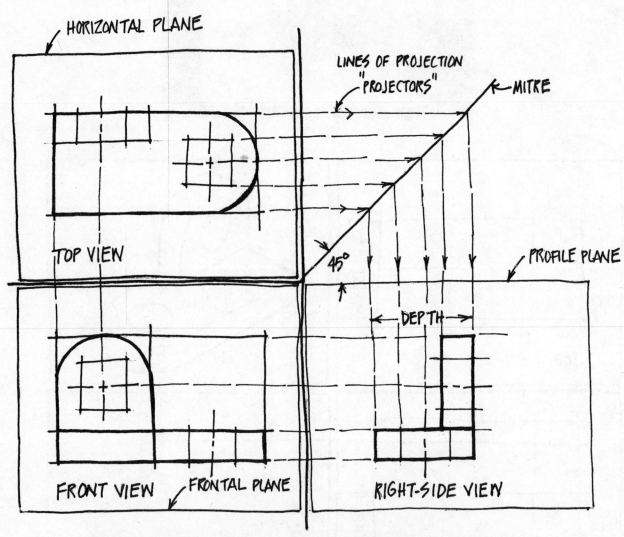

FIG. 4.2 Sketch a mitre line to assist you in the construction. With the assistance of this line, transpose the depth and important features of the object by projecting onto the other planes of projection.

5. To transpose the depth dimensions, draw projectors -to the right, until they hit the mitre line, and then downward- locating the important features of the right-side view.

6. Draw light construction lines to aid in sketching circles. For example, sketch a centered square around the location of circles. Outline the prominent features of the part: curves, changes in direction, etc..

7. Finish the drawing by heavily darkening the visible lines. Lightly darken the hidden lines. Erase all construction lines (see Figure 4.3).

Standard Paper Sizes

Ordinarily, it is necessary to sketch or plot orthographic multiview, pictorials and other drawings on a standard sheet of paper. The following is a list of the ANSI standard paper size designations. All dimensions are given in inches (1 in. = 25.4 mm):

TYPE	WIDTH	LENGTH
A	8.5	11.0
B	11.0	17.0
C	17.0	22.0
D	22.0	34.0
E	34.0	44.0
F	28.0	40.0

The international (ISO) paper sizes are listed below (all dimensions

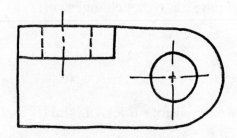

TOP VIEW

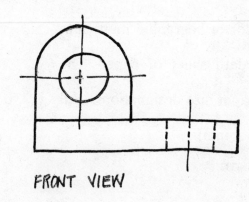

FRONT VIEW

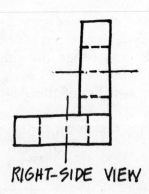

RIGHT-SIDE VIEW

FIG. 4.3 Finish the sketch by heavily darkening the visible lines. Lightly darken the hidden (dashed) lines. Erase the construction lines.

are given in millimeters):

TYPE	WIDTH	LENGTH	
(Nearest U.S. type)			
A0	841	1189	E
A1	594	841	D
A2	420	594	C
A3	297	420	B
A4	210	297	A

Scales

Consider that you have to draw or sketch an object, device, or system larger than the standard sheets of paper listed above. The obvious choice is to reduce or "scale-down" the drawing.

Scaling is the process of drawing an object to a specified size. The object may be drawn to the same size: full scale (1:1). The object may be reduced in size (i.e., making it appear smaller, by using a different scale). For example, a part may be reduced in half by a ratio of reduction equal to 1:2 or half scale. The very small device, like a microchip, may be enlarged (i.e., making it appear larger than the actual size).

In computer graphics we do not have to be that concerned about scaling until the drawing is ready to be plotted. Reason: CADD systems have the capability of zooming-in or out the display as desired. As we will see in Chapter 8, all units remain the same after zooming (i.e., the actual dimensions of the object do not change). Nevertheless, it is important to be familiar with the different types of scales and learn how to use them. For example, you might be required to scale a missing distance from an existing set of working drawings; or to hand sketch a device to scale.

Metric scale is the international system of measurements. The SI or "Le Systeme International d'Unites, is the accepted form of the metric system.

This scale is labeled in each of its faces as follows: 1:1 FULL SIZE; 1mm calibration equals to 1mm, 1:2 HALF SIZE; each division equals 2 mm. Other ratios available are: 1:5, 1:25, 1:33 1/3, 1:75, etc. Each of these metric scales can be used for other ratios. For example, the 1:1 could be used as: 1:10, 1:100 and other multiples or divisible of 10. Figure 4.4 contains some examples of its use.

Engineers scale is graduated in decimals. One inch is divided in 10, 20, 30, 40, 50, and 60 parts. To set measurements at half scale you will utilize the 20 scale and so on so forth (see Figure 4.5). Each of these scales could be used for other ratios. For example: 1"=10', 1"=0.1", etc.

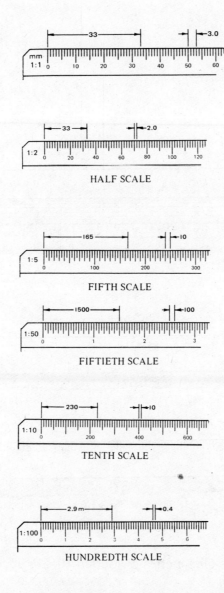

FIG. 4.4 Metric scales. Labeled in its surfaces, as follows: Full 1:1, Half size 1:2, etc. (Courtesy of McGraw-Hill, Source: Jensen/Helsel, Engineering Drawing and Design, 1979)

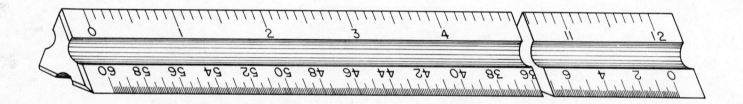

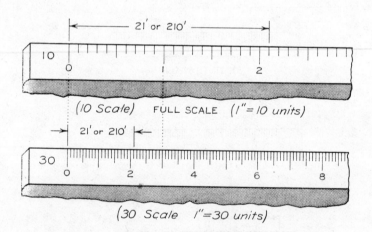

FIG. 4.5 Engineers scale. One inch is divided in 10, 20, 30, etc. parts. (Courtesy of McGraw-Hill)

In the <u>Architects scale</u> the major divisions represent feet and its sub-

divisions are inches. The main ratios are: 16 FULL SIZE (each

division is 1/16 inch; 3"=1'-0"; 1 1/2"=1'-0"; 1"=1'-0"; 3/4"=1'-0";

1/2"=1'-0", 3/8"=1'-0"; 1/4"=1'-0"; 3/32"=1'-0"; 1/8"=1'-0"; 3/16"=1'-

0". Some examples of the architects scale use are shown in Figure 4.6.

Computer-Aided Sketching

As stated earlier, making a freehand sketch only requires pencil and

paper. However, Computer-Aided Sketching requires several

computer graphics tools and knowledge of the idiosyncracies of the

CADD system been used.

CADD software packages like AutoSketch, AutoCAD and CADKEY

can be used to produce high quality sketches and conceptual drawings.

As with freehand sketching, the goal is to rapidly produce a drawing

to communicate and stimulate ideas. Although a computer sketch may

take slightly longer to construct it has the advantage of being available

for recall, modification, and reproduction on a printer or plotter. The

adaptation of a computer to quick sketching is limited only by the

user's knowledge on the manipulation tools provided by the CAD

system at hand.

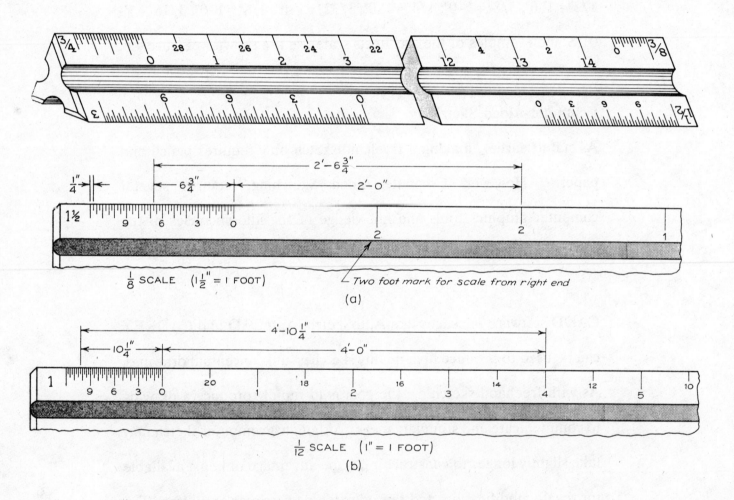

FIG. 4.6 Architests scale. The major divisions represent feet and its subdivisions inches. (Courtesy of McGraw-Hill)

92

Chapters 7 through 12 presents a fairly detailed discussion on sophisticated microcomputer and mainframe CADD packages like AutoCAD, CADKEY and ICEM. These comprehensive software packages provide you with dozens of commands, menus, options and functions to produce any type of engineering drawing or sketch you can imagine. However, it will take you some time to be completely familiar with all their capabilities.

In this section we have selected AutoSketch as our prototypical sketching package since it is user-friendly package. It provides fewer menu options, therefore it is ideal for some of the exercises discussed here. Although the special geometric construction operations described are those available to AutoSketch, you will find many similarities among the CAD software available in the market. For example, the AutoCAD and CADKEY systems provide a [SKETCH] command and entity dragging options (see Chapter 9) that allows some degree of "freehand" sketching with the hand-cursor. Entity dragging refers to the ability of the system to move or modify an object as a rough approximation of that object is shown on the screen. A rough approximation follows the movements of the handcursor or pointing device. This capability is supported by AutoSketch to assist you in visualizing the shape desired.

AutoSketch

In order to develop a computerized sketch in the shortest possible time maximum use must be made of the available system's predefined elements. AutoSketch utilizes <u>objects</u> or predefined elements such as points, lines, circles, arcs, and complex elements such as boxes, polygons, text, curves.

All these objects can be quickly generated in the drawing without the need to generate the individual components and entities within the object by simply selecting from a list of available menus and options. Figure 4.7 (a) illustrates AutoSketch menu bar at the top of the screen. Figure 4.7 (b) shows a display of an schematic diagram and the pull-out submenu for the [DRAW] option. Figure 4.7 (c) displays a bike design with the [ASSIST] pull-out submenus. Notice that this pull-out menus appears as windows in "top" of the drawing without erasing the display.

With the aid of these graphics tools non-standard figures such as ellipses can be constructed with the aid of curve approximation functions. Fractional portions of these objects, such as a 270 degree arc of a circle, may be generated by removing the desired portion with the certain operation. Additional speed may be gained through the use of various special functions. A grid of dots, with adjustable

94

```
Draw Change View Assist Settings Measure File          2%  23:14
```

```
Box  First Corner:
```

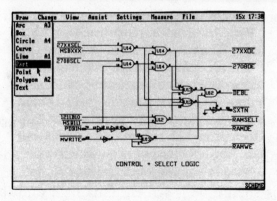

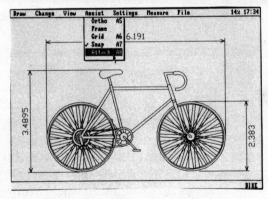

FIG. 4.7 (a) AutoSketch Menu Bar at the top of the screen, **(b)** Schematic diagram produced on AutoSketch. Notice [DRAW] pull-out menu, **(c)** Bike display and the [ASSIST] menus.

spacing may be superimposed over the drawing area as a reference for to do "approximate scaling" and to maintain correct sketch proportions.

In addition, the systems's [SNAP] function can be used to restrict the cursor position to only the certain predefined grid points. Orthogonal [ORTHO] functions can be used to limit line orientation to either horizontal or vertical positions, and is helpful when sketching construction lines.

Several example problems have been designed for the student who has access to a microcomputer based CAD system with an input device such as a mouse, handcursor, puck and/or digitizing pad.

Example 4.2 Drawing Two Concentric Ellipses with AutoSketch

1. Activate the Autosketch drawing [GRID], setting x and y spacing equal to one grid unit.

2. With the solid line activated select the draw [LINE] function and construct a rhombus (or parallelogram) shown in Figure 4.8 (a). The vertical sides of the rhombus should be 4 screen units high and the smallest internal angle about 60 degrees.

3. Construct a diagonal line across the long axis of the rhombus.

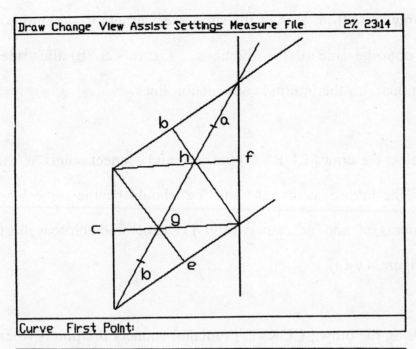

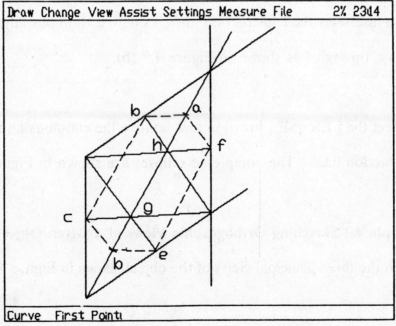

FIG. 4.8 (a) Rhombus drawn with the [LINE] function, **(b)** Internal construction lines.

4. Draw lines from each of the short axes corners to the mid point of the opposite side of the rhombus. Figure 4.8 (b) illustrates the rhombus with the internal construction lines.

5. Select the draw [CURVE] function and connect points "a" through "f". The line segments "ah" and "bg" should be the same length as segments "hf" and "ge" respectively. The generated ellipse is illustrated in Figure 4.9 (a).

6. Using the draw [CURVE] function connect the points where the ellipse intersects the construction lines inside the rhombus adjacent to points a through f as shown in Figure 4.9 (b).

7. Select the [ERASE] function and remove the rhombus and all the construction lines. The completed ellipses are shown in Figure 4.10.

Example 4.3 Sketching Orthographic Views of a Given Object.
Sketch the three principal views of the object shown in Figure 4.11 (a).

The development of multiview orthographic projection follows a process similar to that used in freehand sketching. First, the overall dimension of the object are defined. This can be accomplished in a

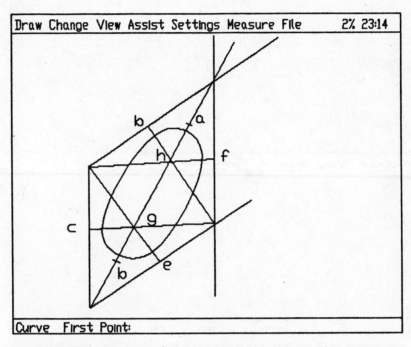

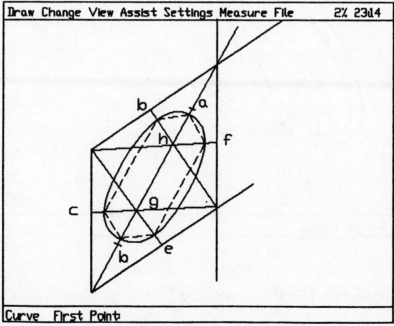

FIG. 4.9 (a) Use of the [CURVE] function, **(b)** Connecting points where the ellipse intersects the construction lines inside the rhombus.

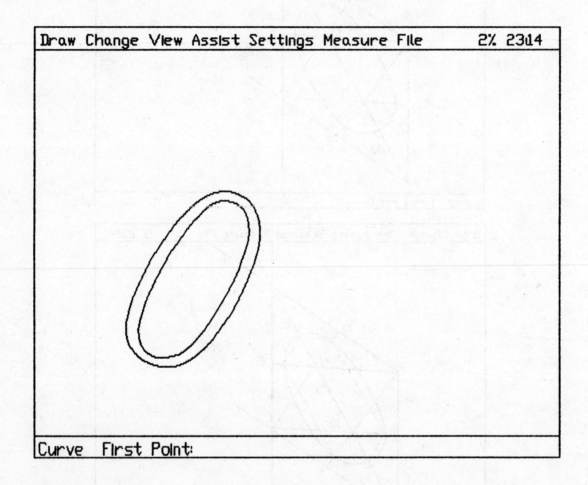

Draw Change View Assist Settings Measure File   2% 23:14

Curve   First Point:

FIG. 4.10 Select the [ERASE] function to remove construcion lines.

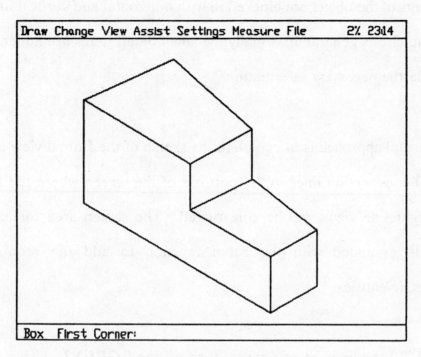

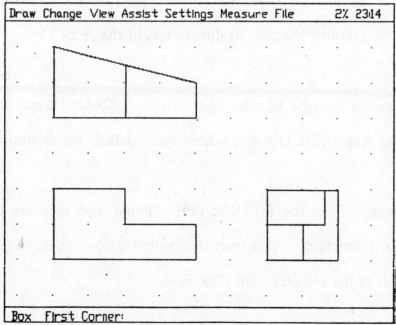

FIG. 4.11 (a) & (b) Sketching orthographics views of a given object.

single step by using the draw [BOX] function. Next the major elements of the object are blocked in with horizontal and vertical lines and the circles generated. Finally the small detail items are added to provide the necessary information.

One useful approach is to complete the sketch of the frontal view and extend construction lines to the portions of the screen where the top and right side views will be constructed. The screen area for each view is expanded with the zoom function to add the required geometric entities.

1. [SET] the linetype to dot and turn off the [GRID]. Using the box function outline the overall dimensions of the front view.

2. Change the linetype to solid and turn the [SNAP] function on. Select the draw [POLYGON] function and outline the frontal view.

3. Select dot from the [LINETYPE] menu and turn on the [ORTHO] function. Construct horizontal and vertical lines of projection to the top and right side views.

4. Select the [ASSIST] menu and turn off [ORTHO]. Change the linetype back to solid and expand the area for the right side view.

5. Draw the right side view.

6. Using the view menu select last view. Expand the area for the top view and complete it.

7. Select the erase function and remove all construction lines. The final sketch is illustrated in Figure 4.11 (b).

Example 4.4 Sketch an Isometric from Given Orthographic Views

Sketch an isometric drawing from the orthographic views of the telephone hand set shown in Figure 4.12.

This problem is approached by applying the basic techniques of isometric drawing (see Chapter 5). Start by drawing a "scaffold" box. The measure angle function is helpful in determining the correct line orientation. Once the initial construction lines for scaffold have been placed the copy function is used to reproduce the parallel line structure required for the three dimensions of the box.

Example 4.5 Sketch the Orthographic Views for Given a Perspective Drawing

Sketch the orthographic views for the bathroom cabinet given in Figure 4.13. Apply the techniques discussed in the previous examples.

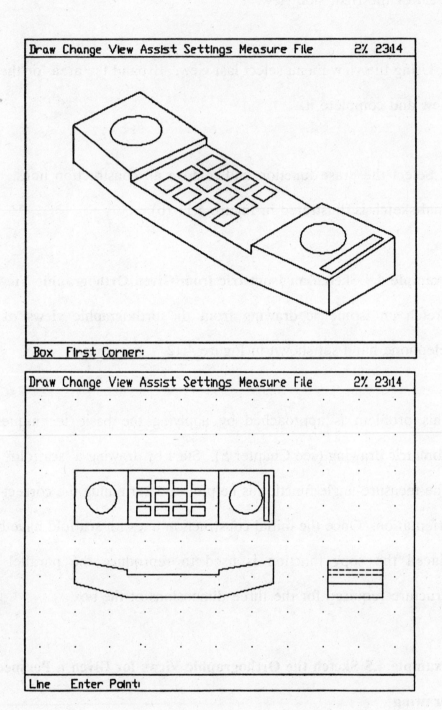

FIG. 4.12 Sketch an isometric from given orthographic projections.

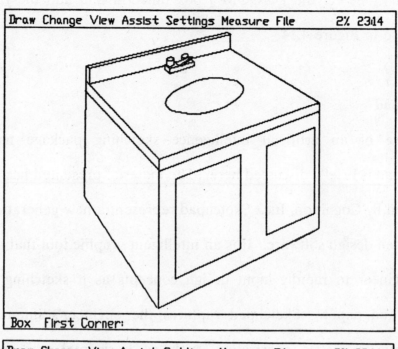

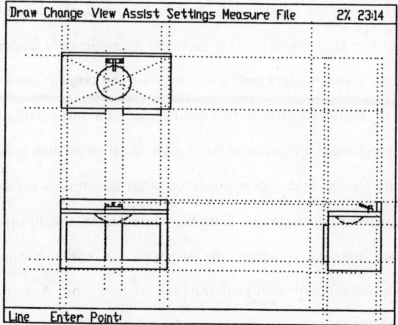

FIG. 4.13 Sketch orthographic projections from a given perspective.

Use the draw box function to reduce the number of operations necessary. Select the [ZOOM] box function and add the faucet displayed in Figure 4.14.

Sketchpad

The use of an artificial intelligence sketching package named Sketchpad is briefly discussed here. The material presented has been provided by Cognition, Inc. Sketchpad represent a new generation in integrated design software. It is an intelligent graphic tool that allow the engineer to rapidly input design concepts as if sketching with pencil and paper. Sketchpad captures the engineer's intent and preserves geometric constraints, such as horizontal, tangent or collinear. For example, if a line is sketched approximately tangent to a circle, the system understands it was meant to be tangent and stores it as such. Sketchpad will automatically maintain this relationship, even when changes are made to the design. Sketchpad also provides immediate feedback to the engineer on what constraints are being applied, in this case, tangency. Since Sketchpad automatically updates the sketch after each change, the engineer can easily create and update the models with extremely complex relationships. As shown in Figure 4.15 the sketched geometry can be combined with engineering equations. In addition the systems provides an on-line help with engineering books as illustrated in Figure 4.16. The help features are

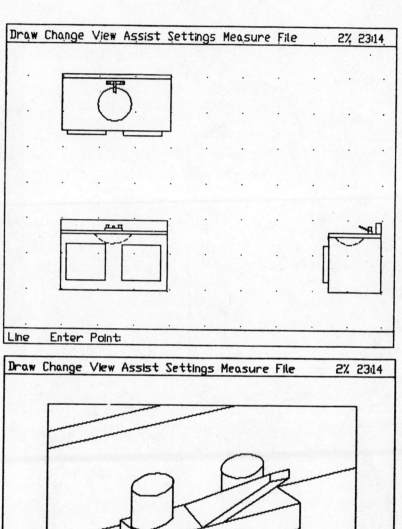

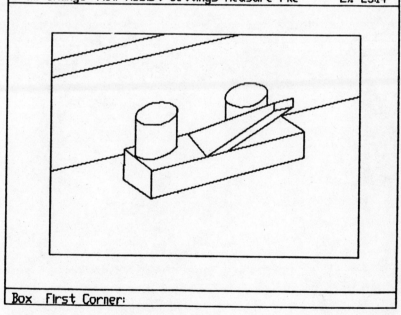

FIG. 4.14 Checking minor details with the [ZOOM] function.

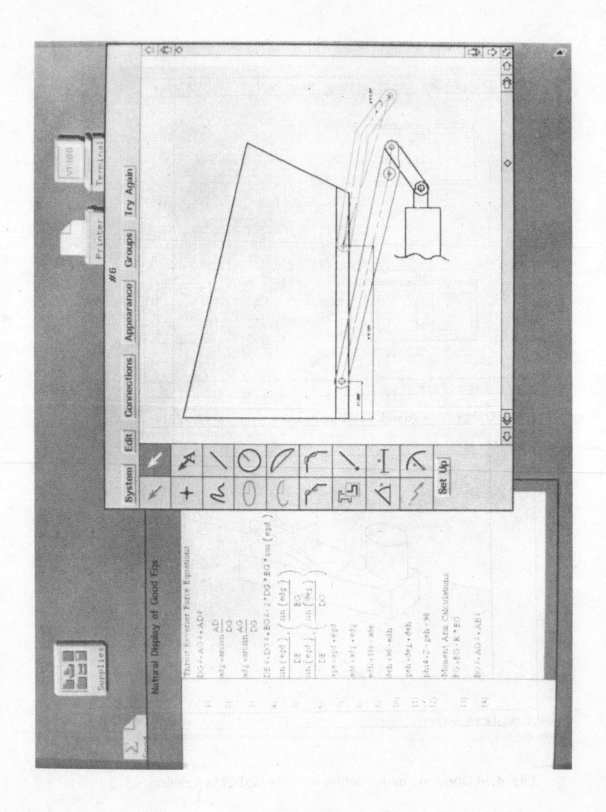

FIG. 4.15 Combining sketched geometry with engineering equations for integrated engineering design. (Courtesy of COGNITION, Inc.)

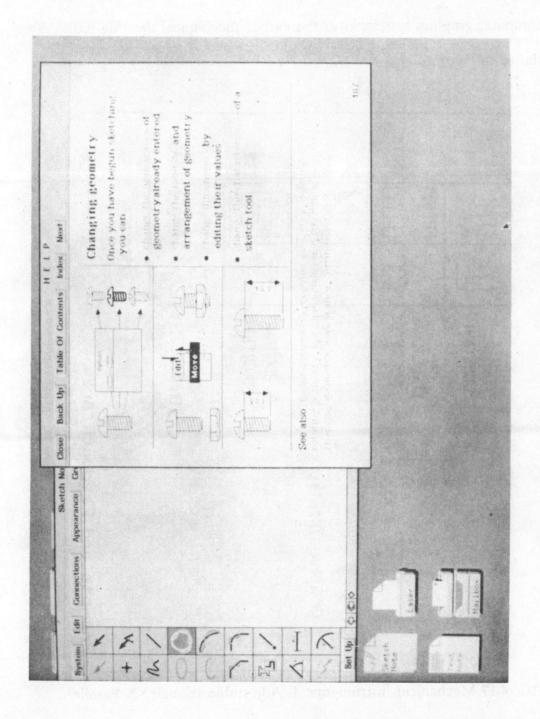

FIG. 4.16 On-line context-sensitive help to make the design process more effective. (Courtesy of COGNITION, Inc.)

context-sensitive to make the engineering design work more productive. After this discussion, it is clear to see the advantages of computer graphics systems over the earlier mechanical drafting tools shown in Figure 4.17.

FIG. 4.17 Mechanical instruments: 1. Adjustable triangle, 2. Parallel slide, 3. Flat scale (Courtesy of McGraw-Hill).

PROBLEMS

Sketch the orthographic multiviews in the following problems. Refer to the concepts discussed in Chapters 3 and 4. Solve the problems by using freehand sketching. Use a scale to obtain the proportions and measurements. Your instructor might assign you to try the same exercises using a package like AutoSketch or the SKETCH command available in AutoCAD and CADKEY.

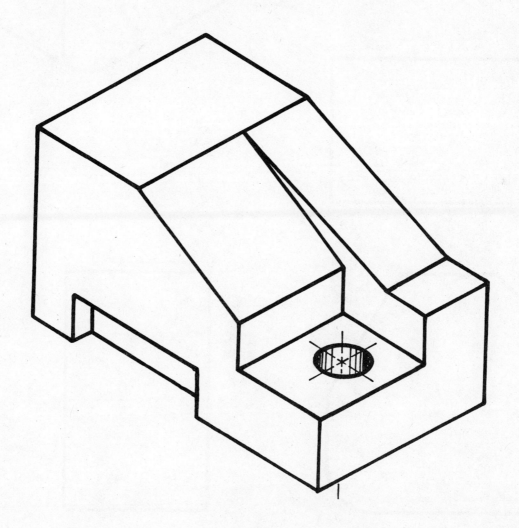

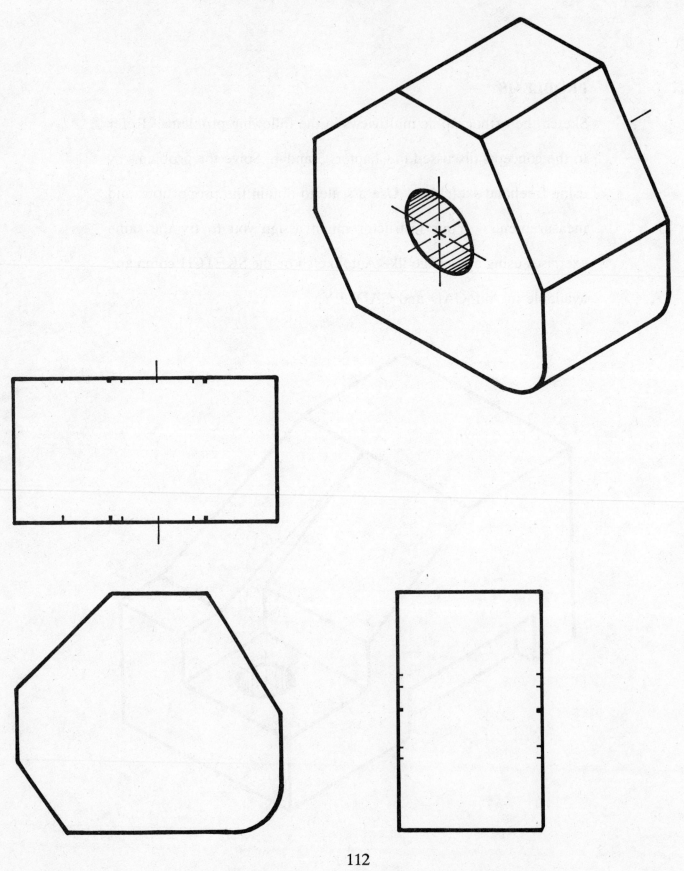

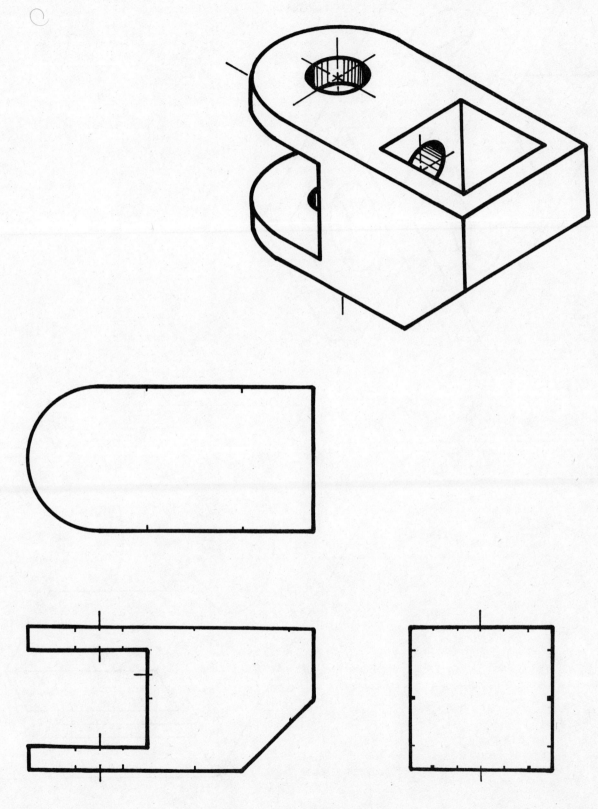

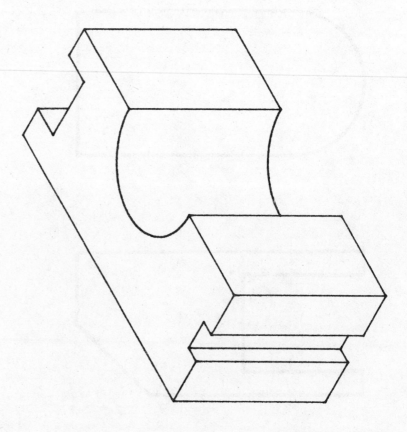

114

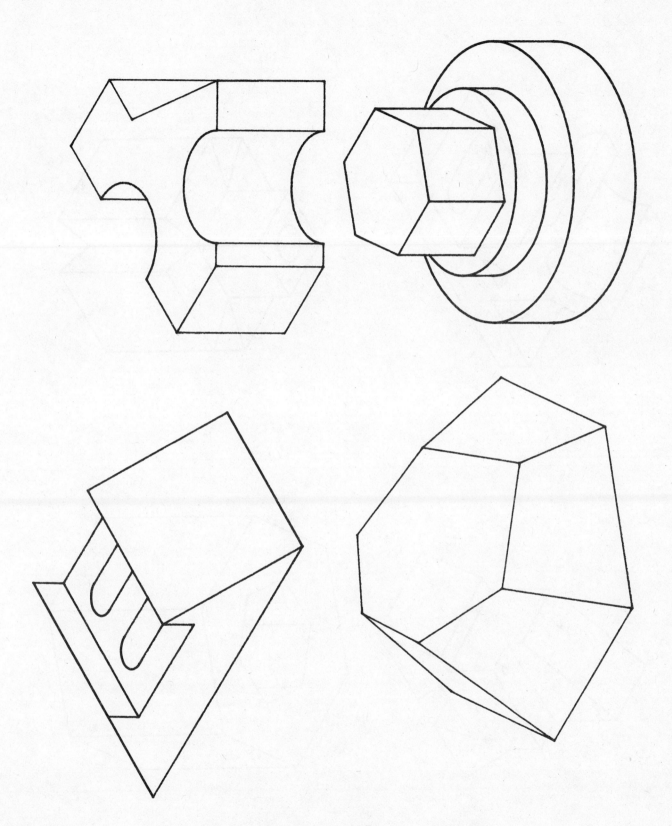

115

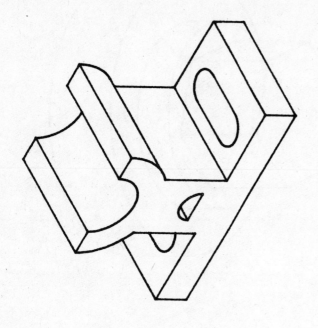

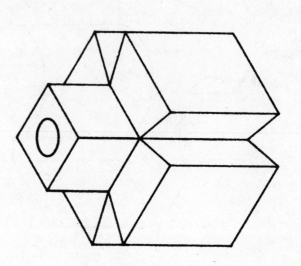

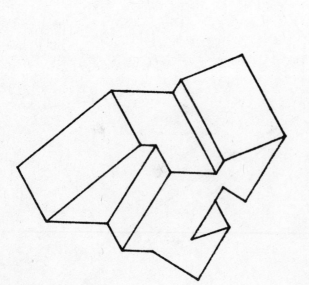

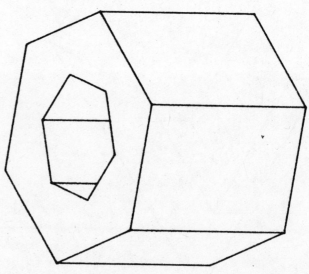

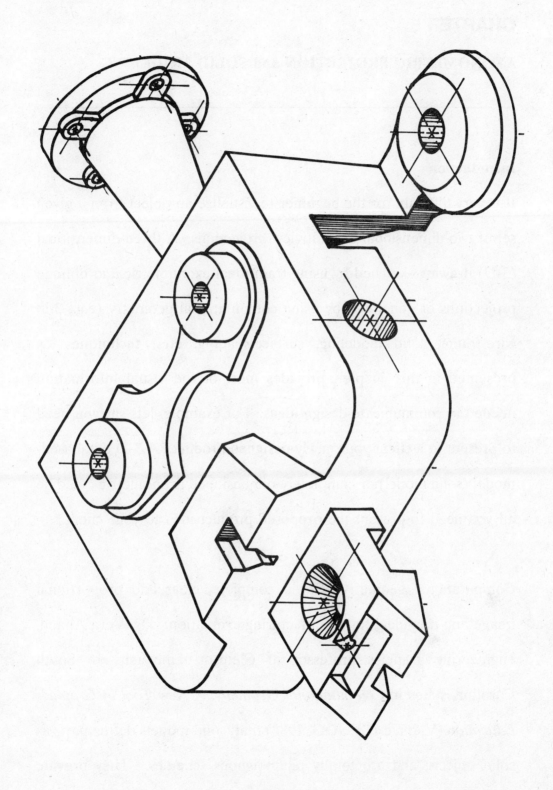

CHAPTER 5

AXONOMETRIC PROJECTION and SOLID MODELING

Introduction

It is very difficult, for the beginner to visualize an object from a given set of two-dimensional or multiview projections. A three-dimensional (3-D) drawing sketched by using traditional axonometric and oblique projections or generated by using computational geometry (e.g., 3-D wire-frame, solid modeling, surface-shading, etc.) techniques, as presented in this chapter, provides most of the visual information needed to communicate design ideas. For example, lets say you need to present to a client your newly-designed product. A 3-D databased-model (solid model) or completely-dimensioned axonometric could be all you need to present the proposed product idea to your client.

Computational geometry offer a complete, clear and proportional image and it is ideal for manufacturing evaluation. Dr. Vera Anand, engineering graphics professor at Clemson University in South Carolina, states in *Computational Geometry: A New Tool in Graphics Education* (Vienna: ICEGDG, 1988) that "solid models define parts as solid objects, and are totally unambiguous schemes. They provide information about mass properties, such as moments of inertia, centroids, etc., and theoretically contain enough information for the definition of part programs for NC (Numerical Control) machines. These models can be considered to be a key factor in the full integration of CAD and CAM (Computer-Aided Manufacturing)."

Designer's Use of 3-D

Such 3-D geometric models facilitate the designer task to "sell" a product idea to a client, particularly if the client is not familiar with 2-D drawings. For example, if you were a structural engineer discussing the details of a steel structure with your client, an axonometric drawing or a solid model, as illustrated in Figure 5.1, would allow you to get your idea across. Architects use axonometrics to represent space, as illustrated in Figure 5.2. In a similar way, an engineer communicates a modification to the backing assembly illustrated in Figure 5.3.

The flexibility and quickness of creating traditional axonometric and oblique sketches proves to be useful in the early stages of the design process. Solid modeling is valuable in the remaining stages of the design process, since geometric models are databased.

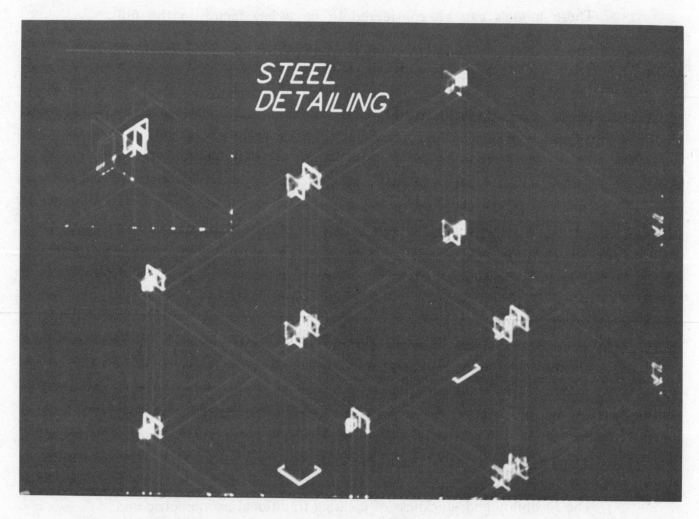

FIG. 5.1 Axonometric (isometric) projection of a steel structure. Including 3-D detailing for visualization of a connection. (Courtesy of GE/ CALMA.)

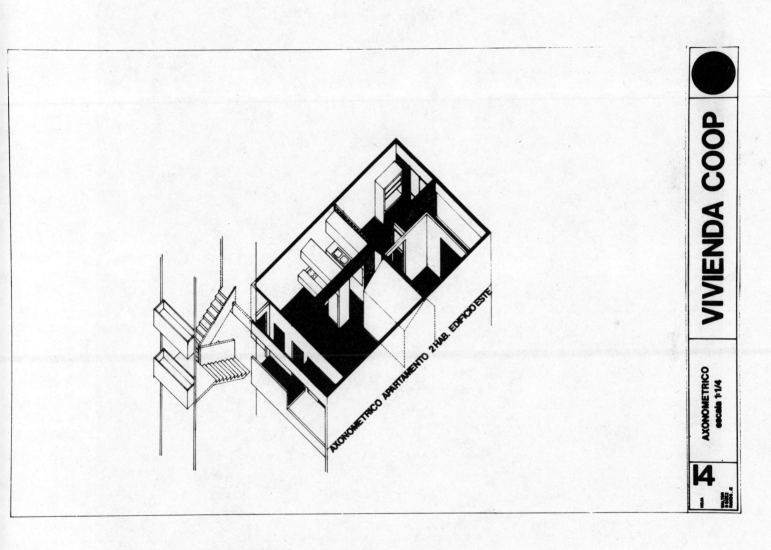

FIG. 5.2 Hand-made axonometric drawing of an interior space.

FIG. 5.3 Computer generated axonometric drawing used to communicate design modifications to a backing assembly. (Courtesy of CADKEY / Microcontrol Systems and T. Sandzimir, Inc.)

They are Pictorials

Both axonometrics and solid models are classified as **pictorials** since they show more than one face of the object in a given view or display. In Chapter 3, we discussed another type of pictorial: perspective projections. As you remember, these were very realistic images that emulate our binocular vision. In perspective projection, the depth-feature guidelines of the object converge to one or more vanishing points. In axonometric projection (being orthographically-based) the depth-feature guidelines remain parallel and never converge. Axonometric drawings are easier to construct than perspectives.

Axonometric Projection

The type of orthographic projection in which the object is positioned, inside an imaginary transparent box, so that three faces of the object are displayed on the planes of projection is named **axonometric projection**. Since it is a type of orthographic projection, its lines-of-sight (visual rays) are perpendicular to the projection plane.

It is very simple to draw an axonometric, simply imagine rotating the object about two of its axes. In doing so, the faces of the object will appear inclined with respect to the plane of projection. (Remember: In multiview orthographic projection, the object's faces are parallel to the plane of projection, and only one principal face is displayed per projection plane. In axonometric, you see three faces of the object.) Theoretically, the axes of an axonometric projection could make any angle with each other except 90 degrees. Obviously, if the axes were to make ninety degrees the result would be an orthographic view.

Visualization Exercise

To visualize an axonometric, pick the thicker book in your library (a dictionary will do). Place the book on a table parallel to the edge of a table, sit down and look straight at the book from its front view. The front face of the book is now parallel to an imaginary picture plane (running along the edge of the table) located between you and the book. Now, stand up and look at the book from the top. Turn the book 45 degrees relative to the picture plane. Then look at the side view. Draw an imaginary diagonal line across the side view of the book. Tilt up the book until the diagonal of the side view is horizontal. Notice that the front view of the book becomes an axonometric (you are now able to see three faces of the object).

Foreshortening

Notice in the previous exercise that the faces, views, and axes of the book appear foreshortened, since the object is inclined with respect to the projection plane. Of course, the degree of foreshortening will depend on the angle of inclination with respect to the projection plane. For practical purposes the scale is foreshortened about 80%, on each of the affected axes. Due to the inclination, the rectangular faces of the object (book) will appear as a parallelogram.

Axonometric Drawings

Axonometric drawings resemble axonometric projections, but the distances along the axes are measured in true length. This makes the construction much easier, since there is no need to calculate the degree of foreshortening on the axes.

In his book *Engineering Drawing with Creative Design* (New York: McGraw-Hill, 1968), author H. E. Grant states that "axonometric projection, although prepared in an entirely different manner, is basically an orthographic view of a tilted part." Note how concretely Professor Grant show us the theory of axonometric drawings:

> The theory of any axonometric drawing is best explained by referring to a cube. Figure N-1 (a) shows a cube turned 45 degrees on its base. In (b) the side view has been tilted until the diagonal of the cube is horizontal and appears as a point in the front view. The front view becomes an *isometric projection*. The *same* view could have been obtained without turning the cube by finding the true length of the diagonal in the primary auxiliary view; the diagonal will be in its point view in secondary auxiliary view. The *same* view could have been obtained in still another way by using a special 81/100 scale to measure the lengths of the edges vertically and at 30 degrees upward to the left and right, since all edges of the cube foreshorten equally in isometric projection.
> *Isometric drawing* takes advantage of the equal foreshortening of *all edges* of the cube. The foreshortened measurements may be replaced with true-

length measurements to obtain the same picture of the cube draw to a larger scale, as shown in N-1 (c). Since it is easier to use full-scaled measurements, isometric drawing is used in practice.

Heavier lines designate the pivoting corner as shown in N-1 (b) or (c). The three edges of the cube related to the pivoting corner are called *axes*. The pivoting corner may be placed at the bottom, as shown in (d).

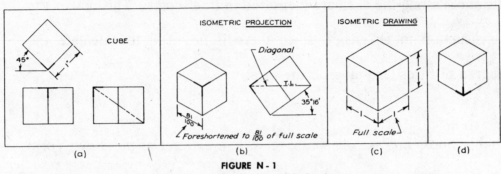

FIGURE N - 1
Isometric projection and isometric drawing.

(Courtesy of McGraw-Hill)

Types of Axonometric Projections

Axonometric projections are classified by the degree of inclination between the object's axes and the projection planes. The three types of axonometric projections are: ISOMETRIC, DIMETRIC and TRIMETRIC.

Isometric Projection is obtained by positioning the object axes at equal angles with respect to the plane of projection. The word isometric, comes from the greek "isometros", and it means equal measure. Expanding: An isometric projection is a type of axonometric

126

projection, where the edges (i.e., axes) and faces of the object are equally projected onto a projection plane. That is, the three principal axes and faces are equally inclined to the projection plane. Axes can be placed in several positions, but they always make equal angles between themselves.

Figure 5.4(a) illustrates the positioning of the axes to produce an isometric projection of a cube.

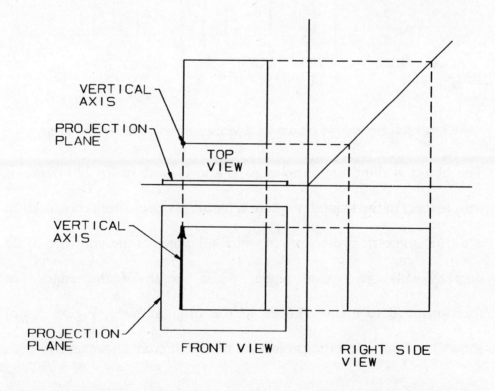

FIG. 5.4 (a). Positioning of axes to produce an isometric projection of a cube. In this original position, the frontal view is parallel to the frontal plane of projection.

127

Notice that the object have been revolved 45 degrees -see Figure 5.4(b)- through the vertical axis, and then tilted about the horizontal axis.

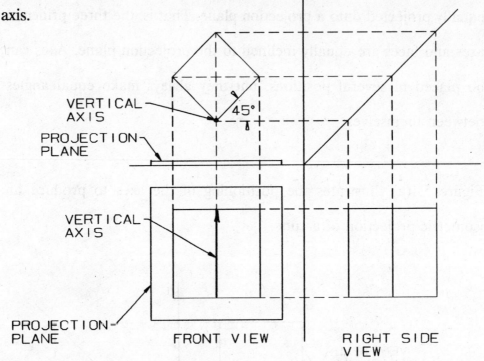

FIG. 5.4 (b). Rotate the object 45 degrees around the vertical axis.

The object is tilted until angles A, B and C each make 120 degrees, with respect to the frontal projection plane. The resulting construction is a true isometric projection, in which all edges of the cube are 35.26 degrees with the frontal plane. The length of the edges are foreshortened to about 81.6 % of the original size. Figure 5.4(c) shows the final isometric projection obtained from this exercise.

As mentioned earlier, since it is awkward to work with foreshortened sides, the preferred procedure is to draw an isometric with sides

128

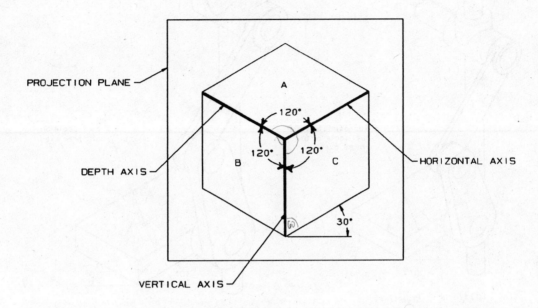

FIG. 5.4 (c). Isometric projection obtained after tilting the object around the horizontal axis until angle A, B and C are equal to 120 degrees.

enlarged as opposed to using the foreshortened sides. To do this, simply construct the isometric axes and measure actual width, height and depth along the axes, rather than the projected image of the lines. Figures 5.5(a) and 5.5(b) compares an isometric projection with an isometric drawing. Figure 5.5(c) shows the manual construction of the circular base for a cylinder. Notice the circle is projected as an approximate ellipse on its isometric view.

129

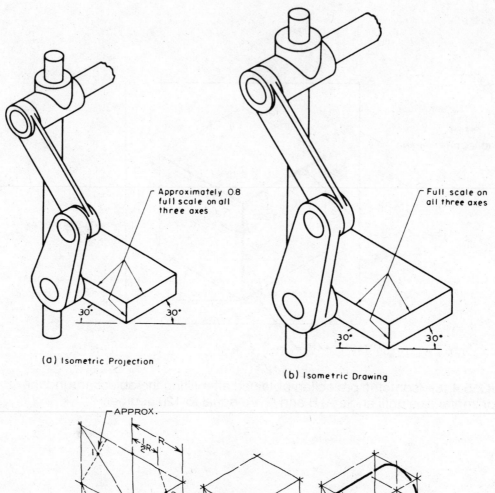

Approximately 0.8
full scale on all
three axes

30°   30°

(a) Isometric Projection

Full scale on
all three axes

30°   30°

(b) Isometric Drawing

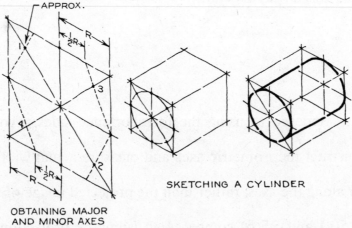

APPROX.

$\frac{1}{2}R$

R

1

3

4

2

$\frac{1}{2}R$

R

OBTAINING MAJOR
AND MINOR AXES

SKETCHING A CYLINDER

FIG. 5.5 Comparison of (a) isometric projection with an (b) isometric drawing. Courtesy of ASME and ANSI.) (c) shows the manual construction of the cylindrical elements (Courtesy of McGraw-Hill.)

130

Example 2.2: Isometric Construction

Based on the multiview projections depicted in Figure 5.6, produce an isometric drawing.

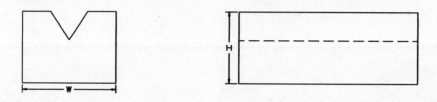

FIG. 5.6 Draw an isometric, given the front and right-side views of an object.

Solution:

1. Start by drawing an imaginary box, big enough to enclosed the object. With the assistance of a 30-60 degree triangle, construct a vertical line and two 30 degrees inclined lines from an arbitrary point in a horizontal reference line, as shown in Figure 5.7(a).

2. Layout the overall depth, width and height of the object. Draw the inclined surfaces or faces of the object, as if you were projecting them onto the isometric box planes (b).

131

3. Establish the end points of the groove (c).

4. Reinforce the visible lines of the object and delete unnecessary construction and hidden lines (d).

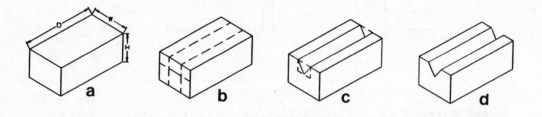

FIG. 5.7 Computer-aided sketching of an isometric drawing. **(a)**. draw an imaginary box, **(b)**. layout dimensions and features, **(c)**. establish end points of the groove, and **(d)**. reinforce visible lines, delete hidden-lines and construction lines.

Dimetric Projection

This is a type of axonometric projection in which two of the object's axes make equal angles with the plane of projection. The third axis makes a different angle with the frontal plane. Therefore, it is foreshortened at a different ratio than the other two axes. Dimetric projections are rarely used. In some cases they are used to explode views of devices which have predominant frontal features (see Fig.5.8).

132

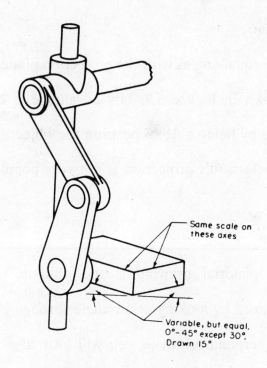

Same scale on
these axes

Variable, but equal.
0°- 45° except 30°.
Drawn 15°

FIG. 5.8 Dimetric Projection.

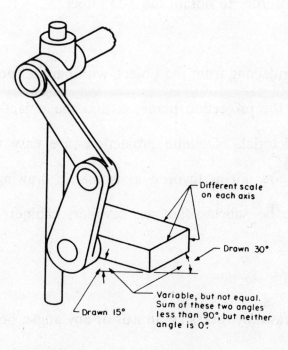

Different scale
on each axis

Drawn 30°

Variable, but not equal.
Sum of these two angles
less than 90°, but neither
angle is 0°

Drawn 15°

FIG. 5.9 Trimetric Projection. No two axes make equal angles with the projection plane. (Courtesy of ASME and ANSI.)

Trimetric Projection

No two axes make equal angles with the projection planes in **trimetric projection,** as shown in Figure 5.9. Its advantage is obviously the flexibility obtained by being able to position the object in almost any direction. Nevertheless, this projection is not very popular.

Oblique Projection

Another type of pictorial drawing is the oblique. An **oblique projection** is produced by looking at an angle through the projection plane, instead of perpendicularly-as you will look at a frontal view. Hence, it is <u>not</u> a type of orthographic. There is no need to rotate or tilt the object in order to obtain the 3-D effect.

The result of projecting from the object, with parallel projectors that are oblique to the projection plane, is that the object's image will appear as a pictorial. Oblique projections are easy to construct. However, they are not as favored as isometric drawings. Oblique projections can be subclassified as: cavalier, cabinet and general oblique.

A **cavalier** is drawn by recessing an axis at any angle, between 0 and 90 degrees -with respect to the horizontal- and utilizing true length measurements, as shown in Figure 5.10. Lines-of-sight, in cavalier

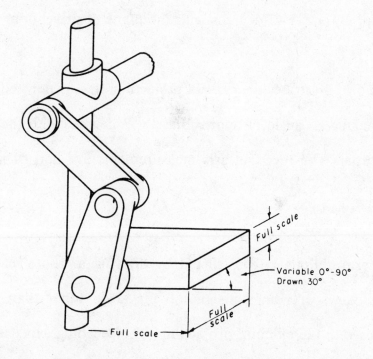

FIG. 5.10 Cavalier -oblique projection. Drawn by recessing an axis, at an angle between 0 and 90 degrees, and utilizing true length measurements. (Courtesy of ASME and ANSI.)

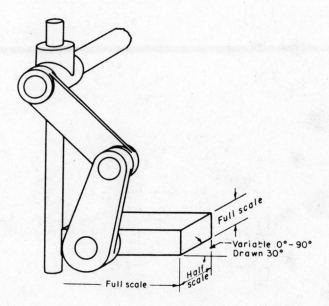

FIG. 5.11 Cabinet -oblique projection. The receding axis measurements are half the actual size. (Courtesy of ASME and ANSI.)

projections, are at 45 degrees with the plane of projection.

Figure 5.11 illustrates the **cabinet** projection. It is generated by visual rays making an angle of approximately 63 degrees with the plane of projection. The receding axis measurements are half of the actual size.

A **general oblique** is constructed by drawing a true size view, say frontal view; with lines-of-sight at any angle other than 45 or 63 degrees with the plane of projection. The receding axis contains the depth features of the object, as illustrated in Figure 5.12. The depth scale will be other than the true length and half size ratio.

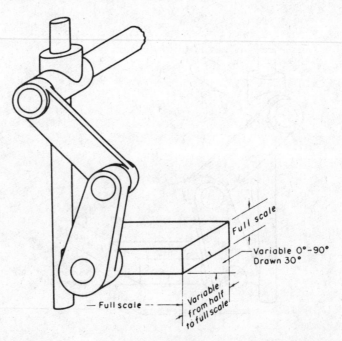

FIG. 5.12 General oblique projection. Constructed by drawing a true size view and lines-of-sight other than 45 or 63 degrees with the plane of projection. Receding depth axis scale will be other than true or half size. (Courtesy of ASME and ANSI.)

Solid Modeling

Probably the best way to visualize the way solid modelers work is think back when you were playing with building blocks (see Fig. 5.13). You would combine various cubes, cylinders and so forth to create more complex constructions. Solid modelers operate in a similar fashion as it allows you to combine a variety of simple shapes into complex objects.

The material that follows present the concepts of solid modeling represented by the software package: ICEM Solid Modeler (ISM). The material has been reproduced (an adapted) from the *ICEM Solid Modeling Manual* (Publication No. 60000147) by written permission of Control Data Corporation.

 BOX - PARALLELEPIPED

WEG - RIGHT-ANGLE WEDGE

 ARB - ARBITRARY POLYHEDRON

CYL - RIGHT CIRCULAR CYLINDER

SPH - SPHERE

FIG. 5.13 Some basic primitives. They are the builiding blocks in ISM. (Courtesy of Control Data Corporation)

Solid Modeling is the process of creating solid geometric primitives, combining the primitives together into a solid model using boolean operations, viewing the solid model, and performing various analysis functions on the geometry.

ICEM Solid Modeling

Solid Modeling uses programs from both ICEM DDN and ICEM Solid Modeler. You start the solid modeling process at ICEM DDN menu 15.4 Solid Modeling.

1. While in ICEM DDN, you can create solid primitives; combine the primitives into solid models, display the solids, and modify the solids.

2. You can then transfer the solid geometry into the ICEM Solid Modeler using ICEM DDN menu 15.4.5 BRANCH TO I.S.M. At the same time, you are moving into the ICEM Solid Modeler.

3. Once in the ICEM Solid Modeler, you can display the evaluated solid model, analyze the solid model, escape to the command mode of the modeler, or return to ICEM DDN.

The Modeling Process

There are four steps in the modeling process:

1. Defining the model.

2. Viewing the model.

3. Analyzing the model.

4. Reviewing the results of analysis.

Defining the Model

The model is built from a set of basic three-dimensional shapes. These basic shapes are called primitives, and include spheres, cones, parallelepipeds, cylinders, and so on. You can create solid geometric primitives using all the construction techniques of ICEM DDN. You can then combine the primitives together into a solid model using boolean operations. These operations include Union, Intersection, and Difference.

Viewing the Model

The solid model can be viewed in ICEM DDN, or it can be transferred and also viewed in the Solid Modeler.

- In ICEM DDN, you can view wireframe representations of all the edges and surfaces of the primitives. You can also view faceted (surface shaded) representations of the primitives.

138

- In the Solid Modeler, the boolean combinations of the primitives are evaluated. These evaluated combinations of primitives are called the model. This model can be viewed as a wireframe, faceted, or shaded representation.

By viewing a wireframe or faceted view of the model, you can confirm that the model looks the way it should before executing the more expensive procedures to create a shaded representation. Wireframe views display all edges but no surfaces, and treats all objects as positive space. This results in an image showing detail that, in reality, would not be visible. Faceted views more closely resemble the model, showing approximated surfaces and the results of subtracted objects as negative space. Shaded representations are realistic, three-dimensional pictures of the solid.

Analyzing the Model

The next step is preparing and submitting the model for analysis. Preparing the model for analysis involves providing instructions as to how the analysis is to be done. You may enter these instructions through the menus or with a set of analysis commands that specify what colors to use, the viewing angle, what size the model will appear on the terminal screen, what portion of the model will be visible, whether a perspective or a parallel projection will be used, and so on. In addition, by positioning the simulated light source, you can control the distribution of light and shading on the model and thus create a heightened three-dimensional effect.

Analysis instructions are associated with viewports or frames. (Frames are available only in command mode.) Each viewport or frame can contain a different set of analysis instructions, resulting in different pictures of the model. In this way, it is possible to view the model from all sides in a series of pictures.

Reviewing the Results of Analysis

You can review any of the following analysis results:

- Line drawings

- Shaded drawings

- Outline shaded drawings

- View independent edge drawings

- View dependent edge drawings

- Mass properties listings

You can display up to four analysis results files on the screen at one time, each in a separate viewport. You also have the ability to change colors and lighting levels when a shaded or outline shaded results file is viewed on a color raster terminal. You can display mass properties results as well as output listings or text files on all interactive terminals.

Axes, Rotation, and the Right-Hand Rule

When describing rotation in three dimensions, the relationship between axes and rotation angles needs to be defined. ICEM Solid Modeler uses two conventions to define axes:

Point and Vector   Establishes a point to serve as a reference and a vector based at the point to establish a direction. This convention serves the following:

- BOX, CON, CYL, ELC, GEN, SLB, TER, and REV primitive functions to define a local coordinate system.

- PAN, ROLL, and TILT view manipulation commands in describing view rotation about the axis formed by the aim point and the appropriate vector.

Point 1 and Point 2   Establishes point 1 as the axis start point and point 2 as the axis endpoint. The axis direction is from point 1 to point 2. This convention serves the following:

- REV primitive function when defining an axis about which to revolve a section.

- TURN, ROTATE, ATTACH, and MIRROR commands to define their respective axes.

ICEM Solid Modeler uses the right-hand rule as a convention for determining rotation direction. The following diagram illustrates the right-hand rule.

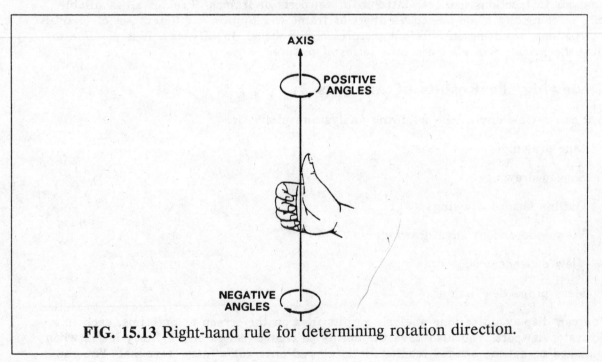

FIG. 15.13 Right-hand rule for determining rotation direction.

(Courtesy of Control Data Corporation)

An axis used for rotation is associated with the commands PAN, ROLL, TILT, TURN, and ROTATE. For each command, the interpretation of the "ANGLE" argument or keyword value follows the right-hand rule. This is needed to specify which rotational direction corresponds to positive angles and which to negative angles.

To use the right-hand rule in these situations, imagine placing the base of the thumb of the right hand at the first point of the axis, with the thumb pointing towards the second point. With the right hand in this position, the fingers curl around in the angular rotational direction corresponding to positive angles. The opposite direction corresponds to negative angles.

Note that this positive angle rotation would appear counterclockwise to viewers on the axis line at a position such that the right-hand thumb is pointing towards them. The same rotation would appear clockwise to viewers at a position on the line such that the right-hand thumb is pointing away from them.

Analysis Accounting and the USER File

During initialization, the Solid Modeler searches your current catalog of files for a file named USER. The USER file, which you create, contains validation and charge information required for processing analysis batch jobs on NOS/VE. If the USER file exists, the validation and charge information is stored and then later retrieved when you enter the ANALYZE command. If the USER file does not exist, the application prompts you for your NOS/VE password, charge number, and project number the first time you enter the ANALYZE command.

Creating the USER File for Analysis on NOS/VE

The USER file should contain one logical line of text which may be continued onto more than one physical line by using the ellipsis (..). The form of the text is as follows:

```
LOGIN,U=username,PW=password,FN=familyname,..
     A=account,P=project
```

- The parameters which are required on the LOGIN statement are site-dependent, but username and password are always required.

- Up to 4 physical lines of text are allowed.

- Consult the SCL for NOS/VE System Interface Manual for more information on the LOGIN command.

Creating the USER File for Analysis on the CYBER 910 Workstation

On the CYBER 910 workstation the USER file is *user* (in lowercase). The information it contains is also slightly different from that on NOS/VE. The first line should contain the NOS/VE user name, NOS/VE password, and NOS/VE family name separated by commas as follows:

```
username,password,familyname
```

An optional second line may contain the NOS/VE account name and project name.

SOLID MODELING

with the ICEM Solid Modeler

Menu 15.4

With this choice, you can create solid geometric primitives in ICEM DDN using all the construction techniques available in ICEM DDN. You can then combine the primitives into a solid model using boolean operations. After the solid model is created, you can transfer the solid geometry into the ICEM Solid Modeler (ISM). You can then use the ICEM Solid Modeler to view and analyze the solid model. The viewing functions in ICEM Solid Modeler allow you to create a polygonal representation from the CSG-Tree of the model which can be viewed in up to four viewports. The analysis function of the ICEM Solid Modeler allows you to analyze the geometry of the solid model using the analysis programs.

The options for analysis are:

- Mass properties

- Shaded pictures

- View-independent edge file generation

- Three-dimensional (3-D) view-dependent edge file generation

Once the data from the edge files is available, you can execute menu choice 4. DDN BRANCH OPERATIONS to transfer the edge geometry back into ICEM DDN. At this point, you can use the drafting, numerical control, and other ICEM DDN functions required to continue with the design and manufacture of your part.

The term *solids* refers to either of two new entity types in ICEM DDN.

- A solid can be any primitive (type 52) created using 15.4.2 CREATE PRIMITIVE.

- A solid can be any boolean combination object (type 51) created using 15.4.3 CREATE OBJECT.

NOTE

Any hexahedron entity created with menu 15.4.1 in any version of ICEM DDN 1.62 or earlier is automatically converted to an ICEM DDN version 2.0 BOX primitive entity. This automatic part update function occurs when an older part is first accessed by ICEM DDN version 2.0. Entities other than hexahedron created with older versions of 15.4 SOLIDS do not need to be changed.

The menu for solid modeling is:

```
SOLID MODELING
1.SOLIDS MODALS
2.CREATE PRIMITIVE
3.CREATE OBJECT
4.MODIFY SOLID
5.BRANCH TO I.S.M.
```

15.4.1 Solids Modals

This menu manages operation modes for solids. Modes for Naming (selections 1 and 2) and Surfaces (selection 3) apply to solids created using menu 15.4 or menu 13 (selections 7, 8, 9, 14 and 15). However, solids properties (selection 4) for menu 13 copies are inherited from the copied solids.

The first sample menu displays the default mode settings at the right of each line except the last.

```
SOLIDS MODALS
1.PRIMITIVE NAMING    STANDARD PREFIXES
2.OBJECT NAMING       STANDARD PREFIX
3.PRIMITIVE SURFACE    DO NOT GENERATE
4.SOLIDS PROPERTIES
```

Another sample display follows, in which the modes have been assigned non-default settings.

```
SOLIDS MODALS
1.PRIMITIVE NAMING    PREFIX = WHEEL
2.OBJECT NAMING       RE-USE BASE NAME
3.PRIMITIVE SURFACE   DO GENERATE
4.SOLIDS PROPERTIES
```

15.4.1.1 Primitive Naming

This menu controls the modals for naming individual primitives. ICEM DDN automatically checks for and rejects duplicate names. When this mode is set, names for this entity type are generated according to the selected method until the mode is reset. All names must be alphanumeric and start with an alphabetic character.

The menu for this section is:

```
PRIMITIVE NAMING
1.STANDARD PREFIXES
2.PRESET PREFIX
3.PROMPT FOR NAME
4.SET WHEN USED
```

Enter:

1   To use standard prefixes. The standard prefixes are BOX, CON, CYL, REV, SLB, SPH, TOR, and WEG. These prefixes come from the mnemonics that appear in menu 15.4.2 Create Primitive. Names for created primitives have eight characters, and are generated in order, as BOX00001, BOX00002, etc.

2   To use a preset prefix that is automatically created each time a primitive is generated.

    `ENTER PREFIX 1-7 CHARACTERS)`   Enter a 1- to 7-character prefix which will be used in 8-character names that are generated in numerical order. The prefix is truncated if necessary to accommodate the numerical sequence part of the names. For example, a prefix of "PREFIX" would generate the names PREFIX01, PREFIX02, ... PREFIX99, PREFI100,...

3   To enter the full primitive name each time a primitive is created. At the time of primitive creation, the system displays:

    `ENTER PRIMITIVE NAME`   Enter a primitive name of up to eight characters.

4   To choose from the three primitive naming techniques each time a primitive is created. At the time of primitive creation, the system displays:

```
PRIMITIVE NAMING METHOD
1.STANDARD PREFIXES
2.PRESET PREFIX
3.PROMPT FOR NAME
```

15.4.1.2 Object Naming

This menu controls the modals for the names of solid boolean combination objects. ICEM DDN automatically checks for and rejects duplicate names. When this mode is set, names for this entity type are generated according to the selected method until the mode is reset. All names must be alphanumeric and start with an alphabetic character.

The menu for this operation is:

```
OBJECT NAMING
1.STANDARD PREFIX
2.PRESET PREFIX
3.PROMPT FOR NAME
4.RE-USE BASE NAME
5.SET WHEN USED
```

1   To use the standard object prefix. Names for created boolean objects have eight characters, and are generated in order, as OBJ00001, OBJ00002, etc. ICEM DDN keeps a record of the highest number in the sequence used for this prefix.

2   To use a preset prefix that is automatically created each time an object is **generated**.

ENTER PREFIX(1-7 CHARACTERS)   Enter a 1- to 7-character prefix which will be used in 8-character names that are generated in numerical order. The prefix is truncated if necessary to accommodate the numerical sequence part of the name. For example, a prefix of "BOOLEAN" would generate the names BOOLEAN1, BOOLEAN2, ... BOOLEAN9, BOOLEA10, ... BOOL1234, ...

3   To enter the full boolean object name each time a primitive is created. At the time of object creation, the system displays:

ENTER OBJECT NAME   Enter a boolean object name of up to 8 characters.

4   To reuse the base name of the object. If the solid selected as the base is a combination object, the name of that object will be reused for the resultant object. The selected base object then becomes an unnamed combination entity. A symbolic **example** of this is:

OBJ = OBJ+A-B

If the solid selected as the base is a primitive, the selected primitive's name cannot be reused for the new object, since primitives must be named. In this case, this option reverts to 15.4.1.2.5 SET WHEN USED.

145

5   To choose from the four solid object naming techniques each time an object is
    created. At the time of object creation, the system displays:

```
OBJECT NAMING METHOD
1.STANDARD PREFIX
2.PRESET PREFIX
3.PROMPT FOR NAME
4.RE-USE BASE NAME
```

Naming Modes

The preset prefix mode can be in effect for primitives and objects concurrently, even
with the same prefix in effect.

Any time either the primitive or object preset prefix mode is selected, the system
examines the name list for the appropriate starting sequence number to create a
unique name.

15.4.1.3 Primitive Surfaces

This menu provides the capability to control whether surfaces are generated for new
primitives. The appearance of each surface is controlled by the modal 15.1.3 SURFACE
PATHS.

The optional curved surface for any sphere, cylinder, torus, cone, or solid of revolution
primitive is a standard surface of revolution entity (type 19, form 0). The planar
surfaces for box, wedge, or slab are ruled surfaces (type 21, form 1).

The menu for this operation is:

```
PRIMITIVE SURFACE
1.DO NOT GENERATE
2.DO GENERATE
3.SET WHEN USED
```

Enter:

1   To not generate surfaces for new
    primitives.

2   To generate all surfaces for each new
    primitive.

3   To set the primitive surfaces option for
    each new primitive before it is
    generated.

At the time of primitive creation, if the preset modal is 3.SET WHEN USED, the
system displays:

```
PRIMITIVE SURFACES
1.DO NOT GENERATE
2.DO GENERATE
```

15.4.1.4 Solids Properties

This operation provides control over the physical properties of density and surface reflectance (see the ASSIGN command in chapter 7) assigned to primitives and objects as they are created in ICEM DDN. You can alter any or all of these modal values. The following is a data entry display with predefined default values:

```
SOLIDS PROPERTIES
1. DENSITY               = 1.0
2. DIFFUSE REFLECTANCE   = 0.5
3. SPECULAR REFLECTANCE  = 0.0
```

This display always shows current values for the modals. Object properties take precedence over the properties of their component primitives and subobjects. Density must be greater than zero. Diffuse and specular reflectance must each be in the range from zero to one.

The ICEM Solid Modeler properties of hue and saturation are calculated from the color associated with each entity (used in color display mode 1.9.1.4 COLOR BY ENTITY COLOR) together with the current color table values.

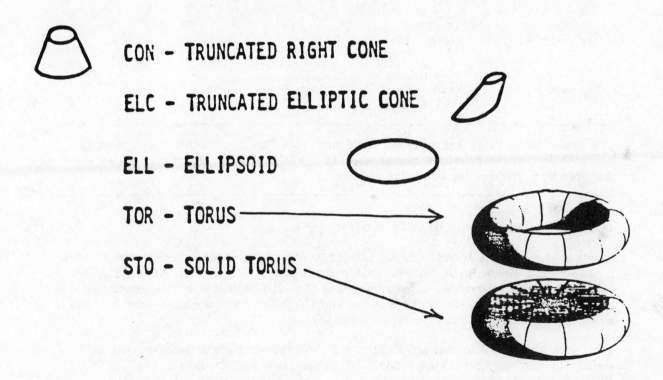

FIG. 15.14 Additional Primitives (see pp. 137)

(Courtesy of Control Data Corporation)

147

15.4.2 Create Primitive

With this choice, you can create the primitive solids box, cone, cylinder, revolution solid, slab, sphere, torus, and wedge.

The menu for this choice is:

```
CREATE PRIMITIVE
 1.BOX               (BOX)
 2.CONE              (CON)
 3.CYLINDER          (CYL)
 4.
 5.
 6.
 7.
 8.REVOLUTION SOLID  (REV)
 9.
10.SLAB             (SLB)
11.SPHERE           (SPH)
12.
13.TORUS            (TOR)
14.WEDGE            (WEG)
```

NOTE
_____

The blank menu items are reserved for future use. The three-letter mnemonics in parentheses are the primitive names used in the ICEM Solid Modeler and also serve as the Standard Prefixes for Primitive naming.

_____

Primitive Data Coordinate Entry

Whether the prompts indicate model (absolute) coordinate input or current-work-view transform coordinate input depends on the setting of 1.15.2 DEFINITION SPACE MODE. Input is interpreted as coordinates of the type indicated by the displayed prompts. This also applies to the DELTA and the LENGTH coordinates for box and wedge primitives, and diagonal corners for box.

The coordinate entry format shown in the following pages for primitive creation is similar to that used for 15.4.4.1 MODIFY PRIMITIVE DATA and for 14.1 DATA VERIFY for primitives. The definition space mode has the same effect on these functions as it does for primitive creation.

148

Primitive Creation

Each primitive's data includes pointers to associated wireframe geometry which is automatically created for each primitive. A set of bounding surfaces is optional for each primitive. A primitive's data includes pointers to any such associated surface geometry. Each associated geometry entity is created as a new entity during the primitive creation process. Entities selected as primitive definition input are duplicated and the duplicate entities are used as associated geometry. Each associated geometric entity has read-only status. This means that you can only select it for non-destructive functions such as 9.8 POINT AT CURVE END and 13.8 DUPL AND TRANSLATE. You cannot select it for alteration functions such as 13.5 TRANSLATE or 12.8 TRIM/EXTEND CURVES.

There are many cases in which the system prompts for a circular arc or an ellipse as part of primitive creation. In most of those cases, a curve less than 360 degrees is automatically considered as a full 360-degree arc for purposes of the primitive definition. The only exceptions to this are circular arc components in Revolution Solid or Slab cross-sections.

The following things should be kept in mind when using the] (operation complete) key and [(operation reject) key.

- If you enter] before the last required entity is selected when the system is in menu 15.4.2 prompting for entity input, creation is halted, and the primitive is not formed.

- Entering [at any time rejects the latest entity selection (if any) for that primitive. This can be repeated to reject each previously selected entity in the reverse order that they were selected. Entering [after all selected entities have been rejected backs up to the input for the preceding parameter.

Immediately after a primitive creation method has been chosen (15.4.2.x.y), the primitive's name is established according to the setting of the primitive naming modal. If 15.4.1.1.4 SET WHEN USED is in effect, the reduced (3-item) primitive naming menu is presented, and naming proceeds for this primitive according to your selection. If 15.4.1.1.3 PROMPT FOR NAMES is in effect, the user is prompted to ENTER PRIMITIVE NAME. Otherwise, the primitive name which is automatically generated by the system is displayed in the dialog area. An example of the display format is NEXT CYL NAME IS PLUG0123. An automatically generated name cannot be changed at creation time, but any solid can be renamed later by 5.11.2 ATTACH NAME TO ENTITY.

1.15.2 DEFINITION SPACE MODE controls whether you are prompted for model (absolute) coordinates or current-work-view transform coordinates.

The data entry prompts in the following sections show the model space input, such as x, dx, y length, z delta, and so on. For work transform space input, these prompts are xt, dxt, yt length, zt delta, and so on.

149

15.4.2.1 Box (BOX)

With this choice, you can create a shape with rectangle or parallelogram faces. The three edges meeting at any corner do not have to be perpendicular to one another, but they do have to point in 3 independent directions.

```
BOX
1.KEY-IN
2.3 LINES AT A POINT
3.CORNER, 3 EDGE POINTS
4.CORNER, 3 EDGE DELTAS
5.CENTER, 3 EDGE LENGTHS
6.2 DIAGONAL CORNERS
```

BOX - PARALLELEPIPED

Enter:

1   To create a box primitive by entering the coordinates.

```
BOX CORNER
1. X =
2. Y =
3. Z =
```
Enter the model coordinates of the box primitive corner point. If the definition space mode is set to transform coordinates, you must enter xt, yt, and zt coordinates.

```
BOX EDGE 1
1. DX =
2. DY =
3. DZ =
```
Enter a vector defining the direction and length of the first box edge line. If the definition space mode is set to transform coordinates, you must enter dxt, dyt, and dzt coordinates.

```
BOX FDGE 2
1. DX =
2. DY =
3. DZ =
```
Enter a vector defining the direction and length of the second box edge line. If the definition space mode is set to transform coordinates, you must enter dxt, dyt, and dzt coordinates.

```
BOX EDGE 3
1. DX =
2. DY =
3. DZ =
```
Enter a vector defining the direction and length of the third box edge line. If the definition space mode is set to transform coordinates, you must enter dxt, dyt, and dzt coordinates.

The box is created with a corner at (x,y,z), and three edge vectors (dx,dy,dz).

2   To create a box primitive using three non-coplanar lines that join at a point.

INDICATE 3 BOX EDGE LINES   Select three non-coplanar finite lines that meet and end at a point.

The box is created with the common endpoint as a corner and the three lines as edges.

3   To create a box with a corner point and three edge points.

INDICATE BOX CORNER POINT   Select the corner point of the box.

INDICATE 3 BOX EDGE POINTS   Select the three endpoints of the edge lines of the box.

The four points must not lie in the same plane. The first point is a box corner, and the lines from that corner to the other three points are edges.

4   To create a box with a corner point and three delta vectors for the edge lines.

```
INDICATE BOX CORNER POINT
```
Select the corner point of the box.

```
BOX EDGE DELTAS
1.X DELTA =
2.Y DELTA =
3.Z DELTA =
```
Enter any three non-zero numbers d1, d2, and d3. If the definition space mode is set to transform coordinates, you must enter dxt, dyt, and dzt coordinates.

The edge vectors are (d1,0,0), (0,d2,0) and (0,0,d3). This input mode creates box faces that are rectangles. If d1 = d2 = d3, the box will be a cube. Menu 1.15.2 DEFINITION SPACE MODE specifies whether these are model or current-work-view transform coordinates.

5   To create a box with a center point and three edge lengths.

```
INDICATE BOX CENTER POINT
```
Select the center point (c1,c2,c3) of the box.

```
BOX EDGE LENGTHS
1.X LENGTH =
2.Y LENGTH =
3.Z LENGTH =
```
Enter any three positive numbers d1, d2, and d3. If the definition space mode is set to transform coordinates, you must enter xt, yt, and zt lengths.

The box corner is at (c1-.5d1, c2-.5d2, c3-.5d3), and the edge vectors are (d1,0,0), (0,d2,0), and (0,0,d3). This input mode creates box faces that are rectangles. If d1=d2=d3, the box will be a cube. Menu 1.15.2 SPACE DEFINITION MODE specifies whether these are model or current-work-view transform coordinates.

6   To create a box with two corner points.

```
INDICATE 2 BOX DIAGONAL CORNER POINTS
```
Select the two corner points (a,b,c) and (A,B,C) of the box.

The box corner is created at

    (min(a,A),min(b,B),min(c,C))

and the edge vectors are as follows:

    (abs(a-A),0,0)
    (0,abs(b-B),0)
    (0,0,abs(c-C))

This input mode creates box faces that are rectangles. If abs(a-A) = abs(b-B) = abs(c-C) then the box will be a cube. Menu 1.15.2 SPACE DEFINITION MODE specifies whether (a,b,c) and (A,B,C) are model or transform coordinates.

151

15.4.2.2 Cone (CON)

With this choice, you can create a solid truncated cone shape. The small end cannot be a point, but can have a very small positive radius. The cone axis, which passes through the circle center points of the two ends, must be perpendicular to the planes of the two circles.

```
CONE
1.KEY-IN
2.2 END ARCS
3.2 END POINTS, RADII
4.WORK PLANE ARC, AXIS DELTA, RADIUS
5.END ARC, DIRECTION LINE, RADIUS
6.2 END DIAMETER LINES
```

Enter:

1   To create a solid truncated cone shape with the coordinates of an endpoint of the cone axis, the cone axis vector, and the two radii of the cone.

The cone is created with an axis line extending from the first endpoint of the cone (x,y,z) to the second endpoint of the cone (x+dx,y+dy,z+dz). The radii must be different from each other, and both must be greater than zero.

CONE END 1 CENTER 1. X = 2. Y = 3. Z =	Enter the coordinates of the first endpoint of the cone axis line. If the definition space mode is set to transform coordinates, you must enter xt, yt, and zt coordinates.
CONE AXIS 1. DX = 2. DY = 3. DZ =	Enter a vector defining the direction and length of the cone axis line. If the definition space mode is set to transform coordinates, you must enter dxt, dyt, and dzt coordinates.
CONE END RADII 1. END 1 RADIUS = 2. END 2 RADIUS =	Enter the two radii of the truncated cone shape.

2   To create a solid truncated cone shape from two arcs of different radii in different parallel planes. The line joining the circle centers must be perpendicular to the planes of the two circles. The line is the cone axis, and the circles are at the cone ends.

INDICATE 2 CONE END ARCS	Select two arcs that define the ends of the cone.

3   To create a solid truncated cone shape from two endpoints and the two radii. The axis line is the line that joins the two endpoints. The two radii must be positive and must have different values.

INDICATE 2 CONE END CENTER POINTS	Select the two end center points that define the cone axis line.
CONE END RADII 1. END 1 RADIUS = 2. END 2 RADIUS =	Enter the two radii of the truncated cone shape.

CON - TRUNCATED RIGHT CONE

ELC - TRUNCATED ELLIPTIC CONE

4   To create a solid truncated cone shape using an end arc that is parallel to the work plane, a length equal to the axis delta, and two radii, one for each end of the cone.

INDICATE CONE ARC PARALLEL TO WORK PLANE Select an arc parallel to the current work plane

CONE AXIS DELTA = Enter a non-zero number D

CONE END 2 RADIUS = Enter a positive radius number R which is not equal to the arc radius.

The arc defines one end of the cone, the axis vector is $(0,0,D)$ in transform coordinates, and the radius is R at the opposite end of the cone from the selected arc.

5   To create a solid truncated cone shape from an end arc, a direction line, and a radius.

INDICATE CONE END 1 ARC Select an arc.

INDICATE CONE DIRECTION LINE Select a line.

CONE END 2 RADIUS = Enter a positive radius number not equal to the arc radius.

The direction line must end in the plane of the arc, and be perpendicular to the plane of the arc; the direction line does not have to go through the arc's center. The entered radius number is the radius of the cone at the opposite end of the axis from the selected arc. The cone axis is defined as the direction line translated to the arc center.

6   To create a solid, truncated cone shape from two end diameter lines.

INDICATE 2 CONE END DIAMETER LINES Select two lines of different lengths.

The line joining the midpoints of the selected lines must be perpendicular to both of those lines. This perpendicular line is the cone axis, and the radii are determined so that the selected lines are end diameters.

153

15.4.2.3 Cylinder (CYL)

This is a solid cylinder shape. The cylinder axis, which passes through the circle center points of the two ends, must be perpendicular to the planes of the two circles.

```
CYLINDER
1.KEY-IN
2.2 END ARCS
3.2 END POINTS, RADIUS
4.WORK PLANE ARC, AXIS DELTA
5.END ARC, DIRECTION LINE
6.2 END DIAMETER LINES
7.AXIS LINE, RADIUS
```

Enter:

1   To create a solid truncated cylinder shape with the coordinates of an endpoint of the cylinder axis, the cylinder axis vector, and the radius of the cylinder.

The cylinder is created with axis line extending from the first endpoint of the cylinder (x,y,z) to the second endpoint of the cylinder $(x+dx, y+dy, z+dz)$. The radius must be greater than zero.

CYLINDER END CENTER 1. X = 2. Y = 3. Z =	Enter the coordinates of the cylinder end center. If the definition space mode is set to transform coordinates, you must enter xt, yt, and zt coordinates.
CYLINDER AXIS 1. DX = 2. DY = 3. DZ =	Enter a vector defining the direction and length of the cylinder axis. If the definition space mode is set to transform coordinates, you must enter dxt, dyt, and dzt coordinates.
CYLINDER RADIUS =	Enter the cylinder radius.

2   To create a cylinder using two end arcs that have the same positive radius. The line joining the circle centers must be perpendicular to the planes of the two circles. The line is the cylinder axis, and the circles are the cylinder ends. The cylinder radius is the common radius of the arcs.

INDICATE 2 CYLINDER END ARCS	Select two arcs that define the ends of the cylinder.

3   To create a cylinder using two end points and a positive radius value. The axis line joins the two points, and the radius is the cylinder radius.

INDICATE 2 CYLINDER END CENTER POINTS	Select the two end center points that define the cylinder axis line.
CYLINDER RADIUS =	Enter a positive radius.

CYL - RIGHT CIRCULAR CYLINDER

4   To create a cylinder using an end arc that is parallel to the work plane and a length equal to the axis delta.

INDICATE CYLINDER ARC PARALLEL TO
WORK PLANE

Select an arc parallel to the current work plane.

CYLINDER AXIS DELTA =

Enter a nonzero current depth D. The arc defines one end of the cylinder and the axis vector is (0,0,D) in transform coordinates.

5   To create a cylinder using an end arc and direction line.

INDICATE CYLINDER END ARC

Select an arc.

INDICATE CYLINDER DIRECTION LINE

Select a line.

The direction line must end in the plane of the arc, and be perpendicular to the plane of the arc; the direction line does not have to go through the arc's center. The cylinder radius is the radius of the arc. The cylinder axis is defined as the direction line translated to the arc center.

6   To create a cylinder using two end diameter lines.

INDICATE 2 CYLINDER END DIAMETER LINES   Select the two end diameter lines.

The two end diameter lines must be of the same length. The line joining the midpoints of the selected lines must be perpendicular to both of those lines. This perpendicular line is the cylinder axis, and the cylinder radius is chosen to be one half the common length of the two selected lines.

7   To create a cylinder using an axis line and a positive radius. The line is the cylinder axis and the radius is the cylinder radius.

INDICATE CYLINDER AXIS LINE

Select the line that defines the cylinder axis line.

CYLINDER RADIUS =

Enter a positive radius.

15.4.2.8 Revolution Solid (REV)

This is a shape obtained by sweeping the area bounded by a planar closed "cross-section" contour 360 degrees about an axis. The axis must be in the same plane as the contour, and can touch the contour, but the infinite extension of the axis must not pass through the interior of the contour.

```
REVOLUTION SOLID
1.AXIS LINE, CURVES
2.ROTATION ARC, CURVES
```

REV - SURFACE OF REVOLUTION

Enter:

1   To create a revolution solid using an axis line and curves that define a 2-D cross-section contour.

INDICATE REV ROTATION AXIS LINE	Select a rotation axis line.
INDICATE REV CROSS-SECTION CURVES	Select appropriate curves for the REV cross-section contour (Refer to the discussion under Cross-Section Contours).

2   To create a revolution solid using a rotation arc and curves that define a 2-D cross-section contour. The revolution solid rotation axis will be through the arc center and perpendicular to plane of the arc. The cross-section is rotated about the axis in place.

INDICATE REV ROTATION ARC	Select a rotation arc.
INDICATE REV CROSS-SECTION CURVES	Select appropriate curves for the revolution solid cross-section contour (Refer to the discussion under Cross-Section Contours).

Cross-Section Contours (REV & SLB)

Allowable curves for a revolution solid or slab cross section contour are line, arc, 2-D Bezier curve, Wilson-Fowler spline (same as entity type 5, rotated cubic spline), string, or composite curve. Composite curves can only contain instances of the other allowable curve types.

Solid primitives cannot use strings or composite curves as such; only individual component curves. Copies of the component curves of strings or composite curves will be created and used in the definition of the cross-section contour.

ICEM DDN automatically orders the curves and checks planarity for cross-section contours to be used in a revolution solid or slab.

In version 2.0, there is a limit on the number of curves that can be in any cross-section contour. The limits are:

* A revolution solid can have at most 75 curves.

* A slab can have at most 115 curves.

For purposes of these limits, a selected string or composite does not count as just one curve, but as the number of components it has.

15.4.2.10 Slab (SLB)

This is a shape obtained by extruding the area bounded by a planar closed "cross-section" contour a "thickness" distance in one of the two directions perpendicular to the plane of the contour.

```
SLAB
1.POINT, CURVES
2.DIRECTION LINE, CURVES
3.WORK PLANE CURVES, THICKNESS DELTA
```

SLB - ARBITRARY SLAB

Enter:

1   To create a slab using a point and curves that define a 2-D cross-section contour.

INDICATE SLAB POINT

Select a point.

INDICATE SLAB CROSS-SECTION CURVES

Select appropriate curves for the slab cross-section contour (refer to the discussion under Cross-Section Contours).

The point must not be in the plane of the contour. The perpendicular distance from the point to the plane of the contour is the slab thickness, and the point location gives the sweep direction.

2   To create a slab using an line and curves that define a 2-D cross-section contour.

INDICATE SLAB DIRECTION LINE

Select a line.

INDICATE SLAB CROSS-SECTION CURVES

Select appropriate curves for the slab cross-section contour (refer to the discussion under Cross-Section Contours).

The line must be perpendicular to the contour plane, and one line endpoint must be in the contour plane. The slab thickness is the line length, and the line location gives the sweep direction.

3   To create a slab using work plane curves and a thickness delta. This is an input option relating to the work space (transform coordinate system) associated with the current work view, and in particular to the current work plane.

INDICATE CURVES PARALLEL TO WORK PLANE

Select appropriate curves for the slab cross-section contour (refer to the discussion under Cross-Section Contours).

SLAB THICKNESS DELTA =

Enter a nonzero delta D. The sweeping thickness vector is (0,0,d) in transform coordinates.

157

15.4.2.11 Sphere (SPH)

This is a solid sphere shape.

```
SPHERE
1.KEY-IN
2.GREAT CIRCLE
3.DIAMETER LINE
4.CENTER, RADIUS
5.CENTER, SURFACE POINT
```

 SPH - SPHERE

Enter:

1 To create a sphere by entering the coordinates of the sphere center and a radius value. The center is at (x,y,z) and the radius must be positive.

```
SPHERE CENTER
1. X =
2. Y =
3. Z =

SPHERE RADIUS =
```

Enter the coordinates of the sphere center. If the definition space mode is set to transform coordinates, you must enter xt, yt, and zt coordinates.

Enter a positive radius number.

2 To create a sphere using a great circle arc.

```
INDICATE SPHERE GREAT CIRCLE
```

Select a circle arc whose plane contains the sphere diameter. The sphere center point is the arc center point, and the sphere radius is the arc radius.

3 To create a sphere using a diameter line.

```
INDICATE SPHERE DIAMETER LINE
```

Select a finite line which will be a sphere diameter line. The sphere center point is the line midpoint, and the sphere radius is one half the line's length.

4 To create a sphere using a center point and a radius.

```
INDICATE SPHERE CENTER POINT
```

Select the sphere center point.

```
SPHERE RADIUS =
```

Enter the positive radius number.

5 To create a sphere using a center point and a surface point.

```
INDICATE SPHERE CENTER POINT
```

Select the sphere center point.

```
INDICATE SPHERE SURFACE POINT
```

Select any point that will be on the sphere's surface.

15.4.2.13 Torus (TOR)

This is a solid shape, known as a torus, obtained by sweeping a circular or elliptical "cross-section" area 360 degrees about an axis line in the plane of the circle or ellipse. The infinite extension of the line must not touch any point of the cross-section.

```
TORUS
1.KEY-IN
2.ROTATION ARC, SECTION
3.CENTER, SECTION
4.AXIS LINE, SECTION
5.DIAMETER LINE, SECTION
6.CENTER, DIRECTION LINE, 3 RADII
7.ARC, 2 RADII
```

TOR - TORUS

Enter:

1   To create a torus by entering coordinates. The center is at (x,y,z) and the axis line extends from there to (x+dx,y+dy,z+dz) . The torus main radius is the distance from the torus center to the cross-section center. The section radial radius is one half the dimension of the circle/ellipse cross-section measured perpendicular to the torus axis (that is, in a radial direction). The section axial radius is one half the dimension of the circle/ellipse cross-section measured parallel to the torus axis (that is, in an axial direction). For the cross-section to be a circle, the section radial and section axial radii must be the same.

```
TORUS CENTER
1. X =
2. Y =
3. Z =
```
Enter the coordinates of the torus center. If the definition space mode is set to transform coordinates, you must enter xt, yt, and zt coordinates.

```
TORUS AXIS
1. DX =
2. DY =
3. DZ =
```
Enter a vector defining the direction of the torus axis. If the definition space mode is set to transform coordinates, you must enter dxt, dyt, and dzt coordinates.

```
TORUS RADII
1. TORUS MAIN      =
2. SECTION RADIAL =
3. SECTION AXIAL  =
```
Enter the torus main radius, the torus section radial radius, and the section axial radius.

2   To create a torus using a rotation arc and an arc/ellipse section.

INDICATE TORUS ROTATION ARC   Select a rotation arc.

INDICATE TORUS SECTION ARC OR ELLIPSE   Select an arc/ellipse section.

The rotation arc defines the axis about which the section is rotated to sweep out the torus. The axis is the line through the center of the rotation arc and perpendicular to the plane of the arc. The rotation arc does not have to pass through the section. The torus axis must lie in the plane of the section. The section must satisfy the restrictions from the note below.

159

3 To create a torus using a center point and an arc/ellipse section.

INDICATE TORUS CENTER POINT	Select a point as the center.
INDICATE TORUS SECTION ARC OR ELLIPSE	Select an arc/ellipse section.

The point is the torus center. The axis is through that point, in the plane of the section, and perpendicular to the line joining the torus center to the section center. The selected center point must be in the plane of the section. The section must satisfy the restrictions from the note below.

4 To create a torus using an axis line and an arc/ellipse section.

INDICATE TORUS AXIS LINE	Select a line as the axis line.
INDICATE TORUS SECTON ARC OR ELLIPSE	Select an arc/ellipse section.

The line must be in the plane of the section and the infinite extension of the line must not touch any part of the cross-section. The torus center is the point on the infinite extension of the axis line which is closest to the section center. The section must satisfy the restrictions from the note below.

5 To create a torus using a diameter line and an arc/ellipse section.

INDICATE TORUS DIAMETER LINE	Select a line as the diameter line.
INDICATE TORUS SECTION ARC OR ELLIPSE	Select an arc/ellipse section.

The line may be any diameter line of the torus. The midpoint of the line is the center of the torus. The torus axis is perpendicular to the selected line, through its midpoint, and in the plane of the section. The section must satisfy the restrictions from the note below.

6 To create a torus using a center, direction line, and three radii.

INDICATE TORUS CENTER POINT	Select a point as the center point.
INDICATE TORUS DIRECTION LINE	Select a line as the direction line.
TORUS RADII 1. TORUS MAIN = 2. SECTION RADIAL = 3. SECTION AXIAL =	Enter the torus main radius, the torus section radial radius, and the section axial radius.

The point is the torus center. The function of the selected line is to specify the axis direction. The line must have non-zero length but it does not have to pass through the center point.

7 To create a torus using an arc and 2 radii.

INDICATE TORUS MAIN RADIUS ARC	Select an arc.
TORUS SECTION RADII 1. SECTION RADIAL = 2. SECTION AXIAL =	Enter the torus section radial radius, and the section axial radius.

The torus axis will be through the arc center and perpendicular to the plane of the arc. The torus main radius is the radius of the selected arc. The two radius values entered are the section radial radius and section axial radius, respectively.

160

The section is any arc or ellipse entity on the intended torus. The arc and ellipse sections chosen do not have to be full 360-degree arcs, but they are treated as such for purposes of the torus definition. If the section is an ellipse, there is a restriction on its orientation. The major diameter line of the ellipse is the longest line segment from one point on the ellipse to another point on the ellipse which goes through the ellipse center. This line must always be parallel to or perpendicular to the torus axis line.

Another restriction is that a (full) section curve cannot touch or cross the torus axis. This implies, for example, that the value entered for the torus main radius must be strictly greater than the section radial radius.

15.4.2.14 Wedge (WEG)

This is a solid shape obtained by sweeping a triangle in any nonzero vector direction. The legs of the triangle together with the sweep vector do not have to be perpendicular to one another, but they do have to point in three independent directions. This shape is also equivalent to half a BOX which has been cut along a diagonal.

```
WEDGE
1.KEY-IN
2.3 LINES AT A POINT
3.CORNER, 3 EDGE POINTS
4.CORNER, 3 EDGE DELTAS
```

Enter:

1   To create a wedge by entering coordinates. The wedge is created with a corner at (x,y,z) and edge vectors (sx,dy,dz) as entered. The first two edges are the triangle legs, and the third edge vector specifies the sweep.

```
WEDGE CORNER
1. X =
2. Y =
3. Z =
```
Enter the coordinates of the wedge corner. If the definition space mode is set to transform coordinates, you must enter xt, yt, and zt coordinates.

```
WEDGE EDGE 1
1. DX =
2. DY =
3. DZ =
```
Enter a vector defining the direction and length of the first edge. If the definition space mode is set to transform coordinates, you must enter dxt, dyt, and dzt coordinates.

```
WEDGE EDGE 2
1. DX =
2. DY =
3. DZ =
```
Enter a vector defining the direction and length of the second edge. If the definition space mode is set to transform coordinates, you must enter dxt, dyt, and dzt coordinates.

WEG - RIGHT-ANGLE WEDGE

WEDGE EDGE 3
1. DX =
2. DY =
3. DZ =

Enter a vector defining the direction and length of the third edge. If the definition space mode is set to transform coordinates, you must enter dxt, dyt, and dzt coordinates.

2   To create a wedge using three lines that meet and end at a point.

INDICATE 3 WEDGE EDGE LINES

Select three non-coplanar finite lines that meet and end at a point.

The wedge is created with the common endpoint as a corner. The first two lines determine the triangle, and the third line specifies the sweep.

3   To create a wedge by using a corner point and three edge endpoints.

INDICATE WEDGE CORNER POINT

Select the corner point.

INDICATE 3 WEDGE EDGE POINTS

Select the three endpoints.

Select four points, not all of which are in the same plane. The first point is the corner; lines from the corner to the second and third points determine the triangle; and the line from the corner to the last point specifies the sweep.

4   To create a wedge by using a corner point and three edge delta distances.

INDICATE WEDGE CORNER POINT

Select the corner point.

WEDGE EDGE DELTAS
1.X DELTA=
2.Y DELTA=
3.Z DELTA=

Enter any three nonzero numbers d1, d2, and d3. If the definition space mode is set to transform coordinates, you must enter delta xt, yt, and zt coordinates.

The edge vectors defining the triangle are (d1,0,0) and (0,d2,0); the vector (0,0,d3) specifies the sweep. Menu 1.15.2 SPACE DEFINITION MODE specifies whether these are model or current-work-view transform coordinates. This input mode creates the triangle of the wedge as a right triangle.

15.4.3 Create Object

With this choice, you can combine solid objects by using the boolean combination operations; union, difference, and intersection. Each time you enter this menu only one object is created, but you can select any number of combination operations in any order while you are in this menu.

Follow these steps in creating an object:

1. Select the base solid; that is, the object to start with when applying the subsequent object creation operations.

   INDICATE BASE SOLID   Select the base object or primitive.

2. Name the new object if it is not automatically set by the the object naming modal. ICEM DDN displays:

   OBJECT NAMING METHOD   Select a naming option.
   1.STANDARD PREFIX
   2.PRESET PREFIX
   3.PROMPT FOR NAMES
   4.RE-USE BASE NAME

   or

   ENTER OBJECT NAME   Name the object.

   or

   NEXT OBJECT NAME IS name   The object is automatically named by
                                          the system.

3. Choose one of the three operations from the Combination Operation menu described below, and select the set of solids for combination.

   Completing this step yields a new base solid.

4. Repeat the third step with the same or different operations.

   Enter] at the Combination Operation menu to end new object creation. Using a menu string to go to another menu also ends object creation. The base solid resulting from this step becomes the named object.

The order of solid combination is the order of selection. Symbolically, this follows according to the rule of combination to the left if selected objects are written from left to right. For instance, the object X with the base solid A written $X = A + B*C - D - E$ means $X = (((A + B)*C) - D) - E$.

In order to see the physical results of these operations, you must branch to the ICEM Solid Modeler (Refer to 15.4.5 BRANCH TO I.S.M.). In the ICEM Solid Modeler, you can view the physical results by using analysis processing or interactive faceted viewing. In addition, you can use analysis processing to calculate the mass properties of the solid.

Combination Operation Menu

With this menu, you can unite, subtract, or intersect selected solids to the base solid. The menu for this operation is:

```
COMBINATION OPERATION
1.UNION
2.DIFFERENCE
3.INTERSECTION
```

Enter:

1   To add selected solids to the base solid.

This operation adds the selected solids to the latest base solid. The resulting solid volume equals the total solid volume of the base and the selected solids. A symbolic example is BASE+S+T.

2   To subtract selected solids from the base solid.

This operation subtracts the selected solids from the latest base solid. The resulting solid volume equals the solid volume of the base with that of the selected solids removed. A symbolic example is BASE−S−T.

3   To intersect selected solids with the base solid.

This operation intersects the latest base solid with the selected solids. The resulting volume equals that which is contained in the base solid and also in every one of the selected solids. A symbolic example is BASE*S*T.

NOTE

A solid entity can be used directly in the definition of up to 30 objects.

If a solid has been used this many times, then in order to select it again for object creation, some previous object it was used for must be deleted. For purposes of this limit, only solids selected during the creation of an object are directly used by the object. For example, if

    GASKET = BOX1 − HOLES

where

    HOLES = CYL1 + CYL2

then CYL1 and CYL2 are directly used in HOLES but not in GASKET. BOX1 and HOLES are directly used in GASKET.

Object Creation Example

You can control the number of separate objects that are created for a particular solid model, as illustrated by the following example of removing two cylindrical holes from the union of two boxes.

First, assume default modal settings in a new part, and secondly, assume that you have created the boxes and cylinders. The default naming mode names them, BOX00001, BOX00002, CYL00001, and CYL00002 . Three creation methods are used for the final object. Figure 15.15 shows the starting primitives and the final resulting object using any of the following three methods.

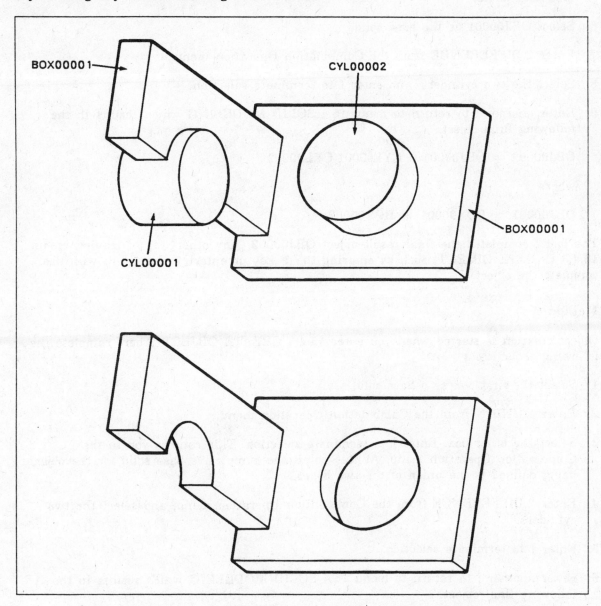

FIG. 15.15 Object creation example (Courtesy of Control Data Corp.)

165

Method 1

Object creation is started when you enter 15.4.3 CREATE OBJECT. Then, complete the following sequence:

1. Select the first box as a base solid.

2. Enter 1.UNION from the Combination Operation menu.

3. Select the other box, and enter] (operation complete) to terminate selection.

4. Enter another] to complete object OBJ00001. This returns you to menu 15.4 SOLID MODELING.

5. Restart object creation by entering 3.CREATE OBJECT again from the Solid Modeling menu.

6. Select OBJ00001 as the base solid.

7. Enter 2.DIFFERENCE from the Combination Operation menu.

8. Select the two cylinders, and enter] to terminate selection.

9. Enter another] to return to menu 15.4 SOLID MODELING which results in the following final object.

   OBJ00002 = OBJ00001 − CYL00001-CYL00002

   where

   OBJ00001 = BOX00001 + BOX00002.

The last] completed the final result object OBJ00002. Any other way of leaving menu 15.4.3 CREATE OBJECT, such as entering the F key or entering Control-P, will also complete the object.

Method 2

Object creation is started when you enter 15.4.3 CREATE OBJECT. Then, complete the following sequence:

1. Select the first box as a base solid.

2. Enter 1.UNION from the Combination Operation menu.

3. Select the other box. Enter] to terminate selection. This returns you to the Combination Operation menu. At this point, the cumulative base solid for the object being defined is the union of the two boxes.

4. Enter 2.DIFFERENCE from the Combination Operation menu, and select the two cylinders.

5. Enter] to terminate selection.

6. Enter another] to return to menu 15.4 SOLID MODELING which results in the following final object.

   OBJ00001 = BOX00001 + BOX00002 − CYL00001 − CYL00002.

166

Method 3

Object creation is started when you enter 15.4.3 CREATE OBJECT. Then, complete the following sequence:

1. Select the first box as the base solid.

2. Enter 2.DIFFERENCE from the Combination Operation menu. Select the first cylinder. Enter] to terminate selection. Enter another] to complete object OBJ00001. This returns you to menu 15.4 SOLID MODELING.

3. Restart object creation by entering 3.CREATE OBJECT from the Solid Modeling menu.

4. Select the other box as the new base solid.

5. Enter 2.DIFFERENCE from the Combination Operation menu. Select the other cylinder. Enter] to terminate selection. Enter another] to complete object OBJ00002. This returns you to menu 15.4 SOLID MODELING.

6. Restart object creation for a third time by entering 3.CREATE OBJECT, and select OBJ00001 as the base solid.

7. Enter 1.UNION from the Combination Operation menu. Select OBJ00002.

8. Enter] to terminate selection, and enter another] to return to menu 15.4 SOLID MODELING, which results in the following final object.

    OBJ00003 = OBJ00001 + OBJ00002

    where

    OBJ00001 = BOX00001 − CYL00001

    and

    OBJ00002 = BOX00002 − CYL00002.

The following things should be kept in mind when using the] (operation complete) key and [(operation reject) key.

- Enter] to terminate selection and return to the Combination Operation menu.

- Enter [before any selection has been made to rechoose the operation.

- Enter] before any selection has been made to return to the 15.4 SOLID MODELING menu.

- Enter [to cancel the most recent solid selection in a set. This can be repeated to reject each previously selected solid in the reverse order of selection.

- Enter [after all selected solids have been rejected to rechoose the operation.

- Enter] after all selected solids have been rejected to return to the 15.4 SOLID MODELING menu.

167

15.4.4 Modify Solid

This menu modifies the definition and representation of existing primitives or objects.

```
MODIFY SOLID
1.MODIFY PRIMITIVE DATA
2.GENERATE SURFACES FOR PRIMITIVES
3.DELETE SURFACES FROM PRIMITIVES
4.MODIFY PROPERTIES
```

15.4.4.1 Modify Primitive Data

You can use this operation to change any primitive by keying in replacement data. The meaning of displayed and input data is determined at the start of this operation according to the definition space mode (1.15.2).

INDICATE PRIMITIVE TO MODIFY   Select a single primitive for modification.

The primitive type, name, and all modifiable key-in data for the selected primitive are displayed. Any displayed numerical data can be changed, but the type and name are shown only for reference. (Use 5.11 NAMED ENTITIES for all name changes.)

```
PRIMITIVE TYPE = CYLINDER
PRIMITIVE NAME + CY00001
CYLINDER END CENTER
 1.X = 1.5000
 2.Y = 2.0000
 3.Z - 0.0000
CYLINDER AXIS
 1.DX = 0.0000
 2.DY = 3.0000
 3.DZ = 0.0000
CYLINDER RADIUS = 1.6000
```

After data modification changes have been completed, all wireframe and surface (if any) geometry associated with the primitive is updated to reflect the new definition data. If no changes are made, no associated geometry updates will take place, and ICEM DDN displays the message NO DATA CHANGES MADE.

For primitive types box, cone, cylinder, sphere, torus, and wedge, the data displayed for modification is the key-in data as for primitive creation by key-in.

For the revolution solid primitive type, only the axis line can be changed. The start and end coordinates are displayed for modification. An example is:

```
PRIMITIVE TYPE = REVOLUTION SOLID
PRIMITIVE NAME = REV00001
AXIS END 1
 1.X = 1.7000
 2.Y = 0.0000
 3.Z = 0.0000
AXIS END 2
 1.X = 1.7000
 2.Y = 3.5000
 3.Z = 0.0000
```

For the slab primitive type, only the thickness and direction can be changed. Enter a positive number to change the thickness of the slab, or enter a negative number to change both the thickness of the slab and the direction of projection (extrusion) of the slab from its defining section. The defining section end of the selected slab is highlighted in the work view. An example is:

```
PRIMITIVE TYPE = SLAB
PRIMITIVE NAME = SLB00001

(NEGATIVE THICKNESS REVERSES DIRECTION)
SLAB THICKNESS = 2.5000
```

 GSU - GENERAL SURFACE

TER - TERRAIN SURFACE

15.4.4.2 Generate Surfaces for Primitives

This operation generates a complete set of boundary surface entities for the selected primitive(s). The modal 15.1.3 SURFACE PATHS controls the appearance of these surfaces. The surfaces are considered to be part of the primitive entity via pointer references. Any primitive already including surface pointers is ignored for this function.

INDICATE PRIMITIVES OR OBJECTS   Select primitives and/or objects and the system automatically generates surfaces for the selected primitives and for all primitives in the selected objects.

15.4.4.3 Delete Surfaces from Primitives

This operation deletes all surfaces (if any) pointed to by the selected primitive(s). Any primitive not containing surface pointers is ignored for this function.

INDICATE PRIMITIVES OR OBJECTS   Select primitives and/or objects and the system automatically deletes surfaces of the selected primitives and of all primitives in the selected objects.

NOTE

If only one or two specific surfaces are needed from a primitive, the recommended procedure is to produce all the surfaces with 15.4.4.2 GENERATE SURFACES FOR PRIMITIVES, duplicate the desired surface(s) with 13.8 DUPL AND TRANSLATE (using translation vector (0,0,0)) and then delete the original surfaces with 15.4.4.3 DELETE SURFACES FROM PRIMITIVES.

15.4.4.4 Modify Properties

You can use this operation to alter any or all of the physical properties (density, diffuse reflectance, and specular reflectance) for the selected primitives and/or objects.

```
MODIFY PROPERTIES
1.DENSITY
2.DIFFUSE REFLECTANCE
3.SPECULAR REFLECTANCE
```

Enter:

1 To specify changes in density.

DENSITY = nnn

The current value for the density modal is displayed. Enter the new value. Density must be greater than 0.

2 To specify changes in diffuse reflectance.

DIFFUSE REFLECTANCE = nnn

The current value for the diffuse reflectance modal is displayed. Enter the new value. $0 \le diffuse \le 1$

3 To specify changes in specular reflectance.

SPECULAR REFLECTANCE = nnn

The current value for the specular reflectance modal is displayed. Enter the new value.. $0 \le specular \le 1$

Any combination of properties can be changed for the selected solids. After entering all replacement values for the properties and], you are prompted to INDICATE SOLIDS TO MODIFY, and the changes specified are applied to the selected primitives and objects. Object properties take precedence over the properties of their component primitives and subobjects.

The ICEM Solid Modeler properties of hue and saturation are calculated from the color associated with each entity (used in color display mode 1.9.1.4 COLOR BY ENTITY COLOR) together with the current color table values.

15.4.5 Branch to I.S.M.

This menu choice transfers control to the ICEM Solid Modeler (ISM), passes solids data to the ICEM Solid Modeler, passes the current ICEM DDN viewing information to the ICEM Solid Modeler, and allows the current ICEM DDN part to be filed before the branch to ISM takes place. All solids entities (primitives and objects) in the current part are transferred, though there is a "no data" option available. If the current view display in ICEM DDN consists of one, two, or four views, the same views are displayed in the ICEM Solid Modeler. If more than four views are currently displayed in ICEM DDN, the first four ICEM DDN views are displayed in the ICEM Solid Modeler.

The ICEM Solid Modeler provides the capability to branch back to ICEM DDN. Control returns to menu 15.4 SOLID MODELING.

The branch menu is:

```
BRANCH TO I.S.M.
1.FILE - SEND SOLIDS DATA
2.      - DO NOT SEND DATA
3.DO NOT FILE - SEND SOLIDS DATA
4.           - DO NOT SEND DATA
```

All four choices cause a branch (transfer of control) to the ICEM Solid Modeler. The complete documentation for ICEM Solid Modeler operations is in the chapter titled ICEM Solid Modeler.

Enter:

1   To file the current part in ICEM DDN and send all solids (primitive and object) geometry to the ICEM Solid Modeler workspace. This is for keeping the ICEM DDN and ICEM Solid Modeler solids data equivalent.

2   To file the current part in ICEM DDN and branch quickly to the ICEM Solid Modeler (with an empty ICEM Solid Modeler workspace) for viewing analysis results or checking analysis job status.

3   To not file the current part in ICEM DDN and send all solids (primitive and object) geometry to the ICEM Solid Modeler workspace. This is for keeping the ICEM DDN and ICEM Solid Modeler solids data equivalent.

4   To not file the current part in ICEM DDN and branch quickly to the ICEM Solid Modeler (with an empty ICEM Solid Modeler workspace) for viewing analysis results or checking analysis job status.

NOTE

A primitive or object without a name is given a name when you branch to the ICEM Solid Modeler. The names are assigned using the preset prefix naming modal if this is the current setting of the modal, else the standard prefix naming modal will be used. One way to produce an un-named solid is with 5.11.3 DETACH NAME FROM ENTITY. Another way is from name conflicts during a Part Merge or Independent Restore. Pattern operations may yield unnamed solids as well.

A primitive or object with a name longer than eight characters (This is done with 5.11.2 ATTACH NAME TO ENTITY) cannot keep that name in the ICEM Solid Modeler. ICEM DDN allows up to ten characters in a name, but the ICEM Solid Modeler only allows up to eight. The rightmost one or two characters are dropped off automatically before the solid is sent. If the resulting 8-character name is already being used, another unique name is assigned.

PROBLEMS

Manually sketch the isometric drawings in the following problems.

Then generate a solid model for each of the problems.

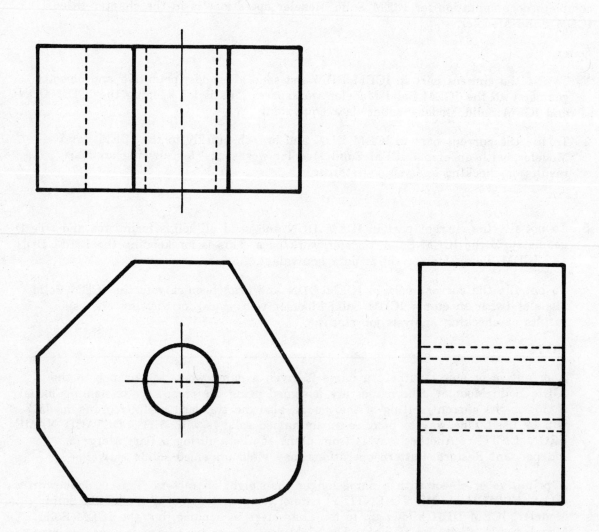

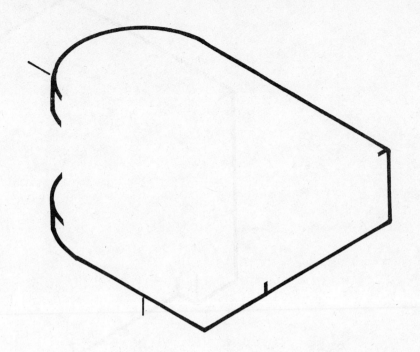

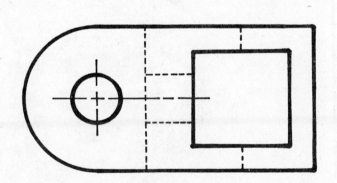

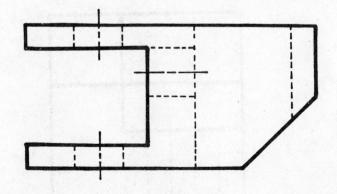

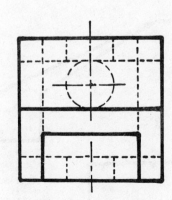

173

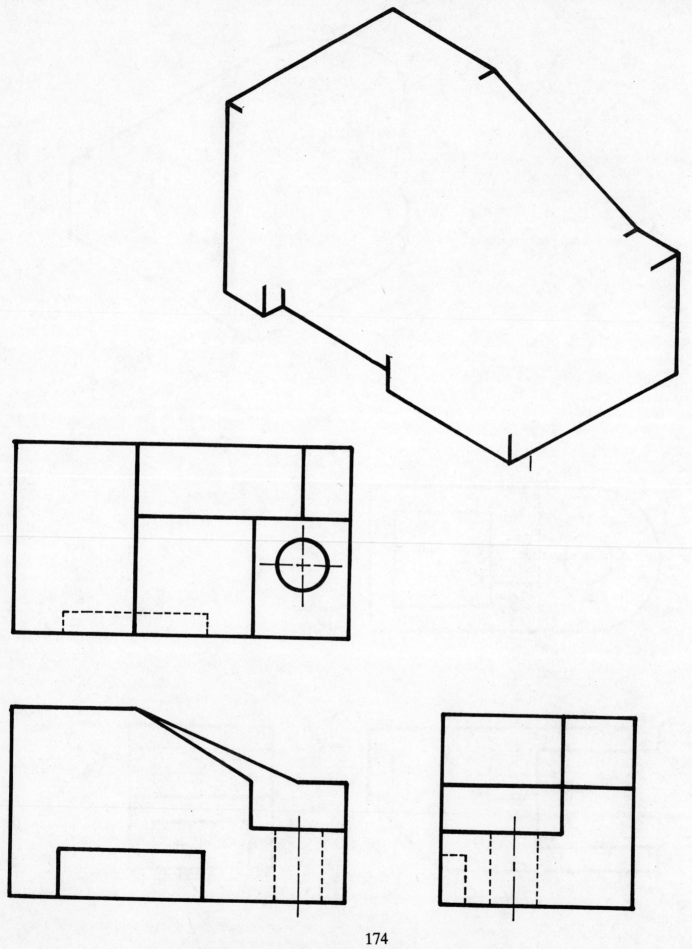

174

CHAPTER 6

SPATIAL GEOMETRY and VISUALIZATION

Introduction

An engineer should be able to visualize a project, device or object from given set of plans, production drawings or any other 2-D representation as well as from a 3-D representation. The first step in visualizing an object is to analyze the drawings.

Analyzing the drawings mean to study the drawings and determine all the spatial distances and relationships not explicitly provided on the drawings (e.g., non-dimesioned oblique lines, angles, missing lines, inconsistencies, etc.) This information will be used in the construction and manufacturing process. For example, an engineering construction manager may spend several days to "read" (analyze) a set of construction plans, for a project, in order to determine all the distances, angles, material quantities and operations involved in the project. In the same way, a manufacturing engineer may require to understand and fully visualize every single detail of a new product or device before beginning the manufacturing process. Rarely will he or she have the opportunity to meet with the designer to thoroughly visualize the new device. The designer might assist the visualization process by building a prototype, solid model or by sketching a pictorial. However, this is more the exception than the rule.

Visualization

The ability to form a mental image of an object and draw sketches of any pictorial (e.g., perspectives, axonometrics, obliques) is indispensable to the engineer. This human ability to think in three-dimensions is called **visualization**.

Some people seem to have a natural talent to visualize objects. We might ask: Is this visualization ability a natural gift or the product of a trained mind? Maybe, it is a combination both, in diverse degrees of intensity. It is possible to use some axiomatic principles, rules and logic to analyze solid geometry. Learning the basic principles of descriptive geometry should facilitate the visualization process. As stated by B. Leighton Wellman in *Technical Descriptive Geometry* (New York: McGraw-Hill, 1957):

> "traditionally, descriptive geometry has been taught as a course in visualization. The emphasis has been placed on imagination, and therefore the unimaginative student has been foredoomed to failure. Years of experience have convinced the author that this approach is faulty. Descriptive geometry is a science based on sound facts and should be taught as a course in logical reasoning. Visualization must follow, not precede reasoning. Imagination can aid, but must not determine, the solution.
>
> The visualization of an object from a multiview drawing should be based on logical conclusions derived from observation and accurate analytical thinking. There must

176

be no guess or flights of imagination. Students have frequently said to the author: 'I can't *imagine* what this new view should look like, so I can draw it?' The answer has always been: 'Good! Since you have no preconceived idea, you can go ahead and draw the view without prejudice. Follow exactly the rules and principles that you know apply here. When the view is finished, you'll see what it looks like and you'll know it is right.' In this method of teaching, the student is taught to depend solely on established facts."

In this chapter, you will learn that the winning combination is to use both: **logical reasoning** and **constructive imagination**. The axiomatic approach assists in this process.

As mentioned in the preface, the axiomatic approach serves in devising resolutions -in synthesis- and in analyzing the existing engineering graphics strategies. The main tools of axiomatic theory are definitions, conditions, and axioms. **Axioms** are postulates and propositions generally recognized as truth. In the context of this discussion, they are utilized to describe general rules that allow you to infer a solution to a visualization problem.

The user of this approach think in terms of the logical relationship among the orthographic views of the object; assisted by his/her imagination. The eminent scientist-Albert Einstein, once said: "Imagination is more important than knowledge, for knowledge is limited...". Notwithstanding, imagination without a basic knowledge of the facts is useless in our technologically oriented society. The following section describes some of the definitions, conditions and axioms necessary for the axiomatic-aided visualization procedure.

Definitions, Conditions and Axioms

Several definitions and axioms will guide our discussion. Keep in mind that these principles apply to multiview orthographic projections. To simplify the discussion, views will be named by the plane in which they have been projected (e.g., frontal, horizontal, profile, ... instead of top, front, right-side, ..., respectively.).

Definition 1: <u>Aligned Views</u> are views placed side by side, so that their corresponding points are placed on the same projection line.

Definition 2: <u>Adjoining Views</u> are views that share a common boundary (i.e., folding line or edge view of the projection plane).

Definition 3: <u>Adjacent Views</u> are two aligned adjoining views.

Definition 4: <u>Related Views</u> are two views contiguous to a common intermediate orthographic view between them. They are adjacent to the same view (see Figure 6.1).

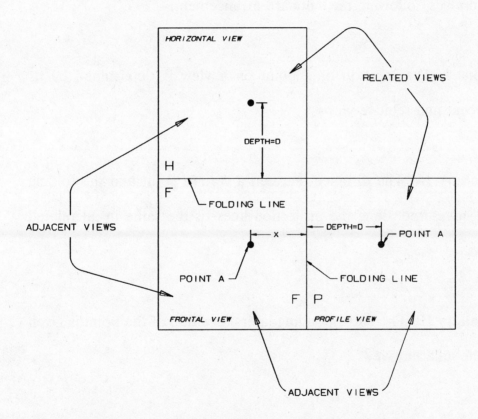

FIG. 6.1 Representation of a projected point. Adjacent views are two aligned adjoining views. Related views are two views contiguous to a common intermediate view.

Condition 1: Lines-of-sight are at right angles with the projection plane.

Condition 2: Lines-of-sight of corresponding adjacent views are perpendicular to each other.

Condition 3: All adjacent and related views are aligned between themselves, following the standard arrangement.

Axiom 1: The location of a point on a view is determined by its adjacent and relative views.

Corollary 1A: The distance between a certain point and the folding line -measured along the projection lines- is the same in all related views.

Corollary 1B: The corresponding lateral position of the point is given by the adjacent view.

Explanation: Observe, in Figure 6.1, the representation of a point projected on the Horizontal, Frontal and Profile planes of projection. Notice that the depth D between point A and the folding lines H/F and F/P, is the same in the related views, namely: the horizontal and profile views. Of course, the adjacent view -namely frontal view- gives the corresponding lateral position of the point along the horizontal (X) axis.

Axiom 2: Two contiguous plane surfaces on a view are not on the same plane.

Explanation: Contiguous surface areas on an orthographic view are separated by visible lines. This visible lines indicate a change in the direction of the plane or curved surface. Therefore, the adjacent surface is at a different depth, elevation or inclination.

Axiom 3: Inclined or curved surfaces appear flat on the orthographic projection.

Example 6.1 Contiguous and Inclined surfaces
Determine the relative position of two contiguous surfaces and sketch an isometric to show how it is visualized.

1. Figure 6.2 (a) illustrates top, front and right-side views of an object. Notice that both the top and front views of the object display two contiguous surfaces. From the top view, surface "abcd" is adjacent to

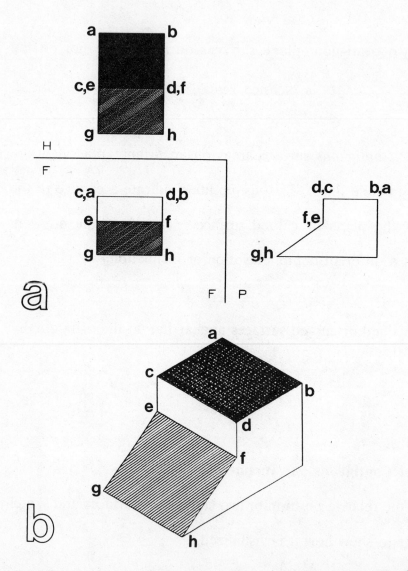

FIG. 6.2 (a) Contiguous surfaces are at different elevation or depth. Surface "abcd" is above inclined surface "efgh". (b) Pictorial obtained from the spatial analysis.

surface "efgh". Notice that visible line "cd" or "ef" separates the surfaces. This indicates that these surfaces are at a different elevation or inclination. The profile view provides the relative height or elevation of the surfaces. In this case, surface "abcd" is above "efgh". Notice also that "efgh" is inclined relative to "abcd". Both surfaces appear to be flat from the front and top views.

2. Figure 6.2 (b) depicts a pictorial obtained from the preceding simple spatial analysis and visualization process.

Auxiliary Projections

Another type of orthographic projection is the auxiliary projection - commonly called auxiliary view. **Auxiliary projections** are orthographic views inclined to the principal planes of projection. Their objective is to display the true shape of an object's feature that is not parallel to any of the principal planes of projection, as illustrated in Figure 6.3. A **primary auxiliary view** is constructed by drawing an imaginary auxiliary plane of projection parallel to the inclined surface, and projecting its features onto that surface -similar to drawing multiviews.

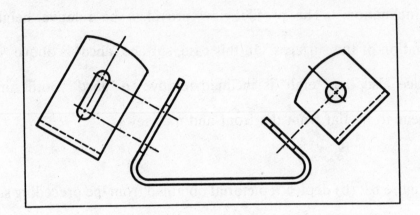

FIG. 6.3 Auxiliary views are orthographic views inclined to the principal planes of projection. (Courtesy of ASME and ANSI.)

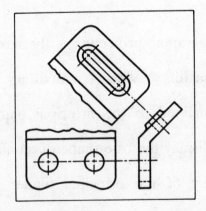

FIG. 6.4 Primary auxiliary view are generated by projecting points from the given partial front and right-side views. (Courtesy of ASME and ANSI.)

184

Consider Figure 6.4: The partial front view and right-side profile view are given. Notice that a primary auxiliary view has been generated by projecting points from the right-side view; the width of these points is obtained from the front view.

Secondary auxiliary views and sections can be constructed if a surface of an object is inclined and does not appear as an edge view (i.e., when you look at a sheet of paper from the border, it looks like a thin line) in any of the principal planes of projection. These views are not normally used in working drawings, but they are utilized in descriptive geometry to find information about the object.

Missing Views and Lines

Sometimes it is difficult to visualize the 3-D shapes to be manufactured. To make things worse, it is not unusual to find that there are **missing views** and **missing lines** in the drawings. However, it is possible to visualize these incomplete drawings by utilizing certain principles of descriptive geometry and the power of constructive imagination.

Example 6.2 Missing Lines

Given the frontal and profile views of an object find the missing line on the incomplete auxiliary view, as shown in Figure 6.5 (a).

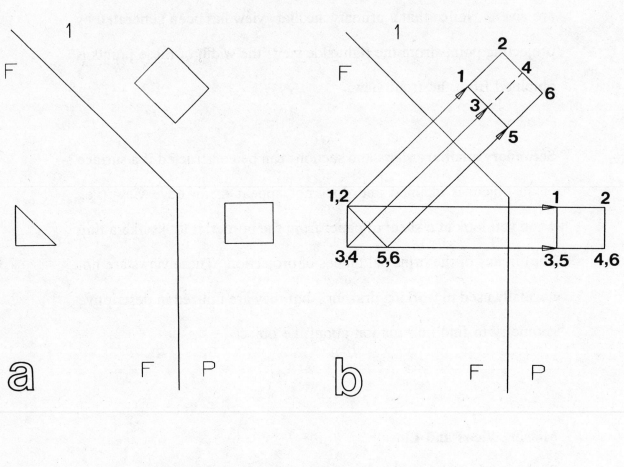

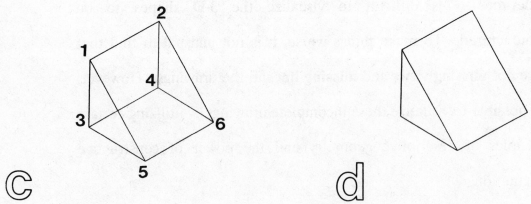

FIG. 6.5 (a) Given the frontal and profile views, find the missing line on the auxiliary view. (b) The position of missing line 3-4 is found by projecting points 3,4. Wire-frame and isometric are given in (c) and (d).

Solution

1. Draw projection lines from the frontal view to the two related views (i.e., auxiliary 1 and profile), to determine the corresponding aligned points at the object's intersection points. Notice that points 1, 2 -in the frontal view- are aligned with 1, 2 on the profile and auxiliary views, as illustrated in Figure 6.5 (b).

2. Find the position of the missing hidden line 3-4, on the auxiliary view, by projecting points 3,4 from the front view. The depth of points 3 and 4, on the auxiliary view, is obtained from the profile view (i.e., since those views are related).

3. Although not necessary, Figure 6.5 (c) displays a 3-D wire frame model of the visualized object. Figure 6.5 (d) shows the isometric construction that correspond to the completed orthographic views.

ANSI Principles on Space Geometry and Analysis

The following pages contain some important spatial geometry principles that will assist you in the knowledge-based visualization process. They have been reproduced as a courtesy of the publisher, ASME, and in collaboration with ANSI, from ANSI Y14.3-1975. In the problem section of this chapter we will be requested you to develop ten new axioms based on the presented ANSI principles.

SPACE GEOMETRY

Definition. Space geometry is the science of graphically solving problems involving space distances and relationships. (Space geometry is also referred to as descriptive geometry, or engineering geometry.) The most popular and practical method of solution is that in which the principal views are supplemented by auxiliary views. Four basic types of views are employed:

(1) the true length view of a line

(2) the point view of a line

(3) the edge view of a plane

(4) the true view of a plane.

Phantom Lines and Notation

A phantom line, usually between adjacent views, is:

(1) an edge view of a plane of projection,

(2) the intersection line of adjacent projection planes (a folding line, or hinge line), or

(3) an artificial device employed as an aid in construction.

NOTE: It is helpful in visualizing space relationships to think of each phantom line as representing a 90° bend between the adjacent projection planes, or in other words, the observer's direction of viewing has changed by 90° when going from one view to the adjacent view. It is standard practice to represent the phantom line with two short dashes and one long dash alternately. The line may be labeled with letters or numerals as desired.

In the construction of auxiliary views the consistent and accurate transfer of distances from one related view to another is facilitated by the use of the phantom lines. Several phantom lines are shown in Figure A1. A height dimension, such as X, measured

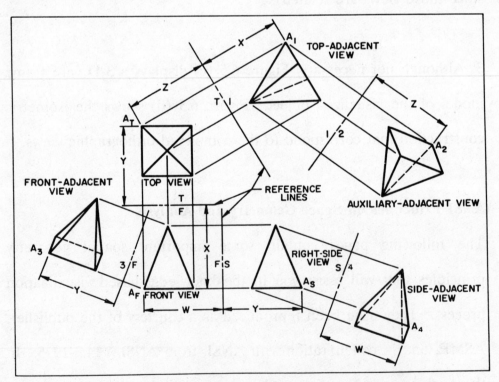

FIG. A1   STANDARD USE OF REFERENCE LINES BETWEEN VIEWS

ANSI Y14.3-1975

from the phantom line, must be the same in both the front view and the related top-adjacent view. Similarly, distance Y must be the same in all views that are adjacent to the front view. Any side-adjacent view must show the same width dimension W as that shown in the front view. Distance Z illustrates the correct measurement for an auxiliary-adjacent view.

The letters T, F and S shown beside the phantom lines and as subscripts for points, signify TOP, FRONT and SIDE views from which the auxiliary views are developed. The numbers 1, 2, 3 and 4 signify the auxiliary views projected from the top, front or side views or from other auxiliary views.

For symmetrical objects the phantom line is on an axis of symmetry. See Figure A2.

True Length View of a Line

The true length of a line segment is the actual straight-line distance between its two end points. The projection of a line will be in true length if in the adjacent view, the projection of the line is parallel to the phantom line between the views. A line that is in true length in a principal view is called a principal line (lines AB and CD in Figure A3).

An oblique line (line BC in Figure A3) is not in true length in any principal view. Its true length is found in a primary auxiliary view, such as view 1 or 2 in Figure A3, if the phantom line is parallel to the line in the given views.

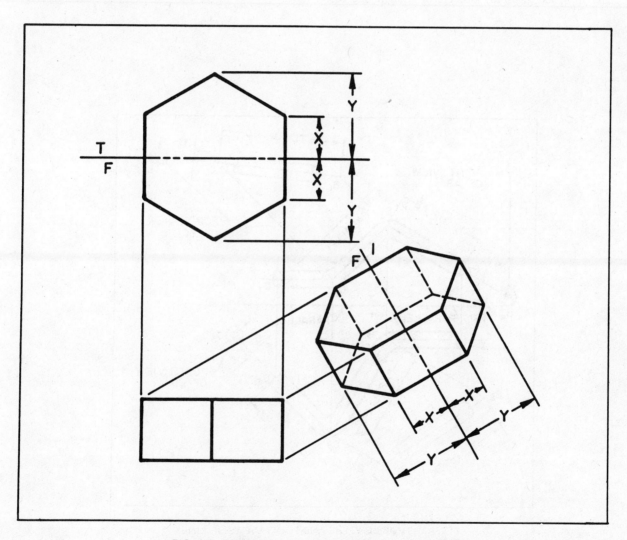

FIG. A2 SYMMETRICALLY PLACED REFERENCE LINE
ANSI Y14.3-1975

189

Point View of a Line

A view with the direction of sight parallel to a straight line in space provides a point view of the line. See Figure A3. A point view of a line is adjacent to a true length view, and the phantom line is perpendicular to the true length projection of the line. The point view appears in a secondary auxiliary view as the line is in true length in a primary auxiliary view. See line B_1C_1 and point B_3C_3 in Figure A3.

Edge View of a Plane

A view with the direction of sight parallel to a plane in space gives the observer a straight line or edge view of the plane. An edge view is obtained whenever *any* line in the plane appears as a point.

If any line of the plane is in true length in one view (line A_TB_T or assumed line A_FE_F in Figure A4), then a point view of that true length line will also show the plane as an edge (view 1 or view 3 in Figure A4).

True View of a Plane. A true view is the direction of sight perpendicular to a plane. See Figure A4, views 2 and 4. A true view of a plane is adjacent to an edge view, and the phantom line is parallel to the edge view.

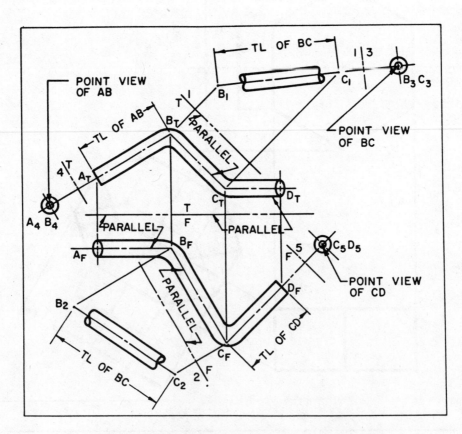

FIG. A3 TRUE LENGTHS AND POINT VIEWS OF LINES

ANSI Y14.3-1975

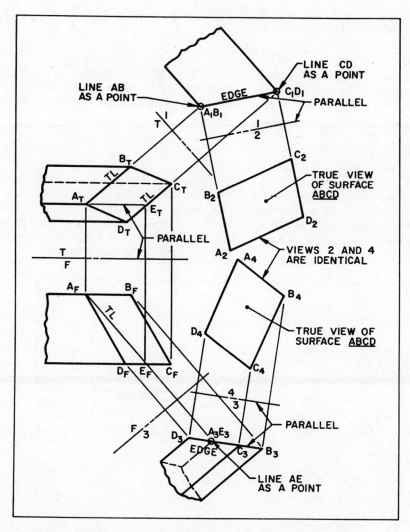

FIG. A4 EDGE AND TRUE SIZE VIEWS OF A PLANE SURFACE

ANSI Y14.3-1975

191

SPACE ANALYSES AND APPLICATIONS

General. To make a space analysis it is usually helpful to simplify the problem by reducing it to terms of points, lines, and planes. A pipe can be considered in terms of its center line, or a plane surface can be treated by using only three points, a point and a line, or two lines that lie in the plane surface.

Clearance Between a Point and a Line

In a view of the point and line which shows the line as a point, the clearance between the line and point will be in true length. View 2 of Figure B1 shows the clearance between oblique line AB and point C.

By an alternate method, the point and line can be treated as a plane, and in the true view of the plane, the perpendicular distance from the point to the line is the clearance. See Figure B2.

Clearance Between Two Lines. In a view of the two lines which shows one of the lines as a point, the clearance between the two lines will be in true length as the perpendicular distance from the point to the line. View 2 of Figure B3 shows the clearance between oblique lines AB and CD.

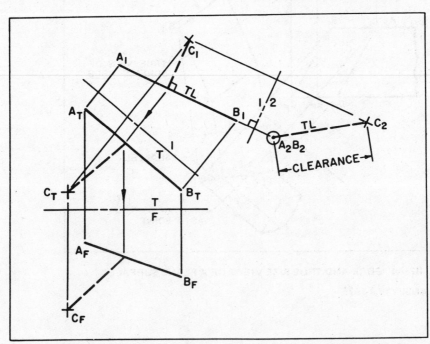

FIG. B1   CLEARANCE BETWEEN A POINT AND A LINE (POINT METHOD)

ANSI Y14.3-1975

192

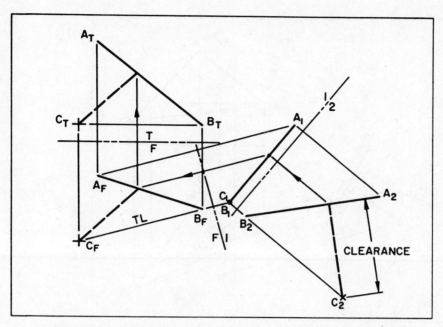

FIG. B2 CLEARANCE BETWEEN A POINT AND A LINE (PLANE METHOD)

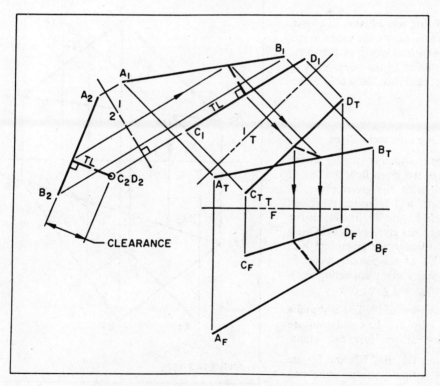

FIG. B3 CLEARANCE BETWEEN TWO OBLIQUE LINES
ANSI Y14.3-1975

193

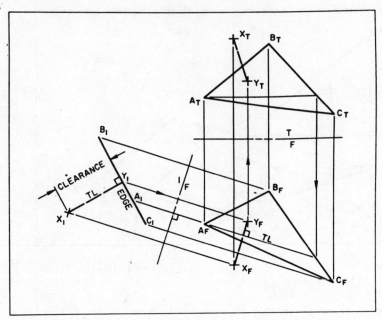

FIG. B4 CLEARANCE BETWEEN A POINT AND A PLANE

Clearance Between a Point and a Plane. In a view of the point and plane which shows the plane as an edge, the clearance will be in true length as a perpendicular distance from the point to the edge. View 1 of Figure B4 shows the clearance between plane ABC and point X.

Point of Intersection of a Line and a Plane

When a vertical plane, which is an edge in the top view, is passed through the given line, the line of intersection of this plane with the given plane, as observed in the front view, will intersect the given line at the piercing point. In Figure B5, line MN is the line of intersection between the given plane ABC and the vertical plane passed through the given line XY. Line MN intersects line XY at the piercing point P. It is equally effective to pass a plane appearing as an edge in the front view through the given line.

Alternate Method. A view of the line and plane showing the plane as an edge can be used to locate the point of intersection of the line and plane.

The planes in Figures B5, B6, B7, and B9 are considered to be opaque with a corresponding visibility of lines in each case.

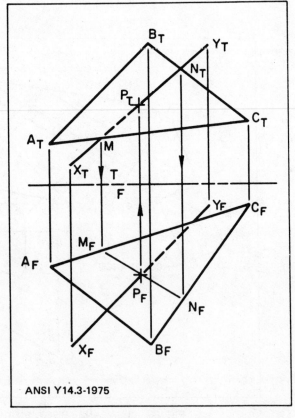

ANSI Y14.3-1975

FIG. B5 INTERSECTION OF A LINE AND PLANE
(PIERCING POINT)

194

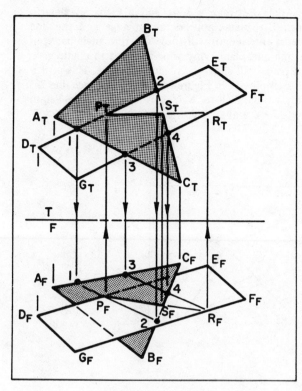

FIG. B6 INTERSECTION OF TWO PLANES

Line of Intersection of Two Planes

If the points are determined where two lines in one plane pierce another plane, a line connecting the piercing points will be the line of intersection of the two planes. Figure B6 shows the line of intersection, PR, of planes ABC and DEFG as if plane ABC were extended in area. PS is the segment of the line of intersection common to the bounded planes.

Alternate Method. A view of two planes showing one of the planes as an edge, will locate the line of intersection. Figure B7 shows the line of intersection PR of planes ABC and DEFG by this method.

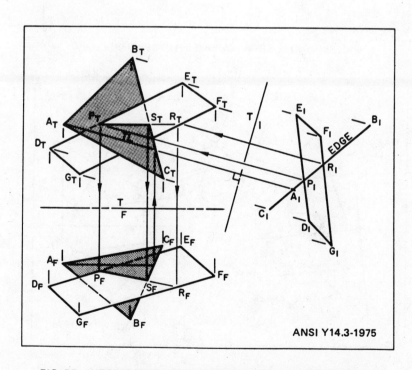

ANSI Y14.3-1975

FIG. B7 INTERSECTION OF TWO PLANES (ALTERNATE METHOD)

195

Angle Between Two Intersecting Lines. Two intersecting lines form a plane whose true view is found by the method of A6. The angle between the two lines will be shown in the true view. In Figure B8, the true size of the angle ABC is found at B_2.

Angle Between a Line and a Plane. A view in which the plane appears as an edge and the line appears true length will show the true angle between the line and plane. Any view adjacent to a true view of a plane will show the plane as an edge. This principle is employed in Figure B9 where reference line 2-3 is drawn parallel to X_2Y_2 to obtain a true length view of XY and an edge view of plane ABC in view 3.

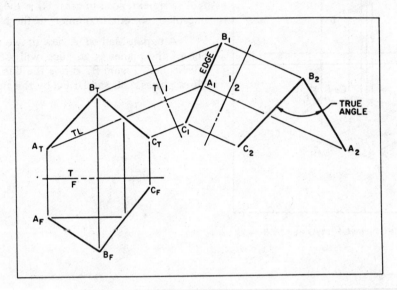

FIG. B8 ANGLE BETWEEN TWO INTERSECTING LINES

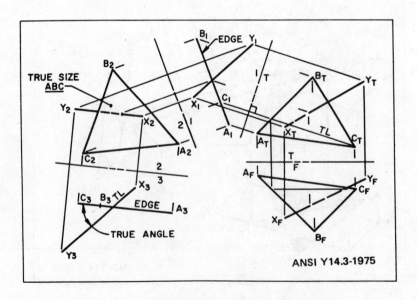

FIG. B9 ANGLE BETWEEN A LINE AND PLANE

196

Angle Between Two Planes. The line of intersection between two planes is first identified or found by the method of B6. A view of the two planes with the line of intersection appearing as a point will show the required angle. Both planes will appear as edges in this view. View 2 of Figure B10 shows the angle between planes M and N.

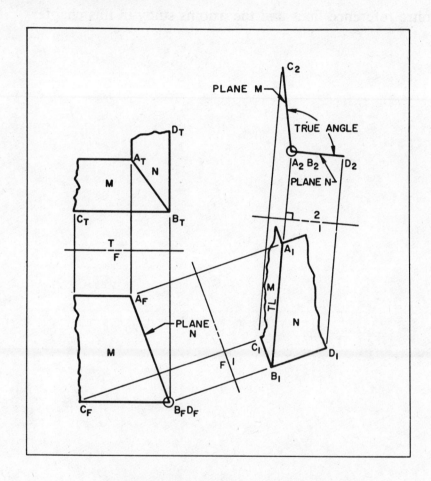

FIG. B10 ANGLE BETWEEN TWO PLANES
ANSI Y14.3-1975

197

PROBLEMS

1. Develop ten new descriptive geometry axioms based on the space geometry and spacial analysis concepts presented.

2. Sketch the missing views and auxiliary views by using projection lines, mitre reference lines and the axioms study in this chapter.

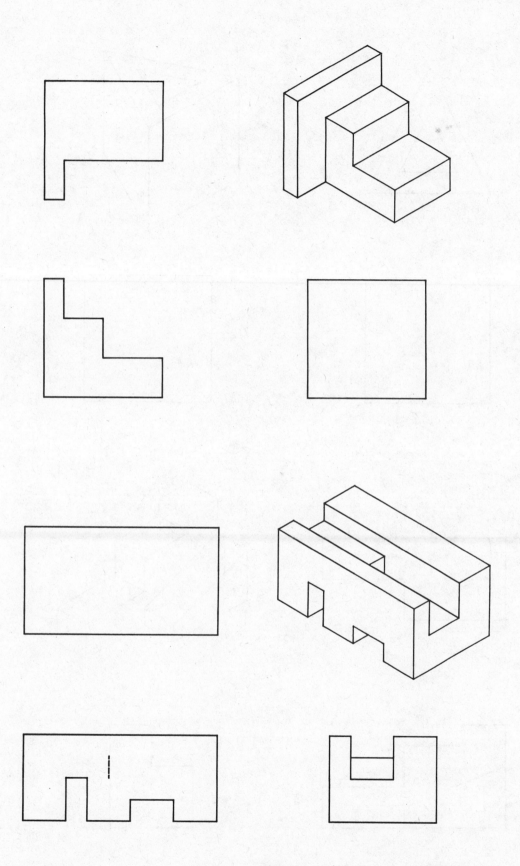

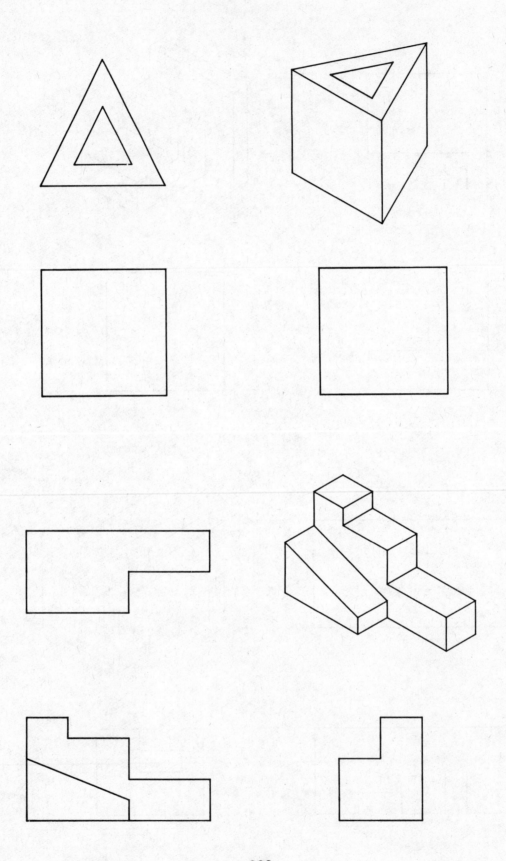

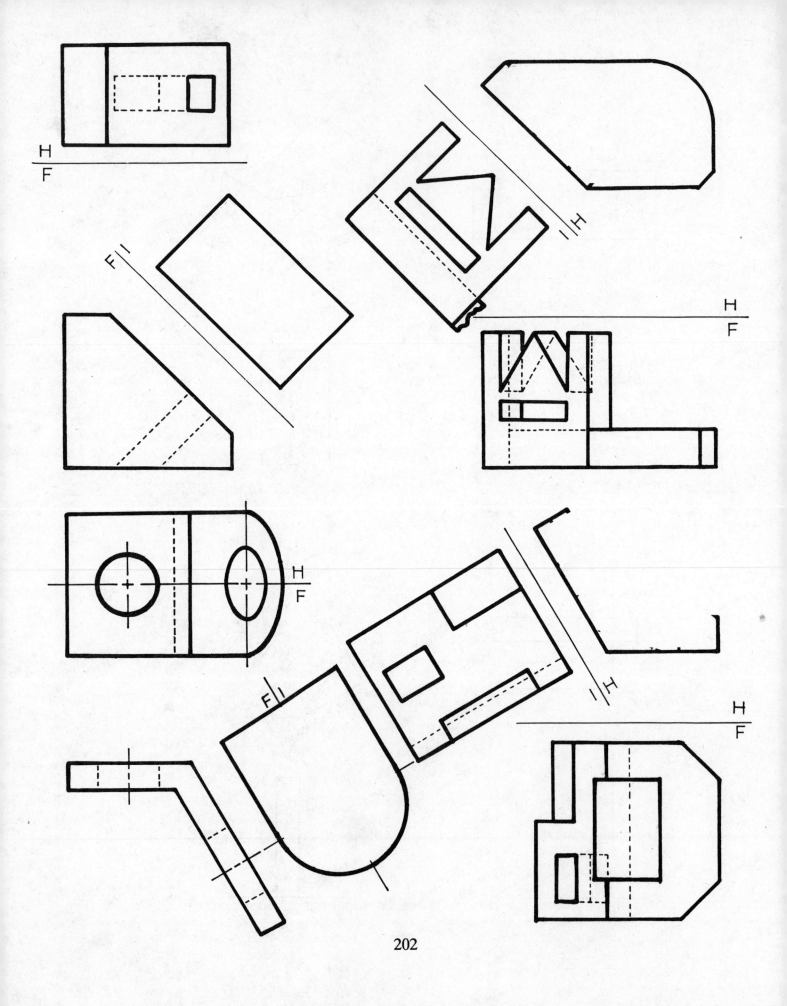

CHAPTER 7

COMPUTER GRAPHICS TOOLS

Introduction

This chapter provides a description of the major computer hardware and software tools utilized in engineering computer graphics and CADD. It reviews some of the terminology covered in previous chapters and provides additional nomenclature and principles. The chapter describes the major computer components and some indispensable computer operations. Emphasis has been placed on the microcomputer and workstation environment, although mini and mainframe computers are discussed as well.

Computer System Components

A computer graphics system consists of various interdependent mechanisms: graphics software and hardware -used to generate, digitize, display, print and/or plot characters and visual images.

The computer workstation illustrated in Figure 7.1 is loaded with

FIG. 7.1 An example of a detail drawing produced in standalone CAD station. (Courtesy of Adage, Inc.)

204

CADD software that allow the user to generate visual images on the screen. The CADD <u>software</u> is simply the collection of coded instructions or programs employed by the system hardware to execute certain operations. Software programs direct or "tell" the computer what to do, after you have entered a command. The CADD software packages provide the necessary user interface (menu of options) to allow us to design devices and systems as shown in Figure 7.2.

<u>Hardware</u> refers to the physical equipment that makes up a computer system. Figure 7.3 illustrates several hardware devices used in a typical Professional Engineering (P.E.) office. The figure shows a large digitizing table and stylus used to input infromation onto the system.

Computers contain electronic circuits that operate by storing and transmitting electrical signals. With the aid of software, computers are capable of manipulating information very quickly. The computer graphics system performs the following operations: input, processing and output. In the microcomputer environment, these operations are handled by the following components (i.e., larger systems have similar components):

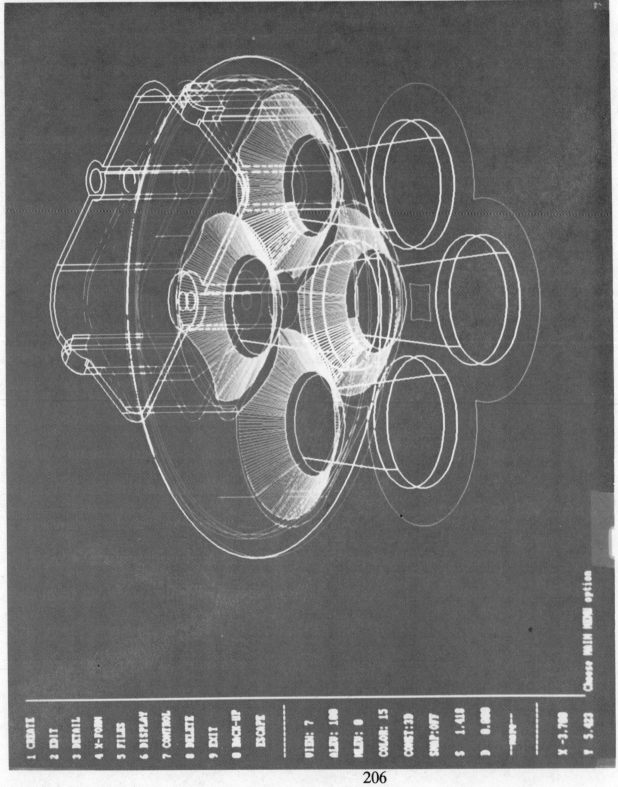

FIG. 7.2 Carburetor designed with a CADD system for the personal computer. (Courtesy of PFB Concepts and CADKEY / Micro Control Systems, Inc.)

FIG. 7.3 The P.E. office computer configuration consists of: CPU, monitor, digitizing tablet, plotter/printer (Courtesy of Arrigoni Computer Graphics, Inc.)

1. The processing is handled by the system unit which houses the electronic components that control and transfer of data and perform the arithmetic and logic calculations (see Figure 7.4). The system unit plays a major role in the computation process; for example, its central processing unit (CPU) is a microprocessor that directs computational activities and examines every instruction. The system unit's internal clock coordinates computer circuit responses. ROM (Read-Only-Memory) and RAM (Read-and-Write Memory, misnamed Random-Access-Memory) microchips provide the internal memory that holds the instructions and stores the programs while the computer is operating; power supply to convert alternate current to direct current; ports to connect input/output attachments, as discussed below (see Figure 7.5).

2. The input/output is handled by peripheral devices which are part of the equipment assembly connected to the computer. Peripherals like input devices (e.g., keyboard, digitizer, mouse, light pen, stylus) and output devices (e.g., screen's monitor, printer, plotter) are attached to the computer. The output consists of alphanumeric characters (i.e.,numbers and letters) and/or graphical entities (i.e., drawings) displayed on a monitor screen or printer-plotted on paper.

Another important element is the hardware interface. Hardware

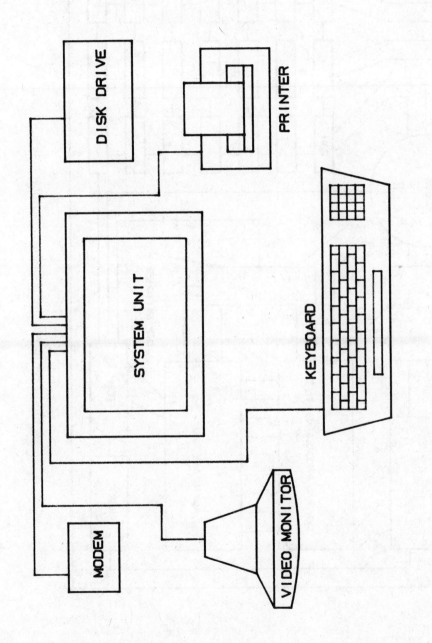

FIG. 7.4 Microcomputer components.

209

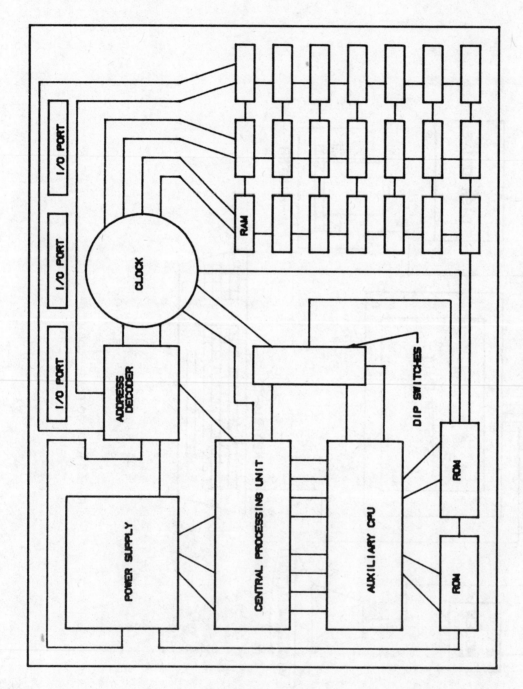

FIG. 7.5 Key elements of the computer's system unit.

210

interfaces are electronic assemblies that connect a peripheral device (e.g., interface cards, cables) to the computer and provide communication between two parts of the system. Interfacing devices link the computer to its associated peripherals.

The Mass Storage Device consists of floppy disks, hard disks or magnetic tape like devices that store large amounts of data. Data in this form is readily available and accessible to the CPU.

Configuration

The peripherals and the computer form a system. The particular characteristics of a system are known as its configuration. It is also associated with the way the hardware is set-up to take advantage of certain software.

Example 7.1: IBM-PC XT Configuration

Typical microcomputer graphic system components are listed below:

Hardware

*   System Unit: Central Processing Unit (CPU) IBM-PC XT or "workalike" microcomputer [512K or 640K RAM user memory] or IBM AT with 512K.

*   Mass Storage Media: One 360KB floppy disk (drive A:), 20 MB harddisk drive (drive C:), diskette and fixed disk adapters or 30

MB hard drive-8Mhz clock speed.

* Keyboard: Standard IBM compatible key and functions layout

* Video Display: Monochrome or color monitor [640 X 400 resolution, color display] or enhanced color display and enhanced graphics adapter (EGA).

* Printer-Plotter: D size (i.e., 24" x 36") pen plotter [e.g., Houston Instrument DMP 52] or a standard size (8 1/2" X 11") laser printer [e.g., Quadlaser] or FX-85 printer.

* Parallel and serial ports.

* Digitizer and pointer: [none]

* Modem: Hayes Smartmodem 2400

Software (installed on harddisk's directories)

* Operating System: DOS 3.x (Disk Operating System)

* Languages: Fortran, Basic

* CADD Packages: AutoCAD (Version 2.x with Advanced Drafting Extensions), AutoSketch or CADKEY, an in-house program.

* Wordprocessing: Wordperfect, Wordstar.

* Electronic spreadsheet: Lotus 1-2-3.

* Communications: Hayes Smartcom II, etc.

* Other: TK!Solver

Each part of the above system is unique in function and is discussed separately below. As stated previously, the discussion focuses mainly on microcomputer graphic systems, since they are more generic.

Central Processing Unit

The Central Processing Unit (CPU) is often referred to as the "brain" of the computer and is divided into two major units and several minor units. The first major unit is the Arithmetic Logic Unit (ALU) which performs the arithmetic computing tasks. The second major unit is the Control Unit, which organizes the processes of the ALU and consequently the functions of the entire computer. Smaller registers, also part of the CPU, provide temporary data storage necessary to the function of the computer as well as advancing the program counter which tells the computer to execute the next program line.

Microcomputers are often described on the basis of their CPU (microprocessor) "word size." There are three main types of popular micro-processors: 8 bits, 16 bits, and 32 bits. As you remember, bit is short for binary digit (0's or 1's). A byte is equal to 8 bits. Simply put: it is the number of bits required to represent a character. Byte and character are used interchangeably. The words referred to here are not words like you are reading but instead are groups of bits which might make up letters or numbers or any type of alpha-numeric

213

character. Each microprocessor picks up the largest amount of bits that it can handle, manipulates them, and returns them to the computer's memory. Simply put, the larger the word size, the fewer cycles it takes for the microprocessor to perform a certain task which means a quicker execution time. An Apple II's CPU is an 8 bit microprocessor, while the IBM PC's CPU is a 16 bit microprocessor which means that the IBM will run faster this Apple model, all other things being equal.

Memory chips hold the information -in bits- encoded as electrical charges and stored in particular locations, called <u>addresses</u>. Instructions come out of the processing unit coded to find a particular address as a series of electrical pulses. The address code travels on parallel wires named <u>address bus</u>. The information returns to the CPU on parallel data bus wires.

Another microprocessor characteristic often used to describe the rate at which it can perform functions is its <u>clock speed</u>. A microprocessor's clock is much faster than the clock used to tell time, and functions at 5-10 MHz. Obviously, the higher the clock speed, the quicker the microprocessor does its job. Consequently, in terms of speed, the larger the word size and the higher the clock speed, the faster the microcomputer.

214

Internal Memory

The next pieces of microcomputer hardware to be discussed are the parts which store programs and data which the user plans to use in the near future. Also included here is the part of the internal memory which cannot be altered either by the computer or by the user, since it is essential for the proper functioning of the computer.

Read-Only-Memory

Read-Only Memory (ROM) is the permanent memory which resides within the microcomputer on a set of silicon chips. "Written" on the chips are very basic instructions essential to the operation of the computer. Without the instructions contained in ROM, the computer would not know what to do when first switched on, and would be useless. Most ROM information tells the computer to look to a certain input device or a certain place in memory where the computer will get additional information. Consequently, this memory can only be read by the computer and never can be written over by the computer.

Read-and-Write Memory

Read-and-Write Memory was previously labeled: Random Access Memory However, Random Access Memory is a misleading phrase. Its acronym RAM, is still used to indicate Read-and-Write Memory. RAM is the memory space within the computer where programs and data are manipulated. RAM is like ROM, in that it is contained in chips. Programs or data can be loaded into RAM by using any of the various input devices discussed earlier. This memory is called random access memory because the computer has the ability to look at any one part of it (memory address) without looking at any of the other memory. RAM is volatile memory; that is, its contents are not retained when the computer is turned off. In addition, information in RAM can be written over, if desired.

Mass Storage

Mass storage is relatively permanent media where programs and data are kept. Information is stored on a mass storage device by changing the polarity of a very small section of magnetic film which has been applied to either a plastic or metal base. This means that any device which generates a magnetic field has the potential to erase information in mass storage. Also, over the life of the storage device, the polarity of the particles of metallic oxide will wear off and the stored data will gradually be lost. Consequently, it is a good idea to have a backup disk or tape, itself renewed every few years, made so that information will not be lost.

Two of the most popular disks are: hard disks, which are aluminum disks covered with microscopic magnetic particles, and floppy disks or diskettes, which are thin plastic disks covered with magnetic particles. Many microcomputers use both types. Both types of disk storage require the user to install a card in one of the microcomputer's slots. This is called a disk controller card and is needed for the computer to transmit or get data from a disk.

Hard Disk

Hard disks are becoming increasingly popular for microcomputers as their cost drops. They are preferred because of their ability to store large quantities of data (i.e., measured in MB megabytes or 1,048,576 bytes) and recall that information very quickly. From time to time the data on a hard disk can be lost (due often to user error), so hard disks are often "backed up" by copying their information onto floppy disks or tape cassettes. Hard disk drives are also referred to as fixed disk drives, since the disk is sealed. Fixed disk drives are faster than diskette drives, but the user cannot change them with the easy of floppies.

Tape storage, in the form of small cassettes, is recognized as being a reliable method of keeping information and is used today to backup data for hard disks because of tapes large storage capacity.

217

Floppy Disk

Floppy disks or diskettes are very popular among microcomputer users, and come in three sizes: 8", 5-1/4", and 3-1/2". Eight inch is declining in popularity partially because of the large size of the disk and also because of the increasing efficiency of the smaller disks. The middle size is a double-sided/double-density (DS/DD) disk, with a typical capacity of 360K bytes (i.e., one K bytes equals 1024 bytes). It is also available as a double-sided/high density (DS/HD) diskette that will store 2 MB of data. The small, 3-1/2" diskettes, used on the PC portables, are gaining popularity, since they can hold 350 pages of information (a type written page contains about 2000 bytes).

Video Display

The screen monitor is the most prominent output device of the interactive graphic system. Although there are several types of video monitors, the CRT is the most widely accepted design in the microcomputer environment. The Cathode Ray Tube (CRT) closely resembles a small TV screen. It is a very versatile output device and typically is able to display both text and graphics (pictures or graphs generated by computer programs).

The Refresh CRT device consists of the following components: connecting pins, base, electron gun, focusing device, horizontal and vertical deflection plates, and phosphor coated screen. The end pins connect the base to the system. The electron gun emits a beam of electrons that goes through the focus and deflection devices. The latter device directs the electron beam to predefined points on the screen to form a glowing image. The image is refreshed continuously to keep the phosphors glowing.

Two types of refresh CRT are: raster and random scan. Raster-scan operates by shooting the electron beam all over the screen. The beam will be turned on or off to concur with the specified drawing. Random-scan video monitors handle the task by directing the beam to specific points on the screen.

The quality of the generated picture depends on the resolution; that is, the optimum number of points that can be displayed on the screen. Screen resolution is given by the number of points per centimeter plotted vertically or horizontally. Another important characteristic is the aspect ratio which refers to the proportion of vertical to horizontal points needed to generate equal length lines on the screen.

The monitor is connected to the system through a video card, often purchased separately from the computer. This card is installed in the microcomputer, and the monitor is plugged into the card. This card transforms the computer's output into a language the monitor can understand. Some cards are designed to display graphics output, some designed for color output, some for very high resolution, and some inexpensive ones for just adequate (i.e., low resolution) display quality. Cards provide flexibility of choice for the typical microcomputer. This variety gives the consumer a better selection and chance to customize the computer to his or her needs.

Modem

Modem is short for MOdulator-DEModulator, and it is a device which enables a computer to "talk" to another computer. A modem takes output from its computer (or terminal), translates it into audible tones (modulates the output) and sends it along telephone lines (see Figure 7.6) to another computer's modem which translates the audible tones into electric pulses that its computer can understand (demodulates the data). A modem can, for example, connect a person using a microcomputer in Atlanta, Georgia with a mainframe computer in San Juan, Puerto Rico. Modems are very popular with microcomputer users as they enable the user to gain access to the vast memory and capabilities of a mainframe.

Modems come in two basic types: external and internal. Both have several parts in common with one another. Both must have a "jack"

220

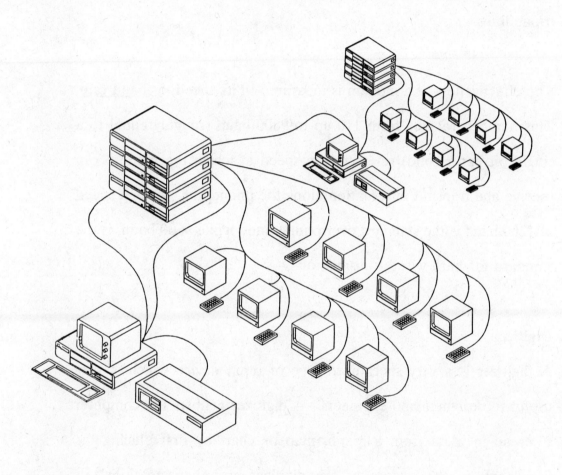

FIG. 7.6 A computer system network connecting several hardware devices. (Courtesy of SAIDS, Inc.)

for the phone line. Both must have some form of interface (connection) with the computer. The major difference is that the external modem sits alongside the computer and the internal modem is built on a card and sits within the computer. Both have software which enables the microcomputer to take advantage of the modem's capabilities.

The effectiveness of a modem is measured in its speed, or <u>baud rate</u>. This number, ranging from 110 up to 9600 baud (roughly equal to a single bit per second) refers to the speed at which the modem can receive and transmit information along the phone line. A high speed of 1200 baud is the standard over phone lines, while 9600 baud, is the standard for hard wired transmission.

Digitizer

A digitizer is a very specialized type of input device which is very useful to designers and engineers. A digitizer enables the computer to "read in" data from a graph, map or chart by first placing the document on the surface of the digitizer and then "marking" its boundaries by placing a hand-held cursor (i.e., pointer, stylus, mouse) on the corners of the document and pressing a button on the cursor. The user can then use the cursor to read in the desired data points within the predetermined boundaries. Although digitizers are quite expensive, their worth is easily seen when dealing with large irregular documents.

In addition, digitizers can be used to circumvent the computer's keyboard as a shortcut for inputing commands especially for some graphics-oriented programs. Typically some sort of stylus, light pen or cursor is used to point out the command desired by the user. When the light pen contacts the surface of the digitizer, the command associated with that area on the digitizer is executed.

Printer

The printer is a popular output-only device. Most printers fall into one of three main categories: dot-matrix, letter-quality (daisy-wheel), and laser printers. Dot matrix printers are inexpensive, fast, and are usually able to print graphic output. Their main disadvantage is that when operated at top speed their print quality may not be acceptable for some jobs. At lower speeds, however, even relatively inexpensive dot-matrix printers are able to print nearly as cleanly as a letter-quality printer. Letter-quality printers work much like a typewriter does giving very clear text but at a slow speed. They are usually unable to print graphics but are preferred for text printing. Most letter-quality printers in use today are of the daisy-wheel variety. A daisy-wheel printer has a printing element which is shaped like a daisy with the various characters located at the end of each petal. To print a character the printer rotates the daisy-wheel to the proper position, and a small hammer strikes the end of the petal on its back, pushing the character against a ribbon and then against the paper.

Laser printers are the newest printing development and are rapidly gaining in popularity. Although they are very expensive, advantages like tremendous speed, quality, and quietness are worth the cost. Most of the graphs and drawings in this book were produced with a laser printer. Laser printers work like some popular copying machines, even using the same laser engine to guide the print head to the prescribed point.

Plotter

A plotter is an output device which has the ability to draw intricate shapes and designs on paper, vellum, mylar, or transparent film. Maps, graphs, blueprints and other charts can be generated on the plotter easily and with very high quality. Plots are expensive but perform printing/drawing tasks very well in minute detail. Plotters draw by using small ink pens with as many as fourteen different colors and pen widths. The computer tells the plotter to pick up a certain pen, move it to a certain point identified with x-y coordinates, put the pen down, and draw based on instructions from the computer. Flatbed plotters operate by holding the drawing surface fixed on a flat bed and moving the print head on the surface to create the desired picture. There are also drum plotters which function by moving the drawing surface in one direction (the Y-direction) and the pens in the other direction (the x-direction). The drawing surface is rolled by means of a revolving drum.

Monitor Programs

Every CPU chip has an instruction set built into it. The instruction set is a list of commands to which the chip can respond. These instructions are very technical and would be nearly impossible for a user to program (particularly in machine language, which is a series of 0's and 1's). Consequently, one of the first programs that must be written for a new CPU chip is a monitor (not to be confused with the CRT). The monitor program watches for input, such as characters typed in from a keyboard, and routes it to a desired destination such as the CRT or a RAM memory location. Similarly, the monitor program handles output, such as to a diskette or printer.

The monitor program is a major part of an operating system developed for a CPU chip. The operating system is a file manager that is the main link between the user and the microcomputer. It provides user access to the computer's capabilities.

Microcomputer Operating Systems

The operating system of a microcomputer controls the way the computer utilizes it resources. <u>DOS</u> is one of such systems. Operations with this management system usually involves storage using floppy disks, hence the name: DOS (Disk Operating System). DOS manages the flow of information between what is stored on the disks and the computer's memory. DOS is used to perform the following file operations: formatting new disks, sorting into similar groups, copying, deleting unused files, listing of files and backing-up files for safekeeping.

DOS, as any other operating system, must be running in the system unit before a computer can begin any application program. When you see a prompt like this:

C> or A>

DOS is ready to accept commands. To change from a default drive C to drive A, enter:

_____

C> A:

_____

and vis-versa. The following sections discusses some indispensable DOS commands.

DIRECTORY

The DOS command **DIR**, short for directory, instructs the microcomputer to read a disk library of files and to send that list to the screen display. For example, entering:

C> DIR

---

will display all the files that reside on the hard-disk of your microcomputer. In addition, it displays sub-directories, free bytes, number of files, bytes in each file, date and time when those files were created. It also possible to obtain file information in an specific drive (e.g., entering { **DIR A:** } will display files on drive A. The DOS command { **DIR/W** } will display filenames in a compact manner fashion, say file listings in five columns -rather than one single column- without the bytes per file information. If you want to display one page of files listings at a time enter { **DIR/P** }. In other words, the system will wait for you to press a key before displaying the next page of information.

FORMAT

The DOS FORMAT command prepares a new floppy disk to store

files. If you reformat a used disk, it will destroy the existing information in it. Issue

the command:

C> FORMAT A:

---

to prepare a floppy disk located in drive A. In a high-capacity drive the command is { **FORMAT A: /4** }.

DISKCOPY

This command provides the capability to copy the contents of an entire floppy disk (SOURCE DISK) onto another (TARGET DISK), provided the source disk is not copy-protected. This operation will delete any existing files on the target disk. For example the DOS command:

C> DISKCOPY A: B:

---

copies the contents of the disk on drive A onto the disk on B. To avoid accidental erasure, of the source diskette, cover the write-protect notch with a special tab or foil tape that comes with the disk's box.

228

COPY

The COPY command allows you to copy a specific file or several designated files from one diskette onto another. For example, if you need to copy a drawing file named LAYOUT.DRW, on a disk (in drive A), onto a disk in drive B enter:

C> COPY A:LAYOUT.DRW B:

If you need to copy all the files on the source disk in A to a disk in B enter:

C> COPY A:*.* B:

ERASE

The command ERASE delete specific files from a directory. To delete a file named { A:LAYOUT.DRW }, simply enter { **ERASE A:LAYOUT.DRW** } at the DOS prompt.

Computer Programming Languages

The operating system of a computer permits the user to perform only limited, file managing types of tasks. Computer programming languages enable the user to tell the computer specifically what is to be done. As seen below, there are many different types of languages, each with its own specialty.

There are two major types of computer programming languages: general purpose and special purpose. <u>General purpose</u> languages are designed so that the user can create a program to perform almost any task he wants done by the computer. <u>Special purpose</u> languages, on the other hand, permit programming on a limited, specific-purpose basis. Special purpose languages perform their limited number of functions more efficiently than a general purpose language performs those same functions, but have many fewer functions in their vocabulary. An example of a special-purpose language is dBASE III, developed by the Ashton-Tate Company as a data base manager.

There are three major characteristics of computer programming languages which will be used to describe the most popular ones. A language can be "threaded" if the user can define the computer functions, and "non-threaded" if the user must use a pre-defined list of commands. A programming language can also be "structured" or "unstructured." The most extreme degree of a structured language is one which has no GOTO statement at all, because all the "branching" of the program is implicitly embodied in the program. A **GOTO**

230

statement is a statement that transfers the execution of a program to another part in the program. A language can also be "compiled" or "interpreted." A program line in an interpreted language is translated from the language to the computer's machine language, executed, and the computer then proceeds to the next line in the program. In a compiled language, the computer translates the entire program into machine language (compiles it), and stores this machine language version of the program in memory. When the user tells the computer to run a certain program in a compiled language, it runs this "compiled" version. Compiled languages tend to run programs much faster then interpreted languages, because they have less work to do to the program when they run it. They are suitable for large, complex programs. For simple programs interpreted languages are easier to use; if a program fails to run, most interpreters will provide helpful error messages and the user can re-run the corrected program without going to the trouble of recompiling it.

General Purpose Languages

General purpose languages enable the user to do whatever he desires, within limits. These are very popular with students, since a course in a general purpose language is often a student's first introduction to computers.

BASIC

BASIC, the Beginner's All-purpose Symbolic Instruction Code, has been a very popular language ever since its introduction at Dartmouth College in the mid-1960s. BASIC programming is easy to learn, since most of its commands are single-word commands taken from everyday English. It is a non-threaded, fairly unstructured language, and is usually interpreted, although there are compiled versions of BASIC. Although it is a relatively slow language, it is very popular because of its simplicity. Most microcomputers can be programmed in BASIC or BASICA (Advanced BASIC). The example of BASIC code is listed below, will produce a colorful and never ending loop, full of "Good Afternoon"'s labels:

```
100 PRINT "Good Afternoon";
150 COLOR 14,1
200 GOTO 100
```

FORTRAN

FORTRAN stands for FORmula TRANslation, and is a language developed for use by scientists and engineers. Its commands are very similar to those of BASIC, with more emphasis on numerical work, and it is always compiled. FORTRAN is non-threaded and relatively unstructured. It is popular on large computers and is also used on microcomputers. FORTRAN is an older computer language, and was one of the first "English-like" languages. Standardized FORTRAN versions include FORTRAN V and FORTRAN 77 and are more structured.

PASCAL

Pascal is a slightly newer computer language which is beginning to receive wide use in all fields. Named for the French mathematician Blaise Pascal and developed at the University of California at San Diego, Pascal is a very readable language like BASIC but is highly structured. It is a non-threaded, compiled language used mainly on microcomputers. Pascal is widely used in graphics applications.

COBOL

COBOL, the COmmon Business Oriented Language, is an older language, like FORTRAN. It resembles older versions of FORTRAN, in that it is compiled, unstructured, and is also non-threaded. Most COBOL programs are long, but they execute very quickly. Because of the program length, COBOL is very popular on large computers, where there is no shortage of memory space. Because of the memory requirements of COBOL programs, the language is rarely used on microcomputers. ANSI COBOL is recognized as the standard version.

FORTH

Forth is a new language, designed to appeal to BASIC users, but it is more efficient than BASIC. It is a structured, threaded language which is usually compiled. There is no standardized form of Forth, so many different "dialects" exist. It is also the only major threaded language, permitting the user to define terms and functions, if desired.

C

The C programming language is popular among professional computer programmers. C is compiled, non-threaded and relatively structured. Its increasing popularity is due in large part to its close association with the UNIX operating system developed by Bell Laboratories.

Special Purpose Languages

Special purpose languages are becoming increasingly popular as they become better able to accomplish more and more with greater ease. Discussed below are two of the most popular types of special purpose languages.

Data Base Managers like dBASE III (short for data-Base Manager, 3rd edition) can take user defined input data, mathematically manipulate it (if necessary), and put the data into a blank form

234

designed by the user and kept in the computer memory. The package dBASE III uses a very specific language and is called a "command-driven" application which means that the user must know the commands or have an instruction manual handy to use it. In contrast, "menu-driven" programs present choices to the user one screenful at a time.

Spreadsheet Programs like Lotus 1-2-3 are designed to be flexible to meet the needs of many different types of users. Spreadsheets are large blank grids of rows and columns. They allow the user to fill the individual "cells" with column headings, row titles, the data, and the results of calculations which can be performed on the data. Spreadsheets are excellent for manipulating and reducing large quantities of data quickly and easily with little error. This is in sharp contrast to the tedious and error-prone method of giving the data manipulation and reduction job to a technician. The macro command capability allows you to develop and write programs. For example, it is possible to mimic a sequence of keystrokes to create a graph from given data. Also you can control the flow of the program with its math and logic functions. This command language is much simpler than BASIC, and you have access to their assembly language speed, predefined formatting and functions. Examples of these function are: **@TAN(x), @IF(Cond,x,y), @TRUE**; the first function calculates the tangent of an angle, the second will determine the truth value of a formula, and the last will perform certain operation if certain condition is present (i.e., the @ sign is an identifier to the program, it "tells" LOTUS

1-2-3 that what follows is a function).

CADD Software

Certain CADD packages contain special and general purpose languages, that allow the user to program certain tasks. AutoCAD, CADKEY, VersaCAD and MicroCADAM are examples of a microcomputer graphics packages which meets this criteria. They can be utilized by all engineering technology fields and

can augment or replace everyday drafting tasks performed by draftsmen.

AutoCAD

AutoCAD is one of the most popular programs that provides CADD capabilities for microcomputers. It was initially a two-dimensional based graphics package. The latest version has 3-D capabilities, several solid modeling interfaces (e.g., RoboSolid) and programming capabilities. AutoCAD is menu-driven and can be used by those with a minimum of computer experience. Until the advent of AutoCAD,

CAD capabilities were available only on mainframes and minicomputers. AutoCAD can be used with many engineering design programs, and can be used separately, if needed. It is particularly suited for mechanical, industrial, structural and architectural work.

The user can create, display, store, retrieve, edit, print and plot engineering graphics. The user can create plane geometry to determine the object position (x,y), then add the z-axis coordinates and perform hidden line removal.

The main programs of a graphics package are the drawing editor, plot program and several utilities. The user selects utilities from the main menu displays as soon as the package is loaded. The graphic editor operates on a continuous loop -prompting you for a command. When the command is entered, it prompts for the values of the appropriate parameters. A 16-bit microcomputer -running AutoCAD- should be configured with at least 512KB of RAM, an 8087/287 math coprocessor (to increase its speed), one floppy disk drive and a fixed disk.

CADKEY

CADKEY is a "true" three-dimensional based micro CADD package. The creation process of a device begins by defining x, y, and z coordinates. In other words, the user creates a 3-D wire frame model, instead of drawing separate orthographic projection. In 2-D packages, an axonometric is constructed by extrusion. An extrusion can be defined as a copy of the 2-D outline shape placed at a different depth -lines are generated so as to connect the copy and its original- giving the impression of a 3-D drawing.

With this drafting package, you can look at the views of the object with a keystroke function. Then, a "pattern file" is generated for each of the orthographic views needed. The software also facilitates the definition of auxiliary views to determine the true shape of an inclined plane. Menu driven options and commands allow the user to access any task without backing out of the currently used function. CADKEY open database provides a link between its files and external programs (i.e, interface programming) as illustrated in Figures 7.7 and 7.8.

CADKEY provides a three-dimensional shading and hidden-line removal program module called Solid Synthesis. This module can be used to produce solid images (see Figure 7.9), animation and calculate mass properties of mechanical parts.

IGES Translator Module

CADKEY's IGES (Initial Graphics Exchange Standard) Translator provides 3-dimensional bi-directional data exchange between CADKEY and major CAD/CAM vendors' systems. It has already been used to communicate product data between a CADKEY workstation and CAD systems such as Computervision, Intergraph, CALMA, McAuto, and Gerber and has proven to be both fast and accurate.

The CADKEY IGES Translator serves as a versatile and powerful tool allowing a micro-based CADD workstation operating CADKEY software to exchange 3-dimensional product definition data with mini, super-mini, or even mainframe CADD/CAM systems. This ability within CADKEY makes the potential of true CADD integration a reality. The CADKEY workstation can now exchange all CADKEY geometric modeling entities with the highest possible level of integrity. The attributes and accuracy of data is maintained during IGES transfer and translation. The Translator is bi-directional and will allow transfer of data from other CADD/CAM systems to CADKEY as well.

IGES COMMUNICATIONS

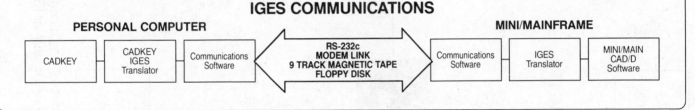

CADKEY Advanced Design Language (CADL)

CADL provides ASCII input and output to CADKEY via easy to read and write disk files. With CADL, external programs interface easily to CADKEY. All 2-D drawings, 3-D design, and text database information generated in CADKEY can be used for applications such as finite element analysis, spreadsheet calculations, database communication, numerical control, bill of materials, and more. Numerous interfaces have already been written in these areas, with more being constantly added. (Contact your CADKEY representative for the latest list.)

Data Interchange Format (DXF)

CADKEY can both read and write information in the DXF format now used in a wide variety of applications programs, including commonly used 2-D drafting systems. With the DXF Interface, users are able to transfer their 2-D drafting files and upgrade to three dimensions with CADKEY.

FIG. 7.7 Promotional literature showing CADKEY's IGES Translator Module, CADL and Data Interchange Format (DXF) capabilities. (Courtesy of Micro Control System, Inc.)

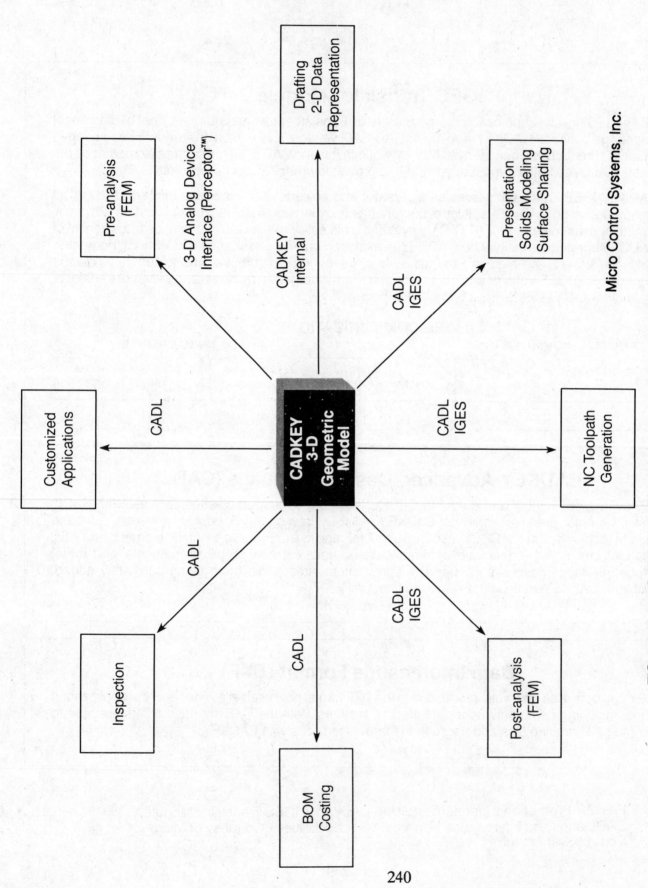

FIG. 7.8 Using CADKEY's 3-D geometric model as a centralized database of information, designers are able to utilize CADL and/or IGES translator to link to other programs.

Drafting
2-D Data
Representation

Pre-analysis
(FEM)

3-D Analog Device
Interface (Perceptor™)

CADKEY
Internal

Presentation
Solids Modeling
Surface Shading

CADL
IGES

Micro Control Systems, Inc.

Customized
Applications

CADL

CADKEY
3-D
Geometric
Model

CADL
IGES

NC Toolpath
Generation

Inspection

CADL

CADL

BOM
Costing

CADL
IGES

Post-analysis
(FEM)

240

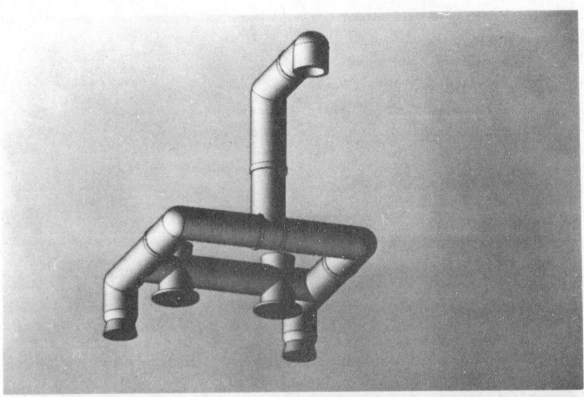

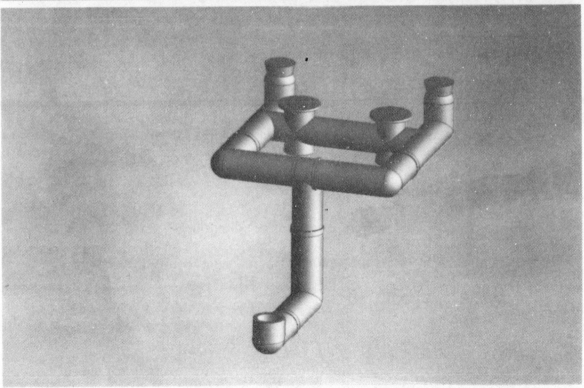

FIG. 7.9 Solid models generated with Solid Synthesis, a 3-D shading software module for use with CADKEY.

241

Mainframe and Mini Computer Systems

One drawback with graphics-based microcomputer work is the tremendous amounts of memory space required to display and manipulate CADD generated drawings. Although 640K bytes of storage seems like a lot, it doesn't go far with CADD work. Consequently, the full potential of microcomputer-based CADD will not be realized until the memory space of microcomputers can be expanded greatly. At the present time, CADD packages have to be written carefully to make the most of memory and mass storage space.

There is no question that the capabilities of CADD software are enhanced by utilizing a more powerful system. The main frame system are unique, since they are normally configured around other existing hardware and communication network.

Example 7.2: Mainframe Facilities

This section discusses one example of such large scale systems: specifically the facilities used by the Engineering Computer Graphics Program at Georgia Tech.

System units: The central computing facility system consists of several Control Data Corp. (CDC) CYBER's workstations (see Fig. 7.10).

242

The CYBER 910-300 graphics workstations are single-user/multi-user computer systems that provide very cost-effective ways to run highly interactive CAD/CAM applications and produce real-time three-dimensional graphics.

CYBER 910-300 workstations are highly integrated systems incorporating an applications processor, graphics processor, communications support, peripheral support, and operating software. They are designed to serve as both personal workstations and as nodes in a network.

These workstations meet the needs of professionals requiring high performance graphics for applications such as mechanical design, visual simulation, solids modeling, finite element modeling, PCB and VLSI design, and mechanical or electrical engineering analysis.

Benefits

The CYBER 910-300 workstations provide fast and predictable response, large amounts of available memory, extensive computing power, multi-windowing, multi-tasking, and powerful real-time high resolution graphics.

The stand-alone capabilities are especially effective for performing highly interactive graphics applications. This allows host computers in a network to do what they do best: support high performance peripherals, manage data, and process large scale analyses.

FIG. 7.10 Control Data CYBER   (Courtesy of Control Data Corp.)

243

These workstations and other terminals are connected through a network to other mainframe computers like: CDC CYBER 990, CDC CYBER 855 and CDC CYBER 830. There are many other systems on campus, namely: IBM 4381, two IBM 4341, a Pyramid 90x, two AT&T 3B20 systems, among others, located in different buildings.

Terminals: Hundreds of CDC Viking 721s terminals, AT&T UNIX PC's and IBM-PC's are used mainly as visual displays for interactive engineering graphics. Several CDC 790, Tektronics 4115B, SUN/3, IBM 5080, Apollo and other workstations are used for more sophisticated graphics, finite element analysis and solid modeling.

Printers and Plotters

Printing is produced on the following devices: Xerox 8790 laser printer (output: 70 pages per minute) and the Xerox 9700 for quality graphics and large fonts. Plotting is done on several CalComp and Hewlett Packard brand devices.

Network: Interactive access to these machines is provided by the campus network (GTNET). The network consists of a series cables, fiber optics, and microwave links carrying information. Dial-up access to the GTNET is provided at a baud rate of 300, 1200 and 2400 bps (bit per second). From most of the terminals, the users connect by turning on the terminal, pressing the RETURN or NEXT key several times and key-in the following after the NOS prompt > >:

> >Connect *OCS CYBER D

then, pressing RETURN once more. When the system is being heavily used the network will respond with "All resource ports busy". You start to appreciate the PC environment when this happens!

Software: CYBER runs the Network Operating System (NOS), the Virtual Environment (NOS/VE) and UNIX* (VX/VE) operating system. The IBM 4381 runs the VM/CMS and MVS operating systems, the Pyramid runs both System V and Berkely UNIX, and the AT&T 3B20s run System V UNIX. All major computer programming languages are available (e.g. FORTRAN, PASCAL, C, BASIC, ASSEMBLER, PL/1, etc.). CADD software available: AutoCAD, CADKEY, COMPUTERVISION, INTERGRAPH, CADAM, CATIA, CAEDS, IBM graPHIGS (advanced graphics application programming interface, PHIGS (Programmers Hierarchical Interactive Graphics System) and ICEM DDN. This latter mainframe package is discussed below.

ICEM DDN

Integrated Computer-Aided Engineering and Manufacturing for

Design, Drafting and Numerical Control (ICEM DDN) is a mainframe/supermini computer based CADD package. It enables the construction of two and three-dimensional geometries. The geometries include: splines, conics (ellipses, hyperbolas, parabolas), strings, triangles, rectangles, hexagons, surfaces, and solids used in engineering design. EDL (Engineering Data Library) manages ICEM software as shown in Figure 7.11. It controls engineering data so that the storage and movement of information is handled automatically.

The engineering data generated by ICEM can be analyzed to determine: weight, volume, surface area, moment of inertia, and radius of gyration for a given object.

Summary

As long as people have had to count and read, they have had to compute and search for information. This activity was performed manually in the early days of civilization. In current times, microcomputers and other machines are employed to perform fast calculations and to produce engineering drawings. In the future, we might utilize some form of "artificial brain", that will provide instant solutions to our engineering technology problems.

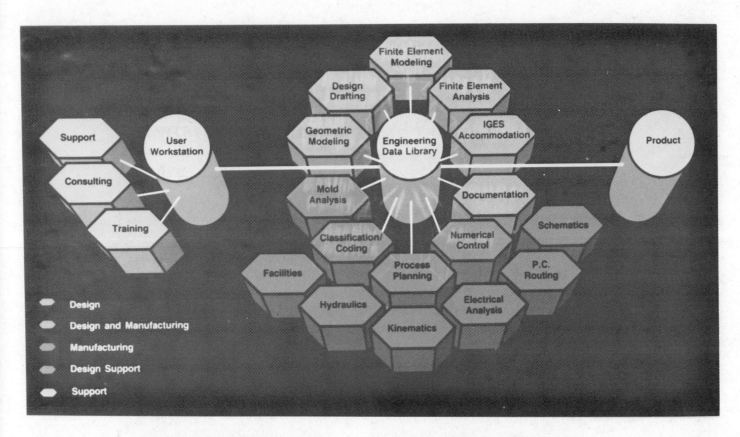

ICEM integrates CAD/CAM activities under a single computerized design management and control system.

The ICEM application management system and shared data base provide convenient access to a wide range of engineering and manufacturing applications. As shown above, these range from geometric modeling to numerical control and release to manufacturing.

Final documentation can be generated with additional data transmitted into or out of the system through the Initial Graphics Exchange Specification (IGES). The ICEM Engineering Data Library (EDL) manages and controls engineering data so that storage and movement are handled automatically.

The data storage and retrieval function of EDL allows massive amounts of parts geometry and other data to be contained in a single data base. Information can be shared, retrieved, added and deleted interactively or in batch mode. Multiple users from geographically dispersed locations can access the same data. You save time, save money and significantly increase the productivity of design, drafting and manufacturing personnel.

The ICEM system of data management and access enables configuration control of the design and added security of all information in the data base.

FIG. 7.11 Engineering Data Library (EDL) manages the ICEM software modules. (Courtesy of Control Data Corp.)

247

CHAPTER 8

GEOMETRIC ENTITIES and COORDINATE SYSTEMS

Introduction

After studying a set of construction plans or engineering detail drawings, it becomes evident that drawings are composed of the basic elements of Interactive Engineering Graphics: points, lines, circles, and character strings (text). These and other similar graphical primitives and entities are generated by the geometric construction capabilities within CADD systems.

This chapter contains a description of the geometric entities that form all drawings. Included are the commands, menus and submenus operations utilized to specify coordinate systems, grids and basic entity description as well as how to store them for later retrieval. The material is presented in a self paced, step by step, tutorial fashion. Subsequent chapters will explain the geometric construction and drafting operations.

In each of the following sections, there is an explanation of the

248

terminology utilized by CADD systems. Follow the examples on the menu selection process and entity construction procedures. Pay particular attention to the different ways to input information and how to respond to the system prompts.

Geometric Entities

Perhaps the most fundamental element of Interactive Engineering Graphics is the **geometric entity**. Geometric entities are uniquely defined units of information. They are predefined elements that can be used to draw on the screen by specifying certain commands. These fundamental building blocks are also known as **primitives**. They have specific characteristics and properties. The user of a computer graphics system can distinctively generate and select one of these entities without confusing it with another. As illustrated in Figure 8.1 (Drw. File: UNIQUE ENTITIES), a triangle can be created with three line-segments (entities). Each entity can be moved, changed or erased (deleted), independently of the other elements on the display. For example, the circle entity can be deleted without affecting the rest of the entities in the display.

The system assigns a unique sequential number to each graphic element automatically. The system operator can assign a name and some attributes to each entity. Each entity has a graphical and numeric representation. An entity is created, stored and deleted by

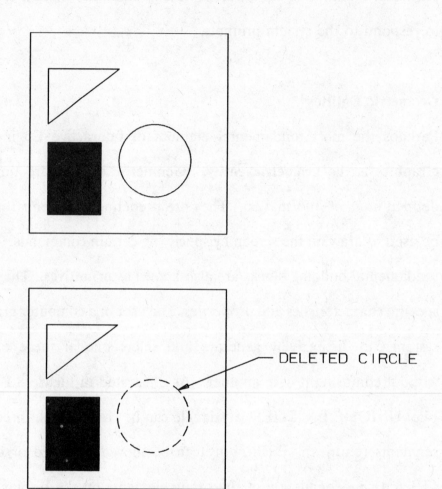

FILE: UNIQUE ENTITIES

FIG. 8.1 Several unique entities (lines) can be created to form triangles, squares, etc. A circle (entity) has been deleted.

interactively following and responding to a series of prompted queries.

Prompts

A system **prompt** is a request for information needed to complete a computer graphics operation. When prompted, you need to input some data like coordinates values, numerals or characters. Occasionally, you might have to respond to prompts by indicating certain selected entities. Reason: the system will utilize the data and information to create the geometric entities. Also you can control the system and manipulate your displayed drawings by responding to this prompt.

The systems prompts are the result of an algorithmic procedure that follows a sequence of predefined steps. This procedure is requesting data, from you, to create output primitives. Computer scientists and engineers expend many hours developing these algorithms and translating them into an specific programming language like FORTRAN, GPL (Graphic Programming Language), PASCAL or C.

Display algorithmic procedures direct the output device (computer screen) to generate specific points and lines at designated locations on the monitor. The system requests digitized or keyboard input through a series of prompts. The coordinate input obtained is utilized by the system to carry out an operation. The system invokes special display generation algorithms to construct the entity or shape on the monitor's screen.

Using Prompts to Create Entities

Usually after responding to a prompt you have to press an acknowledge key:

{ **NEXT** }, { **ENTER** }, { **RETURN** } or a graphical arrow symbol similar to this:

{ **<---** }. With this action, you instruct the system to carry out the operation. The following examples illustrate the prompts in two CADD packages.

The first is the popular <u>AutoCAD</u>, a microcomputer graphics system for IBM-PC compatible (work-alike) computers. The second is mainframe software sytem called <u>ICEMDDN</u>, Integrated Computer-Aided Engineering for Manufacturing, Design, Drafting and Numerical Control. This software package is used on CDC CYBER super-mini and mainframe computers.

Notation Conventions for the Examples

The following conventions have been adopted in this book to define the way to enter data -from the keyboard or pointing device (e.g.,

252

puck, mouse, digitizer with stylus)- into the computer system. The term **ENTRY** refers to the instructions given by the textbook to enter data. When needed, we will offer an explanation, reason or note for the entry called **COMMENT**. Occasionally, the asterisk symbol (*) will call your attention to a comment.

1.   { } Two braces enclosing text symbolizes the need to enter the data enclosed within the braces. It could also indicate the selection of certain entity location, menu selection, or function key to be press.

2.   **CTRL** or caret symbol (^) means that you should hold down the control key while pressing another funtion key.

3.   **SHIFT** means that the shift key is holded down while pressing the upper alphanumeric keyboard definitions.

4.   [ ] When necessary square brackets are used here to enclose messages offered by the system.

5.   < > Corner brackets means that the system is prompting you with a default value.

Example 8.1: AutoCAD Command Prompt Responses.

This example assumes the following configuration: 640 K bytes RAM (Random-Access Memory), IBM-PC compatible, 1 floppy disk drive (i.e., designated as A:) and 20 MB hard disk drive (i.e., designated as C:) with DOS (Disk Operating System) and AutoCAD fully installed. Lets start at the beginning.

STEP 1: Turn on the microcomputer; you will see the following Disk Operating System (DOS) prompt:

C>__

STEP 2: Go to the AutoCAD subdirectory by typing its designated name after the system command prompt:

C> { CD AUTOCAD } { ENTER }

With this action you have Change Directory (CD) to the AutoCAD directory. The name of the directory might be different; names like AUTOCAD, ACAD, AC or CAD are commonly used. However, the last three have the advantage of reducing the number of characters to be typed.

STEP 3: Enter the command {ACAD} to load the AutoCAD package to memory, for instance:

C> { ACAD } { RETURN }

After a short time ... the MAIN MENU is displayed. This menu provides access to the eight different interactive graphics tasks listed below:

AUTOCAD Copyright by AutoDesk, Inc.

Main Menu

0. Exit AutoCAD

1. Begin a NEW drawing

2. Edit an EXISTING drawing

3. Plot a drawing

4. Printer plot a drawing

5. Configure AutoCAD

6. File utilities

7. Compile shape/font description file

8. Convert old drawing file

Enter Selection:___(blinking cursor)

STEP 4: Lets respond to the new prompt: [Enter Selection:]. Start a new drawing by keying task { 1. Begin a NEW drawing } and pressing { **ENTER** }; followed by the name of a drawing {**Sample1**} and pressing { **ENTER** }. The filename cannot be more than eight characters long.

Enter Selection: { 1 } { **ENTER** }

Enter NAME of drawing: { **A:Sample1** } { **ENTER** }

The preceding input is illustrated in Figure 8.2 (Display File: AUTOCAD).

Wait while the system prepares a drawing file. This programming sequence will save or store the new generated drawing file on a formatted floppy disk, located on drive A. Notice that AutoCAD clears the screen and gets into the drawing editor. AutoCAD command prompt, [Command:], is displayed at the bottom of the screen. The ROOT MENU is then displayed on the right side of the graphics display, as illustrated in Figure 8.3.

STEP 5: Now draw a LINE by inputing the following:

```
                A U T O C A D
Copyright (C) 1982,83,84,85 Autodesk, Inc.
Version 2.17k (10/18/85) IBM PC
Advanced Drafting Extensions 3
Serial Number:
EVALUATION VERSION -- NOT FOR RESALE

Main Menu

    0.  Exit AutoCAD
    1.  Begin a NEW drawing
    2.  Edit an EXISTING drawing
    3.  Plot a drawing
    4.  Printer Plot a drawing

    5.  Configure AutoCAD
    6.   File Utilities
    7.  Compile shape/font description file
    8.  Convert old drawing file

Enter  selection: 1

Enter NAME of drawing: SAMPLE1
```

FIG. 8.2 Main AutoCAD menu. From which {1}, has been selected to start a new drawing named {A:Sample1}.

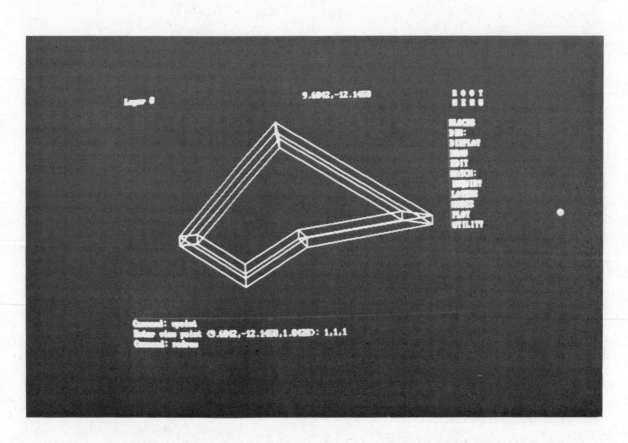

FIG. 8.3 Display of AutoCAD root menu.

Command: { **LINE** } { **ENTER** }

From point: { **0.5,0.7** } { **ENTER** }

To point: { **2.8,5.8** } { **ENTER** }

To point:

Figure 8.4 (Drw. Display: SAMPLE1) shows a printer plot of the line, as created on the screen monitor; some labels have been added for explanation purposes. A print plot is normally obtained by entering { END }, selecting { 4. Printer Plot a drawing }. If you do this, the system will prompt you with the default all the prompted messages (i.e., press {RETURN} several times).

Another way is to input [Command:] { PRPLOT } and accept all the defaults by pressing { RETURN } after each prompted query.

Example 8.2: ICEMDDN System Prompts.

STEP 1: In the main frame computer environment, you will turn the terminal on and follow the log-in procedure provided by the institution's computer services division (this example illustrates one of such systems: the CDC CYBER system environment at Georgia Tech). Usually, you will enter the procedure (PROC) file that will ATTACH or GET the CADD package. **ATTACH** is the Network Operation

259

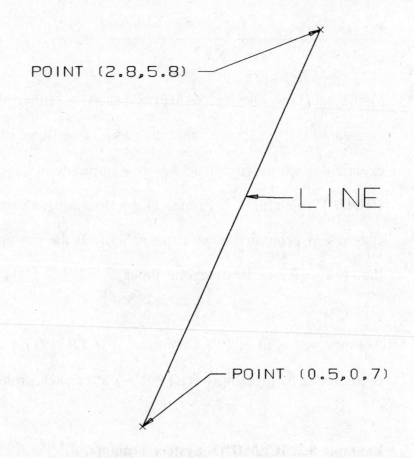

POINT (2.8,5.8)

LINE

POINT (0.5,0,7)

FILE: SAMPLE1

FIG. 8.4 Printer-plot of a line (A:SAMPLE1) generated with AutoCAD.

Procedure (NOS) way to establish communication with a direct access

permanent file. **GET** is used to call indirect access files in

the NOS environment.

STEP 2: Now the user enters the name of the PROC file, in this

example we assume the PROC file name: ICEM.

/ { ICEM }

The system responds by displaying the ICEM Menu:

ICEM Menu

1. Enter ICEM Design Drafting Application

2. Enter ICEM Schematics Application

3. Enter ICEM Facilities Application

4. Enter ICEM Hydraulics Application

5. Enter ICEM Solid Modeler Application

6. Enter Engineering Data Library

SELECT BY NUMBER OR TYPE Q TO QUIT ? ____

STEP 3: Enter { 1 } to obtain another level of menus:

ICEM Design Drafting Menu

1. Enter ICEM Design Drafting

2. Send ICEMDDN plot file to plotter

SELECT BY NUMBER OR TYPE Q TO QUIT ? ____

STEP 4: Enter { 1 }, followed by a { NEXT }:

STEP 5: Enter ICEMDDN Library File <default DDNLIB> ?____

and press

{ NEXT }, to accept the creation of the direct access file name
DDNLIB. Any other names are equally valid. The first time the
system will ask: CREATE?, to which you will respond { Y }, for yes!

STEP 6: Then, enter the BAUD RATE { 9 } { NEXT }. Comment:
This selects 9600 BAUD. For instance:

[ENTER BAUD RATE].

{ 9 }

The system displays:

ICEMDDN VERSION R1.6

COPYRIGHT CONTROL DATA CORPORATION

1978,1979,1980,1981

1982,1983,1984,1985

WELCOME TO ICEMDDN

GRAPHIC TERMINAL TYPE

1. TEKTRONIX 4014

2. TEKTRONIX 4105

3. TEKTRONIX 4107

4. TEKTRONIX 4109

5. TEKTRONIX 4113

6. TEKTRONIX 4114

7. TEKTRONIX 4115

8. TEKTRONIX 4125

9. CDC VIKING 721

10. CDC IEW 790 WITH TEKEM

STEP 7: Enter the terminal type, for instance: { **9** }, to select the Viking 721. Then select { **1** } or { **2** } to turn the TABLET on or off respectively. Wait, until the system displays the [ENTER PART NAME].

STEP 8: Type { **SAMPLE2** } and press { **NEXT** }. After [SHEET NUMBER =], enter { **1** }. Ignore for a while the { UNITS OF MEASURE } prompt. And enter { **M** }, to turn on the menu. Select now the units of measure. For instance: { **2** }, if the ENGLISH SYSTEM is desired. Select the ANSI 1982 standards. Then the computer shows the MAIN MENU:

ICEMDDN L=0 V=1 D=0.00 P=0 C=0

1.MODALS & FONTS

2.BLANK/UNBLANK

3.DELETE

4.FILE/EXIT

5.SPECIAL FUNCTIONS

6.DATA BASE MANAGEMENT

7.INPUT/OUTPUT/REGENERATION

8.DISPLAY CONTROL

9.POINT

10.LINE

11.ARC/CIRCLE/FILLET

12.OTHER CURVES

13.ENTITY MANIPULATION

14.DATA VERIFY

15.ADVANCED DESIGN

16.DRAFTING

17.NUMERICAL CONTROL

18.ANALYSIS

19.SI/US/RESIZE ____

STEP 9: Select { **10** } to get the LINE submenu. Then { **2** } to key-in some coordinates. Enter { **1** } to select a type of coordinates. The different

264

types of coordinates will be explained later. It will suffice to mention

that [XT1 =] stands for horizontal transform coordinate number one.

The following prompts appear on the terminal:

_____

1. XT1 =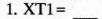

2. YT1 =

3. ZT1 = 0.0000

4. XT2 =

5. YT2 =

6. ZT2 = 0.0000

_____

The system might prompt you with previous values of XT, YT AND

ZT; but you can simply ignore them and input the desired coordinates,

as shown below.

1. XT1 = { **1.46** } { **NEXT** }

2. YT1 = { **2.56** } { **NEXT** }

3. ZT1 = 0.0000

4. XT2 = { **0.6** } { **NEXT** }

5. YT2 = { **0.5** } { **NEXT** }

6. ZT2 = 0.0000

Enter { **SHIFT**] } OR { **DATA** } to indicate: OPERATION COMPLETE. A line will appear on the screen as illustrated by Figure 8.5 (Drw. File: SAMPLE2).

Geometric Manipulation

Points, lines, circles are examples of entities that are easily created on the screen. By utilizing certain preprogrammed control functions it is possible to change the depth at which these entities are to be drawn. It is also possible to rotate, copy, move and rescale the entity by means of the geometric manipulation utilities.

Zooming, that is, enlarging or decreasing the size of the displayed part is utilized extensively to obtain a better picture. The portion of the drawing displayed can be magnified or shrunk. This is referred as **zoom-in** ("blow up") or **zoom-out** ("back off"), respectively. Sometimes it is necessary to **zoom-in** order to select an entity within a **part** (see Figures 8.6, 8.7 and 8.8, Displays Files: CLASP, ZOOMIN and ZOOMOUT). When entities are grouped together, they form a **part**. A drawing is then, a graphic representation of one or more parts.

When you start drawing on the screen or digitizing on the tablet each entity is recorded as a 3-D set of cartesian coordinates. This analytic geometry based system is responsible in part for the capability of displaying multiple views of a line created in a single orthographic

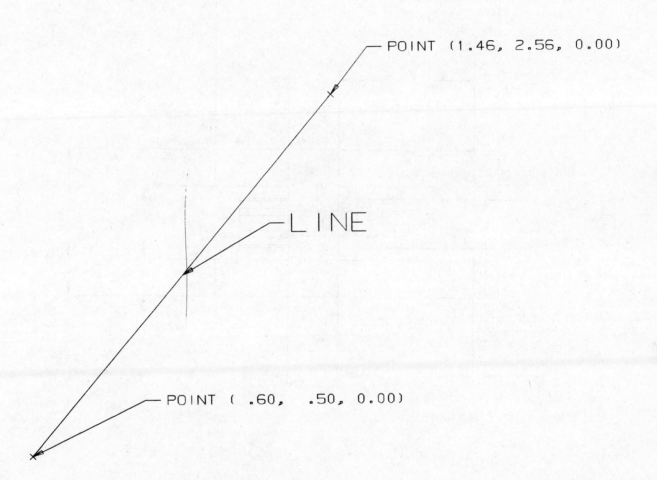

POINT (1.46, 2.56, 0.00)

LINE

POINT (.60, .50, 0.00)

FILE: SAMPLE2

FIG. 8.5 Printer-plot of line (SAMPLE2) created with ICEM DDN.

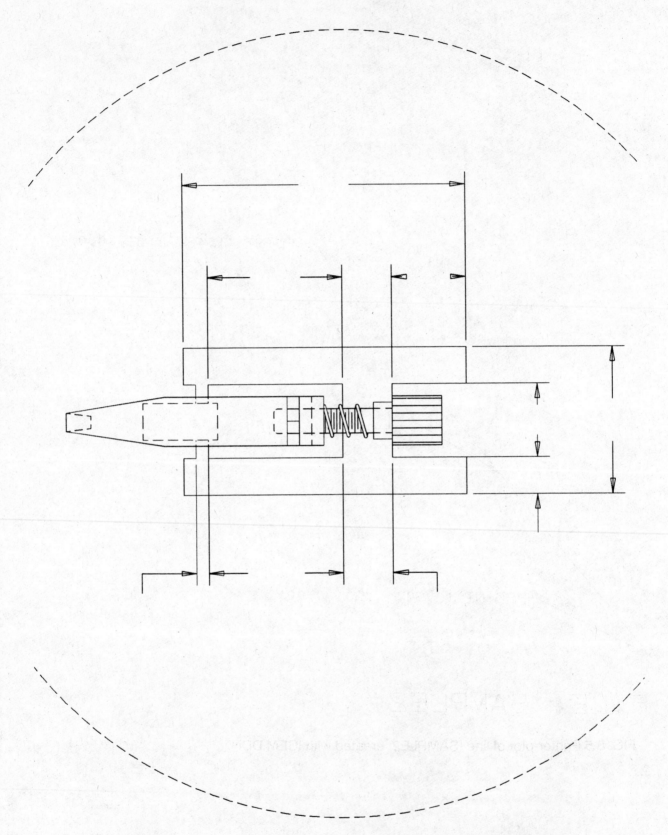

FIG. 8.6 Drum clasp device design shown within its original boundary limits.

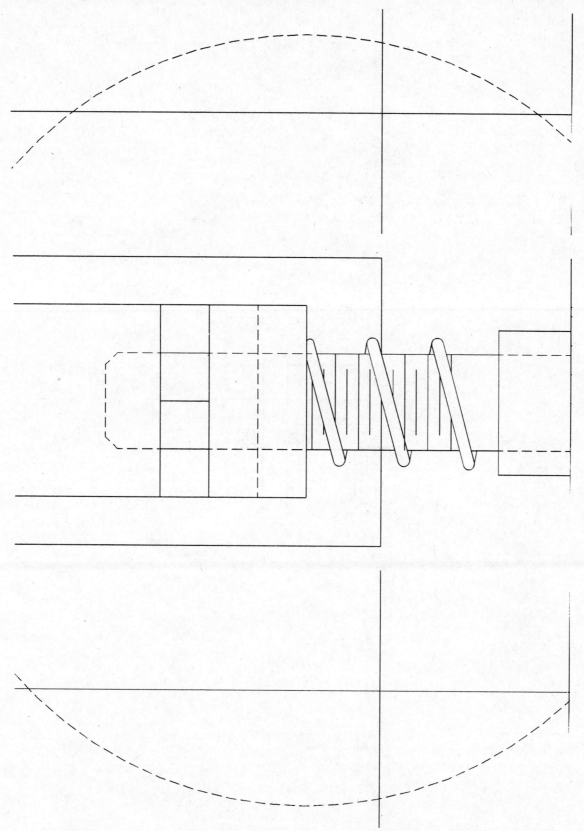

FIG. 8.7 Zooming-in ("blow up") a portion of the clasp device to obtain a closer look.

269

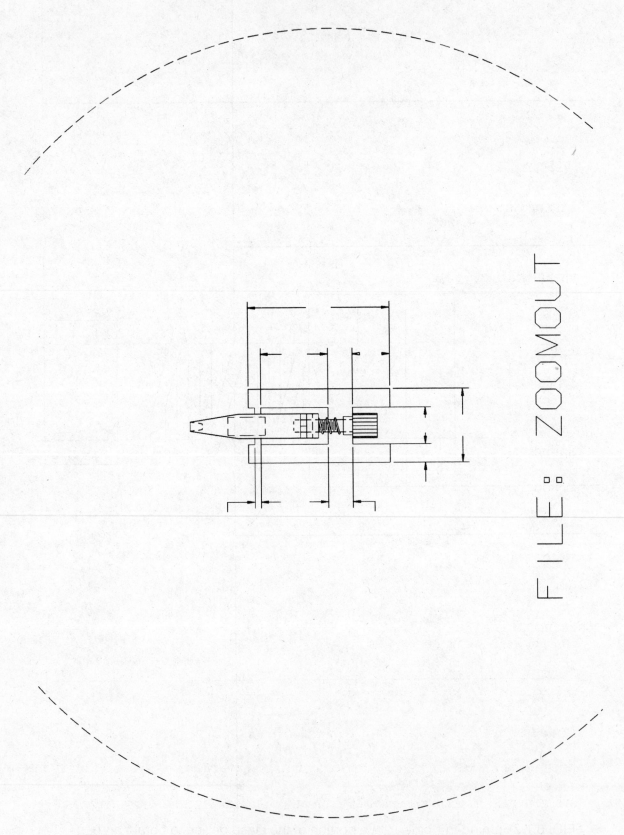

FILE: ZOOMOUT

FIG. 8.8 Zooming-out ("back off") to display the entire part and add entities beyond the original boundary limits.

work view (see Figure 8.9, Drw. File: WORK VIEW). A **view** is a display of coordinate geometry. The **work view** is the orthographic view in which the line was originally created or accepted.

List of Entities

The following is a list of the main geometric entities available on virtually all systems:

Points

Lines and traces

Circles and arcs

Splines, strings and polylines

Leader

Labels

Notes and text

Shapes, patterns and polygons

Section lining and solid filled

Figure 8.10 (Drw. File: ENTITIES), illustrates some of these entities. In addition, CAD systems may contain several drafting entities (i.e., linear dimensions, circular dimensions, angular dimensions, etc.) which are generally associated with the Computer-Aided Drafting program module of the computer graphics system.

Coordinates

TOP VIEW

A   B

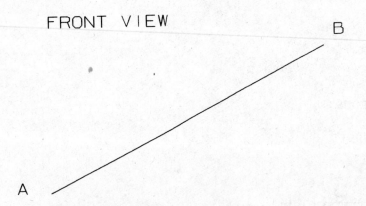

FRONT VIEW   B

A

THIS IS THE WORK VIEW IN WHICH LINE
AB WAS CREATED

FIG. 8.9 The work view, is the active view in which entities are currently
been created. For example line AB was created in the front view.

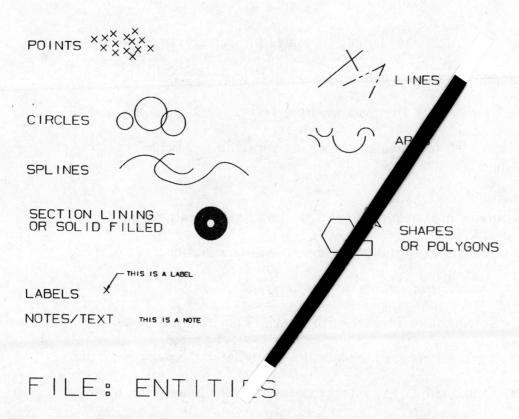

POINTS

CIRCLES

SPLINES

SECTION LINING
OR SOLID FILLED

LABELS

THIS IS A LABEL

NOTES/TEXT   THIS IS A NOTE

LINES

AR

SHAPES
OR POLYGONS

FILE: ENTITIES

FIG. 8.10 Geometric entities available in virtually all systems. One system designates, a series of connected lines: <u>polyline</u>; where another will named <u>string</u>.

In previous examples, the system prompts requested some coordinate values. **Coordinate values** X, Y and Z represent a position in space and are the construction elements of the Cartesian coordinate system. The Cartesian coordinate system is the foundation of geometric construction.

Rene Descartes, the famous seventeenth century mathematician, developed the analytic geometry concept of locating a point on a given plane by means of the distance from two perpendicular axes. The term cartesian coordinates honors his efforts in this field.

Coordinates are an ordered set of absolute or relative data values which indicate a location in space at a distance from a set of axes. Joining coordinate points within a graph allows us to visualize algebraic equations in geometric terms. The idea is to establish a correspondence between the location of a point in the work space and a set of numbers (x,y,z). The cartesian system is used for locating points and positioning entities relative to other parts of the drawing.

Three reference axes orient objects in the three dimensional space. The horizontal x-axis or axis of **abscissas**, is a horizontal line extending indefinitely to the left and to the right of a perpendicular line called **ordinate** or y-axis. The vertical y-axis extends indefinitely up and down, the z-axis extends in and out. The z-axis is also designated as the **depth** axis. All these axes meet at a location named the origin.

The **origin** is a reference location from which distances are measured. This origin is at coordinates (0,0,0). Normally, this origin is at the lower left corner of the display or computer graphic monitor screen. Figures 8.11, 8.12, 8.13 and 8.14 (Drw. Files: ISOCARTESIAN, FCARTESIAN, TCARTESIAN and RSCARTESIAN) show the standard four views (see Figure 8.15) of the Cartesian coordinate system. If you display the CADD system's GRID or AXIS, you can actually count marked off units of measure along the axes and locate coordinate points.

Two dimensional CADD packages define points by designating x- and y- axis values. Three dimensional systems require the x-, y-, and z- axis coordinate locations. However, a user might start a drawing file by specifying a 2-D plane and latter project the entities into the z- axis (depth). A three dimensional based systems will assume a default value of $Z=0$, until you project the entities in the work space.

Various computer systems refer to different types of cartesian coordinates. Different output devices demand various coordinate systems. The following articles explain the main types of coordinate systems utilized by CADD packages.

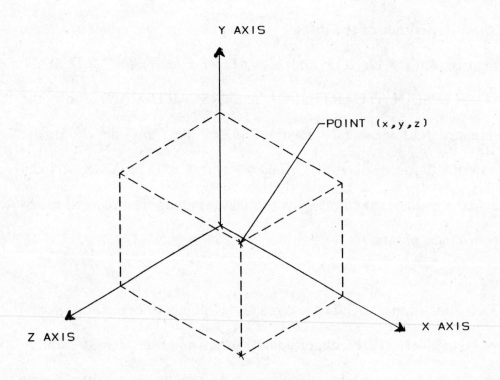

THIS IS A 3-D OR ISOMETRIC DISPLAY OF
THE CARTESIAN COORDINATE SYSTEM.

FILE: ISOCARTESIAN

FIG. 8.11 Isometric display of a cartesian coordinate system, indicating the location of point (x,y,z).

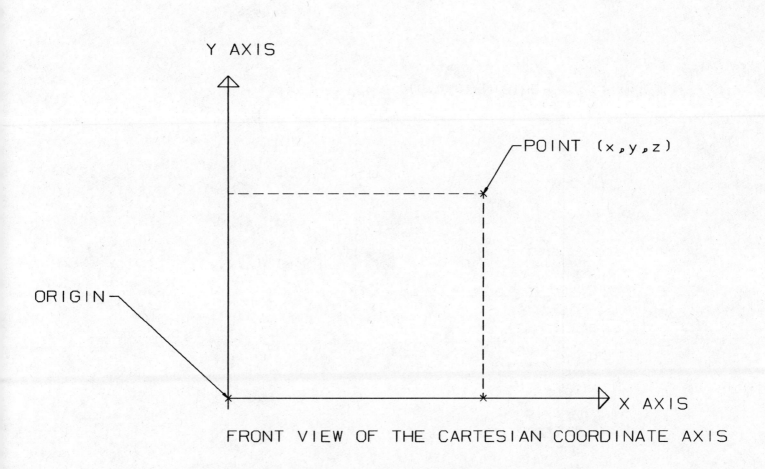

FRONT VIEW OF THE CARTESIAN COORDINATE AXIS

FILE: FCARTESIAN

FIG. 8.12 Relative location of the cartesian axes in front view.

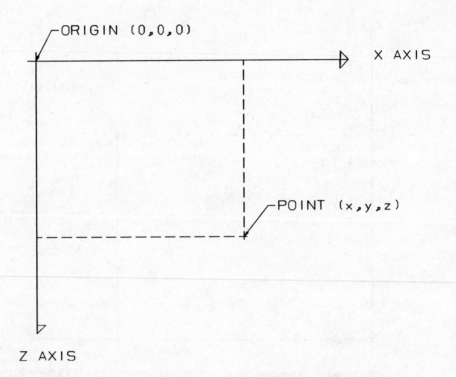

ORIGIN (0,0,0)

X AXIS

POINT (x,y,z)

Z AXIS

TOP VIEW OF THE CARTESIAN COORDINATE SYSTEM

FILE: TCARTESIAN

FIG. 8.13 Relative location of the cartesian axes in top view.

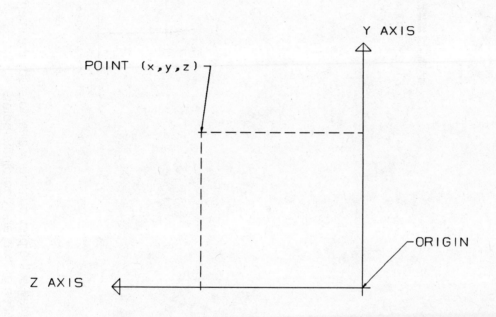

RIGHT SIDE VIEW OF THE CARTESIAN COORDIANTE SYSTEM

FILE: RSCARTESIAN

FIG. 8.14 Relative location of the cartesian axes in right-side view.

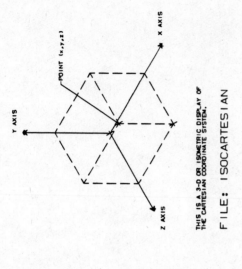

TOP VIEW OF THE CARTESIAN COORDINATE SYSTEM

FILE: TCARTESIAN

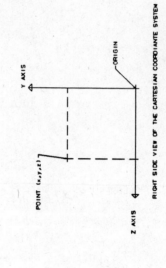

THIS IS A 3-D OR ISOMETRIC DISPLAY OF
THE CARTESIAN COORDINATE SYSTEM.

FILE: ISOCARTESIAN

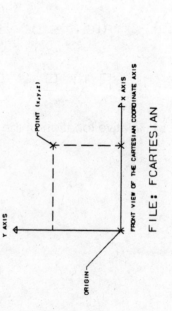

RIGHT SIDE VIEW OF THE CARTESIAN COORDIANTE SYSTEM

FILE: RSCARTESIAN

FRONT VIEW OF THE CARTESIAN COORDINATE AXIS

FILE: FCARTESIAN

FIG. 8.15 Redisplay of the previous four views, to study the interrelationship
and relative location of axes and coordinate points.

280

World Coordinates

World coordinates refer to real coordinates designated by the user. They are not limited by the constrains of an specific output device. For example, you could enter a complete building site layout that comprises several acres. Or you could input an integrated circuit layout that is only a few inches long. When you specify these coordinates, the system automatically converts them to device coordinates. When drawing on a sheet of paper, it necessary to scale the drawing so it will fit within the limits. However, in the CAD system, you can input the real world coordinates and the system will make the necessary adjustments by converting them to device coordinates.

Device Coordinates

Device coordinates are the screen coordinates on the video monitor. These are the coordinates used by the output device. Many software packages convert world coordinates to normalized device coordinates to make the system flexible.

Normalized Device Coordinates

Normalized device coordinates allows the accommodation and interface of different types of output devices. Initially coordinates are assigned values between 0 and 1. For example world coordinate x= 100 may have a normalized device coordinate of x= 0.1. Normalized coordinates are then transformed to integer device coordinates (i.e., x=1). The maximum coordinate values are governed by the characteristics and capabilities of the device in question.

Model Coordinates

Model coordinates are integrally linked to the drawing or part. In the Model Coordinate System (MCS), entity position and orientation remains fixed with respect to the model geometry. The part is defined relative to axes "attached" to it. Therefore, model coordinates are always the same regardless of the view. Model coordinates indicate the point displacements along the horizontal, vertical, and depth axes associated with the part being created. They are part oriented. Creating a three dimensional part with model coordinates requires first the definition of an origin (X=0,Y=0,Z=0). The origin designates the location of the axes, which will serve as the reference to all entities created from there on. [Note: CADKEY uses the term "world coordinates" to refer to these model space coordinates. However, this is not to be confused with the general definition of WORLD COORDINATES.]

Example 8.3 Model Coordinates

Figure 8.16 (Drw. File: MODELCOORD), illustrates a 3-D wire-frame model formed by the following coordinate points:

O (0,0,0)

A (17,0,0)

B (17,0,-8)

C (9,14,-7)

Notice that even after rotation of this object around the Z-axis, coordinates remained with the same values.

Transformed Coordinates

Transformed coordinates are also coordinate displacements along the horizontal, vertical and depth axis. These coordinates are associated with the drawing; and are defined locations relative to the terminal screen, rather than the drawing itself. For instance the lower left of the screen may be the origin, with the x-axis running along the bottom of the screen. The Y- axis along the vertical left side of the screen. Z- axis "coming in or out" of the monitor's screen. For the purpose of this discussion, transform coordinates will be designated by the variables XT, YT and ZT.

In the **Working Coordinate System (WCS)**, coordinates are work plane oriented. The **Work Plane** is the plane in which 2-D entities are constructed. WCS coordinates can be specified at any position of orientation as illustrated in Figure 8.17 (Display File: WCS). In some

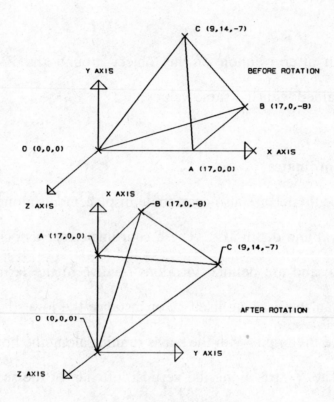

FILE: MODELCOORD

FIG. 8.16 Model coordinates are always the same, regardless of the view or orientation changes.

284

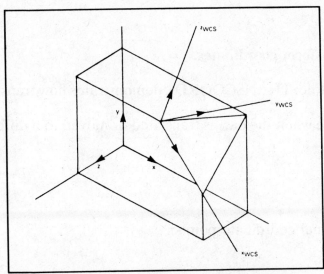

**Example use of the Working
Coordinate System (WCS)**

FIG. 8.17 Working coordinates can be specified in any position of orientation.
For example, the XY plane can be aligned normal to a vector (Courtesy of
GE/CALMA).

285

cases, the XY plane can be aligned: normal to a vector, with a plane defined by three points or to existing geometry. For example, in the Calma Design Drafting Manufacturing (DDM) system three types of WCS coordinates are available, namely: cartesian, cylindrical and spherical as illustrated in Figure 8.18 (Display File: DDM). Normally, mini and PC based CADD systems support cartesian and polar coordinates. Most engineering applications only require the cartesian and polar capabilities.

Example 8.4 Transform coordinates.

Figure 8.19 (Drw. File: TRANSCOORD), demonstrates how transform coordinates change when the part is translated or moved to a different position.

The part has original coordinate points:

E (0,0,-5)

F (4,0,-5)

G (0,0,-12)

H (0,3,-12)

Moving the part 12 units to the right (i.e., translation) draws new X coordinates: 12, 16, 12 and 12 for vertices E, F, G and H, respectively. Rotating the part will result in different coordinates for all points.

286

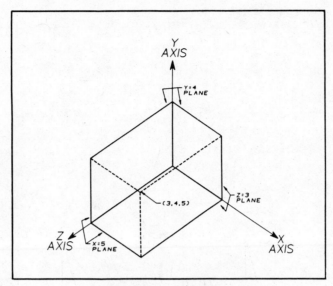

Cartesian coordinate system

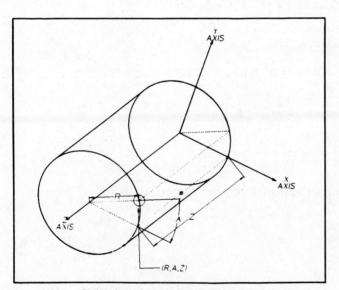

Cylindrical coordinate system

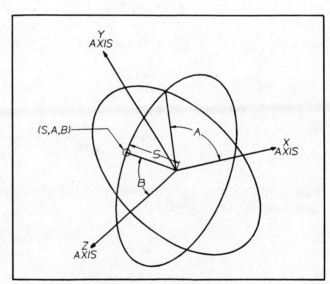

Spherical coordinate system

FIG. 8.18 Comparison of the **(a)**.cartesian, **(b)**. cylindrical and **(c)**. spherical coordinate systems. (Courtesy of CALMA).

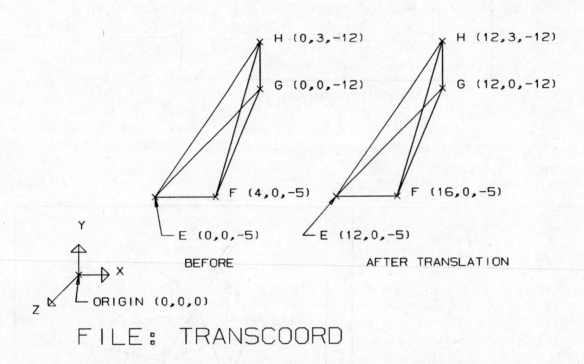

FILE: TRANSCOORD

FIG. 8.19 Transform coordinates change when the part is translated or rotated or moved to a new poistion.

Absolute or View Coordinates

Absolute or View coordinates terms are used by several graphics packages (e.g., AutoCAD and CADKEY, respectively) to refer to coordinates input through the keyboard, digitizer or mouse, where the origin could be defined close to the lower left corner of the screen. You may specify a point by typing in the (X, Y, Z) values. For example, { 4.5,6.254,10.98 } specifies a point with an X coordinate of 4.5 units to the right, a Y coordinate of 6.254 units up and a Z coordinate of 10.98 units outwards (towards you).

Relative Coordinates

Relative coordinates are coordinates referenced to a prior specified coordinate. You may specify a point a distance from the last coordinate. Entities are defined at a specified displacement in the X, Y, Z directions from the selected based point using either model or transform coordinates. When relative coordinates are specified along the horizontal, vertical or depth axis they are **relative delta coordinates**. **Relative polar coordinates** are specified from a base point as a distance and angle from the previous point.

Example 8.5 ICEMDDN Relative Delta Coordinates.

The ICEMDDN software package is used here to illustrate Delta coordinates. Figure 8.20 (Drw. File: DELTACOORD), shows an existing point (4.5, 5.6). Let's assume you want to construct another

289

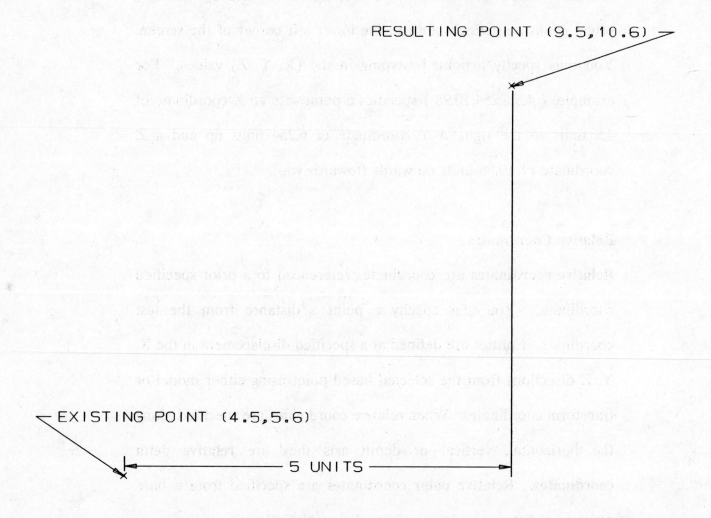

RESULTING POINT (9.5,10.6)

EXISTING POINT (4.5,5.6)

5 UNITS

FILE: DELTACOORD

FIG. 8.20 Relative delta coordinates are coordinates referenced to a prior specified location.

point at a horizontal displacement of 5.0 units and a vertical displacement of 5.0 units to the right of the point. Resulting point is located at coordinates (9.5,10.6).

Example 8.6 AUTOCAD Relative Coordinates.

This example illustrates AutoCAD use of relative coordinates. Assuming that you have just finished inputting point {3.5,6.7} and you want to locate a point at 2 units to the right and 3 units down. The screen will show the prompt lines,

---

Command: { **POINT** }

Point:{ **3.5,6.7** }

In response to the coordinate sequence prompt, you will type:

{ **@2,-3** } (i.e., input the @ symbol followed by the x and y relative displacement). A point will be created 2 units to the right and 3 units down from existing point (3.5,6.7), resulting in point (5.5,3.7).

Polar Coordinates

Polar coordinates are another useful way to locate a point in a plane. These coordinates are constructed by first fixing an origin point and an initial ray.

A **ray** is a half-line consisting of a vertex and points of a line on one side of the vertex (i.e., an origin and positive X-axis is a ray). A point, P, can be located by polar coordinates (radial distance, angle). Where, **radial distance** is the directed distance from origin, O, to point, P, and the **angle** is the directed angle from initial ray to line OP. In geometry and trigonometry, the angle is positive when measured counterclockwise (CCW).

Example 8.7 AUTOCAD Polar Coordinates

Using polar coordinates you can specify a point at a distance and angle from a previous reference point. In AUTOCAD this is performed by the "@distance<angle" function. The coded instruction:

{ @5.7<46.3 }

---

displays a point 5.7 units from the last specified point, at an angle of 46.7 degrees measured counterclockwise. Most CADD packages will designate counterclockwise (CCW) angles as a positive angles.

Establishing Reference Points

Experienced designers and computer graphics end-users recognize the importance of establishing reference points in the generation of engineering graphics. Point construction, facilitates the creation and production process of engineering drawings and graphs. Therefore, it it is helpful to become familiar with the point generation methods available and to understand the process involved in their display and manipulation.

Despite vast amounts of interactive graphics information, the literature rarely refers to these geometric entities. Contained herein is an effort to articulate the point generation techniques and vocabulary.

Engineering devices and systems can be graphically represented by solid models and orthographic projections. Two and three dimensional finite element models are utilized to describe the spatial relationship between the components of these devices and systems. The advent of computer graphics systems has reduced the time and long term costs associated with the generation of engineering drawings and construction plans.

Computer pictures of the engineered devices and systems are interactively displayed, on the screen, with output primitives and elements like: points, lines, arcs and text (character strings). Points are the simplest geometric components of engineering graphics drawings. However, this is debatable since lines are the most basic graphic primitives of interactive graphics systems.

The underlying descriptive geometry theory of points is discussed here in conjunction with a series of point construction and manipulation operations.

Definition

Points designate a unique position in the computer workspace. They are defined by the three dimensional cartesian coordinate system. Algorithmic procedures and computer graphics programming routines for generating points provide the basic tools for construction drawings. A point is a geometric entity defined and stored as an element of the geometric data base. Therefore, points are available as a reference to use in other operations.

Points are the basic building blocks for the creation of computer images. In many instances, the drafter or designer begins a drawing by constructing guide points along the imaginary outline of the given part. Two connected points define a line, a series of joined lines form a plane. Plane surfaces are combined to form a volume.

Descriptive Geometry of Points

The conceptual foundations of engineering graphics are a result of Gaspar Monge's developments in descriptive geometry. **Descriptive Geometry** is the study of graphical representations and spatial relationships between geometric entities. The concepts were

294

originally utilized in the 18th century to solve problems associated with the design of french military fortifications.

In the present, the underlying theory is used by engineers and computer programmers to develop mathematical algorithms that determine points of intersection between two planes, true distances between points and other spatial relationships among the various components of a device or structure. Although some CADD systems are able to perform many of these operation automatically, it is necessary to understand the fundamental descriptive geometric principles. Reason: To be able to use and/or interpret the results. Another purpose is to develop new design procedures.

Theoretically, a point is defined by its location and has no dimensions. For convenience, the interactive graphic system displays a small lighted dot (.), star (*) and cross (x) or (+). It keeps track of the point locations by storing its world, device, relative, absolute, transform or model coordinates.

Point Projection

System generated orthographic projections of a point with coordinates (6.0, 5.5, -0.75), are illustrated in Figure 8.21 (Drw. File: POINT PROJECTION). The Top, Front and Right Views are obtained by projecting the point into the walls of an imaginary transparent box.

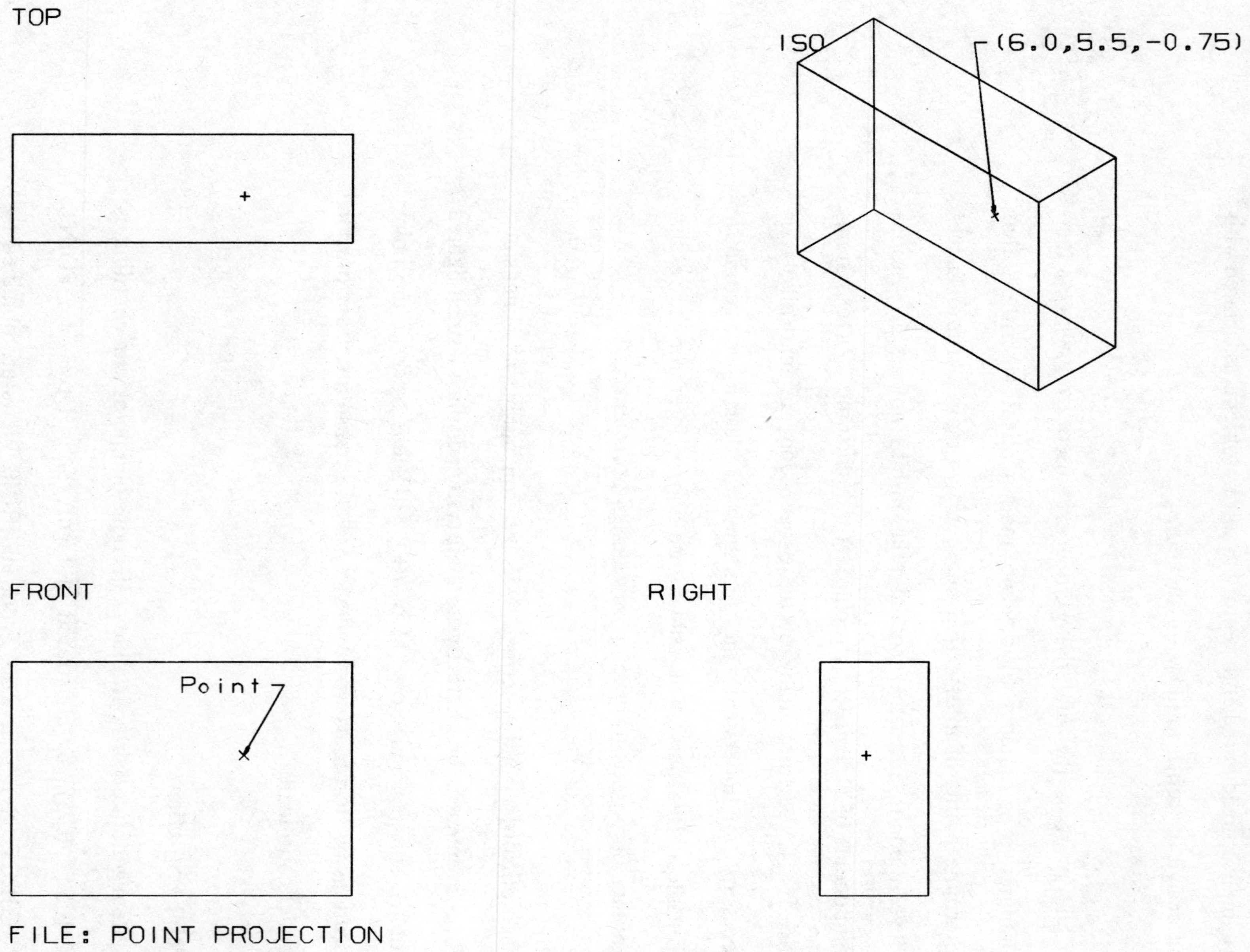

(6.0,5.5,-0.75)

ISO

TOP

+

RIGHT

+

FRONT

Point

×

FILE: POINT PROJECTION

FIG. 8.21 Top (horizontal), front (frontal) and right-side (profile) views are obtained by projecting the point onto the walls of an imaginary transparent box.

The box walls are unfolded and removed to represent the point's **planes of projection.**

In descriptive geometry, the terms: Frontal (F), Horizontal (H) and Profile (P) designate the folding lines for the Front, Top and Right Side orthographic views, respectively. As illustrated in Figure 8.22 (Drw. File: EIGHT VIEWS), the point can be projected in other views like: Back, Left, Bottom, and Auxiliary Views. However, the point can be perfectly represented with the standard projections mentioned earlier. To emphasize this, the other views labels have been omitted.

Traditional Construction

Traditionally, points are projected into planes of projection by the following procedure:

Step 1: Determine the x, y and z coordinates of the point.

Step 2: Locate the front projection of the point (Frontal X-Y plane), by plotting the (x,y) coordinates of the point.

Step 3: Draw a projection line (projector) from the previous point, across and perpendicular to the X axis of the Horizontal X-Z plane.

Step 4: Draw the point projection on that plane, by measuring the depth z, along the projector drawn in step 3.

Step 5: Follow a similar procedure, to locate the point projection on other planes. Alternativelly, use a 45 degree **mitre line,** to transfer the

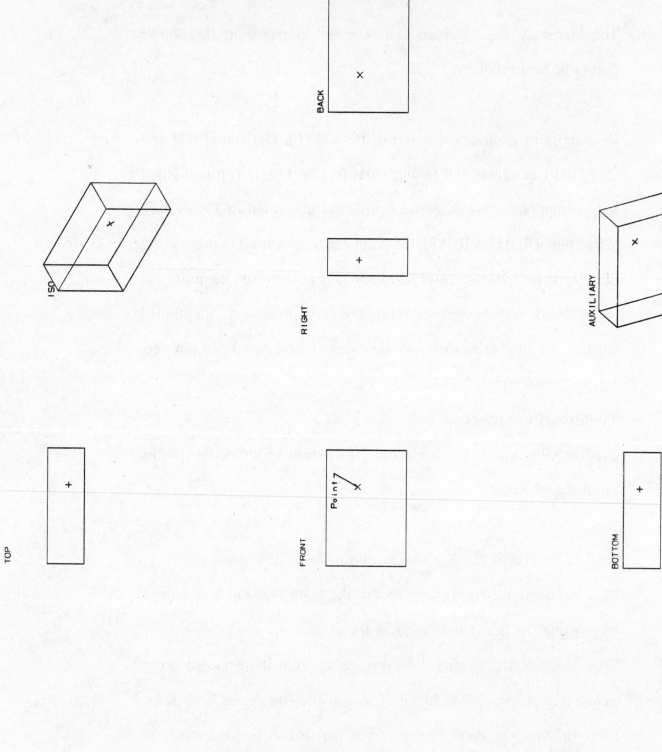

FIG. 8.22 Computer-generated orthographic views of a point.

298

depth dimensions of the point.

Computer Generated

In computer graphics, the displayed image of a point on the screen is implemented by converting coordinate information into the appropriate instructions to the video monitor. You enter the requested information in response to a series of prompted messages provided by the graphics software package present in the computer memory. The software converts this information data into a code that matches the display configuration. Access to the point construction capabilities is gained by the main menu or the POINT commands.

Initial points are created at the default depth $Z = 0.0$, unless otherwise stated. If the system is set on the construction modal, you will be requested for more data for the creation of additional points. If not, the system returns to a higher level menu (or command line). The point is displayed on the screen after entering the data points. In the case of the Cathode Ray Tube (CRT), an electron beam will hit and illuminate a phosphor dot at the specified position.

On the raster device, a point is plotted by setting a bit value equal to 1 (on) at the specified location. The point is displayed when the electron beam encounters a 1 in the frame buffer.

If the task is to be performed on a random-scan monitor, the instructions to create a point are stored in a display file. Coordinates are converted to voltage deflections that move to the specified location.

Point Construction Methods

Point construction methods are utilized on drawings for a number of reasons. For example, if you were to draft the ROM (Read Only Memory) CARD shown in Figure 8.23 (Drw. File: SCHEMATIC DIAGRAM), you might want to first locate an origin, the outer limits of the drawing, and all marked points. You would then proceed by creating lines and patterns referenced to these points. Another application is shown in Figure 8.24 (Display File: SIMUFLOW) where point symbols on a graph represent the relation between pressure drop and time at a given fill rate.

Points can be defined by a series of different inputing methods. The capabilities of the software will determine the number of options that you have available. In general, it is possible to generate a point by indicating coordinate locations, delta increments, or polar measurements (angles and their measurements).

Several construction methods allow the user to create points using other existing geometric entities like circles and curves. Additional

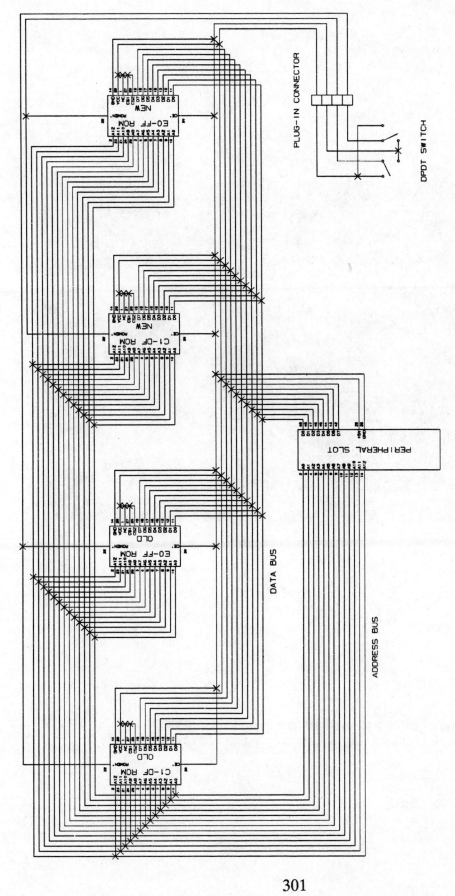

FIG. 8.23 Points are used in the generation of the outline of this ROM schematic diagram.

301

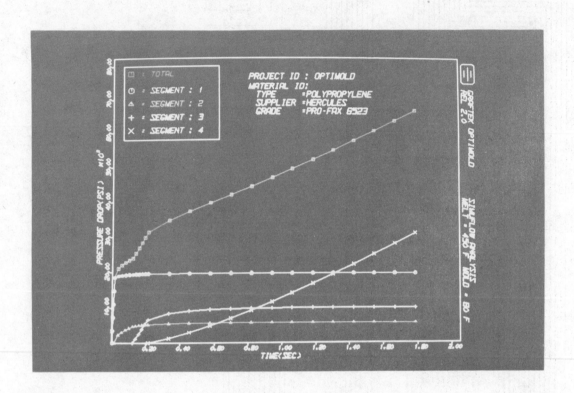

FIG. 8.24 Different points and markers are used to construct the graph. This a semiflow graph of pressure drop vs. time at a given fill rate. (Courtesy of Graftex.)

point creation capabilities include: designating a point of tangency on a curve, intersections, vector measurements and using parametric equations. So the user has more than one option to input points. The allows him or her the flexibility to generate points using the most convenient method for the particular application.

The POINT submenu or command is a subset within the main menu (root menu). The graphic software package will control the passageway to the POINT facility. Each system has its own set of procedures to access the point generation capabilities. Some examples will illustrate the route to point creation. First, we will take a look at a PC based program (AutoCAD) and then to a Supermini or Mainframe modular sample program (ICEMDDN).

Example 8.8: Point command for AutoCAD

Instruct the system to display the point input prompt. Assume you have selected the { Begin a NEW drawing } option from AutoCAD's MAIN MENU.

Solution

Type-in { POINT } after the [Command:] prompt, as illustrated below:

Command: { **POINT** } { **ENTER** }

303

Point:

_____

Example 8.9: Point submenu for ICEMDDN

Select the point submenu. Assume you have logged-in to a CDC
CYBER computer and found your way into ICEMDDN's MAIN
MENU.

Solution

Hold the { **CTRL** } key down press { **P** }, to display the point
submenu shown below, or select the POINT submenu from the MAIN
MENU.

_____

POINT

   1. SCREEN POSITION

   2. KEY-IN

   3. POLAR

   4. DELTA

   5. VECTORED

   6. CIRCLE CENTER

   7. ON A CIRCLE

   8. CURVE END

   9. INTERSECT 2 CURVES

  10. SPLINE POINTS

11. ON A LINE

12. CURVE NORMAL

13. BEARING DISTANCE

14. ON A CURVE

15. SURFACE POINTS

16. SPHERICAL

17. FAN POINTS

18. INCREMENTAL POINTS

19. MODIFY REPLACE

The following articles discusses some of the typical point construction operations. Each of the operations include some terms and concepts that apply to most of the interactive graphic systems available at the micro, mini and mainframe environments.

Screen Position or Pointing

Selection of entities by screen position or pointing consists of specifying a point using a graphic inputing device (e.g., stylus with digitizing tablet, light pen, puck, mouse, joy stick, etc.). Some users prefer to use the term locator rather than pointer, but it means the same thing.

To generate a point in this fashion you move the pointer on the tablet surface until the crosshairs on the screen are at the point you wish to draw. Then, you press the stylus against the tablet or press the pointer pick button. The position is read. Coordinate values are recorded and stored for that point. A lighted point (or mark) appears on the display. Some times the system draws a small lighted x or + to indicate the location of the point. Display of an x or + avoids confusing the point with one of the dots on a displayed GRID.

Grid

A **grid** is a frame of reference that can be display on the screen at any time to help you with your drawing. It consists of a series of construction dots, named **grid dots**, that are independent of your drawing file. You see them on the screen but they will not show when you plot the file. They are reference points evenly spaced in the X and Y axes. The user sets the grid by using the GRID command (AutoCAD) or by selecting the grid activation and display from the MODES or MODALS submenu (ICEM DDN) or the specific command in your system.

If the grid is activated, your point will snap to the closest grid dot. **SNAP** (AutoCAD) instructs the system to grasp the closest dot on the grid. When you invoke this capability, the system set up the smallest recognizable increment as you move the locator around the displayed grid. The following examples demonstrate grid and snap set up procedures for two popular CAD systems. Remember to press the { ENTER } key after each response.

Example 8.10: Setting up a GRID on AutoCAD

There are two ways to set up the grid. One procedure consist of selecting the MODES keyword from the ROOT MENU and picking GRID from MODES, using a mouse. The other method is described as follows:

Command: { **GRID** } { **ENTER** }

On/Off/Value(X)/Aspect <0.0000>:

To change the setup, you may opt to enter the new desired spacing values between grid points after the prompt line, for instance:

On/Off/Value(X)/Aspect <0.0000>: { **0.25** } { **ENTER** }

The preceding input will change the grid settings to quarter inch spacings.

It is also possible to change the **Aspect** ratio between X and Y values by entering letter { **a** } after the prompt line. In this way you can have

different spacing in the workplane. In addition the system provides a "toggle switch" (i.e., pressing function key F7, Ctrl G) feature so that the user can turn on and off the grid display.

SNAP command allows you to activate the grid points. Specified points will grasp the closest dot on the grid. The SNAP operation is set up by selecting MODES from the ROOT MENU and SNAP from the MODES submenu. A toggle (i.e., F9, Ctrl B, etc.) activates the snapping feature. You may also elect to turn on the snapping by commanding the system to do so. This task is carry out by **modifiers**, that invoke alternate forms of a command for instance:

Command: { **SNAP** }

On/Off/Value/Aspect/Rotate/Style: { **ON** }

Value and Aspect on the SNAP prompt line have a similar function as in the GRID command. The **Rotate** function permits snapping polar coordinate values. **Style** allows you to select an isometric grid as opposed to the standard snap.

Example 8.11: Setting up the grid on ICEMDDN

STEP 1: Select { **MODALS AND FONTS** } submenu from the MAIN MENU

STEP 2: Pick { **GRID** } submenu from the MODALS AND FONTS submenu

STEP 3: Turn { **GRID ACTIVATION** } on

STEP 4: Turn { **GRID DISPLAY** } on

To change the grid parameters, follow this procedure:

STEP 5: Select { **GRID PARAMETERS** } submenu

Default values will be displayed

GRID DXT= 0.2500

GRID DYT= 0.2500

STEP 6: Input new grid spacing

STEP 7: From the GRID RANGE submenu, pick **FULL SCREEN.**

STEP 8: Accept X-GRID INCREMENTS =4.0000

Y-GRID INCREMENTS =4.0000

STEP 9: REPAINT the screen if necessary

Automatic Input

Various systems also allow you to input points through screen touch panels ("tough screen"), voice recognition, and devices that automatically enter the 3-D information by photographical and scanning devices.

Automatic Document Scanning (ADS) allows to transport existing drawings engineering drawings to your CAD system (see Figure 8.25, Display File: ADS). In this way it is possible to perform modifications and revisions to old paper drawings. Scanned drawings provide the capability of telecommunicating drawings to other users of these data.

Key Board Pointing

Using the cursor control keys, the user can move the cursor around the screen. These keys are useful when your hardware configuration does not include other interactive input devices. Also, keyboard pointing can be used when the need for precision arises. With the cursor keys, you can select a precise dot without the SNAP feature. Nevertheless, by combining snapping and cursor keys, the user can successfully replace the need for additional peripheral devices.

Several hardware/software configurations let you manipulate the cross hairs, fast or slow, as demanded. This operation is performed by holding down the shift or control keys in combination with the arrow keys. This is true in the Control Data Corporation's (CDC) ICEMDDN/ Viking 721 configuration. In the microcomputer environment (i.e, PC configurations), namely the typical IBM PC

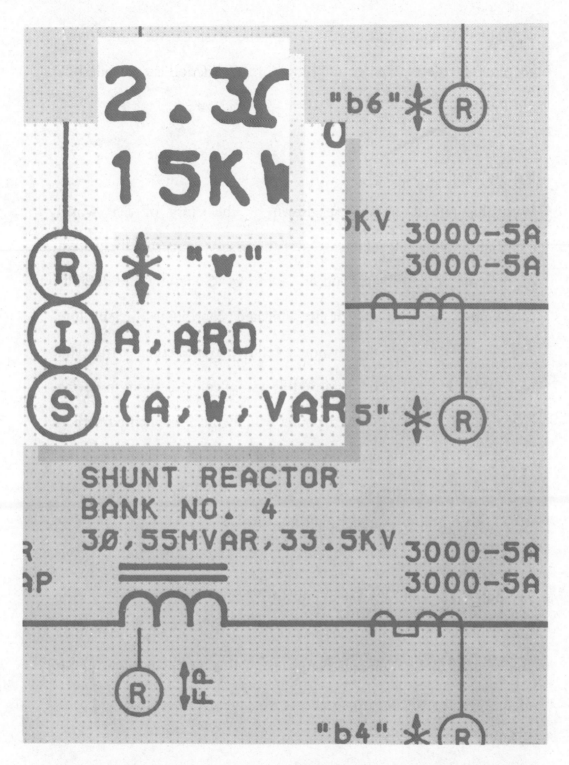

FIG. 8.25 Automatic document scanning allows to transport existing engineering drawings to the CAD system. (Courtesy of Control Data Corp.)

workalike computer using AutoCAD; the Fast Cursor function is governed by the Pg Up key and Slow Cursor function is controlled by the PgDn key.

Key-in Numeric Values

With this option, points are drawn by the entry of real world coordinate values. In some cases, it is necessary to instruct the system on the type of coordinates you are entering. Generally, the default-coordinates are absolute or transformed coordinates. Absolute coordinates will create display points relative to the screen. After you type-in the real world coordinates, the system converts them to device coordinates, so the generated points will fit on the specified screen limits. Of course, the user can associate the input coordinates to the drawing shape or part being created by specifying model coordinates. However, not all systems provide this option.

Example 8.12: Entering coordinates with AutoCAD.

Locate a point at absolute coordinates (7.85, 10.67), then draw another point 5 units to the right and 2 units up relative to the previous point.

Solution

From the ROOT MENU, select DRAW command and reply to the Command prompt as shown below:

Command: { **POINT** } { **ENTER** }

Point:{ **7.85,10.67** } { **ENTER** }

Command:

A bright lighted mark (**+**) emerges on the screen. This is just a construction symbol. If you REDRAW, i.e., {Command:**REDRAW**} an absolute point will be displayed on the monitor. Specify another point, 5 units to the right and 2 units up, as shown below:

Command: { **POINT** } { **ENTER** }

Point: { **@5,2** } { **ENTER** }

Command:

A distinctive delta point appears, after entering relative coordinates @5,2.

Example 8.13: ICEMDDN Key-in Operation.

List the sequence steps necessary to key-in point coordinates.

313

Procedure

Step 1: From the MAIN MENU select {POINT} or press { **Ctrl P** }

Step 2: Then select the { **KEY-IN** } choice

Step 3: Respond to the definition of space prompt. This permits the selection of the type of coordinates to use.

DEFINITION SPACE

1. TRANSFORM COORDINATES

2. MODEL COORDINATES

Step 4: Select { 1 } to create coordinates relative to the screen or { 2 } to generate coordinates tied to the part being drawn. Lets assume you selected transform coordinates. The system responds with a second prompt, as follows:

---

1. > XT=____

2. YT=____

3. ZT=0.0000

In other words, "Please I need input... give me some values."

Notice the > symbol preceding the coordinates, this is an indication of the coordinate being requested.

Step 5: As you input transform coordinates: XT, YT, ZT ; the system moves the > indicator. ZT = 0.0000, default value, is displayed but can be changed by key-in the header { 3.}, followed by the new ZT value.

Step 6: Pressing the { **OPERATION COMPLETE** } control key {] }

or

{ **DATA** }, tells the system you are ready to do something else. The system acknowledges by going to a higher level menu.

Utilizing model coordinates, to create points follows a similar procedure.

Enter the X, Y, AND Z coordinates of the position at which the point is to be displayed. Notice below that depth coordinates default to zero.

---

1. > X =

2. Y =

3. Z = 0.0000

Polar

Additional methods will allow the user to generate points. Lets take a look at some of these procedures. Have in mind that in each of described methods, input is possible by either pointing with a stylus, keyboard pointing or keying coordinates.

The **polar** operation procedure allows creation of a point at a specified distance and angle from certain reference point on a baseline. The reference point is the vertex. And the baseline is the horizontal imaginary line from which the angle is measured. Counterclockwise (CCW) angular measurements are designated positive (+) angles. Likewise, clockwise (CW) angles are negative. With this choice, the user will input the radial distance, angle and indicate reference entity from which the point is to be generated.

Example 8.14: Relative Polar Coordinates with AutoCAD.

Create a point 6 units away from reference point (3,9) at an angle of 65 degrees CCW.

Solution

The POINT operation follows:

Command: { **POINT** } { **ENTER** }

Point: { **3,9** }

Command: { **POINT** }

Point: { @6<65 }

Example 8.15: ICEMDDN Polar Coordinates Procedure.

Describe the method to create polar points using ICEMDDN.

Procedure

Step 1: First select the { **POINT** } submenu from MAIN MENU or {Ctrl P}.

Step 2: Pick { **POLAR** } and respond the indicate point prompt:

INDICATE POINT

1.ANGLE=

2.RADIUS=

Step 3: Indicate the existing point with the pointer.

Step 4: Enter the angle between the baseline and the new point. The angle should be specified in degrees.

Step 5: Enter the radial distance from the base point to the new point.

Step 6: Enter { **OPERATION COMPLETE** }.

A new point will be created relative to the base point at the specified angle and distance. The system will return to the [INDICATE POINT] sequence if the [CONSTRUCTION MODAL] is enable. If you turn off this system modal, it will go back to the "POINT" submenu.

Delta or Relative Displacements

With this option it is possible to generate points at designated locations relative to another point. It is similar to the polar coordinates, but here

the point is created by entering increments along the X and Y axis. The increment is called a **DELTA**. Namely, delta X (DX), delta Y (DY) and delta Z (DZ).

Vectored

In the Engineering Statics field, forces are described by their magnitude, direction and point of application, therefore termed **vectors.** A similar concept is used here to define a point at a specified distance from a base point. With the vectored-point procedure the user specify the direction by selecting an existing line. The point is defined in the direction parallel to the line and towards the positive horizontal direction if a positive value is entered. A negative distance

318

tells the system to create the point towards the negative X direction. In other words, a positive numeral generated a point along an imaginary line, parallel to the selected vectorial line and at the stipulated magnitude from the base point.

Example 8.16: Point generation for the nodes of a truss.

Enumerate some of the methods available to draw the joints (i.e., "points" at the intersection) of the plane truss illustrated in by the creation sequence in Figure 8.26, 8.27 and 8.28 (Drw. Files: TRUSS REFERENCE POINTS, TRUSS MEMBERS and TRUSS LOADS).

Solution

1. Delta

2. Vectored

3. Polar

Center of a Circle

This capability allows you to draw a point that corresponds to the center of an existing circle or arc. The single step method to generate this entity consists of indicating the arc or circle whose center is to be defined.

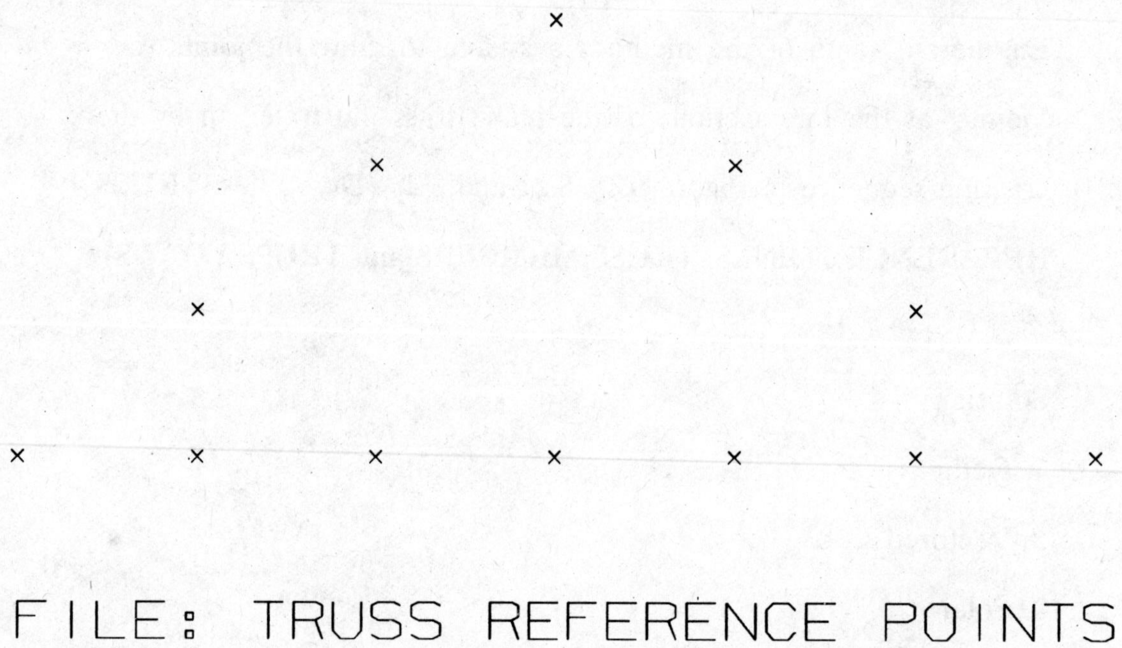

FILE: TRUSS REFERENCE POINTS

FIG. 8.26 Points (x marks) are useful in the generation of the nodes of a structural truss.

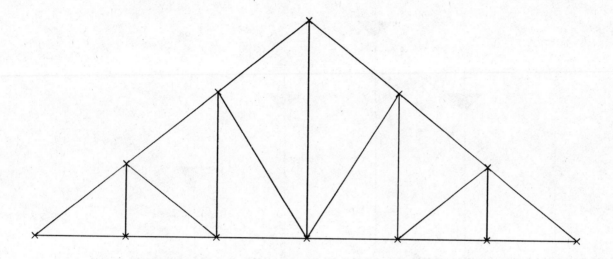

F I L E : TRUSS MEMBERS

FIG. 8.27 Lines and other entities can be easily drawn from these reference points to form the truss members.

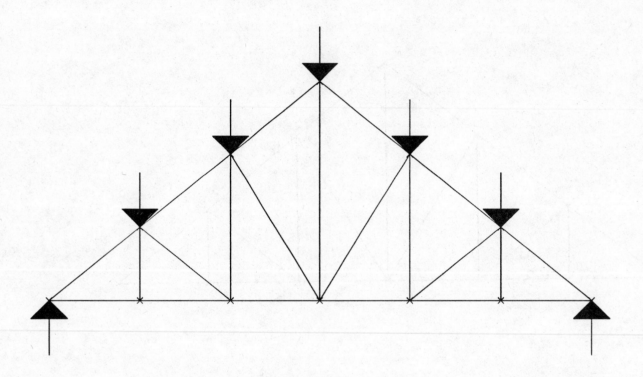

FILE: TRUSS LOADS

FIG. 8.28 Truss loads are added to the drawing utilizing points as a reference location.

Along the circumference

If available, this option let you draw a point at a specified angle on the edge of a selected arc or circle. You will indicate the arc entity and then specify multiple points along the circumference of the circle or arc. First, use the pointer to select the circle or arc around whose edge are points to be drawn. Then, enter the angle at which the point is to be defined. A positive value signals the system to create a point measured counterclockwise from a line that passes through the center of the circle, parallel to the horizontal axis. Other points are specified along the arc's edge in the same fashion without having to indicate the arc again.

Intersecting Curves

Sometimes it is helpful to be able to create a point at the intersection of two curves or lines. In this case, each curve is selected individually. The system's algorithm defines the point at the nearest position used to select the curves. A point is generated at the first curve, on the second curve, at the current depth or at the true intersection of the two curves. The definition of curves includes: lines, arcs, conics and splines. Of course, if no intersection is found the system will indicate so by displaying a message like: [NO INTERSECTION FOUND].

On a Spline

Points along a two or three dimensional spline are created with this operation at the original points used to define the spline. This allows you to recreate the points even after you have deleted them. The pointer is normally utilized to indicate the spline.

On a Line

Also you can create points on an existing line at a certain displacement along the horizontal, vertical or depth axes. With this choice you select the line and enter a displacement along one of the axes.

Normal and Tangent

The **tangent** to a circle is illustrated in Figure 8.29 (Drw. File: TANGENT), where the line is making contact at a single point. The line is merely touching but not intersecting the curve. Notice the line perpendicular to the tangent. It is defined as the **normal**.

Certain geometric construction dictate you to locate a point at the intersection of a curve or along a normal to a curve. The **CURVE NORMAL** option is used to define a point at the intersection of a curve and a line that passes through a point and is normal to the curve. In cases where the curve does not extend to the normal, the point is then drawn on an imaginary extension of the curve. Certain

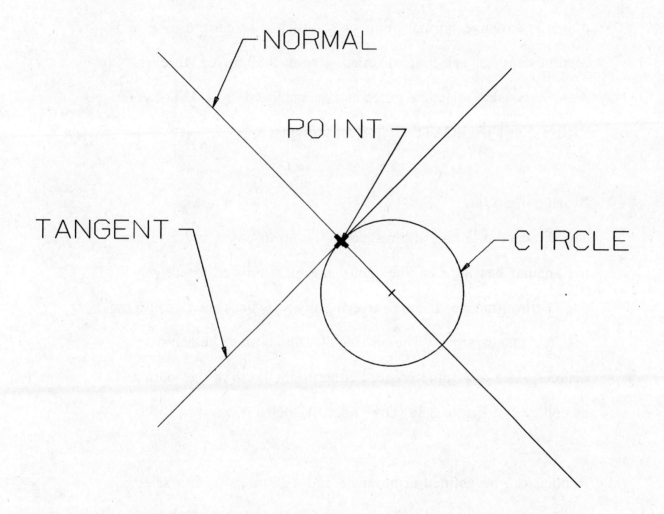

FILE: TANGENT

FIG. 8.29 A point marks the tangent to an arc; the line is merely touching but not intersecting the curve.

systems allow the user to either select a screen position or select an existing point and a curve to define a work plane curve normal point.

Very cultured software packages let you define a true three dimensional curve normal point by selecting a screen position and current depth or selecting an existing point and curve. In each of these cases the selection procedure is managed by [INDICATE POINT] or [INDICATE CURVE] prompts.

Bearing of a Line

The direction of a line with respect to the north/south axis is termed the **angular bearing** of a line. This concept is utilized extensively in engineering practice. In land surveying, property lines are establish by specifying the bearings. The bearing of a line is an angle less than 90 degrees, since you can referenced either to the north or the south axis as depicted in Figure 8.30 (Drw. File: BEARING).

A point can be defined at an angle and a distance from a selected existing point. After choosing the { BEARING/DISTANCE } submenu or command, indicate the reference point. Pick the major direction { NORTH } or { SOUTH }. Then enter any angle in degrees, minutes and seconds, provided it does not exceed 90 degrees. The angle is measured from an imaginary N-S line parallel to the Y-axis and passing through the existing point. The next steps consist of:

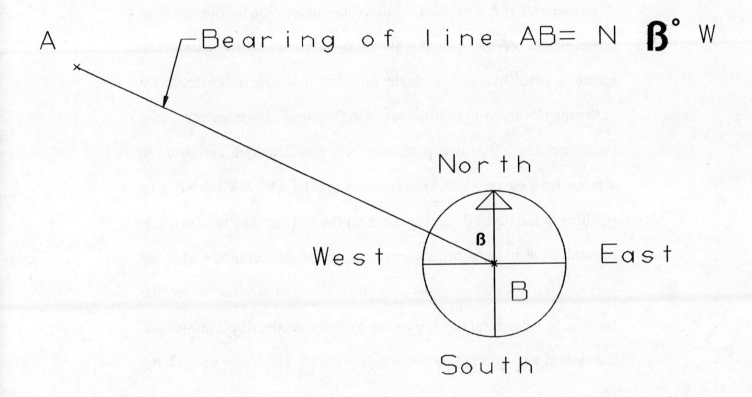

FIG. 8.30 A point can be defined at an angle and a distance by indicating the bearing/distance of the line with respect of a reference point.

key-in the distance from the reference point and the new point. And indicating the East/West direction. In other words, indicate whether the new point is to be to the right (east) or to the left (west) of the existing point.

Parametrically

A **parameter (t)** is a variable whose value determine an operation or characteristic of the system. By using parameters the system can locate a point by using a single number, t; which is the basis for generating 2- and 3-D coordinates. CAD system curves are measured parametrically. That is, a parameter will give a unique definition of a point on a curve. You may create a point { ON A CURVE } by pointing at the desired existing curve on the screen. The system might respond by displaying the parametric values of the start and end of the curve. One alternative that you have is to enter a value where the point is to be generated. If you opt to enter on the displayed values, the system will respond by creating a point at one of the ends of the curve.

Other Options

Points can be generated on a surface, using the following methods: normal to a surface, piercing point to a surface, curve-finite plane, curve surface, and specifying parameters. A point can be generated on a sphere, relative to the center of the sphere. Also, there are algorithms to create one or more points along a continuous curve, namely **fan points,** and to generate these entities by selecting the curve and typing increments along the curve. However, these methods are only available on larger systems like ICEM DDN, CATIA, etc.

Device Independent Points

The point creation process is many times dependent on the intrinsic characteristics of the computer system. However, it is possible to develop standard graphic packages that are device independent (i.e., a program may be used in different hardware). The **Graphical Kernel System (GKS)** is an international standard package that allows programs to be used independently of the hardware devices utilized. It is a "kernel" or core system of functions to provide device independence. Application programs developed in certain computer languages (e.g., BASIC, FORTRAN, C) may call GKS routines. In GKS, point primitives are generated as **polymarkers** types like: small dot (.), star (*), circle (o) and cross (x) or (+). Graph plots of data points can be generated by using these and other marker types as shown in Figure 8.31 (Display File: OUTPUT ENERGY). In addition to the type of marker displayed, color and scale **attributes** can be set. Attributes will govern the properties of the point graphical primitives. To draw a number of point markers defined by world coordinates, Fortran, Basic and C languages specify one array of X coordinates and one of Y coordinates. GKS function is: Polymarker (in:n, in:points).

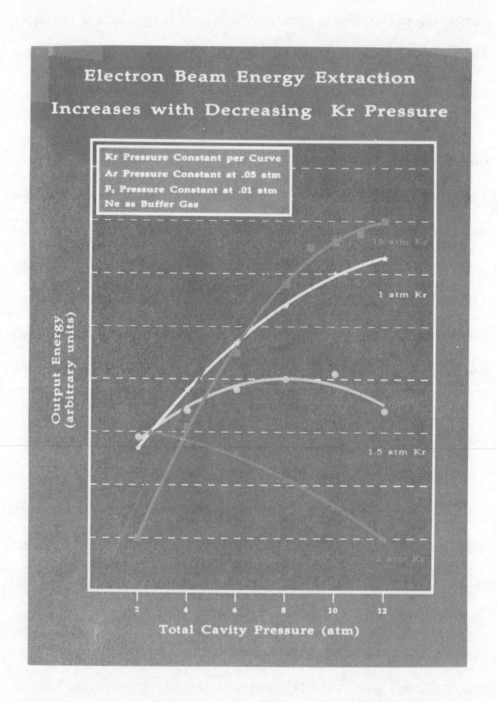

FIG. 8.31 In GKS, points are generated as polymarkers. Graph plots of data can be generate by using different markers. (Courtesy of Precision Visuals.)

Much more remains to be discuss in this area, but that is beyond the scope of this introductory presentation.

Graphing

From his or her research activities the engineer compiles information and gathers data. This data is usually represented in graphical form using rectilinear (see Figure 8.32), logarithmic, semialgorithmic, polar graphs as well as different types of charts. As an engineering student you will have to solve problems, present, document and support your solution by using graphs. The old paraphrased "engineering" saying "a graph worth 10^3 words" applies here. Graphs can be used to represent mathematical functions as well as empirical experimental data. The advantages of using graphs for equation visualization and empirical data representation are shown in Figure 8.33 and 8.34.

Two types of data plotting graphs will be discussed here: polar and semilog. The first type is based on the <u>polar</u> coordinate system which consists of two coordinates, namely the polar angle coordinate and the radius vector coordinate. Together they specify the position of any point in the plane. Polar coordinates are measured from a fixed reference axis called the <u>polar axis</u>. The <u>polar angle</u> is the angle formed by the polar axis and the radius vector as illustrated in Figure 8.35. Notice that the graph outline consists of concentric circles and radial vector lines with the origin (0,0) at the center.

331

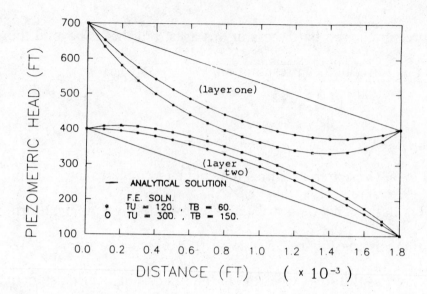

FIG. 8.32 Graph compares analytical and numerical results for a two layer confined aquifer system. (Courtesy of M.M. Aral)

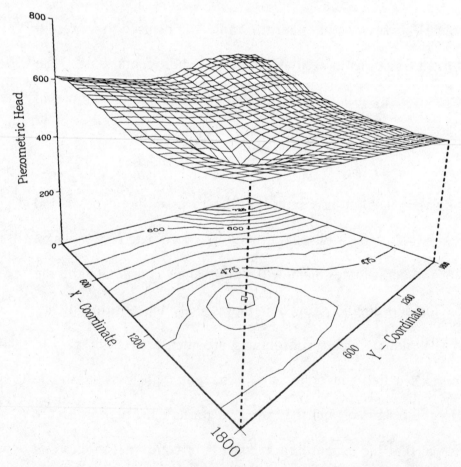

FIG. 8.33 Numerical results for an unconfined aquifer. (Courtesy of M.M. Aral)

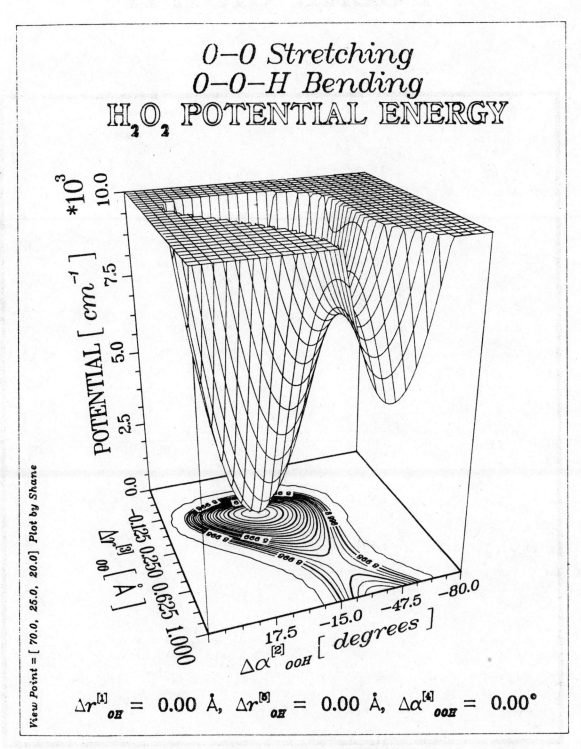

FIG. 8.34 Real potencial energy well graph. (Graph produced by student S. McWhorter based on research data provided by T. Uzer)

POLAR GRAPH

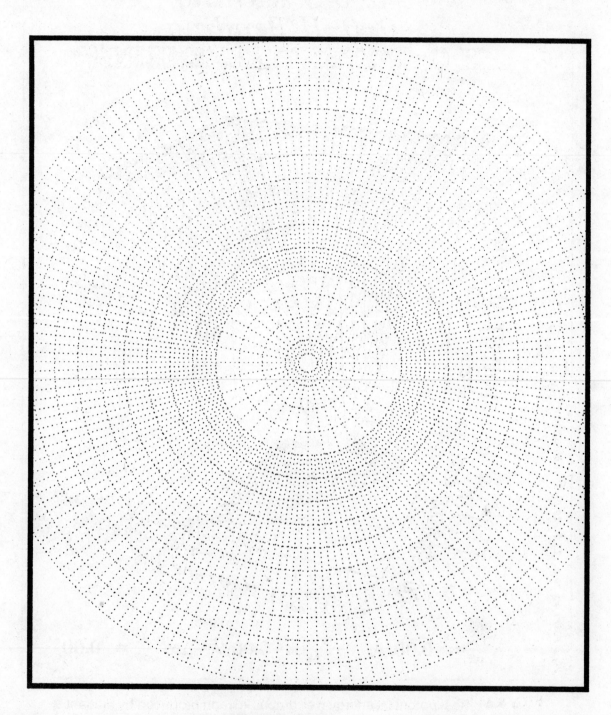

FIG. 8.35 Polar Graph

Logarithmic graphs will allow you to plot the equation $Y = a X^b$ as a straight line. Semilogarithmic graphs, as shown in Figure 8.36, have one axis with equal spacing and the other with logarithmic spacing. By looking at a semilogarithmic curve-slope you can tell the rate of increase or decrease for the data plotted.

Summary

Several geometric entities and coordinates definitions and concepts have been presented here. Including some of the most elementary geometric entity construction procedures. The user can assign names and attributes to each of the primitives generated by the system. The system prompts are the result of an algorithmic procedure. Display procedures direct the output device to generate specific entities at designated locations on the monitor. Several CADD packages were utilized to illustrate the creation of geometric entities and their geometric manipulation capabilities. It is necessary to become familiar with all the coordinate systems supported by CADD systems. Reason: coordinate systems provide the underlying foundation for CADD geometric construction and contribute to the understanding of more advanced graphics procedures.

It is difficult to overstate the importance of point generation in engineering. Reference points are constructed to guide the creation of

SEMILOG GRAPH

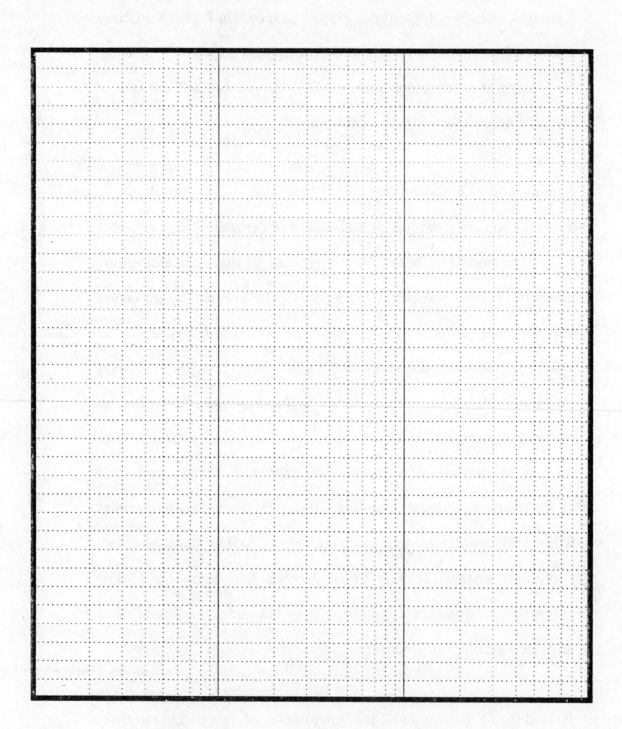

FIG. 8.36 Semilog Graph

complex engineering drawings. Initially, points can be used to set the limits of the drawings. Points can be used to trace the path of graphs and curves.

Grid dots provide a frame of reference and scale. The descriptive geometry definition of points have been presented here in conjunction with a series of techniques to create points. Several point construction examples were presented to illustrate the different methods and capabilities of CADD systems.

PROBLEMS

Using the computer graphics available plot the following graph.

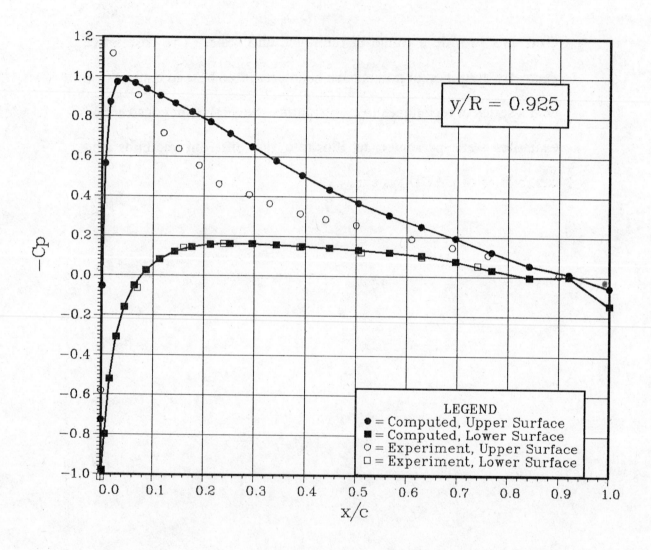

Pressure Distribution

(Graph courtesy of Georgia Tech)

POLAR GRAPH

θ	r
0	0.
30	11.
60	12.
90	0.
120	-22.
150	-42.
180	-50.
210	-42.
240	-22.
270	0.
300	13.
330	11.
360	0.

The data to the left is to be plotted in polar form. Polar form means "angle versus distance from the origin." The first column is angles in degrees, and the second column is the data as a function of angle about the origin. The data is plotted by pointing from the origin at the specified angle and marking a point along the line at that angle and at the distance specified by the second number. After all the points have been plotted, a smooth curve is drawn through them.

When a distance is negative, that means go backwards at that angle.

Determining the proper scale is important. Mark the outer boundry of the circle as just bigger than the biggest value of the data. The circles denoting distance from the origin should be well marked. The angles around the circle should also be well marked from 0 to 360.

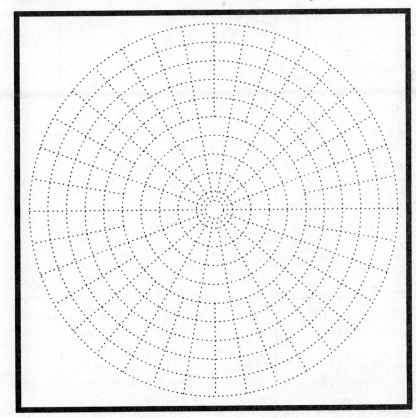

339

SEMILOG GRAPH

The data on the left is to be plotted on a
semilog graph. A semilog graph has equally-spaced
marks on one axis, and log-spaced marks on the
other axis. Semilog graphs are usually associated
with frequency measurement, as the human ear
reponds logarithmically to pitch. In our case,
the left column should be plotted on the log axis.

10	1
1010	23
2010	43
3010	63
4010	83
5010	103
6010	123
7010	143
8010	164
9010	184
10010	204

Each dark line is a factor of ten, and each
line in-between counts up to the next dark line by
multiples of the value of the previous dark line.
In our case, the first dark line would be 10, the
next 100, the next 1000, etc. In log graphs, the
lower values are of more importance. Log graphs
are used when the higher values of data are
mathematically "boring."

The values of the grid lines should be well
marked, as the reader should be able to recover
your data from the graph. A smooth curve should
be fitted to the points graphed.

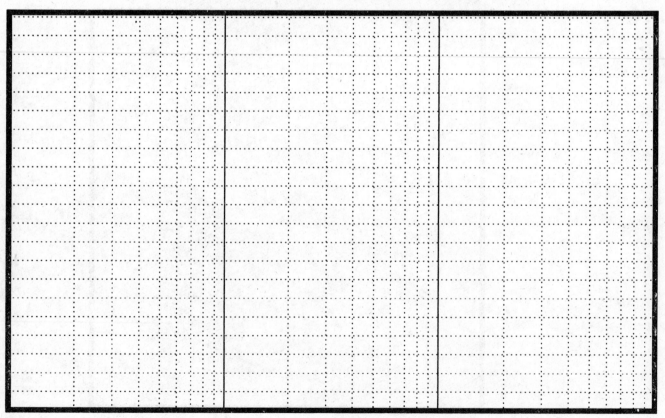

CHAPTER 9

MICROCOMPUTER-BASED CADD TUTORIAL

Introduction

In the preceding chapter we discussed geometric entities, several types of graphical coordinate systems and generic ways to establish reference points. The purpose of this chapter is to learn the basic procedures required to perform geometric construction operations in the microcomputer-based CADD environment. The chapter contains a description of the functions and human-interface menus utilized by microcomputer CADD packages for the creation of lines, arcs, circles, curves and other entities. Included hereinafter are extended examples (or tutorials) for specific microcomputer and mainframe graphics-based systems.

Notation Conventions

The following conventions have been adopted in this chapter:

1. **ENTRY** refers to the instructions given by the textbook to enter data.

2. **COMMENT** refers to an explanation, reason or note for the entry.

341

3.   { } Two braces enclosing alphanumeric characters symbolizes the need to press the function key within the braces, for example:

ENTRY

Command: { **LINE** } { **ENTER** }

COMMENT

This instructs you to type the command "LINE", then press the "ENTER", "RETURN" or "NEXT" key to enter the command.

The braces could also indicate the selection of certain entity location, menu or function key to be press, as illustrated below:

ENTRY

{ **F1** }

COMMENT

This action instructs you to press the F1 key, to flip the screen.

Another case of the use of braces is to pick entities with a mouse or puck, for instance:

ENTRY

{ PICK entity 1-2 }

COMMENT

This action indicates you to move the crosshairs to "entity 1-2" and press the pointer, puck, mouse, hand cursor or stylus to capture the entity.

---

4. **CTRL** or caret symbol (^) means that you should hold down the control key while pressing another function key, for instance:

ENTRY

{ CTRL C } or **{ ^C }**

COMMENT

You need to hold down the control key while pressing the C key to, for example, cancel a command.

---

5. **SHIFT** means that the shift key is to be hold down while pressing the upper alphanumeric keyboard definitions, as illustrated below:

343

ENTRY

{ SHIFT @ }

COMMENT

You should hold down the shift key while pressing the "@" (at) sign.

6.   [ ] Square brackets are used here to enclose messages offered by the system, as shown below:

ENTRY

[Command:]

COMMENT

This is the command queue prompt, offered by the CAD system user interface, to request an specific instruction from you.

7.   < > Corner brackets means that the system is prompting you with a default value, as follows:

ENTRY

Text height: <0.25>

COMMENT

In this entry option you have two options: either to accept the "0.25" default value suggested by the system or enter any other desired "text height".

AUTOCAD EXTENDED EXAMPLE

Setting-up Layers

This section presents detailed description of some basic AutoCAD set-up commands and operations like: listing current layers, creating new layers, setting layer color number and linetype, making a layer current, turning layers on or off. Several illustrative examples of these operations are given.

AutoCAD's "**LAYER**" Command allows you to define and set different drawing layers. A <u>layer</u> is defined as a transparent overlay display. It perform a similar function as the plastic transparencies used in overhead projectors (i.e., you can overlay several transparencies in top of each other). The objective of defining layers is to be able to draw, display and plot some features of an object independent from other features. For example, you might have a building floor plan in one specific layer and the electrical plan in another separate layer; or say,

345

visible lines in one layer and dimension lines in another. In this way you could either display both of them or one at a time. It is convenient to specify the name and attributes (i.e., color and linetype) desired for each layer rather than specifying the attributes of each entity individually.

Getting Ready

Lets turn the computer on and create a sheet layout with several predefined layers, linetypes, colors, settings, units and line border. This layout could be used for the remaining drawing exercises. Figure 9.1 shows the plotted sheet layout in an American National Standard Size A (8.5" X 11") or International Standard A4 (210 mm X 297 mm) paper. It is assumed here that you are working on an IBM-PC or equivalent/compatible system with 640K and AutoCAD is installed in the hard-disk. Also it is assumed you have formatted a double sided/double density floppy disk (see Chapter 7). The following sequence of steps allows you to set-up a file drawing that you could use in the exercise section of this chapter.

Example 9.1 Logging-in and Executing the LAYER Command

To start turn power on or boot the system. You will see the following system prompt:

[C: >____]

346

FIG. 9.1 LAYOUT file plotted with a 6mm pen on A size paper on a HP 7475A Plotter.

This DOS prompt let you know that drive C is ready to accept instructions.

{ CD AUTOCAD } { ENTER }

This operation changes the hard-disk directory to your AutoCAD system directory, i.e., in this example we have assumed that your directory name is "AUTOCAD". The Disk Operating System will respond with another prompt.

[C: AUTOCAD > ___]

{ ACAD } { ENTER } { ENTER }

With this action you have entered the command to call AutoCAD (in some cases, you do not need to press the last "ENTER"). You will see AutoCAD main menu.

Wait for a few seconds until your system processes the operation. From the main menu select:

{ 1 } { ENTER }

At this point you have selected [Begin a NEW drawing] from the main menu. Insert a formatted disk on drive A and key-in the following, after the [Enter NAME drawing:] message:

{ A:LAYOUT } { ENTER }

* This operation creates a filename called "LAYOUT" in the floppy disk located in drive A. The file name could be eight characters long. If there is an existing file named "LAYOUT", the system will respond:

Warning! Drawing a:layout already exists. Do you want to replace it with the new drawing? <N>___].

If you answer { **Yes** }, the system will substitute the old file. If you answer { **No** }, enter a different name for this exercise, like: { **LAYOUT2** }.

Wait!

You have to wait until AutoCAD loads the ACAD.mnx menu file. The system set up a default layer 0, meaning that you will be able to draw with continuous solid lines.

* <u>NOTE ON HOW TO QUIT THIS EXERCISE</u>: If you want to interrupt this exercise, at any time, press { ^C } and type { END } at the command prompt. This will save your drawing under the file name given in step 5, and exit AutoCAD. If instead you want to quit without saving press { ^C } and type { QUIT } at the command prompt, then respond { Y } to the message [Do you really want to discard all changes to drawing?___].

At the command prompt type:

{ LAYER } { ENTER }

* You have entered the "LAYER" command to verify that the default layer 0, is set with continuous lines.

The LAYER Prompt

In response to the above exercise, AutoCAD user interface responds with one of the following prompts, depending on your software version:

Version 2.1

_____

[?/Set/New/ON/OFF/Color/Ltype/Freeze/Thaw:___]

_____

Version 2.5 and 2.6:

_____

[?/Make/Set/New/ON/OFF/Color/Ltype/Freeze/Thaw:___]

_____

Notice that each prompt line option is separated by a delimiter (/). The question mark "?" allows you to request a list of one or more layer names. Selecting the "Make" option will create a layer or make an existing layer current, so that you can draw new entities using the attributes in that layer. Similarly, the "Set" option also makes an existing layer current, but does not create new ones. The usual way of creating new layers is to redefine them by using the "New" option. A specific layer can be either "ON" or "OFF", meaning that the layer would be visible or invisible to the user, respectively. The "Color" and

"Ltype" options are used to specify the color number and linetype attributes associated with the layer. With the "LAYER" prompt "Freeze" it is possible to ignore the entities on specified layers from been displayed or plotted when regenerating the drawing. Since they have been frozen the system does not waste time calculating them. Finally, the prompt option "Thaw" reverses the freezing effect.

Example 9.2 Listing Current Layers

To obtain a list of the current layers, enter the { LAYER } command and press the question mark "?" as follows:

{ SHIFT ? } { ENTER }

AutoCAD responds with the following prompt:

[Layer name(s) for listing < * >:___]

Notice that the default value is an asterisk (*). This means: "list all the predefined layer names", in other words is a wild-card similar to the one used in DOS (see Chapter 7). Now accept the default offered by the system:

{ ENTER }

With this action you have requested a listing of all the layer names. AutoCAD displays the following layer and returns to the layer prompt:

```
Layer name State   Color Linetype
---------------- -------- --------------- ---------------
0        On        7 (white)   CONTINUOUS
```

Current Layer:0

[?/Make/Set/New/ON/OFF/Color/Ltype/Freeze/Thaw:__]

Example 9.3 Defining the Sheet Layout

In order to define our sheet layout (Drawing file a:layout) lets start by entering different drawing layers. We will create on layer for each of the types of drawing lines shown in Figure 9.2. The objective here is to associate certain layers with linetypes that would facilitate the tasks of generating drawing similar to those shown in Figure 9.3. In this way we can draw visible lines in one layer call "VISIBLE", hidden lines in a layer called "HIDDEN", the dimension lines in the "DIMENSION" layer and so on so forth. Lets start by typing:

{ NEW } { ENTER }

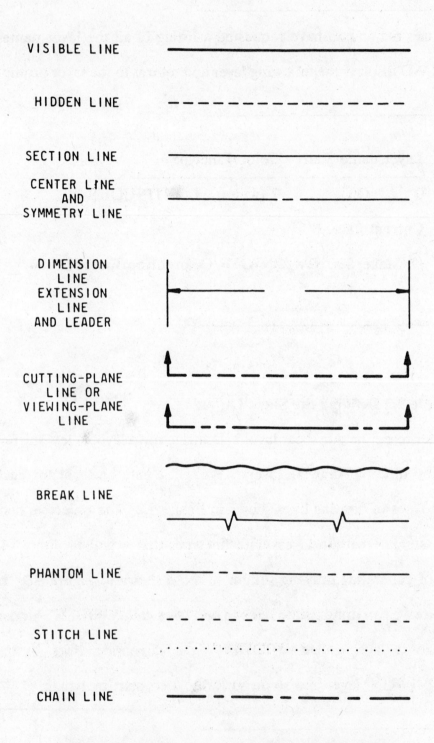

FIG. 9.2 Linetypes to be defined on separate layers.

354

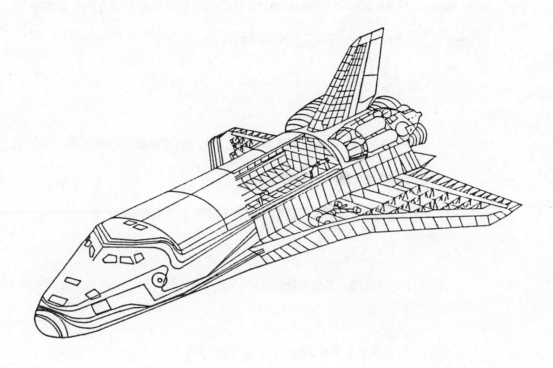

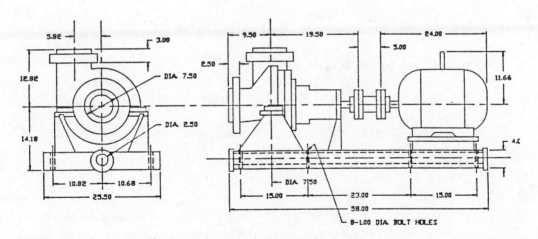

Motor/Pump Mechanical Assembly

FIG. 9.3 Drawings make use of AutoCAD's layers capabilities to allow plotting of linetypes independent of each other. (Courtesy of AutoDesk, Inc.)

As mentioned before, this commands AutoCAD to accept a series of new layers. Now lets create a layer for each of the linetypes given in Figure 9.2. At the prompt [New layer name(s):___] type:

{

VISIBLE,HIDDEN,SECTION,CENTER,DIMENSION,

CUTTING,BREAK,

PHANTOM,STITCH,CHAIN } { ENTER }

[

?/Make/Set/New/ON/OFF/Color/Ltype/Freeze/Thaw:

]

{ ? } { ENTER } { ENTER }

Notice that the screen displays a listing of all the layers you have created, all layers default to CONTINUOUS linetypes, WHITE color and have been turned ON. To change the default linetype for the layer named HIDDEN layer, the following dialogue is offered:

[?/Make/Set/New/ON/OFF/Color/Ltype/Freeze/Th

aw:___]

{ LTYPE } { ENTER }

[Linetype (or ?) <CONTINUOUS>:___]

356

{ HIDDEN } { ENTER }

[Layer name(s) for linetype HIDDEN <0>:___]

{ HIDDEN } { ENTER }

Notice that the word HIDDEN is used for both the layer name and the linetype. Now lets change linetype for center, phantom and stitch lines as follows:

[

?/Make/Set/New/ON/OFF/Color/Ltype/Freeze/Tha

w:___]

{ LTYPE } { ENTER }

[Linetype (or ?) <CONTINUOUS>:___]

{ CENTER } { ENTER }

[Layer name(s) for linetype CENTER <0>:___]

{ CENTER } { ENTER }

[

?/Make/Set/New/ON/OFF/Color/Ltype/Freeze/Tha

w:___]

{ LTYPE } { ENTER }

[Linetype (or ?) <CONTINUOUS>:___]

{ PHANTOM } { ENTER }

357

[Layer name(s) for linetype PHANTOM <0>:___]

{ PHANTOM } { ENTER }

[

?/Make/Set/New/ON/OFF/Color/Ltype/Freeze/Tha

w:___]

{ LTYPE } { ENTER }

[Linetype (or ?) <CONTINUOUS>:___]

{ DOT } { ENTER }

[Layer name(s) for linetype DOT <0>:___]

{ STITCH } { ENTER }

Now lets change the predefined white colors (Comment: It is suggested that you execute this step even if you don't have a color monitor.)

[

?/Make/Set/New/ON/OFF/Color/Ltype/Freeze/Tha

w:___]

{ COLOR } { ENTER }

[Color:___]

{ BLUE } { ENTER }

[Layer name(s) for color 5 (blue) <0>:___]

358

{ 0,HIDDEN,DIMENSION,STITCH } { ENTER }

[

?/Make/Set/New/ON/OFF/Color/Ltype/Freeze/Tha

w:___]

{ COLOR } { ENTER }

[Color:___]

{ RED } { ENTER }

[Layer name(s) for color 1 (red) <0>:___]

{ CENTER,BREAK,PHANTOM,SECTION } { ENTER

}

[

?/Make/Set/New/ON/OFF/Color/Ltype/Freeze/Tha

w:___]

In AutoCAD you can control the color of individual entities in one layer, by using the command "COLOR", however lets set the color to correspond to the layer's specified color.

{ ^C }

[Command:]

{ COLOR } { ENTER }

[New entity color <default>:]

{ BYLAYER } { ENTER }

{ LAYER }

[

?/Make/Set/New/ON/OFF/Color/Ltype/Freeze/Tha

w:___]

{ ? } { ENTER }

[Layer name(s) for listing < * >:] **{ ENTER }**

The following listing reflects all the changes performed in the last step:

Layer name	State	Color	Linetype
0	On	5 (blue)	CONTINUOUS
VISIBLE	On	7 (white)	CONTINUOUS
HIDDEN	On	5 (blue)	HIDDEN
SECTION	On	1 (red)	CONTINUOUS
CENTER	On	1 (red)	CENTER
DIMENSION	On	5 (blue)	CONTINUOUS
CUTTING	On	7 (white)	CONTINUOUS
BREAK	On	1 (red)	CONTINUOUS
PHANTOM	On	1 (red)	PHANTOM
STITCH	On	5 (blue)	DOT
CHAIN	On	7 (white)	CONTINUOUS

Current layer: 0

[?/Make/Set/New/ON/OFF/Color/Ltype/Freeze/Thaw:___]

Notice above that the current layer is 0. Lets make the <u>VISIBLE</u> layer, the current layer. As you remember, being current means that all entities created in such layer will have the same definitions of that layer, entities will be displayed on the screen with the same color, linetype and other attributes. We comment that even when all layers are presently on, you can only draw in the layer that is current.

{ SET or MAKE } { ENTER }

[New current layer <0>:___]

{ VISIBLE } { ENTER }

[

?/Make/Set/New/ON/OFF/Color/Ltype/Freeze/Thaw:___]

Before proceeding, save your work:

{ ^C } { SAVE }

[File name <a:layout>:___]

{ ENTER }

[Command:___]

{ F1 } { ENTER }

The purpose of that last operation was to flip the screen to the graphics editor display.

Setting UNITS and LIMITS Parameters

Before starting your line drawing it is convenient to specify the standard units and limits to be used. The units are controlled by the systems default values until you change them with the "UNITS" command. AutoCAD provide both linear and angular units capabilities are available for the standard measurement systems: Scientific (e.g., 1.46+02), Decimal (e.g., 16.70), Engineering (e.g., 2'-4.6"),. Architectural (e.g., 2'-4 1/2"). AutoCAD Version 2.6 added a fractional choice named: Fractional (e.g., 17 1/2).

The objective of the "LIMITS" command is to specify the drawing boundaries. In other words, you will designate the screen's display that will correspond with the plotted area of the sheet layout. This command affects the portion of the visible grid and the zooming-all operations (see "GRID" and "ZOOM" commands in Chapter 8). However, the "LIMITS" command does not modify the current drawing screen's display other than the area of grid covered on the screen.

Example 9.4 Setting UNITS and LIMITS

Now lets set the units and limits of our sheet layout drawing. This can

be accomplished by entering:

[Command:___]

{ UNITS } { ENTER }

[Systems of units:

    1. Scientific

    2. Decimal

    3. Engineering

    4. Architectural

    5. Fractional

Enter choice, 1 to 5 <2>:___]

{ ENTER }

[Number of digits to right of decimal point (0 to 8)

<4>:]

{ ENTER }

[Systems of angle measure:

    1. Decimal degrees

    2. Degrees/minutes/seconds

    3. Grads

    4. Radians

    5. Surveyor's units

{ ENTER }

[Number of fractional places for display of angles (0 to 8) <0>:___]

{ 2 } { ENTER }

[Direction for angle 0.00:

    East   3 o'clock = 0.00

    North 12 o'clock = 90.00

    West   9 o'clock = 180.00

    South 6 o'clock = 270.00

Enter direction for angle 0.00 <0.00>:___] { ENTER }

[Do you want angles measured clockwise? <N>___]

{ ENTER }

[Command:___] { LIMITS } { ENTER }

[ON/OFF/<Lower left corner> <0.0000,0.0000>:] { ENTER }

_____

With this action we accept the default coordinate values: x=0, y=0, as the lower left corner limits of our drawing, giving us some room at the bottom of our screen.

[Upper right corner <12.0000,9.0000>:] { **10.9,8.3** } { **ENTER** }

We have set our upper limit to x=10.9 in. (277 mm), y=8.3 in. (210 mm). This limits are within the boundaries of a standard A4 or A size papers (297 mm X 210 mm and 11.0" X 8.5", respectively).

{ **F1** }

This latter action allows us to flip back to the graphic editor. Save your drawing file { **SAVE** } or end the session { **END** }.

Geometric Construction Operations

The most common geometric operations are executed by issuing the "POINT", "LINE", "ARC", "CIRCLE", "DOUGHNUT" (or "DONUT"), "POLYGON", "ELLIPSE", "POLYGON", "TEXT" and "DTEXT" commands. Of course you can also select each of these operations from AutoCAD's tablet overlay shown in Figure 9.4 or from the "DRAW" user-interface menu. To select a menu option you have to either use the arrow cursor manipulation keys and the [INS] insert key or use a handcursor pointing device. Any of the functions and

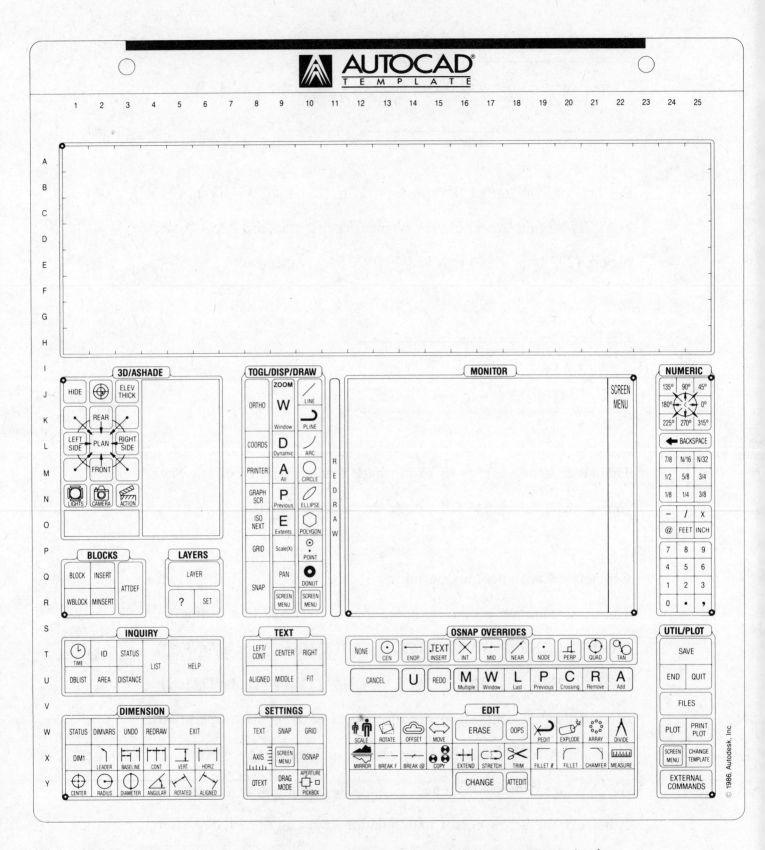

FIG. 9.4 AutoCAD template for version 2.6 (Courtesy of AutoDesk, Inc.)

commands listed in Figure 9.5 can be executed in several ways. For example, by selecting the "POINT" function or entering the [POINT] command, the system displays a point-entity based on coordinate input (x,y), as discussed in Chapter 8 (with AutoCAD version 2.6 you would be able to define 3-D points). Similarly, the "LINE" command allows you to draw straight lines between two plane "points". AutoCAD refer to these locations as "points", however it should be clear that they are actually coordinate positions (x,y) or (x,y,z).

Example 9.5 Generating the Layout Border Lines
We are finally ready to start drawing our sheet layout border.

[Command:] { **LINE** } { **ENTER** }

[From point:] { **0.6,0.6** } { **ENTER** }

[To point:] { **9.6,0.6** } { **ENTER** }

Please continue entering the other coordinate points of the lines.

[To point:] { **9.6,7.2** } { **ENTER** }

[To point:] { **0.6,7.2** } { **ENTER** }

[To point:] { **0.6,0.6** } { **ENTER** }

367

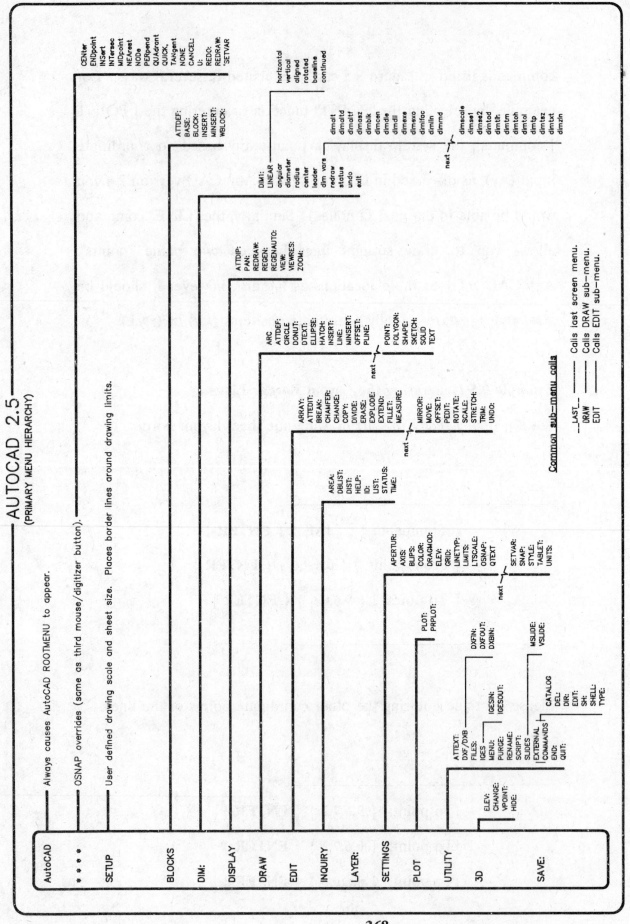

FIG. 9.5 AutoCAD's primary menu hierarchy. Submenus are associated with each of the items in the main root menu.

368

Assuming that you could only see the lower left corner, you would have to perform the following step:

[To point:] { ^C }

[Command:] { ZOOM } { ENTER }

[

All/Center/Dynamic/Extends/Left/Previous/Window/<Scal

e(X)>:]

{ E }

{ SAVE]

With this final operation we finish our drawing file "LAYOUT".

AutoCAD Commands

The following pages contain an alphabetical listing of AutoCAD's geometric construction commands and manipulation functions provided as a courtesy of AUTODESK, INC.

Refer to the following brief description of AutoCAD's commands and functions:

AUTOCAD COMMANDS

APERTURE	Controls the size of the object snap target box
ARC	Draws an arc of any size
AREA	Finds a polygon's area and perimeter
ARRAY	Makes multiple copies of selected objects in a rectangular or circular pattern
ATTDEF	Creates an Attribute Definition entity for textual information to be associated with a Block Definition
ATTDISP	Controls the visibility of Attribute entities on a global basis
ATTEDIT	Permits editing of Attributes
ATTEXT	Extracts Attribute data from a drawing
AXIS	Displays a "ruler line" on the graphics monitor
BASE	Specifies origin for subsequent insertion into another drawing
BLIPMODE	Controls display of marker blips for point selection
BLOCK	Forms a compound object from a group of entities
BREAK	Erases part of an object, or splits it into two objects
CHAMFER	Creates a chamfer at the intersection of two lines
CHANGE	Alters the location, size, or orientation of selected objects. Especially useful for Text entities
CIRCLE	Draws a circle of any size
COLOR	Establishes the color for subsequently drawn objects
COPY	Draws a copy of selected objects
DBLIST	Lists database information for every entity in the drawing
DELAY	Delays execution of the next command for a specified time
DIM	Invokes dimensioning mode, permitting many dimension notations to be added to a drawing
DIM1	Allows one dimension notation to be added to a drawing, then returns to normal command mode

DIST	Finds the distance between two points
DIVIDE	Places markers along a selected object, dividing it into a specified number of equal parts
DOUGHNUT	Draws rings with specified inside and outside diameters
DONUT	Same as DOUGHNUT.
DRAGMODE	Allows control of the dynamic specification ("dragging") feature for all appropriate commands
DTEXT	Draws text items dynamically
DXBIN	Inserts specially-coded binary files into a drawing. Special-purpose command for programs such as CAD/camera
DXFIN	Loads a drawing interchange file
DXFOUT	Writes a drawing interchange file
ELEV	Sets elevation and extrusion thickness for subsequently-drawn entities. Used in 3D visualizations
ELLIPSE	Draws ellipses using any of several specifications
END	Exits the Drawing Editor after saving the updated drawing
ERASE	Erases entities from the drawing
EXPLODE	Shatters a Block or Polyline into its constituent parts
EXTEND	Lengthens a Line, Arc, or Polyline to meet another object
FILES	Performs disk file utility tasks
FILL	Controls whether Solids, Traces, and wide Polylines are automatically filled on the screen and the plot output
FILLET	Constructs a smooth arc of specified radius between two lines, arcs, or circles
GRAPHSCR	Flips to the graphics display on single-screen systems. Used in command scripts and menus
GRID	Displays a grid of dots, at desired spacing, on the screen
HATCH	Performs cross-hatching and pattern-filling
'HELP or '?	Displays a list of valid commands and data entry options or obtains help for a specific command
HIDE	Regenerates a 3D visualization with "hidden" lines removed
ID	Displays the coordinates of a specified point
IGESIN	Loads an IGES interchange file

IGESOUT	Writes an IGES interchange file
INSERT	Inserts a copy of a previously drawn part (object) into the current drawing
ISOPLANE	Selects the plane of an isometric grid to be the "current" plane for orthogonal drawing
LAYER	Creates named drawing layers and assigns color and linetype properties to those layers
LIMITS	Changes the drawing boundaries and controls checking of those boundaries
LINE	Draws straight lines of any length
LINETYPE	Defines linetypes (sequences of alternating line segments and spaces), loads them from libraries, and sets the linetype for subsequently drawn objects
LIST	Lists database information for selected objects
LOAD	Loads a file of user-defined Shapes to be used with the SHAPE command
LTSCALE	Specifies a scaling factor to be applied to all linetypes within the drawing
MEASURE	Places markers at specified intervals along a selected object
MENU	Loads a file of Drawing Editor commands into the menu areas (screen, tablet, and button)
MINSERT	Inserts multiple copies of a Block in a rectangular pattern
MIRROR	Reflects designated entities about a user-specified axis
MOVE	Moves designated entities to another location
MSLIDE	Makes a slide file from the current display
OFFSET	Allows the creation of offset curves and parallel lines
OOPS	Restores erased entities
ORTHO	Constrains LINE drawing so that only lines aligned with the current grid can be entered
OSNAP	Enables points to be precisely located on reference points of existing objects
PAN	Moves the display window
PEDIT	Permits editing of polylines
PLINE	Draws connected line and arc segments, with optional width and taper

PLOT	Plots a drawing on a pen plotter
POINT	Draws single points
POLYGON	Draws regular polygons with the specified number of side
PRPLOT	Plots a drawing on a printer plotter
PURGE	Removes unused Blocks, text styles, layers, or linetypes from the drawing
QTEXT	Enables Text entities to be identified without drawing the text detail
QUIT	Exits the Drawing Editor and returns to AutoCAD's Main Menu, discarding any changes to the drawing
REDO	Reverses the previous command if it was U or UNDO
REDRAW	Refreshes or cleans up the display
REGEN	Regenerates the entire drawing
REGENAUTO	Allows control of automatic drawing regeneration performed by other commands
RENAME	Changes the names associated with text styles, named views, layers, linetypes, and Blocks
RESUME	Resumes an interrupted command script
ROTATE	Rotates existing objects
RSCRIPT	Restarts a command script from the beginning
SAVE	Updates the current drawing file without exiting the Drawing Editor
SCALE	Alters the size of existing objects
SCRIPT	Executes a command script
SELECT	Groups objects into a selection-set for use in subsequent commands
SETVAR	Allows you to display or change the value of system variables
SH	On MS-DOS/PC-DOS systems, allows access to internal DOS commands
SHAPE	Draws pre-defined shapes
SHELL	Allows access to other programs while running AutoCAD
SKETCH	Permits free-hand sketching
SNAP	Specifies a "round-off" interval for digitizer point entry so entities can be placed at precise locations easily

SOLID	Draws filled-in polygons
STATUS	Displays statistics about the current drawing
STRETCH	Allows you to move a portion of a drawing while retaining connections to other parts of the drawing
STYLE	Creates named text styles, with user-selected combinations of font, mirroring, obliquing, and horizontal scaling
TABLET	Aligns the digitizing tablet with coordinates of a paper drawing to accurately copy it with AutoCAD
TEXT	Draws text characters of any size, with selected styles
TEXTSCR	Flips to the text display on single-screen systems. Used in command scripts and menus
TIME	Displays drawing creation and update times, and permits control of an elapsed timer
TRACE	Draws solid lines of specified width
TRIM	Erases the portions of selected entities that cross a specified boundary
U	Reverses the effect of the previous command
UNDO	Reverses the effect of multiple commands, and provides control over the "undo" facility
UNITS	Selects coordinate and angle display formats and precision
VIEW	Saves the current graphics display as a Named View, or restores a saved view to the display
VIEWRES	Allows you to control the precision and speed of Circle and Arc drawing on the monitor by specifying the number of sides in a Circle
VPOINT	Selects the viewpoint for a 3D visualization
VSLIDE	Displays a previously-created slide file
WBLOCK	Writes selected entities to a disk file
ZOOM	Enlarges or reduces the display of the drawing

In addition , the AutoCAD user

can perform certain immediate operations

by pressing the following

keys:

1. { CTRL C } cancels an operation

2. { CTRL B } toggles the [SNAP] mode on or off

3. { CTRL O } toggles the [ORTHO] mode on of off

4. { CTRL G } toggles the [GRID] on or off

5. { CTRL D } toggles the coordinate display

6. { CTRL E } toggles the "ISOPLANE' left, top or right

7. { CTRL T } toggles the tablet mode on or off.

AUTOCAD EXTENDED EXAMPLE II:

CREATING AN ISOMETRIC VIEW DRAWING

To start a file, turn on the computer and go to the directory that contains the AutoCAD system, say [CD AUTOCAD], and press the {RETURN} key. After the introductory message, press {RETURN} twice and the Main Menu will appear. From the Main Menu choose number "1" to Begin a NEW drawing by typing [1] at the prompt:

———————————————

     Enter Selection:>>

———————————————

followed by a {RETURN}. The following prompt will appear:

     Enter NAME of drawing:>>

type [BRACKET], and press {RETURN}. Now the drawing editor appears in the screen.

In this example the isometric drawing of an engineering bracket will be created. At starting, the top view will be created using an isometric grid. Then, a thickness for the element will be specified. The following steps will guide you to set a specific grid and specific increments at which the cursor will snap. Select the Settings submenu. Select the {SNAP} mode from this submenu. The prompt will ask for the snap spacing. Type [.5]. Select the snap mode again and choose {STYLE}; then the {ISOMETRIC} mode. Select the grid mode from the Settings submenu and turn it on. Press {RETURN} to get off the

376

Snap Setting command.

When developing isometric drawings in AutoCAD, it is needed to specify in which isoplane is the user working in. To do this go to the **{ISOPLANE}** Command. The prompt is as follows:

LEFT/TOP/RIGHT/<TOGGLE>:

Use the **{RETURN}** key to go to the default option that appears in square brackets. The system will toggle in to the next Isoplane clockwise. At the previous prompt you can also type the first letter of the corresponding face which is **[T]** for Top in this example.

Select the **{PLINE}** command by either typing the word at the Command prompt followed by the **{RETURN}** key or by selecting it from the DRAW menu with the mouse or digitiser. The PLINE Command stands for polyline; therefore the box will be define as one entity. This is necessary to later on redifine the thickness of the element. Now draw a box as shown in Figure 9.6 which dimensions are 4.5" X 2". Remember that grid spacing is .5". Now select the **{ELLIPSE}** submenu from the DRAW menu. When this prompt appears:

<Axis endpoint 1>/Center/Isocircle:

---

choose the **{ISOCIRCLE}** Command. This command is only available in isometric drawings with the snap mode on. The orientation and

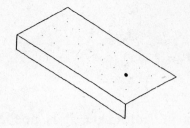

FIG. 9.6

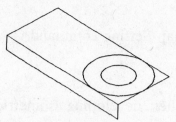

FIG. 9.7

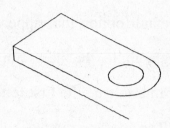

FIG. 9.8

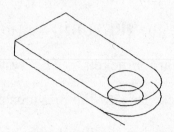

FIG. 9.9

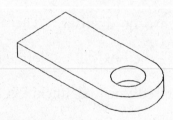

FIG. 9.10

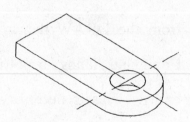

FIG. 9.11

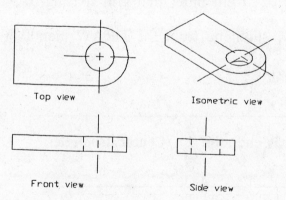

Top view

Isometric view

Front view

Side view

FIG. 9.12

axis dimensions are preset by the AutoCAD system. The next prompt is:

Center of Circle:

Select the point on the grid as shown in Figure 9.6:
At the following prompt:

< Circle radius >/Diameter:

---

enter the radius value, {1.0}, using the keyboard or select the midpoint of the top line of the box's right face.

Use the same procedure to draw a second ellipse inside this one of radius {.5}. At this point, the drawing should look like Figure 9.7. The next step is to erase the left half of the outside ellipse. The best way to do this is to "break" this half ellipse two to prevent from erasing the opposite half of the ellipse. Go to the BREAK submenu of the EDIT menu. The AutoCAD software breaks elements in a counterclockwise direction, therefore the beginning and end point of the element to be broken should be selected in that order. At the prompt:

Select object:

---

select the midpoint of the half of the ellipse that is to be erased, and press {RETURN}.

The next prompt is:

Enter second point (or F for first point):

Now, select the intersection of the ellipse with the front face of the drawing. This will erase that quarter of the ellipse. Follow the same procedure to erase the other quarter of the ellipse but be sure of selecting the element in a counterclockwise direction. If an unwanted segment of the circle remains in the screen it can be erase as well with the ERASE Command. Note that when you select an object to be altered AutoCAD turns it into segmented lines. This is to let the user know which element the system pick to be altered. Use the {BREAK} Command to erase those sections that are not needed on the top view. The user is able to toggle the Grid and Snap modes on or off with Functions 7 and 9 respectively to help in the selection of objects. The {ZOOM} Command in the DISPLAY menu might be very helpful for this step. To zoom your view call the {ZOOM} menu and type a new scale, [2], at the following prompt:

All/Center/Dynamic/Extents/Left/Previous/Window/ < Scale(X) > :

At this point your drawing should look like the Figure 9.8.

Now, go to the {3D} menu and select the {CHANGE} command. The following prompt appears:

Select objects:

Type **[WINDOW]**, press **{RETURN}**, and select two diagonally opposite corners of a box that includes all the elements of the drawing. At this point the prompt appears:

Properties/<Change Point>:

Type **[P]** for properties. Now the system will ask for the type of "Change" that you want to perform. Type **[THICKNESS]** and press **{RETURN}**. Now enter new thickness for the element. This will be **[.5]**. Press **{RETURN}** twice to accept the thickness value and to exit the [CHANGE] command. To be able to visualize the thickness of the bracket use the View Point Command. Type **[VPOINT]**. The following prompt appears:

Enter view point <0.000,0.000,1.000>:

Try the following location:

      0.000,-.500,.500 [RETURN].

At this point your drawing should look like Figure 9.9.

Enter the **{HIDE}** Command again to hide all those lines that are not needed in this view. The drawing should look like Figure 9.10 at this point.

Now you need to draw center lines to the Isometric view. To create center lines or other types of lines as well, it is necessary to change the active linetype. So far the linetype has been CONTINUOUS. Call the {LINETYPE} Command and at the prompt:

?/Create/Load/Set:

---

type "?" and press RETURN.

At this new prompt:

>File to list <ACAD>:

---

press {RETURN}.

The system will show the type of lines it has for each case loaded. Check that under the name [CENTER] is the center line needed. If so, type S for setting a linetype. At the prompt:

New entity linetype (or?)<BYLAYER>:

---

type [CENTER]. Create the center lines needed and change the linetype back to [CONTINUOUS]. Check that your drawing looks like Figure 9.11 at this point. From the Main Menu choose {SAVE} to keep all changes done so far.

CREATING THREE VIEWS FROM AN ISOMETRIC DRAWING

To create in AutoCAD the three standard views of an 3D isometric drawing the user needs to copy that file just created to a 2D file device independent. Therefore the first thing to do is to reconfigure your plotter setup. Go back to the Main Menu and choose selection {5} to [Configure the Plotter] again. The plotter configuration is [ADI] plotter. The output format is the [AutoCAD DXB] file option. You may accept all the default values listed except for the one at the following prompt:

Plotter steps per drawing unit &LT1000>:

At this prompt type "2900" to have more accuracy in the isometric drawing copy. After you set the new configuration answer yes to keep all changes. Your file AutoCAD DXB format can be read now as a 2D drawing where the user can make all the changes needed and add the three standard views of the drawing. Return to the file "BRACKET" and choose the {PLOTTER} {PLOT} Command as if you were plotting a hard copy. At the following prompt:

Enter Filename for Plot <\acad\bracket>:

---

to send the drawing to a file on disk instead of plotting it. Accept the default filename and the extension DXB will be given automatically.

383

Open a new file called Brack2D. Select the {Dxf/dxb} submenu from the {UTILITY} menu and then the Dxbin submenu. The current prompt will be:

_____

DXB file:

_____

type [Bracket]. At this point the system will look for the DXB file and copy the image as a 2D model. The drawing will be copied in the lower left hand corner of your working space. To follow the engineering conventions lets move the isometric drawing to the top right corner of the drawing limits. Call the {MOVE} Command and at the prompt:

_____

Select object:

_____

type [WINDOW], then select two diagonally opposite corners of the drawing. At this point the following prompt appears:

_____

<Base point or displacement>/Multiple:

_____

Select the left lower corner of the bracket. At this prompt:

_____

Second point of displacement:

_____

select the point in the top right corner where you want the base point to be moved to. This drawing is 2D, therefore, when configuring the snap and grid modes the setting is Standard instead of Isometric.

At this point the user may go back to the original file, i.e. BRACKET, to see the three standard view he or she is about to draw. The VIEWPOINT Command enables the user to see the drawing from different locations. The type of drawing displayed by the system is called Wire Frame, and it helps the user visualize a three dimensional object. On the other hand, this Wire Frame Drawings would obscure some parts in the drawing depending on the user's point of view. Type **[VPOINT]** at the Command prompt of the "Bracket" file. The following prompt appears:

Enter view point < 0.000,0.000,1.000 >:

Try the following locations:

     0.866,-.500,0.000   FOR RIGHT VIEW

     -.866,-.500,0.000   FOR FRONT VIEW

     0.000,0.000,1.000   FOR TOP VIEW

Use the {HIDE} Command if you want to suppress the hidden lines of the drawing. In each of these view the user may print what is displayed to have a hard copy when creating those views in the "Brack2d" file. Now the user is be able to create the three standard views. Figure 9.12 is of great help to estimate the location of each one of the views. In case of difficulty look back at the notes on that specific step.

PLOTTING YOUR DRAWING

Go back to the Root Menu and save the drawing, typing the {SAVE} Command. Accept the default name. Select the {PLOT} Command and choose printer if that is the available device. At the prompt:

_____

What to plot - Display, Extents, Limits, View, or Window<D>:

_____

type [D] for Display. Accept all default values except for the drawing rotation and hidden lines removal. The drawing needs to be rotated 90 degrees clockwise to fit the regular 8.5" x 11" paper horizontally, and hidden lines should be removed when plotting. Your plot should look like Figure 9.12.

AUTOCAD EXTENDED EXAMPLE III
This exercise has been provided as a courtesy of AUTODESK, Inc.

1. First, let's setup a 1-unit coordinate grid an make it visible.
Command: **snap**.
Snap spacing or ON/OFF/Aspect/Rotate/Style <1.000>:1.0
Command: **grid**
Grid spacing (X) or ON/OFF/Snap/Aspect <0.000>:on
Note that the indication "snap" has been added
to the status line to remind you that snap mode
is on (see Fig. 9.13).

2. Now we will set the elevation and thickness
for the base plate of our mechanical part, and
draw the plate.
Command: **elev**
New current elevation <0.000>:0
New current thickness <0.000>:1

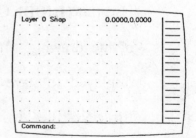

FIG. 9.13

386

```
Command:     pline
From point:   2,2
Current line-width is 0.0000
Arc/Close/Halfwidth/Length/Undo/Width/<Endpoint of line>:   @6<90
Arc/Close/Halfwidth/Length/Undo/Width/<Endpoint of line>:   @6,0
Arc/Close/Halfwidth/Length/Undo/Width/<Endpoint of line>:   8,2
Arc/Close/Halfwidth/Length/Undo/Width/<Endpoint of line>:   close
```

Note that we are viewing the drawing from above, looking straight down at it.

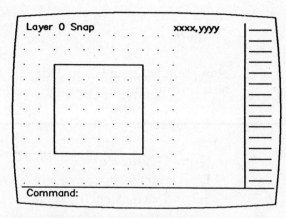

FIG. 9.14 (a)

3. Next we'll place a cylinder on top of the base plate.

```
Command:     elev
New current elevation <0.0000>:   1
New current thickness <1.0000>:   1

Command:     circle
3P/2P/TTR/<Center point>:   5,5
Diameter/<Radius>:   2
```

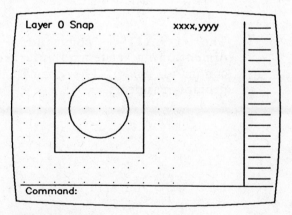

FIG. 9.14 (b)

4. Now let's draw some text, centering it below the rest of the drawing. The dialogue uses the name "Kelvin Throop" for the text, but you can substitute your own name if you like.

```
Command:     elev
New current elevation <1.0000>:   0
New current thickness <1.0000>:   0

Command:     text
Start point or Align/Center/Fit/Middle/Right/Style:   c
Center point:   5,1
Height <0.2000>:   .5
```

387

Rotation angle <0>:   *0*
Text: *Kelvin Throop*

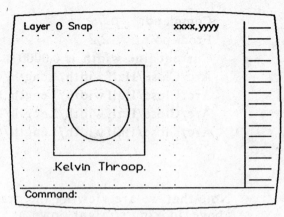

FIG. 9.15 (a)

5.   Now let's measure one side of the mechanical part and add the appropriate dimensioning notation to the drawing.

Command: *dim*

Dim: *vertical*
First extension line origin or RETURN to select: *8,8*
Second extension line origin: *8,2*
Dimension line location: *9,5*
Dimension text <6.0000>:   *(RETURN)*

Dim: *exit*

The "EXIT" command terminates dimensioning mode and returns to regular command mode. The normal "Command:" prompt reappears.

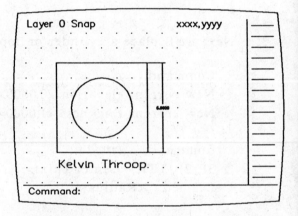

FIG. 9.15 (b)

6.   Next we'll add another cylinder to the drawing, on top of the first one and concentric with it.

Command: *elev*
New current elevation <0.0000>:   *2*
New current thickness <0.0000>:   *3*

Command: *circle*
3P/2P/TTR/<Center point>:   *5,5*
Diameter/<Radius>:   *1.0*

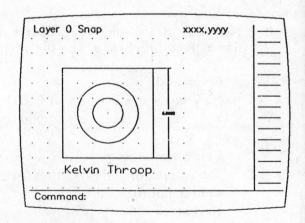

FIG. 9.15 (c)

7. Well, that cylinder has too small a radius. Let's erase it and draw another with a somewhat larger radius.

    Command: *erase*
    Select objects: *(Point to the smaller circle; see page 3)*
    1 selected, 1 found.
    Select objects: *(RETURN)*

    Command: *circle*
    3P/2P/TTR/<Center point>:   *5,5*
    Diameter/<Radius>:   *1.5*

That's more like what we had in mind.

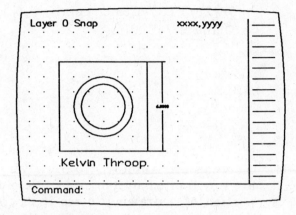

FIG. 9.16 (a)

8. Now let's turn the visible grid off and prepare to draw fillets at all four corners of the base plate. First we'll set the fillet radius to 1 drawing unit.

    Command: *(CONTROL G)* <Grid off>   *fillet*
    Polyline/Radius/<Select two objects>:   *radius*
    Enter fillet radius <0.0000>:   *1.0*

9. Okay, the fillet radius is set. Now let's draw the fillets.

    Command: *(RETURN)*
    FILLET Polyline/Radius/<Select two objects>:   *polyline*
    Select polyline: *(Point to any line of the square)*
    4 lines were filleted

Note that when we press just the RETURN key in response to the "Command:" prompt, AutoCAD repeats the previous command (in this case, FILLET).

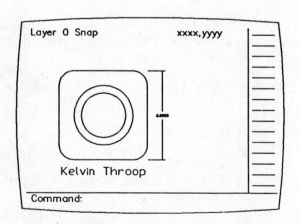

FIG. 9.16 (b)

10. Next we'll add a short circular post to the top of the inner cylinder and near its right edge.

     Command: *elev*
     New current elevation <2.0000>:   *5*
     New current thickness <3.0000>:   *.25*

     Command: *circle*
     3P/2P/TTR/<Center point>:   *6,5*
     Diameter/<Radius>:   *.25*

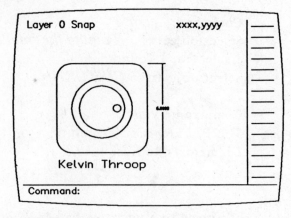

FIG. 9.17 (a)

11. You can use AutoCAD to draw very large, very complex drawings. Drawing size and detail are not limited by the size or resolution of your computer's screen -- you can magnify any portion of a drawing to see it in greater detail. Let's try "zooming in" on a portion of this drawing.

     Command: *zoom*
     All/Center/Dynamic/Extents/Left/Previous/Window/<Scale(X)>:   *w*

This requests a "window" form of zoom. Using the keyboard's arrow keys, move the crosshairs to the point labelled "P1" in the upper illustration shown to the right, and press the RETURN key to specify the lower left corner of the window.

     First corner: *(point P1)*

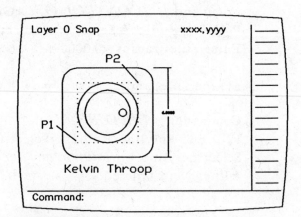

FIG. 9.17 (b)

A "box" now replaces the crosshairs. Use the arrow keys to position the upper right corner of this box at the point designated "P2" in the illustration, and press the RETURN key.

     Other corner: *(point P2)*

The lower illustration to the right shows the resulting display.

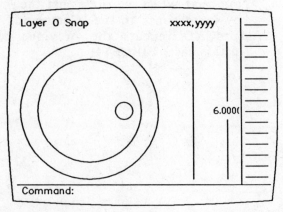

FIG. 9.17 (c)

12. Let's make six copies of the small post, forming a polar (circular) array. For the center point of the array, we'll use the center point of one of the surrounding cylinders.

> Command: *array*
> Select objects: *last*
> 1 found.
> Select objects: *(RETURN)*
> Rectangular or Polar array (R/P):   *P*
> Center point of array: *center*
> of   *(Point to either of the large circles as described below)*

Note that a box has been added to the crosshairs. Position it so one of the large circles passes through the box, but the small circular post does not, and press the RETURN key.

Now that we've defined the array's center point, we can specify how many items it is to contain and how many degrees it should span.

> Number of items: *6*
> Angle to fill (+=ccw, -=cw) <360>:   *(RETURN)*
> Rotate objects as they are copied? <Y>   *n*

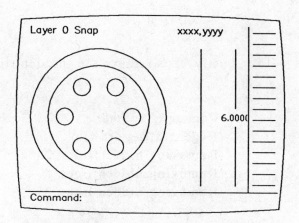

FIG. 9.18 (a)

13. Now we'll return from our magnified view to a full view of our drawing.

> Command: *zoom*
> All/Center/Dynamic/Extents/Left/Previous/Window/<Scale(X)>:   *all*

This "ZOOM All" shrinks the display back so the entire drawing is now on the screen.

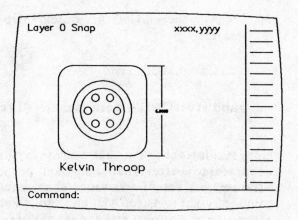

391

FIG. 9.18 (b)

14. Our mechanical part is now complete. Let's view a three-dimensional "wire-frame" representation of it from a point above it, in front, and to the right.

    Command: *vpoint*
    Enter view point <0.0000,0.0000,1.0000>:   *.5,-1,1*

Notice how the drawing reflects the various vertical positions (*elevations*) and heights (*thicknesses*) we specified as we drew the objects.

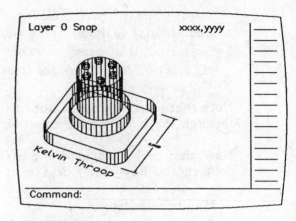

FIG. 9.19 (a)

15. Lastly, let's remove the "hidden" lines from the drawing. (This will take several seconds.)

    Command: *hide*
    Regenerating drawing.
    Removing hidden lines: 25
    Removing hidden lines: 50
    Removing hidden lines: 75

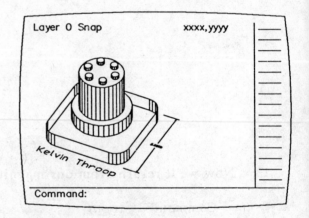

FIG. 9.19 (b)

16. That's the end of this quick introduction to AutoCAD. To save the drawing you have made, enter:

    Command: *end*

and AutoCAD's main menu will reappear.

Congratulations! You have made a three-dimensional model of a mechanical part, dimensionally accurate to better than one part per billion. You can view this part from any point in space, producing a set of drawings that would take weeks to do by hand. Along the way, you've seen some of what AutoCAD can do. Feel free to try this exercise again, changing some of the responses as you go, and see what difference your changes make.

CADKEY EXTENDED EXAMPLE

Introduction

This extended example or tutorial has been provided by the CADKEY division of Micro Control Systems, Inc. The example introduces you to the basic building blocks of this three-dimensional CADD system by providing a step by step procedure to generate the object shown in Figure 9.20. At the beginning, you might want to follow each task step by step in the order which they appear referring to the corresponding illustrations. However, fell free to experiment other approches as you gain experience on the system. Read each prompt and review the screen display as you move along. This will help you understand the geometric construction operation functions. You will be prompted to invoke certain <u>immediate mode</u> commands which allow you to quickly execute certain drawing function. In this task simply hold down the { ALT } or { CTRL } key and simultaneously press the assigned letter.

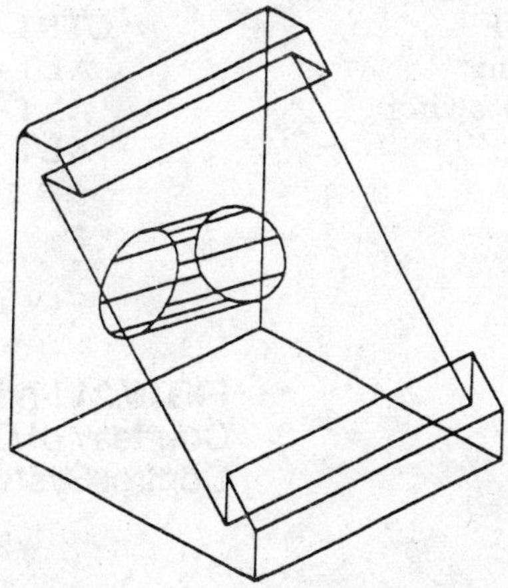

FIG. 9.20 Dovetail 3-D Drawing.
(Courtesy of CADKEY Div. of Micro
Control Systems, Inc.)

This tutorial introduces you to the basic building blocks of this three-dimensional design system. This "hands-on" session has been designed to take you through the construction of a three-dimensional part (as shown below), drawing layout, and dimensioning procedures. It is assumed that you have successfully booted up your system and configured for the correct hardware being used.

Of the tasks described, each one is broken down into a step-by-step format. It is to your advantage to review and understand the system's basic operations described on the next few pages, so that you may move productively through each operation.

<u>Interaction Hints</u>

Use the following guidelines to help you through this "hands-on" tutorial:

1. Follow each task step-by-step in the order which they appear, and refer to the corresponding diagrams on each page.

2. Take the time to read each prompt and review the screen display as you move along. This will help you understand what is going on in the function.

3. When invoking any Immediate Mode commands, remember to <u>hold down</u> the ALT or CTRL key and simultaneously press the assigned letter.

		RECALL last (undelete)	CTRL-U
		REDRAW	CTRL-R
ARROWS IN/OUT	CTRL-A	SCALE with center	ALT-S
AUTO scale	ALT-A	selection MASKING	ALT-M
BACK-1 window	ALT-B	set current COLOR	ALT-X
change DEPTH	CTRL-D	set current LINE TYPE	ALT-T
change VIEW	ALT-V	set current LINE WIDTH	ALT-Y
cursor SNAPPING on/off	CTRL-X	set current PEN #	ALT-Z
CURSOR TRACKING display	CTRL-T	set working LEVEL	CTRL-L
DELETE (single)	CTRL-Q	2D/3D switch	CTRL-W
FILE PART (save)	CTRL-F	VIEW/WORLD coordinates	CTRL-V
GRID ON/OFF	CTRL-G	WINDOW	ALT-W
LEVEL masking	ALT-N	WITNESS LINE	CTRL-B
LINE LIMITS switch	ALT-L	ZOOM-DOUBLE	ALT-D
PAN	ALT-P	ZOOM-HALF	ALT-H

FIG. 9.21 Immediate mode commands.
Courtesy of CADKEY Div. of Micro
Control Systems, Inc.)

At the DOS prompt, move to the \cadkey directory (if you are not there already) by typing:

cd\cadkey

and press RETURN. The \cadkey prompt is displayed. It is in this directory that you may boot up the CADKEY program. This is easily done by typing:

CADKEY

and pressing RETURN. Once the system is initialized you are prompted for a part file name:

Enter part file name ():

Type the file name **template**, and press RETURN. The main screen is now displayed with the Main Menu.

For convenience, we will store a copy of this "empty" part file and recall it later in the system when we need to create another new part. Press the Immediate Mode sequence CTRL-F (hold down the CTRL key and simultaneously press the letter F) to store the current display. You are prompted:

Enter part file name (template):

Accept the default filename in parenthesis (template) by pressing RETURN only. The empty part is automatically stored, and you are ready to begin the new part construction. (If the given file name exists in the part directory, you are prompted to replace the existing file with this new one. Choose YES and continue).

In this first introductory section of the tutorial, we will review the various methods of choosing or selecting options from the screen display. It is suggested that you follow only <u>one</u> type of input method. Then you can repeat these same steps using the other method given when completed. For example, if you have a tablet or mouse as your input device, follow the instructions on how to use these only and use the cursor button to indicate a position or selection.

There are six areas of the screen display which provide you with information relating to menu options, the current status of specific functions, cursor location, as well as where you are in the menu structure.

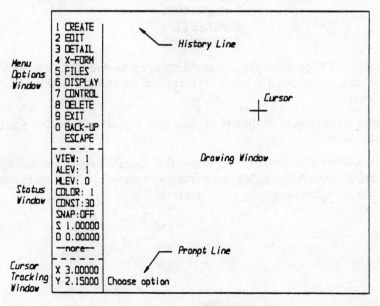

■ **The Cursor**

A cross-like symbol called the "cursor" (+) lies within the boundaries of the *Drawing Window* to make selecting and positioning entities easy and precise. When the keyboard is used as an input device, this cursor is found in the bottom, left corner of the screen.

The intersection point of the two lines that make up the "cross-hair" cursor is used as the selection and position area. The closest entity to this area, within the boundaries of the perimeter of the cursor, is the first to be considered for selection. Selection accuracy and speed are greatly increased when the cursor is placed directly upon a desired entity or position.

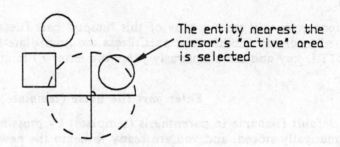

The entity nearest the cursor's "active" area is selected

■ **Selecting From Menus**

The *Menu Options Window* is located in the upper left corner of the screen. Various menus are displayed here each time a function is activated. Each option is numbered, with the numbers corresponding to the function keys located to the left of the keyboard. The Main Menu:

1 CREATE
2 EDIT
3 DETAIL
4 X-FORM
5 FILES
6 DISPLAY
7 CONTROL
8 DELETE
9 EXIT

The **BACK-UP** and **ESCAPE** options are always displayed as the last two options in this window. These allow you to cancel the present operation or return to the Main Menu, respectively, at any time.

The system's command structure is designed so that you are always asked <u>what</u> you want to do, then <u>how</u> you want to do it.

Menu options may be selected in one of two ways: the *function keys* are always available, and the *tablet or mouse select area* is available whenever you have a tablet or mouse installed. You can switch between them at any time, in any function.

The first step in creating the part is to display the X,Y, and Z axes of the screen to use as a visual aide. This is easily done using <u>one</u> of the two methods described next:

Using the function keys

allows the fastest access to the system's powerful functions without the need to move the cursor from the work area.

Locate the function keys (F1-F10). Remember that the F10 key will always return you to the previous menu (or back one step).

Choose the **CONTROL** option, F7, from the Main Menu displayed. Continue to choose the **TOGGLES** option, F3, from the next menu, and then **AXES**, F5. At this point, a new menu is displayed:

DISPLAY
DEFINE

Choose the **DISPLAY** option, F1, then **YES**, F2. The gnomon is displayed in the lower left corner of the screen. Notice that the axes match that of a top view.

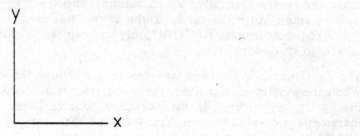

Using a tablet or mouse

allows you to select functions using the cursor.

Move the cursor control to the upper left side of the work area until a marker appears on the right side of a menu option. Choose the **CONTROL** option as follows:

CONTROL ◄

Press the cursor button assigned on your cursor control and the option is selected with the **CONTROL** menu displayed. Continue to select the following options from the menus displayed: **TOGGLES, AXES, DISPLAY, YES.** The gnomon is displayed in the lower left corner of the screen. Notice that the axes match that of a top view.

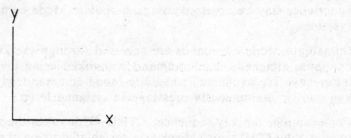

■ Locating Position With the Cursor

Throughout your interaction with the system, you are requested to indicate a position or select entities using the cursor. For this example, change the position of the gnomon just displayed by choosing the **DEFINE** option from the **AXES** menu You are prompted to select a new position for the axes origin. Use the cursor to indicate this position in one of two ways:

| *Using a tablet or mouse* |

move the cursor on the display by sliding the cursor control about the tablet or pad's active area to the upper, left area of the screen, and press the cursor button. At the next prompt, press RETURN only to keep the gnomon's size the same. The gnomon is moved to its new position.

| *Using a keyboard* |

the cursor may only be moved when you are requested to indicate a position. Locate the arrow keys to the right of the keyboard. With the Num Lock key toggled off, use the ↓↑ arrows to move the cursor vertically (top to bottom), and the ⇄ arrows to move the cursor horizontally (side to side). Move the cursor to the upper, left area of the screen and press the space bar. At the next prompt, press RETURN only to keep the gnomon's size the same. The gnomon is moved to its new position.

The Pg Up and Pg Dn keys may be used to change the increment in which the cursor moves. When the system is initialized, the cursor moves at a one-half inch (.5) increment. Each time the Pg Up key is pressed, this increment doubles. When the Pg Dn key is pressed, the current increment is divided by two. You will find these keys useful when positioning the cursor on desired parts of the drawing later on in this tutorial.

■ Interacting with the Status Window Options

The *Status Window* is found directly below the *Menu Options Window*.

The *Status Window* offers information about the current part displayed. You will find these options extremely useful for quick changes or alterations needed when constructing your part. As we move on in the tutorial, a few of these options will be activated using either a keyboard or tablet/mouse using one of the following methods.

| *Using the keyboard* |

Immediate Mode Commands via the Keyboard

Any option found in the *Status Window*, along with commonly used display and drawing functions, may be accessed using Immediate Mode commands from within any function of the system.

Immediate Mode commands are accessed through the keyboard only, even when there is a tablet or mouse attached. Each command is invoked using the CTRL or ALT key and an assigned letter key. To invoke an Immediate Mode command, you must hold down the ALT or CTRL key while simultaneously pressing the assigned letter.

For example, the key sequence, CTRL-G, invokes the **GRID** function. This automatically toggles the GRID which displays a series of dots on the screen for use as a visual aid. Each time this Immediate Mode command is invoked, the grid is toggled on and off. Turn the GRID back off.

If you wish to use a tablet or mouse, consider another convenient method for changing the options in the *Status Window* area, as described next.

| Using a tablet or mouse |

allows you to select and move through a circular stack of windows by choosing the --more-- option. To choose any of the displayed options, move the cursor into the *Status Window* area by sliding the cursor control to the left of the work space on the tablet or mouse. Slide the cursor control forward and backwards until a ◀ marker appears next to the --more-- parameter displayed in this area. Choose --more-- to review the next window.

Now, toggle the grid on by selecting the **GRID** parameter from this second window stack with the cursor button:

GRID:OFF◀

A series of dots appear on the screen for use as a visual aid. Each time the cursor button is pressed, the **GRID** is turned on and off. Turn the **GRID** back off.

■ Instructions and Information

The *Prompt Line* appears across the bottom of the screen. This provides information and instructions to aid you in choosing menu options, entering data, indicating positions, and selecting entities.

The system automatically assigns defaults to some of its functions. Defaults are values or menu options (e.g. YES or NO) which will be chosen if no new value or choice is entered. These defaults usually appear within parenthesis on the prompt line and may be selected by pressing RETURN only. For example when a dimension is created you are prompted:

Accept dimension (YES)?

Pressing RETURN only automatically accepts the YES in parenthesis.

When a position is requested, the prompt line displays two prompts; one for the function, and one for the position method chosen. For example;

Indicate start point   /cursor-indicate position

requests the start position of an entity using the cursor positioning method.

Once a position is designated, the next prompt or instruction appears.

■ Keeping Your Place in the Menu Structure

Across the top of the screen the *History Line* displays the options chosen as you move along in the menu structure. This is a very convenient way to keep your place in the command sequence, especially when you are momentarily interrupted in the course of your work. You will find that each option name, as it is selected, will appear on this line.

You will see the following menus frequently as you move through the tutorial. These menus allow great flexibility in part construction and are reviewed briefly here. As you move through the interactive part of this tutorial, you will be able to choose from each of these menus.

■ **The Selection Menu**

The Selection Menu offers different methods of identifying and operating on existing entities. Each is described:

SINGLE allows single entities to be specified using the cursor. The F10 key may be used to reject those entities selected before RETURN is pressed.

CHAIN allows you to select a series of connected lines and arcs by defining the start and end entities in the chain.

WINDOW allows you to select entities using a window (rubberbox). The cursor is used to specify two corners of this box.

GROUP allows you to select "grouped" entities.

PLANE allows you to select entities by defining a plane using orientation and depth.

ALL DSP allows you to select all entities displayed on the screen, only those specified, or excluding all those specified.

Depending on your CONFIG assignment, a selection marker △ may or may not remain on the screen when an entity is selected. For easy identification, these markers are used in this tutorial, even though they may or may not appear on your display.

■ **The Position Menu**

A standard Position Menu allows you to indicate the position (or location) of an entity in 3D space. You will review this menu throughout the tutorial, since it is an integral part of the system.

An asterisk (*) always appears next to the active position method (the **CURSOR** option is the default). It is not necessary to select from this menu more than once within a function unless you wish to change the method of positioning.

Whenever this menu appears, two prompts appear on the prompt line, divided by a slash (/). The first prompt requests information on the current function, while the second prompt requests positioning information.

Here are the nine position methods available:

1 **CURSOR**
2 **POINT**
3 **ENDENT** (endpoint of entity)
4 **CENTER**
5 **INTRSC** (intersection)
6 **ALONGL** (along a line)
7 **POLAR**
8 **DELTA**
9 **KEYIN**

COORDINATE SYSTEMS

Two types of coordinate systems are available: World and View.

■ View Coordinates

We will begin the part construction in view coordinates.

There are eight defined views (as listed) provided by the system, along with an <u>unlimited</u> amount of user-defined views. View coordinates are relative to the screen; the X axis is horizontal, the Y axis is vertical, and the Z axis points towards you. Each of the eight views are assigned numbers for easy access:

> 1 TOP
> 2 FRONT
> 3 BACK
> 4 BOTTOM
> 5 RIGHT
> 6 LEFT
> 7 ISOMETRIC
> 8 AXONOMETRIC

The TOP view is the first view assigned when the system is initialized. Be sure that the COORDS: parameter in the second stack (select the --more-- parameter to roll through each stack) of the Status Window is set to View (VW). If not, use the Immediate Mode sequence CTRL-V.

■ World Coordinates

World coordinates are the units in which geometric entities are stored. Think of this as a stationary coordinate system in which objects are defined when viewed from any position. In this system, world coordinates are relative to View 1, the top view, sometimes referred to as *Model Space*.

EXITING THE SYSTEM

(Note: Do not exit the system if you wish to continue with the tutorial at this time.)

To exit from the tutorial and return to DOS at any time, press ESCAPE and choose the EXIT option, F9, from the Main Menu.

If you wish to store the current part displayed, choose the YES option, F2, from the exit menu displayed. Enter a part file name (for example, DOVE), and press RETURN.

If you do not wish to store the current part displayed, choose NO to exit the system without storing the part.

DELETING UNWANTED ENTITIES

This function is useful only if you have created unwanted entities on the screen.

Single Entities:

Step 1:   Invoke the Immediate Mode function, CTRL-Q (hold down the CTRL key and simultaneously press the letter Q).

Step 2:   Move the cursor to each entity you wish to erase and press the space bar or cursor button. If you make a wrong selection, press F10, BACK-UP; this causes a # marker to appear on the cancelled selection.

Step 3:   Press RETURN to activate the deletion process of these entities.

Deleting Entity Groups

To delete more than single entities:

Step 1:   Return to the Main Menu (by pressing ESC).

Step 2:   Choose the **DELETE** option (F8).

Step 3:   Choose to **SELECT** entities (F1).

Step 4:   Choose an option from the new menu displayed:

SINGLE   allows you to indicate each entity for deletion (same as CTRL-Q). Press RETURN when the selection process is completed.

CHAIN   allows you to select a set of connected entities for deletion.

WINDOW   allows you to erase entities that are surrounded by a rubberbox. Use the space bar or cursor button to indicate each corner of the window. The entities desired for deletion must be completely surrounded by this rubberbox.

GROUP   allows you to select grouped entities for deletion.

PLANE   allows you define a definition plane.

ALL DSP   allows you to delete everything on the display screen as indicated.

Step 5:   When the deletion process is complete, activate a screen REDRAW (CTRL-R) to "clean up" the screen. The screen is refreshed with all temporary markers erased.

Press ESC to exit this function. If necessary, reconstruct desired entities and continue on.

Deleting Dimensions and Text

Select the dimension or text for deletion by placing the cursor at the bottom, left corner of the furthest, left line of text or dimension.

For example:

_xHELLO   _xR 1.30

402

TUTORIAL: DOVETAIL BRACKET

Task 1: Setting Up the Display

Objective: To assign the display a front view for creating the part.

Command Sequence: ALT-V (View)

When beginning a new part, it is advantageous to set up the screen display with the parameters and attributes needed for creation. The options displayed in the *Status Window* allow you to view the current status of some of these parameters and attributes. Changes may be made to any of those options listed using the cursor control of any tablet or mouse device attached, or by invoking the assigned Immediate Mode sequence.

Step 1:   Press the Immediate Mode sequence, ALT-V or move the cursor into the *Status Window* area and place the cursor symbol next to the **VIEW:** option. Press the space bar or cursor button.

Step 2:   You are prompted for a new view assignment. Enter the value 2 and press RETURN.

Step 3:   The view is changed to a front view (2). The *Status Window* displays the new view assignment :

VIEW: 2

The gnomon has also rotated to display the axes of the current view.

Note: (For those with color monitor setups only) Choose to change the current color assignment to blue by activating Immediate Mode command ALT-X or by placing the cursor next to the **COLOR:** option in the second stack of parameters in the *Status Window*. Activate the color command in one of the following ways:

a) Choose from the color bar by placeing the cursor on the desired color and press the cursor button or space bar.

b) Press RETURN and enter the corresponding numerical value of the desired color.

The current working color is now blue and the *Status Window* area will display the number assigned to blue:

COLOR: 8

Task 2: Create a rectangle (4 X 5 inches)

Objective: To create a rectangle by entering width and height values.

Command Sequence: F1 CREATE, F1 LINE, F7 RECTANG, F2 WID/HT, F9 KEY-IN

Step 1: Press ESCAPE to return to the Main Menu. Choose to **CREATE** (F1) from the Main Menu displayed.

Step 2: Choose to create a line rectangle by selecting the **LINE** (F1) and **RECTANG** (F7) functions.

Step 3: Choose the **WID/HT** (width/height) method (F2) to enter values for the rectangle size.

Step 4: You are prompted for the width value of the new rectangle. Enter the number 4 and press RETURN.

Step 5: You are prompted for the height value of the new rectangle. Enter the number 5 and press RETURN.

Step 6: Choose the **KEY-IN** method (F9) from the Position Menu displayed. This method allows you to determine a position for the new rectangle by keying-in the coordinate values of its lower left corner.

Step 7: Enter a zero (0) value for each coordinate by pressing RETURN at each prompt (the zero value is the default assigned by the system). This positions the bottom, left corner of the rectangle at the home position.

$$XV = 0$$
$$YV = 0$$
$$ZV = 0$$

Note that this positioning method causes only part of the rectangle to appear on the screen. Once we display the complete part within the drawing window, the 0,0,0 position is found at the bottom, left corner of the rectangle.

Step 8: To display the complete part within the *Drawing Window*, invoke an autoscale using the Immediate Mode command, ALT-A.

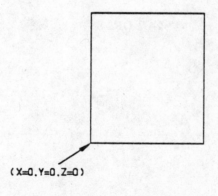

(X=0,Y=0,Z=0)

FIG. 9.22 (a) Home positions of the rectangle.

404

Task 3: Creating line entities

Objective: To create reference lines within the rectangle.

Command Sequence: F1 CREATE, F1 LINE, F1 ENDPTS, F3 ENDENT, F3 PAR/PRP, F2 AT DIST

Lines with Endpoints

Step 1:   Press ESCAPE to return to the Main Menu.

Step 2:   Choose to **CREATE** (F1) a **LINE** (F1) by specifying **ENDPTS** (endpoints, F1).

Step 3:   The Position Menu is displayed offering nine methods for indicating the start and end points of the new line. Choose the **ENDENT** method (F3) to locate the endpoints of existing lines. An asterisk (*) appears next to the selected menu option.

Step 4:   Move the cursor to a line endpoint near the upper left corner of the rectangle and press the space bar or cursor button. The endpoint of the selected line is designated as the start point of the new line. Note that when the cursor is moved, a rubberband line is attached until an endpoint is designated.

Step 5:   Move the cursor to a line endpoint near the lower right corner of the rectangle and press the space bar or cursor button. The endpoint of the selected line is designated as the end point of the new line. With a modal Position Menu, one positioning method can be selected for a variety of tasks; in this case, it was finding the endpoint of an entity.

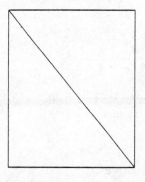

FIG. 9.22 (b) Creating line entity.

Note: If an unwanted entity is created by mistake, use the delete option described on page 7-43.

Parallel Lines

Step 1:   To create a line parallel to the diagonal line, return to the LINE menu using the **BACK-UP** option (F10).

Step 2:   Choose the **PAR/PRP** option (F3) to create parallel lines.

Step 3:   Choose **PARALLEL** (F1) for the line type, and the **AT DIST** option (F2) to position the new line a specified distance from the selected reference line.

Step 4:   Enter a distance value of .5 and press RETURN. When the parallel line is created, it is placed one-half inch (.5) from the line referenced.

Step 5: Move the cursor to line 1 and press the space bar or cursor button.

Step 6: Indicate a position for the new parallel line by moving the cursor to the right of the line referenced and pressing the space bar or cursor button. The new line is created, .5 inches from the reference line on the side selected. Note that it is the same length as the line referenced.

Step 7: Create another parallel line by selecting line 2 as the reference line, and positioning the new line to its left.

Step 8: Select line 3 as the third reference line and position the new line below it.

A total of three new lines are created, parallel to lines 1, 2 and 3.

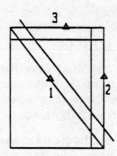

FIG. 9.22 (c) Parallel lines.

Step 9: Invoke the redraw command by holding down the CTRL key and pressing the letter R.

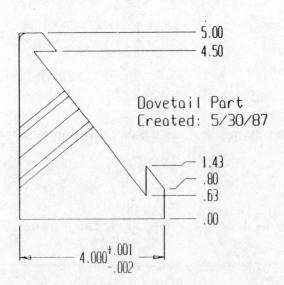

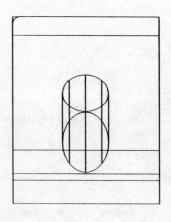

Task 4: Trimming lines

Objective: To trim assigned entities to form the base of the Dovetail bracket.

Command Sequence: F2 EDIT, F1 TRM/EXT, F2 BOTH, F4 DIVIDE, F5 MODAL

Trimming Both Lines

Step 1:   Return to the Main Menu using the ESCAPE key.

Step 2:   Choose to **EDIT** (F2), and **TRM/EXT** (trim/extend, F1) designated lines. The lines have been numbered for your reference.

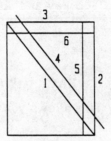

FIG. 9.23 (a) Trimming both lines.

Step 3:   Choose to trim **BOTH** (F2) lines selected.

Step 4:   When selecting lines for trimming, it is important to position the cursor near the desired trimming intersection. In the following diagrams, <u>select each line at the</u> △ <u>selection symbol</u>.

Move the cursor to line 1, indicating the first line for trimming and press the space bar or cursor button. Select line 5 in the same manner. (See diagram A)

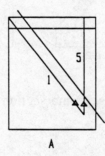

FIG. 9.23 (b) Moving the cursor to line 1 and 5.

Both lines are trimmed at their intersection point.

Step 5:   Trim lines 2 and 4 (diagram B), 3 and 4 (diagram C), 1 and 6 (diagram D) in the same manner.

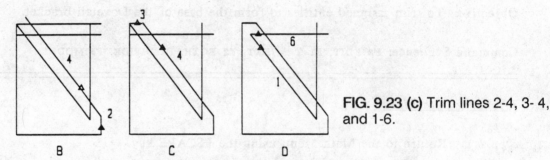

FIG. 9.23 (c) Trim lines 2-4, 3- 4, and 1-6.

Step 6:   To clear the screen of temporary markers, invoke the Immediate Mode command, CTRL-R by holding down the CTRL key and simultaneously pressing the letter R.

Modal Trimming

Step 1:   Return to the TRIM menu using the **BACK-UP** (F10) option.

Step 2:   Choose the **MODAL** option (F5). This allows you to continually trim selected entities to a reference entity.

Step 3:   Move the cursor to line 1, as shown in the figure below. Press the space bar or cursor button. This is the reference entity to which lines will be trimmed.

Step 4:   Select the two lines which intersect this line (lines 2 and 3) on the portion of the line to keep. Remember to press the space bar or cursor button to indicate each line.

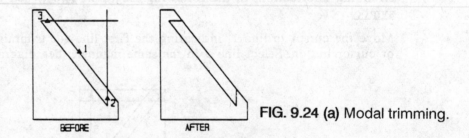

FIG. 9.24 (a) Modal trimming.

Step 5:   Lines 2 and 3 are trimmed to their intersection points with line 1.

Divide Trimming

Step 1:   Once again, return to the **TRM/EXT** Menu (press F10 twice).

Step 2:   Choose the **DIVIDE** option (F4). This function divides a selected line at its intersection points and removes the middle entity.

Step 3:   Move the cursor to the center of line 1, as shown in the next diagram, and press the space bar or cursor button.

Step 4:   Next, select the lines (2 and 3) which intersect this diagonal line by moving the cursor to each line and pressing the space bar or cursor button. Trimming is automatically completed.

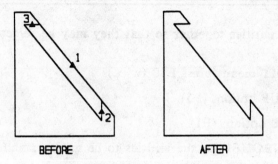

BEFORE   AFTER

FIG. 9.24 (b) Divide trimming.

Step 5:   Redraw the screen using CTRL-R.

Note: It is always good practice to store your part at different times during creation. Invoke the Immediate Mode command, CTRL-F, enter the filename DOVE, and press RETURN. The part is saved and you are returned to your place in the menu structure.

Task 5: Grouping Entities

Objective: To group the inner portion of the dovetail for easier manipulation.

Command Sequence: F2 EDIT, F5 GROUP, F1 MAKE, F6 ALL DSP, F1 ALL

Grouping allows you to link entities together so that they may be selected as a complete unit.

Step 1:   Return to the **EDIT** menu (press F10 twice).

Step 2:   Choose the **GROUP** option, (F5).

Step 3:   Choose the **MAKE** option, (F1).

Step 4:   Enter the name **GROUP1** for the entities to be grouped and press RETURN.

A subgroup is created for the selected entities and is assigned the number 1. There is a maximum of 256 subgroups which may be created for any one group.

Step 5:   Select the entities to group using the **ALL DSP** method (F6), from the Selection Menu displayed. This allows you to select all entities displayed.

Step 6:   Once again, choose **ALL** (F1) so that everything is selected.

The displayed entities are grouped and assigned the name **GROUP1**.

Step 7:   To check that you successfully grouped everything, return to the GROUP menu (F10 twice). Choose to **LIST** the groups created.

A list appears on the screen as follows:

Group Name	# of Subgroups
group1	1

Press RETURN and the part is redisplayed. From this point on, we may select any entity on the part and the complete part is selected.

Task 6: Making Changes to the Display

Objective: To change the display status and part.

Command Sequence: CTRL-R (REDRAW), ALT-V (VIEW), ALT-A (AUTO-SCALE), ALT-H (HALF-SCALE), CTRL-V (VW/WLD)

_____

Throughout the creation of a part, you may find it convenient to reorganize the screen display by clearing out temporary symbols, altering the part size, changing the view, reassigning a new coordinate system, adding levels, etc. Most of these changes may be made without leaving your place in the menu structure via Immediate Mode commands or the *Status Window*.

Step 1: Switch to a new view using the Immediate Mode command, ALT-V or move the cursor into the *Status Window* , place the cursor symbol next to the VIEW option, and press the space bar or cursor button. When prompted, assign view number 7, an isometric view, and press RETURN. Notice how the gnomon is also rotated to the new view.

Step 2: Invoke an Autoscale (ALT-A) to fit the completed part on the screen.

Step 3: Reduce the drawing size to one-half its size using the Immediate Mode command ALT-H.

Step 4: Change the coordinate system from view to world coordinates using the CTRL-V sequence. Choose the **WORLD** (F2) option.

With any of these new assignments, you are always returned to your place in the current menu structure.

411

Task 7: Creating the 3rd Dimension

Objective: To begin transformation of the part into 3D.

Command Sequence: F4 X-FORM, F1 TRANS-R, F3 JOIN, F4 GROUP, F2 BY NAME

Step 1: Press ESCAPE to return to the Main Menu.

Step 2: Transform the part using the **X-FORM** function (F4).

Step 3: Choose to transform the drawing relative to its current position, **TRANS-R** (F1), and **JOIN** (F3) the endpoints.

Step 4: Choose the **GROUP** method (F4) from the Selection Menu displayed to select the grouped part.

Choose to enter the group name (**BY NAME, F2**). Enter the group name:

group1

and press RETURN.

Step 5: When prompted for the number of copies, enter the number 1 and press RETURN.

Step 6: Position a copy of the part at the following location (remember you should be in world coordinates). Press RETURN after each number entered:

dx = 0   dy = -4   dz = 0

Use F10 to back-up if necessary. The part is transformed and joined right before your eyes!

BEFORE

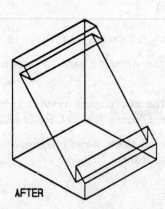

AFTER

Task 8: Adding 3D fillets

Objective: To create arc fillets between selected line and arc entities in the upper left corner of the bracket.

Command Sequence: F1 CREATE, F6 FILLET, F1 TRIM

A fillet allows you to connect potentially intersecting line and arc entities which lie in the same or parallel plane at the same depth. The fillet takes on the appearance of an arc.

Step 1:   To enlarge a corner of the part for easier manipulation, use the ZOOM-WINDOW option, Immediate Mode command, ALT-W. This allows you to create a rubberbox window to surround and enlarge a desired part of the entity.

You are prompted:

Indicate position for 1st window corner

Step 2:   Move the cursor near the upper left corner of the part (point 1), as shown below and press the space bar or cursor button. The F10 key allows you to back-up and reselect a new position if necessary.

Step 3:   With the box positioned, move the cursor upwards and to the right of the part's left corner until the rubberbox completely surrounds the desired corner (point 2). Press the space bar or cursor button.

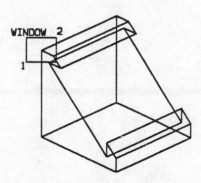

The upper left corner of the part is enlarged to the boundaries of the *Drawing Window*.

Step 4:   Return to the Main Menu (ESC).

Step 5:   Choose to **CREATE** (F1) a **FILLET** (F6).

Step 6:   Choose to **TRIM** (F1) the selected intersection of the new fillet.

Step 7:   Enter a radius value of .2 for the arc fillet and press RETURN.

Step 8:   Proceed to select the designated lines for filleting. Move the cursor to line 1 (as shown on the next page) and press the space bar or cursor button.

Choose line 2 in the same manner. A fillet is created for one corner of the box.

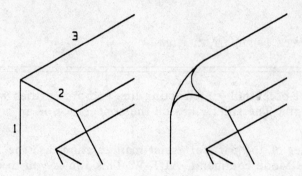

Step 9:   Select lines 2 and 3, and then 3 and 1 using the same procedures described in Step 8.

Step 10:   Return the part to its previous size using the Immediate Mode command ALT-B (BACK-1).

Task 9: Adding a reference entity

Objective: To create a point for use as a reference entity for depth.

Command Sequence: F1 CREATE, F4 POINT, F1 POSITN, F4 CENTER

Step 1:   Return to the Main Menu and invoke an autoscale on the part (ALT-A).

For color monitors only: To keep track of the point entity we are about to create, you may want to change its color. As you already know, there are a few ways to access options in the system, so choose one of these methods for assigning a new color:

1. Use the Immediate Mode command ALT-X.

2. Invoke the **COLOR** option from the *Status Window* area (for tablets and mice only).

For any of these options, cursor-select the color yellow from the color table and press the space bar or cursor button.

Step 2:   At the Main Menu choose to **CREATE** (F1) a **POINT** (F4) on the face of the block for a reference entity.

Step 3:   Position this point using the **POSITN** option (F1) at the **CENTER** (F4) of a selected line.

Step 4:   Move the cursor near to line 1 and press the space bar or cursor button. A point entity (+) is automatically created at the midpoint of this line. Use CTRL-R to redraw the screen.

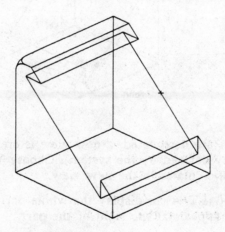

Task 10:   Defining a new view

Objective: To define a new view and add it to the system's view list for future use.

Command Sequence: F6 DISPLAY, F7 VIEW, F2 DEFINE, F1 3-PTS, F3 ENDENT

Although the system supplies us with 8 defined views already, it is sometimes necessary to view created parts in other perspectives.

Step 1:   Return to the Main Menu.

Step 2:   Choose to **DISPLAY** (F6) a new **VIEW** (F7) by defining (**DEFINE**, F2) three points (**3-PTS**, F1).

Step 3:   A new view is defined by indicating a series of three points. Choose the ENDENT method (F3) from the Position Menu to locate these three points.

Step 4:   Use the cursor to select the following endpoints (1, 2, 3) for the new view:

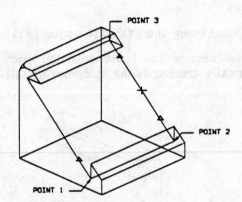

Step 5:   When all three points are designated, a new view is created and assigned view number 9 (since 1-8 are already defined by the system). Choose YES (F2) to change to the new view. The gnomon also rotates to the new view.

Step 6:   Invoke an autoscale (ALT-A) to display the whole part on the screen. Note that the reference point now appears at the right of the part.

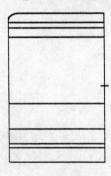

Check that the *Status Window* VIEW prompt assignment is the new view, number 9.

Task 11: Creating a new depth

Objective: To create a new depth using a POINT entity as a reference.

Command Sequence: CTRL-D (DEPTH), F2 POSITN, F2 POINT

The current working depth may be changed at any time within any function.

Step 1:   Invoke the working depth option from within the current function using the Immediate Mode command, CTRL-D.

Step 2:   Of two methods offered for locating this depth, choose the **POSITN** option (F2).

Step 3:   From the Position Menu displayed, choose the **POINT** method (F2). This locates a new position at a selected point entity.

Step 4:   Move the cursor to the point entity on the right side of the part and press the cursor button or the space bar.

Step 5:   The point entity is selected and its depth value is taken on as the current working depth (e.g. 3.123). Check the D option found in the *Status Window* area to view this new depth assignment.

D 3.12348

Task 12: A new circle

Objective: To create a new circle on the front part of the bracket at a new depth.

Command Sequence: CTRL-V (VIEW), CTRL-W (VW/WLD), F1 CREATE, F3 CIRCLE, F2 CTR+DIA, F8 DELTA, F2 POINT

Change the color to purple by activating ALT-X or from within the *Status Window*

Step 1:   Return the coordinate switch back to VIEW coordinates using the Immediate Mode command, CTRL-V and choosing the VIEW option. Set the construction switch to 2D using the Immediate Mode command, CTRL-W. The *Status Window* displays the new settings.

Step 2:   From the Main Menu, choose to **CREATE** a **CIRCLE** by designating its center and diameter (**CTR+DIA**).

Step 3:   Enter the diameter of 1.25 and press RETURN.

Step 4:   To place the circle on the dovetail, choose the **DELTA** (F8) method from the Position Menu displayed. This allows us to position the center of the circle at a delta distance from a designated reference point.

Step 5:   Notice that the Position Menu appears again, this time without the **DELTA** option. Choose the **POINT** method and select the point entity to the right of the part.

Step 6:   Enter in the delta distance from this reference point as follows:

$$dXV = -2 \quad dYV = .5 \quad dZV = 0$$

Press RETURN after each value is entered. The center of the circle is placed at this position and appears on the part with the assigned radius.

Step 7:   Return the part to the isometric view using the Immediate Mode command: ALT-V. Assign the number 7 and press RETURN. The circle appears on the face of the dovetail part.

Step 8:   Return to the Main Menu and choose to **DELETE** the point entity. Choose to **SELECT:ALL DSP** (all displayed):**BY TYPE**. Mask on **POINT** entities and press RETURN to exit the menu. Only the point entity is deleted.

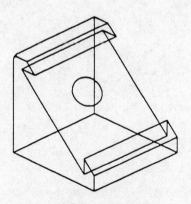

Task 13: Sectioning

Objective: To create a surface intersection using projected mapping techniques.

Command Sequence: F1 CREATE, F4 POINT, F3 SEGMENT - F4 X-FORM, F1 TRANS-R, F3 JOIN,
F6 ALL DSP, F1 BY TYPE, F1 POINT - F2 EDIT, F9 SECTION, F1 TRIM, F6 ALL DSP,
F1 ALL, F1 ENTITY - F1 CREATE, F9 SPLINE, F4 3D CLSD, F3 ENDENT

Sectioning allows you to trim, break, delete, change entities of a part.

Creating Reference Points

Step 1:   Return to the Main Menu and change the view to the new view created, view 9 (ALT-V).

Step 2:   Choose to **CREATE** a **POINT** on a **SEGMENT**, in this case our circle. These points will serve as reference entities and will be deleted later on in this task.

Step 3:   Enter 8 and press RETURN for the total number of point entities to create on the selected arc.

Step 4:   Choose **NO** from the NO/YES menu displayed to not group the points.

Step 5:   Select the circle just created. The points are automatically created on the selected circle.

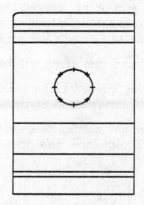

Transforming the Points

Step 1:   Return to the Main Menu. Set the construction switch back to 3D.

Step 2:   Choose to transform (**X-FORM**) the newly created point, relative (**TRANS-R**) to their current position.

Step 3:   Choose to **JOIN** these points with line entities.

Step 4:   Since it would be difficult to select only the point entities, let's take advantage of selection masking. Choose the **ALL DSP** method in the Selection Menu displayed. To select only desired entities, in this case points, choose the **BY TYPE** option.

Step 5:   Choose to mask on **POINT** entities only and press RETURN. Only the point entities are selected.

Step 6:   Enter 1 for the number of copies desired and press RETURN.

Step 7:   Enter the new coordinate position in which to move and join the point entities. Enter a value for each coordinate as follows:

$$dXV = 0 \quad dYV = 0 \quad dZV = -6$$

The points are transformed into the z axis (-6 inches) which is directed into the screen, and therefore not visible. To actually see the transformation, change the view back to a top view; view number 2, using ALT-V. Use ALT-A to display everything on the screen.

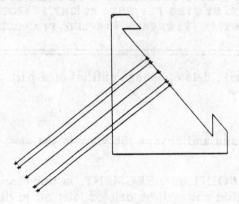

Sectioning the Join Lines

Step 1:   Return to the Main Menu and choose to EDIT the part displayed.

Step 2:   Choose to SECTION and TRIM an area on the part using a defined plane. Select the ALL DSP:ALL options so that all entities are included in the trim.

Step 3:   To define the plane of the sectioning, choose the ENTITY method. This allows you to select an intersecting entity as the definition plane on the part. In this example, choose the left most vertical line on the part as the plane entity.

All entities which pass through this plane will be trimmed.

Step 4:   Indicate the right side of the defined plane entity as the side which will remain. The other side is trimmed to the intersection of the defined plane.

Step 5:   The point entities are no longer needed so delete them using the DELETE:SELECT: ALL DSP:BY TYPE:POINT sequence, and press RETURN. The points are deleted.

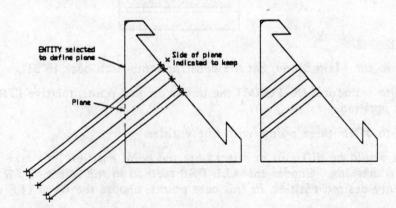

Creating the Spline

Step 1:   Change to view 7, an isometric view using the ALT-V sequence. Enlarge the circle area and its connecting lines on the part using the zoom-window, ALT-W. The enclosed area of the window is enlarged to the size of the screen.

For those with color setups, change the current color using ALT-X to green.

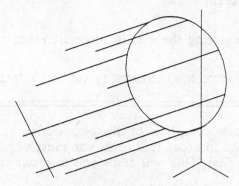

Step 2:   At the Main Menu choose to **CREATE** a **SPLINE** using the **3D CLSD** method. This creates a closed 3D parametric spline.

Step 3:   Indicate the first knot point (1) on the spline by chosing the **ENDENT** method from the Position Menu displayed. Continue to select the endpoint of each line to define the direction of the spline. In this example, the lines are picked in a counter-clockwise direction.

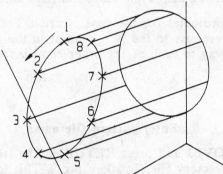

Note that the start point of the spline, or the first node selected only needs to be picked once, it does not need to be indicated as the endpoint also. Press RETURN when all the knot points are selected.

The spline is created in the direction of the selected endpoints. Change to view 9 to see how the new circle (or spline) lies directly behind the first circle created as if a hole has been drilled through the part. You may want to use the ZOOM-WINDOW for a closer look at the circles.

Step 4:   Change to view 5, and auto-scale to view the ellipse.

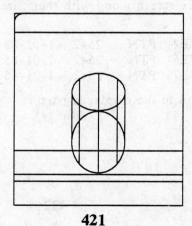

Task 14: Storing the Part in Different Views

Objective: To use pattern files for storing the part in three different views

Command Sequence: F5 FILES, F2 PATTERN, F1 CREATE, F6 ALL DSP, F1 ALL, F9 KEY IN, F5 LST/RTV

The dovetail part construction is now complete. In this next section you will create a drawing layout of the part in three different views. In order to do this you must store the displayed part in each of the three views desired as pattern files. This will allow you to recall each file into the layout part for full display.

Step 1: At the Main Menu choose the **FILES** function. This option allows you to select a method for filing displayed parts. As mentioned, we will store the displayed part as a pattern file so we may recall it into the layout. Choose F2, **PATTERN.**

Step 2: Change to view 2, a front view and choose to **CREATE** a pattern file.

Step 3: Choose to select everything displayed using the **ALL DSP** and **ALL** options.

Step 4: Choose to **KEY-IN** coordinates for the base position. Press RETURN only to enter a default value of 0 in response to the X = prompt in the lower right corner of the screen. Respond in the same way to each of the other coordinate prompts, i.e.:

$$X = 0 \quad Y = 0 \quad Z = 0$$

Step 5: You are prompted:

Enter pattern file name

Enter the file name **DOVE2** and press RETURN. The file is stored as a pattern file in the system's pattern directory file (\cadkey\ptn\). This identifies the pattern in the front view for future reference.

Step 6: Change the view of the current display to View 7 using the ALT-V sequence and autoscale (ALT-A). Repeat steps 2 through 5, only this time store the pattern as file name **DOVE7.**

Step 7: Change the view one more time to view 5 and create a pattern file named **DOVE5.**

At this point a total of three pattern files have been created. To check and make sure all three exist, choose the **LST/RTV** (list/retrieve) option, F3, from the pattern file menu. Press RETURN at the pattern file directory prompt (\cadkey\ptn\). Existing pattern files are displayed on the screen along with their size and date of creation:

DOVE2	PTN	2542	1-01-85	1:33 pm
DOVE5	PTN	2542	1-01-85	1:40 pm
DOVE7	PTN	2542	1-01-85	2:00 pm

Press RETURN to return to the displayed part.

CREATING A PART ASSEMBLY

You have just learned how easy it is to construct a part and patterns using the system. In this part of the session, you will display the part assembly in three different views within a drawing layout. This may sound like a laborious task, however, with the system's powerful design and drafting capabilities, it's a cinch!

A title block may be used when creating a drawing layout (displaying a part in different views) and may be thought of as a "frame" for your part. To retrieve a title block you must begin with a blank screen using the Escape Code sequence:

ESC, F5 FILES, F1 PART, F2 LOAD, F1 NO (do not store current part)

Enter the name of the file you created at the beginning of this tutorial named **Template**, and press RETURN. The empty file is loaded and you are ready to create the part assembly.

Task 15: Retrieving The Title Block

Objective: To retrieve the title block to be used as a frame for the part.

Command Sequence: F5 FILES, F2 PATTERN, F2 RETRIEV, F9 KEYIN

The Sample Files diskette supplies a title block stored as a pattern file name BORDC. This pattern file is not installed automatically on your hard disk, therefore it must be read in separately.

Press ESCAPE to return to the Main Menu.

Step 1: Call up the **PATTERN:RETRIEV** function using the ESCAPE code: ESC-F5-F2-F2. At the prompt:

Enter pattern file name ():

type the following:

BORDC (if it is installed on your hard drive)

or

A:BORDC (if it is on the floppy diskette in drive A)

Press RETURN.

Step 2: Do not group entities in the pattern being retrieved. Choose the **NO** option, F1.

Step 3: You are prompted to enter the **SCALE** factor of the retrieved pattern. Accept the default value of 1 by pressing the RETURN key only.

Step 4: At the next prompt:

Enter rotation angle (0.0000) =>

accept the current rotation angle of 0 by pressing RETURN only.

Step 5: Indicate a base position for the border by choosing the **KEY-IN** option, F9, from the Position Menu displayed. This option allows cartesian coordinates to be entered from the keyboard to indicate a desired position.

When this pattern was stored, the bottom, left corner was chosen as the base position. When the pattern is retrieved, this same corner is used as the reference point of the new base position. Assigning zero (0) coordinate values for the title block location will position this reference point in the lower left corner of the screen (the cursor's home position).

At the first **KEY-IN** option, XV, press RETURN to accept the view coordinate default value of 0. Repeat this procedure for each coordinate:

XV = 0   YV = 0   ZV = 0

Invoke the Immediate Mode command, ALT-A, to autoscale the border.

Task 16: Retrieving Patterns For Display

Objective: To retrieve previously stored patterns for display in order to create a layout of the part in three different views.

Command Sequence: F5 FILES, F2 PATTERN, F2 RETRIEV, F9 KEY-IN, CTRL-X (SNAP), CTRL-G (GRID)

You have already stored the pattern files needed to make up the layout. Retrieve each one as follows:

Step 1:   Return to the **PATTERN** menu.

Step 2:   Turn on the **SNAP** option using the CTRL-X sequence. This causes the cursor to snap to set intervals for locating specific positions.

Step 3:   Turn on the **GRID** option using the CTRL-G sequence. A series of dots is displayed on the screen to visually aid in pattern placement.

Step 4:   Choose to **RETRIEV** from the Pattern Menu displayed. Enter the pattern file name DOVE2 and press RETURN. This is view 2, a front view, of the part layout. (Dimensions are not stored in pattern files so only the basic part appears.)

Step 5:   At the prompt to "group" entities, choose **NO**.

Step 6:   Accept the default values assigned to the scale (1) and rotation prompts (0) by pressing RETURN twice.

Step 7:   The grid and snap features will serve as our guide for placing the first pattern file. Turn on the *Cursor Tracking Window* using the Immediate Mode command, CTRL-T. Once turned on, the cursor's position is displayed in this window as it is moved about the screen.

Move the cursor until the *Cursor Tracking Window* displays the

X 4.0000
Y 3.0000

values and press the space bar or cursor button.

Step 8:   Return to the PATTERN:RETRIEV menu using F10. Enter the name DOVE7, and press RETURN.

Step 9:   Once again, choose **NO** for grouping and enter a default value of .9 for scaling. Accept the current rotation value of 0 by pressing RETURN only.

Step 10:   Use the cursor to indicate a position for the new pattern at the:

X 14.5000
Y 12.0000

position and press the space bar or cursor button. The second pattern is placed at this location.

Note: To delete patterns that are placed in the wrong position, use the **DELETE:SELECT** option (ESC-F8-F1) as described on page 7-43. This is only necessary if you have made an error. Choose the **WINDOW** option and surround the whole pattern for erasure. Return to the FILE:PATTERN:RETRIEV menu to continue.

Step 11: Retrieve the last of the three patterns in the same manner (refer to steps 8 and 9). This pattern file name is DOVE5.

Step 12: Position this pattern using the cursor at the

$$X\ 16.5000$$
$$Y\ \ 3.0000$$

position.

Step 13: When all three patterns are retrieved, turn off the **GRID** (CTRL-G) and **SNAP** (CTRL-X) options and remove unwanted screen symbols using the Immediate Mode command CTRL-R (redraw).

You will notice that the upper left corner of the layout has been left blank. If you would like, create another pattern file of the the dovetail part from a new view and incorporate that using the steps previously followed.

From this point on, you may work on each part separately, or with the whole layout displayed. If you wish to have dimensions displayed with the part in the layout you can assign them now.

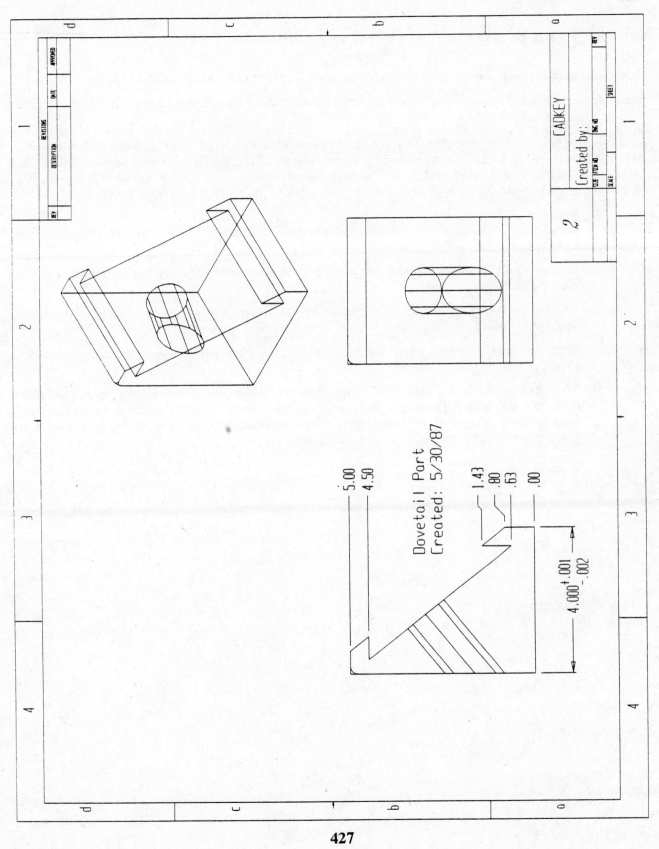

Dovetail Part
Created: 5/30/87

5.00
4.50

1.43
.80
.63
.00

$4.000{}^{+.001}_{-.002}$

CADKEY

Created by:

2

Task 17: Changing Levels

Objective: To activate a new level on which to create dimensions.

Command Sequence: F6 DISPLAY, F3 LEVEL, F1 ACTIVE, ALT-V (VIEW), ALT-H (HALF SCALE)

Before dimensioning one of the parts displayed, let's change the current active level. This will allow us to create dimensions on a different layer than the part construction itself and the flexibility to view the part with or without dimensioning, when desired. The following steps describe how to change the current active level of 1 to 2. The active level is displayed in the *Status Window* as the ALEV: parameter. Note that the system allows you to build up to 256 different levels!

Step 1: Return to the Main Menu. Change the current color assignment to yellow (value number 2) using ALT-X. All text created from this point on will be yellow.

Step 2: Choose to **DISPLAY** a **LEVEL**. A new menu is displayed offering four methods of manipulating levels.

Step 3: Choose the **ACTIVE** option. This option allows you to add a new level to the part. From this point on, all dimensioning will be stored on this new level.

Step 4: Enter the level number 2 and press RETURN. This level is displayed next to the ALEV: prompt in the *Status Window*.

Step 5: To dimension only the front view (found in the lower left corner of the layout) of the part, use the "zoom" feature to enlarge only this section. Use the ALT-W sequence and indicate two corners of the window to surround the complete part. Be sure to leave some extra room around the part for dimensioning.

Task 18: Dimensions

Objective: To dimension the bracket horizontally.

Command Sequence: F3 DETAIL, F1 DIMENSN, F1 HORIZTL, F3 ENDENT

Step 1: Return to the Main Menu and choose the **DETAIL** option.

Step 2: Choose to dimension (**DIMENSN**) selected points of the part.

Step 3: Choose to select **HORIZTL** points as your first dimension.

Step 4: Locate dimension points by choosing the **ENDENT** method from the Position Menu displayed.

Step 5: To select the first point of the dimension, move the cursor near an endpoint of line 1 and press the space bar or cursor button.

The endpoint of the line is located and marked with an X symbol.

Step 6: Select the opposite endpoint of the same line by moving the cursor near the endpoint and press the space bar or cursor button. (Note that the **ENDENT** method chosen is still in effect.)

Step 7: When both points are located, you are prompted for a dimension text position. Move the cursor to the bottom of the part, between the two marked points, and press the space bar or cursor button.

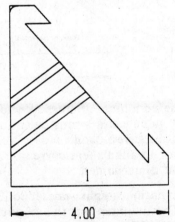

Step 8: The dimension text appears with arrows, witness lines and text. Choose YES from the menu displayed, if the dimension is acceptable. The NO option allows you to place the dimension text once again. Redraw the screen, CTRL-R.

Task 19: Creating ordinate dimensions

Objective: To dimension the distance between the set of lines which join the two circles.

Command Sequence: F3 DETAIL, F1 DIMENSN, F7 ORDINAT, F1 CREATE, F1 ALIGN, F2 VERTICL, F3 ENDENT

Step 1:   Return to the DIMENSION menu and choose **ORDINAT** (ordinate dimensioning).

Step 2:   Choose to **CREATE** the dimensions and **ALIGN** them as we indicate dimensioning positions. This will line up all the dimension values.

Step 3:   Choose to dimension vertically (**VERTICL**) on the part using the **ENDENT** method for positioning.

Step 4:   Indicate the endpoint of a line as shown below. This is the base ordinate position for the dimension. If the correct endpoint is not selected, press F10 and reselect the entity once again.

Step 5:   Next, indicate a text position to the right of the part to place the first dimension value of the ordinates. This base position is displayed as 0. All ordinate dimensioning from this point on is measured and aligned using this position as its base.

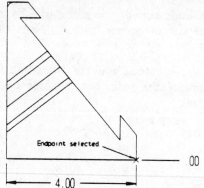

Step 6:   Continue to choose the endpoints of lines as you move up the part as shown below. Once again, press F10 to cancel a wrong selection. As each position is indicated a dimensioning value is displayed. Don't worry about overlapping dimensions; in the next step you will learn how to align them correctly. Press RETURN when all the positions have been selected and dimensioned.

Step 7:   Assuming that the dimension height was set to .3 with an aspect ratio of .5, the dimensions overlap. To straighten out this alignment problem, return to the ORDINAT menu and choose to **MODIFY**.

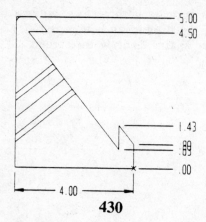

430

Step 8:   Choose to **ALIGN** ordinates from the MODIFY menu. Select any one of the ordinate values displayed, in the lower left corner of the text.

All the dimensions are redrawn and aligned with the correct spacing.

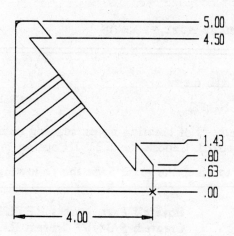

Task 20: Adding notes

Objective: To add a note to the completed bracket.

Command Sequence: F3 DETAIL, F2 NOTE, F1 KEYIN

Step 1: Return to the **DETAIL** menu.

Step 2: Choose to create a **NOTE**.

Step 3: There are three methods of creating notes: reading data in from disk or file, or typing a note using the keyboard. Choose the **KEY IN** option to type a note.

Step 4: You are prompted to enter the text. Type the following and press RETURN after each line of text.

> **Dovetail Part** <press RETURN>
> **Created: 5/30/87** <press RETURN>

Mistakes are easily corrected using the backspace key before RETURN is pressed, or by pressing the F10 key and retyping the text.

Step 5: When the note is completed, press RETURN again.

Step 6: Use the cursor to position the note text to the right of the completed part. Text is displayed to the right of the cursor's center. Press the space bar or cursor button to indicate this position.

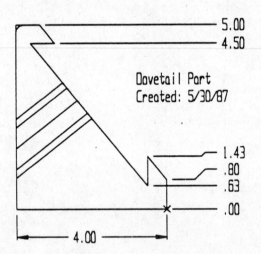

Note: If any part of the dimensions or notes appear off the screen, use ALT-B to return to a full view of the layout and zoom in on the top view once again.

Task 21: Changing dimensions or text

Objective: To alter dimension or note attributes using the **CHANGE** function.

Command Sequence: F3 DETAIL, F7 CHANGE, F1 TXT ATT, F4 ASPECT, F5 DIM REP, F1 DECIMAL, F8 TOLER, F2 TYPE, F1 VALUES

Various parts of a dimension or note (e.g. attributes, position, decimal precision, etc.) may be altered or changed using the **CHANGE** function. Only a few of these options are described here. Feel free to try those options not presented here on your own.

Changing Attributes

Step 1:   Return to the DETAIL menu using F10 and choose to **CHANGE** text attributes (TXT ATT).

Step 2:   There are four attributes offered for change. To change the character aspect ratio of the note (height and width ratio), choose the **ASPECT** option.

Step 3:   Enter a character aspect ratio of .75 and press RETURN.

Step 4:   No changes are made to text until the TXT ATT menu is exited and entities are selected. Choose the **DONE** option from this menu.

Step 5:   The Selection Menu appears. Because there is only a single note to change, choose the **SINGLE** option.

Step 6:   Move the cursor near the lower left-hand corner of the upper, leftmost character of the text (in this case, the D in Dovetail) and press the space bar or cursor button. A selection symbol appears at this location.

Step 7:   Press RETURN. The text is redrawn and takes on the new character aspect ratio assigned.

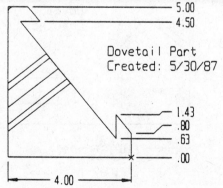

Changing Decimal Precision

Step 1:   Return to the **CHANGE** menu and choose the **DIM REP** then **DECIMAL** options.

Step 2:   A menu appears, offering different decimal precisions (where n represents any value). Choose to change the decimal precision to three places, **n.nnn** (F4).

Step 3:   Choose the **SINGLE** method from the Selection Menu displayed. Move the cursor to the lower left corner of the horizontal dimension text (4.00) and press the space bar or cursor button (4.000).

Step 4:   Press RETURN and the dimension is redisplayed with the new decimal assignment of three places.

Changing Tolerances

Step 1:   Return to the **CHANGE** menu (F10 twice). Choose to change tolerance (**TOLER**) values.

Step 2:   Choose to alter the **TYPE** of tolerance used to the +/- option. This displays both the negative and positive tolerance values with a dimension.

Step 3:   Select the same horizontal dimension (4.000) using the **SINGLE** method from the Selection Menu. Move the cursor to this dimension and press the space bar or cursor button.

Step 4:   Press RETURN and the default tolerance value of .010 is displayed, positive over negative, with the dimensioned part.

Step 5:   To change this value, return once again to the **TOLER** menu (F10 twice). This time select the **VALUES** option.

Step 6:   Choose to change **BOTH** tolerances. Enter a positive value of .001 and press RETURN. Then enter a negative value of -.002 (negative .002) and press RETURN.

Step 7:   Once again, select the same horizontal value (4.000) by choosing the **SINGLE** method from the Selection Menu using the cursor.

Step 8:   The dimension is redisplayed with the new tolerance values.

Step 9:   Invoke an autoscale to return the complete layout to the screen.

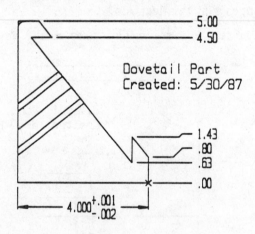

434

Task 22: Turning levels on and off

Objective: To turn on/off a level to display the part with/without dimensioning.

Command Sequence: F6 DISPLAY, F3 LEVEL, F4 LIST

Until now we have created entities on two different levels. The main body of the part is found on level 1, while all dimensioning is found on level 2. To view the part once again without the dimensioning, level 2 can be turned off as follows:

Step 1:   Return to the Main Menu.

Step 2:   Choose to **DISPLAY** the **LEVEL** options.

Step 3:   Choose the **LIST** option to list and turn desired levels on or off.

Step 4:   The first page of levels lists numbers 1-128, with a box surrounding levels 1 and 2. These boxes represent the levels which are currently turned on.

Step 5:   Turn off level 2 by moving the cursor to the number 2 and pressing the space bar or cursor button. (When using the keyboard to move the cursor, use the Pg Up and Pg Dn keys to increase or decrease the movement increment of the cursor.)

Step 6:   Level 2 is automatically turned off.

Step 7:   Press RETURN twice to return to your part. The dimensions are no longer displayed.

Turning Levels On

The same procedure may be followed to turn levels on. A box surrounds selected levels.

Task 22: Saving the Part

Objective: To store the complete drawing layout.

Command Sequence: F5 FILES, F1 PART, F1 SAVE

The drawing layout may be stored as a part file, ESC-F5-F1-F1. Enter the part file name LAYOUT and press RETURN. The part is stored.

This is the end of the tutorial. You have just experienced only <u>some</u> of the basic functions found within the system! If you wish to continue working, press ESC to return to the Main Menu and try out some more functions on your own.

To exit, return to the Main Menu and choose the **EXIT** option.

SOLIDS SYNTHESIS

By extracting solid models from wire-frame geometry, the Solids Synthesis software provides a dynamic extension to CADKEY's 3D-design capabilities in such areas as object rendering, visualization, animation, and determination of mass properties. The CADKEY Advanced Design Language (CADL) serves as the interface between Solids Synthesis and CADKEY. A menu-driven user interface provides complete control over the format, appearance, and orientation of the solid models that are output from the Solids Synthesis process.

THE SOLIDS SYNTHESIS PROCESS

The input data for the Solids Synthesis process is a CADL file that defines wire-frame geometry. As depicted in the illustrations on the following page, Solids Synthesis can perform both synthesis (i.e. extracting a solid model from the wire-frame geometry) and rendering (i.e. manipulating the solid model to produce the desired output display). The following sections provide an overview of these processes.

Synthesis

The synthesis procedure involves transforming the input geometry (e.g. lines, arcs, polylines, polygons) into a collection of planar polygons that define the bounding surfaces of the solid model. A synthesized solid model comprises a full 3D description of a solid, with each surface of the model defined by one or more planar polygons.

Because the synthesis procedure is the most complex task performed by the system, it is essential that the input data file does not include any extraneous geometry. Each feature of the input geometry must contribute to the definition of an object's surface boundaries.

Note: Solids Synthesis is a powerful system; however, available memory may be insufficient for processing extremely large or highly complex designs.

A CADL file containing a synthesized solid model can be input to a CADKEY part, pattern, or plot file. Synthesized solids can be used as input to third-party systems that require polygon/solid representations (e.g. FEA packages).

A previously-synthesized solid model also can be input for rendering by Solids Synthesis. In such cases, you can bypass the synthesis operation and significantly reduce processing time.

Rendering

Solids Synthesis can create multiple renderings, or frames, from the same solid model. Your input (i.e. animation) instructions determine the number of frames that will be output by Solids Synthesis, as well as the format, appearance, orientation, and CADKEY level for each frame of rendered output.

Based on your animation instructions, the system can produce any of the following renderings of the solid model:

-Filled and shaded, with hidden surfaces removed

-Wire frame, with hidden lines removed

-Wire frame, with hidden lines replaced by dashes

Synthesizing a Solid Model

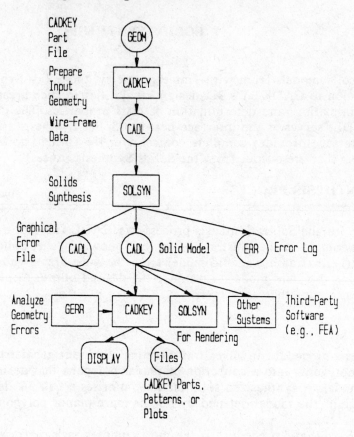

CADKEY Part File

Prepare Input Geometry

Wire-Frame Data

Solids Synthesis

Graphical Error File

CADL — Solid Model — ERR — Error Log

Analyze Geometry Errors

GERR — CADKEY — SOLSYN — Other Systems — Third-Party Software (e.g., FEA)

For Rendering

DISPLAY — Files

CADKEY Parts, Patterns, or Plots

Rendering a Solid Model

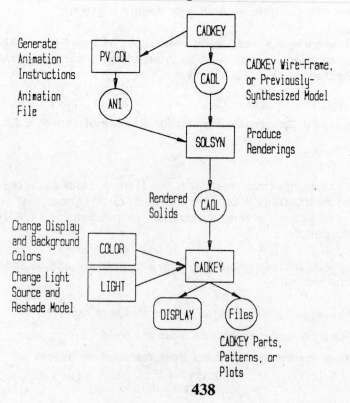

Generate Animation Instructions

Animation File

PV.CDL — CADKEY

CADL — CADKEY Wire-Frame, or Previously-Synthesized Model

ANI

SOLSYN — Produce Renderings

Rendered Solids — CADL

Change Display and Background Colors

Change Light Source and Reshade Model

COLOR — CADKEY

LIGHT

DISPLAY — Files

CADKEY Parts, Patterns, or Plots

A CADL program--PV.CDL--enables you to generate a complete set of animation instructions for rendering the solid model. By selecting the appropriate menu options, you can rotate the solid model to the desired view and specify the type of rendering to be performed. Other menu options allow you to control the color and shading of filled objects, as well as the amount of perspective (if any) to be applied to each rendering of the solid model.

CONTROLLING THE PROCESS

When initiating the Solids Synthesis process, you are prompted to specify which of its major functions the system should perform with the input geometry. Based on these specifications, your Solids Synthesis output may comprise a synthesized solid model, a rendered solid model, or both.

The standard Solids Synthesis configuration includes the geometric tolerances and the color class specifications that the program uses for synthesizing and rendering the solid model. Solids Synthesis menu options enable you to change the default settings for this configuration information.

ANALYZING THE RESULTS

The results of the Solids Synthesis process are output for display and inspection as CADL files. Solids Synthesis output is viewed, manipulated, and analyzed in CADKEY.

A CADL program--COLOR.CDL--allows you to modify the display colors for filled/shaded renderings, and to build a background color for the display. Another CADL program, LIGHT.CDL, enables you to reposition the light source and to reshade the filled/shaded renderings of the solid model.

Throughout the synthesis process, the system monitors its actions, reports status, and maintains an error log. In those cases where the input geometry contains errors or the synthesis procedure fails, the program facilitates analysis of the problem part by generating a graphical error file, a powerful visual debugging tool, that uses color coding to highlight problem geometry. A CADL program--GERR.CDL--provides a menu-driven structure for analyzing the information from the graphical error file.

Refer to the following page for an example of a filled/shaded rendering.

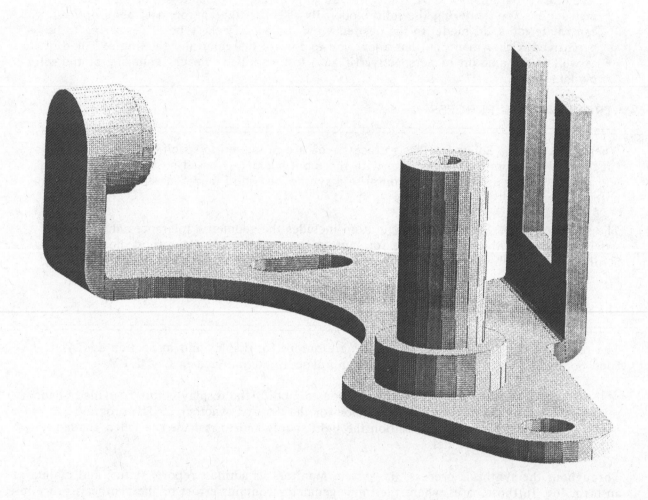

Filled/Shaded Rendering

440

INSTALLATION

The Solids Synthesis software operates on hard disk drive systems that have been formatted with DOS version 2.0 or later. After completing the installation process, you need to make minor modifications to the configuration of your CADKEY program. If you typically work with metric units, you need to change one tolerance factor in the default Solids Synthesis configuration. Instructions for completing each of these steps are detailed in the following sections.

RESTRICTIONS AND NOTES

* The CADKEY Software Interface Module (SIM) must be installed on your machine.

* You must be running CADKEY version 3.02 (or later).

* At least 360KB of free disk space is required to install the software.

* Solids Synthesis operates with DOS version 2.0 (or later).

MAKING BACK-UP COPIES

The master program diskette contains all the files necessary to install and operate Solids Synthesis. Use a blank diskette that has been formatted with DOS version 2.0 (or later) to make a back-up copy of the master program diskette.

CONTENTS OF THE RELEASE

The release includes the following files:

READ.ME	the latest information about the release.
SHLR.EXE	the Solids Synthesis program.
SOLSYN.EXE	a menu-driven program for initiating the Solids Synthesis process.
INSTALL.BAT	the batch file that is used to install Solids Synthesis.
SCONFIG.DAT	the standard Solids Synthesis configuration file.
SMENUS.TXT	the text file for Solids Synthesis menus.
SPMPTS.TXT	the text file for Solids Synthesis prompts.
SHLR.TXT	the default text file for system messages.
PV.CDL	a CADL program that enables users to generate animation instructions.
COLOR.CDL	a CADL program that allows users to modify the colors of shaded models.
LIGHT.CDL	a CADL program that allows users to reposition the light source and to reshade filled/shaded renderings.
SEG.MAC	CADKEY macro utilities for preparing input geometry.
GERR.CDL	a CADL program that facilitates analysis of input geometry errors.
ANI	a sample animation file.
SAMPLE1.CDL	a sample wire-frame design.
SAMPLE2.CDL	a sample wire-frame design.
SAMPLE3.CDL	a sample wire-frame design.

INSTALLING THE PROGRAM

The INSTALL.BAT batch file automatically installs the Solids Synthesis software in the correct directories.

1) Boot up your system on the hard disk drive.

2) Move to your main CADKEY directory:

    cd*directory name (press RETURN)*

3) At the DOS prompt, insert the Master Program Diskette in drive A and type:

    A:INSTALL *(press RETURN)*

Note: During the installation process, the system attempts to create the required directories. The message **"Unable to create directory"** indicates that this step has been omitted because the main CADKEY and \cdl directories already exist.

When installation is complete, the DOS prompt is displayed, and the program leaves you in the main CADKEY directory.

RECONFIGURING CADKEY

Before running Solids Synthesis, you must modify the configuration of the CADKEY program by changing three parameters related to CADL execution and output.

1) Initiate the CADKEY CONFIG program from the main CADKEY directory by typing:

    CONFIG *(press RETURN)*

CONFIG program option 5, **"Set Program Options"**, provides access to a series of prompts that will allow you to redefine the appropriate parameters.

The current setting for each CADKEY Program Option will be displayed in parentheses. Change the settings for three options as described in the following steps. Press RETURN only to accept the default values for the other CADKEY Program Options.

2) Select option 5, **"Set Program Options"**, from the CONFIG menu displayed.

3) In response to the appropriate prompts, change the following parameters:

    -The decimal precision for CADL output must be at least 7 places to the RIGHT of the decimal point.

    -The number of CADL program statement labels supported must be at least 60.

    -The number of register variables supported must be at least 100.

After accepting or changing the CADKEY Program Option settings, you are returned to the CONFIG program main menu.

4) Store the CADKEY configuration settings by selecting option 8, **"Exit w/save"**.

Refer to the CADKEY User Reference Guide for a complete description of the CONFIG program.

442

SOLIDS SYNTHESIS CONFIGURATION DATA

The default configuration for Solids Synthesis comprises the following data:

- Geometric tolerances for synthesizing solid models from wire-frame geometry.

- Color class specifications for producing filled/shaded renderings.

- The maximum number of allowable iterations for the synthesis procedure.

RESETTING THE DEFAULT CONFIGURATION

Like CADKEY's CONFIG program, Solids Synthesis provides a combination of menu options and on-screen prompts that enable you to modify the default settings for the configuration data.

To reset Solids Synthesis configuration data:

1) Access the Solids Synthesis Main Menu from the main CADKEY directory by typing:

SOLSYN *(press RETURN)*

2) Select option 1, **"Reset Default Configuration"**.

The system displays the Configuration Menu, which allows you to select the category of configuration data (i.e. tolerances, color classes, synthesis iteration limit) that you want to modify.

GEOMETRIC TOLERANCES

During the synthesis procedure, Solids Synthesis uses several tolerance factors to evaluate your input geometry. Configuration Menu option 1, **"Tolerances"**, allows you to reset the tolerance factors. With one possible exception, it is advised that you accept the default settings for the Solids Synthesis tolerances.

The tolerance factor that Solids Synthesis uses for determining whether two points are coincident has a default value of 0.000050 inches. If you typically work in metric units, you should rescale this tolerance factor accordingly by entering a positive real number. For example, reset the tolerance to 0.00127 if your base unit is the millimeter.

Note: Relaxing (i.e. increasing) a tolerance may produce unpredictable results, and should not be viewed as an easy solution for a synthesis failure.

Any tolerance changes typically will involve tightening (i.e. decreasing) a tolerance to differentiate finer features of a model. For example, if the program is treating two distinct planes as coplanar, you may need to tighten the coplanar tolerance factor to allow the program to distinguish between the two planes.

Most of the geometric tolerances are defined in radians. These tolerance factors have a default value of 0.001. Real numbers that are greater than 0.0 and less than 1.0 are valid values for these tolerance factors.

Resetting Tolerances

Use the following procedures to reset tolerances. The default value for each tolerance factor is listed in parentheses, and can be accepted by pressing RETURN only.

1) Select option 1, **"Tolerances"**, from the Configuration Menu.

2) Enter the inclination angle (in radians) within which two vectors are considered to be identical in direction (0.001000).

3) Enter the inclination angle (in radians) within which two lines are considered to be colinear (0.001000).

4) Enter the inclination angle (in radians) within which two planes are considered to be coplanar (0.001000).

5) Enter the inclination angle (in radians) within which two entities are considered to be parallel (0.001000).

6) Enter the radius within which two points are considered to be coincident (0.000050).

7) Enter a positive integer to define the maximum number of nested boundaries allowed (21).

After accepting or changing each of the tolerance factors, you are returned to the Configuration menu. You can select another category of configuration data to be modified or you can exit the Configuration menu.

COLOR CLASS DEFINITIONS

Solids Synthesis supports 15 color classes, corresponding to the 15 CADKEY color numbers. Color class 0, a default color class, is applied to any entities that do not reference an active color class. Each color class definition comprises the current status (i.e. active, inactive), an outline color number, and a range of shading color numbers.

As illustrated in the following table, Solids Synthesis processes the color class specifications to determine the correct colors for outlining and shading the filled renderings that it produces from a solid model. Any entities in the input geometry file with a CADKEY color number that matches an active color class number are rendered according to the specifications for that color class. Any entities in the input geometry file with a CADKEY color number that matches an inactive color class number are rendered according to the specifications for color class 0, which is always active.

Color Numbers

The outline color number identifies the CADKEY color that is used for displaying the outline of the polygons that comprise a shaded rendering of a solid. Integers in the range 0-15 are valid values for outline color numbers. An outline number of zero disables outlining.

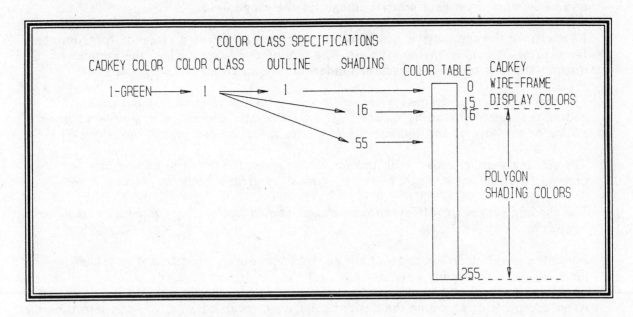

The range of shading color numbers defines the number of shades that can be used for producing a filled/shaded rendering of a solid. The larger the range, the finer the shading that can be applied to the rendering.

Integers in the range 16-255 are valid values for shading numbers. In the default configuration, the 240 valid shading numbers are divided into 6 ranges--16 to 55; 56 to 95; 96 to 135; 136 to 175; 176 to 215; and 216 to 255.

In the default configuration, these ranges of shading colors are assigned to color classes 1 through 6. The default setting for color class 0 is a copy of the default setting for color class 1.

Note: The shading numbers do not define actual colors; they specify a range of values that are mapped to shades of a specified base color when you display the rendered output. After displaying your rendered output, you can use the COLOR.CDL program to change the base colors for any of the color classes that are used in the display.

Resetting Color Classes

Select the **"Color Class"** option from the Configuration menu to access a series of prompts that allow you to change the current status (i.e. active, inactive) of any color class. You also can modify the outline and shading numbers for any of the active color classes. To accept a default value, press RETURN only.

1) Select option 2, **"Color Classes"** from the Configuration Menu.

   The system displays a list of color classes, and identifies the currently-active classes. Color class 0 is always active; this setting cannot be changed.

2) Enter the option number for the color class that you are modifying.

3) Indicate whether or not you want to make the class active/inactive. If you make the class inactive, you are returned to the list of color classes.

If you make the class active, you are prompted to enter an outline color number. The outline number must be a positive integer in the range 0-15.

If you make the class active, you also are prompted to define a range of color numbers for shading objects in that color class. The size of the range defines the number of distinct shades that can be used for rendering objects from that color class.

The shading range is defined by entering values for the starting (i.e. darkest) and ending (i.e. lightest) shading numbers. The starting and ending color numbers always reference the darkest and lightest shades of the specified base color, respectively.

The starting number must be an integer in the range 16-255. The ending number is derived from the same range; however, it must be greater than the starting number.

The shading ranges for different color classes should not overlap, as unpredictable results will occur.

4) Select the next color class to be modified, or select option 16, "Done" to return to the Configuration Menu.

After accepting or changing the desired color class specifications, you can select another category of configuration data to be modified, or you can exit the Configuration menu.

THE SYNTHESIS ITERATION LIMIT

The Synthesis Iteration Limit defines the maximum number of passes that the system can make in attempting to synthesize a solid model. If the specified limit is reached, processing is terminated. A value of zero disables the limit. The default value for the iteration limit is 32.

Setting the iteration limit is a useful debugging tool for those cases where you believe that the input geometry includes errors. For example, by setting the limit at 32 you will allow the program to run long enough to identify most of the errors in the input geometry. Any errors that the program finds are dumped into the ERROR.CDL file, which can be analyzed with the graphical error program (i.e. GERR.CDL).

Resetting the Iteration Limit

To change the iteration limit:

1) Select option 3, "Synthesis Iteration Limit" from the Configuration menu.

2) Enter a positive integer.

The program returns you to the Configuration menu. You can select another category of configuration data to be modified, or you can exit the Configuration menu.

EXITING THE CONFIGURATION MENU

Select option 4, "Done", from the Configuration menu.

You are returned to the Solids Synthesis Main Menu, which allows you to reset the default configuration, process a model, or exit to DOS.

Select option 3, "Exit to DOS".

You are returned to the main CADKEY directory.

PREPARING THE INPUT GEOMETRY

The input data for Solids Synthesis is a CADL file that describes 3D wire-frame geometry with CADL LINE, POLYGON, POLYLINE, and ARC statements. Other CADL data primitives, commands, and expressions may be included in the input file; however, Solids Synthesis ignores these statements and passes them through to the output file unaltered.

Solids Synthesis defines the surface edges of the geometry as straight line segments. An edge formed by an arc is defined as the chord between the two endpoints.

In the synthesis process, the system groups the edges of the wire-frame geometry into boundaries that define surfaces. In other words, the system synthesizes the input geometry to create groups of planar polygons that define the bounding surfaces of the solid object(s). Surfaces that contain holes are defined by more than one boundary.

Reducing Synthesis Processing Time

The synthesis procedure is the most complex, time-consuming task performed by the system. Because each surface of a synthesized solid model comprises one or more planar polygons, you can facilitate the synthesis procedure by representing complex features of your input geometry with polygons. The **CREATE:POLYGON:MESH:GENERAL** option from the CADKEY Main Menu is particularly useful for representing twisted surfaces.

If your input geometry includes a surface that has opposite edges defined by two arcs, two splines, or an arc and a spline, you can simplify the synthesis process by using one of two CADKEY/Solids Synthesis macro utilities to clarify the definition of the surface between these entities. These macros enable you to segment the surface between the two entities into a three-sided or four-sided ruled polygon mesh. You can use this mesh to replace the two entities in the CADL file that describes your input geometry.

The macros are stored in a CADKEY macro library file, seg.mac, in the CADKEY \mac directory.

INPUT REQUIREMENTS

Wire-frame geometry that is being input to the synthesis process must meet the following requirements:

1) All boundaries forming a surface must be planar, and each boundary must be closed. Create a polygon mesh to represent a surface that otherwise would not meet this requirement.

2) Boundaries cannot cross each other; however, they may have common points and edges.

3) The wire-frame model can comprise more than one object. Objects can be nested, and they can contain holes.

4) Each of the objects described by the wire-frame geometry must occupy a finite volume (i.e. the bounding surfaces of each object must be closed).

5) All features of the wire-frame description must contribute to the definition of an object's surface boundaries. Any extraneous geometry must be removed before the geometry is input to the synthesis process. For example, primitives that pierce the volume of an object are not allowed. Similarly, if there are features in the plane of a surface that do not define the boundary of the surface, those features should be removed from the wire-frame geometry.

Note: A CADL file that comprises an all-polygon representation of an object can be input directly to the rendering process without being synthesized. This capability is useful for producing shaded renderings of "surfaces" that do not form solid objects (e.g. geometry that has been created with the CADKEY **CREATE:POLYGON:MESH: GENERAL** function).

DEFINING THE INPUT GEOMETRY

Solids Synthesis input geometry is defined by a CADL file. This CADL file might be output from a CADKEY part file, or it may comprise a previously-synthesized solid model that you plan to input for rendering.

To output a CADL file from an existing CADKEY part file:

1) Load the appropriate part file using the **FILES:PART:LOAD** option from the CADKEY Main Menu.

2) Output a CADL file using the **FILES:CADL:OUTPUT** option.

DISPLAYING THE INPUT DATA

Although it is not required, you will probably find it helpful to display the wire-frame geometry when you are generating animation instructions.

Execute the appropriate CADL file with the **FILES:CADL:EXECUTE** option from the CADKEY Main Menu.

GENERATING ANIMATION INSTRUCTIONS

With your input data defined in a CADL file, you are ready to generate the animation instructions that determine how Solids Synthesis renders the solid model that it creates from your wire-frame geometry. Based on these animation instructions, Solids Synthesis will manipulate the solid model to create one or more renderings of the object.

Each rendering that Solids Synthesis outputs from a set of manipulations is called a frame. Multiple frames can be generated from the same input geometry.

The CADL Preview program, PV.CDL, enables you to generate the animation instructions that define the orientation of the model and the type of rendering for each frame, as well as the number of frames that will be output by the rendering process.

USING THE PREVIEW PROGRAM

To start generating animation instructions, execute the CADL Preview program, PV.CDL.

Like CADKEY, the Preview program menu options are selected by pressing the appropriate function key, or by cursor-selecting the desired option. When you select a Preview program menu option, that selection remains in effect until you select another option from the same menu. For example, if you select a filled/shaded rendering for the first frame of your output, that selection is used for all subsequent frames until you select another option from the RENDER menu.

Preview program menu options allow you to perform such functions as:

- Rotating the geometry to the desired view(s)
- Selecting the type of rendering (e.g. filled/shaded, hidden lines removed) and specifying whether perspective should be applied to the rendering
- Specifying the CADKEY level for each frame of rendered output
- Recording the frame(s)

As in CADKEY, press F10 to back up. Press ESC to exit the Preview program.

Several Preview program menus offer the FRAME option, which allows you to record the animation instructions that you have selected for one rendering of the solid model. After recording the animation instructions for one frame, you can select the animation instructions for the next frame, or you can exit the Preview program.

For example, your rendered output file could comprise a series of frames displaying the solid model in different views that you have created with the ROTATION options. Because the ROTATION menu offers the FRAME option, these frames can be captured without leaving the ROTATION menu.

As you enter your selections, the Preview program stores these animation instructions in a temporary file. When exiting the Preview program, you are prompted to enter a filename for saving your animation instructions.

The following sections describe all of the Preview program menu options.

449

MODE: Controlling CADL Execution

The MODE option is used to specify the CADL execution mode for your rendered output. If the default mode, DRAW, is selected, the rendered solid model is displayed on the screen, but it is not stored in the CADKEY database. Redrawing a CADL file that was executed in DRAW mode will clear the screen.

In NORMAL mode, the rendered model is displayed on the screen and it is entered into the CADKEY database. Select NORMAL mode if you plan to use the solid model in a CADKEY part file or plot file. NORMAL mode also is required for using the LIGHT.CDL program.

If your rendered output comprises multiple frames that will be executed in NORMAL mode you should organize your output by using the LEVEL option to assign each frame to a different CADKEY level.

ROTATION: Positioning Objects

The first six options on the ROTATION menu enable you to rotate objects in the following directions (see the following illustration):

- Top out
- Top in
- Right side out
- Right side in
- Counter-clockwise
- Clockwise

Objects are rotated in precise increments. Select the INCRMNT option to enter a new positive value for the rotation increment, which has a default value of 22.50 degrees.

Select the FRAME option to record the animation instructions that you have entered for one rendering (i.e. frame) of the solid model.

The DONE option returns you to the Preview program main menu.

As you create new views with the ROTATION options, the view number in the status window is updated and the views are recorded in CADKEY. You can access these views by entering the Immediate Mode command ALT-V and the desired view number.

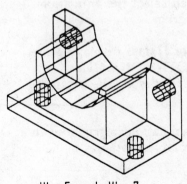
Wire Frame in View 7

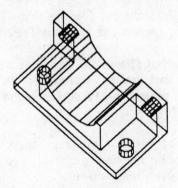
Top Out, 30 Degrees

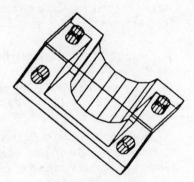
Right In, 30 Degrees

RENDER: Controlling the Appearance of the Solid Model

The RENDER option is used to access a series of menus that provide you with complete control over the format and appearance of each frame that will be output from Solids Synthesis. The RENDER menu offers the following rendering options:

Option	Rendering
HIDDEN	Wire frame, with hidden lines removed (see example).
DASHED	Wire frame, with hidden lines represented by dashes (see example).
FILL	Filled and shaded, with hidden surfaces removed.
PERSPC	Perspective view.

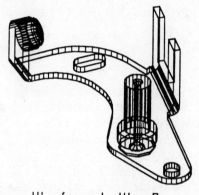
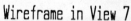

Wireframe in View 7

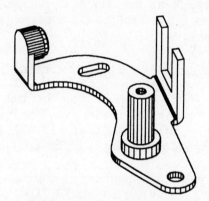

Hidden Lines Removed

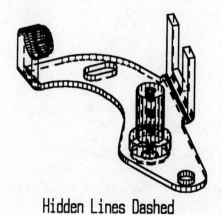

Hidden Lines Dashed

Perspective can be applied to any rendering. The other rendering options (i.e. HIDDEN, DASHED, FILL) are mutually exclusive; selecting one of these options will toggle the previous selection off.

The current rendering selection remains active until you select another rendering option; thus, you may not need to return to the RENDER menu for each frame in your animation file.

Select the FRAME option to record the animation instructions that you have entered for one rendering (i.e. frame) of the solid model.

Select DONE to return to the Preview program main menu.

Controlling Shading and Perspective

If you select a filled rendering, the Preview program automatically displays a menu that enables you to control the shading and color of the solid model. Similarly, if you select the PERSPC option from the RENDER menu, the Preview program offers two options for specifying the amount of perspective to be used in rendering the solid model. These options for controlling the appearance of the solid model are described in the following sections.

LIGHT - Shading the Solid Model

The LIGHT option on the FILL menu is used to define the direction of the light source for filled, shaded renderings. The Preview program gives you the option of defining the direction of the light source in WORLD or VIEW coordinates. The light source is planar and is positioned at infinity, with its rays parallel to the direction that you define.

Define the light source by entering three parameters (X, Y, and Z for WORLD; XV, YV, and ZV for VIEW). Press RETURN only to accept a default value.

Because you are defining a direction rather than an actual position, the magnitude of the values that you enter is unimportant. For example, a light source located at infinity in the positive X direction could be defined in any of the following ways:

$$X = 1.0, \quad Y = 0.0, \quad Z = 0.0$$
$$X = 2.0, \quad Y = 0.0, \quad Z = 0.0$$
$$X = 0.1234, \quad Y = 0.0, \quad Z = 0.0$$

A CADL program, LIGHT.CDL, allows you to change the position of the light source when you display your rendered output.

COLOR - Resetting Color Class Specifications

Selecting the COLOR option on the FILL menu causes the Preview program to display the COLOR menu, which allows you to change the current status (i.e. active, inactive) for any color class, and to change the specifications (i.e. outline and shading color numbers) for any active color class.

Note: When you process the model, any color class specifications that you have stored in your animation file will override the default Solids Synthesis configuration data.

1) Select the color class that you want to activate or redefine.

2) Respond to the prompts by entering an outline color number and a range of color numbers for shading objects in the color class. The outline color number must be an integer in the range 0-15.

   The shading range is defined by entering values for the beginning (i.e. darkest) and ending (i.e. lightest) color numbers. The beginning color number must be an integer in the range of 16-255. The ending color number is derived from the same range; however it must be greater than the beginning color number.

   Press RETURN only to accept the current values, which are displayed in parentheses.

3) Select the next color class to be redefined, or select DONE to exit the COLOR menu and return to the FILL menu.

PERSPC: Specifying the Degree of Perspective

If you have selected a perspective rendering, the Preview program automatically displays the PERSPC menu. The PERSPC menu allows you to define one of two values--LENS or STANDOFF--that Solids Synthesis uses in performing the perspective transformation. The PERSPC menu also offers the NONE option, which allows you to turn off the perspective effect.

The LENS value is a scale-independent parameter that Solids Synthesis uses for calculating the desired degree of perspective. To generate a perspective rendering, the LENS value must be a real number that is greater than or equal to one. The degree of perspective is greater with smaller lens values. Similar degrees of perspective can be obtained for different objects by using the same LENS value.

The STANDOFF value specifies the viewer's distance from the model. This value must be a real number that is greater than the bounding radius of the specified geometry (i.e. the radius of a sphere that would contain all of the specified geometry). The degree of perspective is greater with smaller STANDOFF distances.

If you select a perspective rendering for one frame in your animation instructions, perspective remains in effect for all subsequent frames in the animation file until you select the NONE option from the PERSPC menu.

LEVEL: Specifying the Destination of the Output

Select the LEVEL option on the Preview program main menu to specify which CADKEY level will contain the frame that you are defining. If you use the LEVEL option, you also should select NORMAL mode.

For example, if your rendered output comprises several frames that will be executed in NORMAL mode, you should assign each frame to a different level.

VERSION

Select the VERSION option to display the current version number of the Preview program, PV.CDL.

FRAME: Recording a Set of Animation Instructions

Select the FRAME option to record the animation instructions that you have entered for one rendering (i.e. frame) of the solid model.

After recording the current frame, you can use the other Preview program options to select the animation instructions for the next frame of your output, or you can exit the Preview program.

DONE: Exiting the Preview Program

1) Select DONE to exit the Preview program.

As you enter your animation instructions, they are recorded in a temporary file. When you exit the Preview program, you are prompted to enter a filename for saving your animation instructions. If you enter the name of an existing file, the Preview program will replace the old file with your new animation file.

2) Enter a valid filename and press RETURN.

Note: To generate renderings, your animation file must include at least one FRAME statement. If you attempt to exit the Preview program without recording any frames, the following reminder is displayed on the prompt line:

Animation file has no frames, still exit?

If this message is displayed, select NO to remain in the Preview program.

RUNNING SOLIDS SYNTHESIS

After defining the input geometry and/or generating your animation instructions, you are ready to initiate the Solids Synthesis process. The Solids Synthesis program provides a combination of menu options and on-screen prompts that enable you to specify input and output filenames, select the desired processing options, and start the Solids Synthesis process.

As described in the **Solids Synthesis Configuration Data** section, Solids Synthesis menu options also allow you to modify the default settings for the geometric tolerances, the color class specifications, and the iteration limit that the system uses for synthesizing and rendering your solid model.

If you typically work with metric units, verify that you have modified the default setting for the appropriate tolerance factor before you use Solids Synthesis.

SOLIDS SYNTHESIS PROCESSING OPTIONS

The Solids Synthesis program can perform both synthesis and rendering with your input geometry. In the synthesis process, the software creates a solid model by transforming (i.e. synthesizing) the CADL data primitives that define each bounding surface of the wire-frame geometry into a set of planar polygons. In the rendering operation, Solids Synthesis processes your animation instructions to create the desired rendering(s) of the solid model. The system allows you to specify one or both of these main processing options.

Note: If you specify both of the processing options, you must enter different filenames for your synthesized output and your rendered output. If you enter the name of an existing file, your Solids Synthesis output will replace the contents of that file.

Synthesized Output

If you specify synthesized output, Solids Synthesis outputs a CADL file that comprises an all-polygon, wire-frame representation of the input geometry. This file contains a full 3D description of a solid object, with each surface of the object defined as one or more planar polygons. An animation file is not needed when you specify synthesized output only.

Because a synthesized model consists entirely of CADL POLYGON statements, it can be loaded into any CADKEY part. A synthesized model also can be input for rendering by Solids Synthesis.

If a CADL file containing a previously-synthesized solid model is input for rendering by Solids Synthesis, you can bypass the synthesis procedure and significantly reduce processing time.

Rendered Output

If you specify rendered output, Solids Synthesis processes your animation instructions to create one or more renderings of the solid model. These frames are output for display as a CADL file.

1) Access the Solids Synthesis main menu from the main CADKEY directory by typing:

   SOLSYN *(press RETURN)*

2) Select option 2, **"Process a model"**.

   The system displays a series of prompts, asking you to specify the required filenames and to select the desired processing options. Press RETURN only to accept a default value.

3) Enter the pathname for the directory containing your CADL files (e.g. CDL).

4) Enter the input filename.

5) Indicate whether or not the input data is already synthesized.

6) Specify whether or not synthesized output is required. If so, enter the output filename for the synthesized output. Do not select this processing option if the input data is already synthesized

7) Specify whether or not rendered output is required. If so, enter the output filename for the rendered output.

8) If rendering is required, enter the animation filename. Rendering cannot occur without animation instructions.

9) Indicate whether or not Solids Synthesis should process the model. If you indicate that you do not want Solids Synthesis to process the model, you are given the option of returning to the Solids Synthesis main menu or reentering your processing specifications.

As it processes the input geometry, Solids Synthesis calculates the mass properties of the solid model, and displays a series of status messages. When processing is complete, the system returns you to the main CADKEY directory.

VIEWING THE RESULTS

The results of the Solids Synthesis process are output for display as CADL files. A CADL program, COLOR.CDL, allows you to modify the display colors of filled/shaded renderings. Another CADL program, LIGHT.CDL, enables you to modify the appearance of filled/shaded renderings by repositioning the light source.

DISPLAYING THE SOLID MODEL

To display the synthesized and/or rendered solid model, select the **FILES:CADL:EXECUTE** option from the CADKEY main menu, and enter the appropriate filename.

If your rendered output comprises more than one frame, press RETURN to advance from one frame to the next.

MODIFYING THE DISPLAY COLORS

The CADL Color program, COLOR.CDL, allows you to modify the display colors of filled/shaded renderings. COLOR.CDL also is used to build a background color that will complement the color and shading of the model.

Execute the Color program as a CADL file.

Like CADKEY, the Color program menu options are selected by pressing the appropriate function key, or by cursor selecting the desired option. Pressing F10 allows you to back up. Pressing ESC allows you to exit the Color program.

The Color program main menu offers the following options:

Option	Purpose
CLASS	Specifying a color class and selecting a new base color for that color class.
COLOR	Selecting a new base color for the currently-specified color class.
INTENS	Adjusting the shading (lighter or darker) for the currently-specified color class.
RANGE	Defining a range of shading color numbers.
BACKGD	Building a background color.
DONE	Exiting the Color program.

Each of the above options is described on the following pages.

Note: When you first enter the Color program, color class 1 is the current color class.

CLASS

Select the CLASS option to specify a new base color for any of the active color classes.

1) Select the color class to be reshaded.

2) Select the new base color for the color class from the following menu:

> 1 Red
> 2 Green
> 3 Blue
> 4 Cyan
> 5 Magenta
> 6 Yellow
> 7 White

Any objects that were displayed in shades defined by the specified color class will be displayed in shades of the new base color.

3) Select the next color class, or press F10 twice to return to the Color program main menu.

COLOR

Select the COLOR option to choose a different base color for the currently-selected color class. Any objects that were displayed in shades defined by the specified color class will be displayed in shades of the new base color. When you initiate the Color program, color class 1 is set as the current color class.

Press F10 to return to the Color program main menu.

INTENS

Select the INTENS (i.e. intensity) option to adjust the shading of entities that are shaded with the currently-selected color class. Based on your specifications, the appropriate surfaces will be displayed in darker or lighter shades of the base color for that color class.

You have the following options for reshading objects:

- Press the cursor-down key to display objects in successively darker shades.
- Press the cursor-up key to display objects in successively lighter shades.
- Press PgUp to double the effect of the cursor-movement keys.
- Press PgDn to reduce the effect of the cursor-movement keys by 1/2.
- Press F10 to return to the Color program main menu.

RANGE

Use the RANGE option to define a range of shading color numbers. The range that you define may be within one color class, or it may span more than one color class. You will be prompted to define a range of shading color numbers, and to select the base color that will be applied to that range.

Shading color numbers must be integers in the range 16-255. The ending color number must be greater than the starting color number.

1) Select the RANGE option from the Color program main menu.

2) Enter the starting (i.e. darkest) color number.

3) Enter the ending (i.e. lightest) color number.

4) Select a color from the base color menu. This base color will apply to the range of color numbers that you defined in the preceding steps.

5) Press F10 to return to the Color program main menu.

Any objects with color numbers in the range that you have defined will be displayed in shades of the base color that you have selected.

BACKGD

Use the BACKGD option to build a background color for your solid model. You will build the background color by combining varying amounts of red, green, and blue.

1) Start the process by selecting one of the following colors to be included in the background mix:

> R = Red
> G = Green
> B = Blue

2) As with the INTENS option, scrolling keys are used to vary the intensity of the selected color as follows:

   - Press the cursor-up key to increase the intensity of the selected color.
   - Press the cursor-down key to reduce the intensity of the selected color.
   - Press PgUp to double the effect of the cursor-movement keys.
   - Press PgDn to reduce the effect of the cursor-movement keys by 1/2.

3) Repeat the process for the next color to be included in the background mix, or press F10 to return to the Color program main menu.

DONE

Select DONE to exit the Color program.

The CADL Light program, LIGHT.CDL, allows you to redefine the direction of the light source for filled/shaded renderings. The filled/shaded rendering is reshaded based on the new light source.

The Light program main menu gives you the option of defining the new direction of the light source in WORLD or VIEW coordinates. The light source is planar and is positioned at infinity, with its rays parallel to the direction that you define.

Restrictions and Notes

* To use the Light program, the CADL file that contains your filled/shaded rendering must be executed in NORMAL mode.

* If you plan to input the shaded rendering to a new or existing CADKEY file, you should do so before using the Light program. Do not save a part that has been reshaded with the Light program.

Using the Light Program

Like CADKEY, the Light program menu options are selected by pressing the appropriate function key, or by cursor selecting the desired option. Pressing F10 allows you to back up, while pressing ESC allows you to exit the Light program.

1) With a filled/shaded rendering executed in NORMAL mode, execute LIGHT.CDL as a CADL file.

2) Press F1 to select all shaded entities for processing.

3) Select the method for specifying the light source--WORLD or VIEW.

4) Define the light source by entering three parameters (X, Y, and Z for WORLD; XV, YV, and ZV for VIEW). Press RETURN only to accept a default value.

Because you are defining a direction rather than an actual position, the magnitude of the values that you enter is unimportant. For example, a light source located at infinity in the positive X direction could be defined in any of the following ways:

$$X = 1.0, \quad Y = 0.0, \quad Z = 0.0$$
$$X = 2.0, \quad Y = 0.0, \quad Z = 0.0$$
$$X = 0.1234, \quad Y = 0.0, \quad Z = 0.0$$

The display is reshaded, based on the new light source that you have defined.

CHAPTER 10

MAINFRAME-BASED CADD TUTORIAL

Introduction

The purpose of this chapter is to present an example of the geometric construction and manipulation procedures for mainframe and supermini computer systems. As in micrographic systems, mainframe CADD systems incorporate routines that allows you to generate a three-dimensional representation of the device being modeled.

Mainframe Systems Software

Control Data Corporation's INTEGRATED COMPUTER-AIDED ENGINEERING and MANUFACTURING for DESIGN, DRAFTING and NUMERICAL CONTROL (ICEM DDN) graphics package. ICEM contains software modules (e.g., Basic Geometry, Mechanical Drafting, Geometric Analysis, Extended Geometry and Numerical Control) and special control, database management, analysis, drafting functions similar to those available in other packages. The control functions allows you to change or set the depth, zoom,

461

view and level (layer). Geometric definition functions form the graphics and alphanumeric representation of the part. Geometric manipulation permits rotation, copying and moving objects. Dimensioning, tolerancing, line conventions, detail magnifing, modifing entities and section lining (hatching) are supported by the Drafting functions. Analysis functions are used to link analysis packages for finite-element mesh generation. Finally, Database Management functions allows inspection, editing, manipulation of parts and patterns, storing, retrieving, deleting, copying and listing of parts.

Projected Entities

Projecting groups of entities (i.e., a 2-D geometric configuration) is normally accomplished by copying a set of displayed entities, at a predefined depth. This copy is projected into or out of the screen, relative to a predefined depth. Projectors (i.e., connector-lines) are displayed connecting the two sets of entities, at its intersecting points. In other words, the copy and original shape will be connected by lines, at certain points.

By projecting this two-dimensional geometric configuration, normal to the plane of definition, you can define any three-dimensional object. When you indicate the entities to be projected the system automatically duplicates the 2-D shape, at the specified depth and connects the end points between the shape and its copy. Some systems limit the number of entities that can be projected at once. But obviously you can enter this entities in several small groups. Each group of geometric entities is projected in a similar fashion. The projected entities could embrace points, lines, arcs, circles, ellipse, hyperbolas, parabolas, 2-D and 3-D splines and strings made out of each of these entities as will be illustrated in the following example.

ICEM EXTENDED EXAMPLE

This exercise has been provided as a courtesy of Control Data Corporation. The material has been extracted from ICEM DDN User's Guide (Publication No. 60000146).

In this practice session, you will use many of the basic construction techniques you have already learned as well as some new techniques to create the three-dimensional bracket shown in figure 10-1.

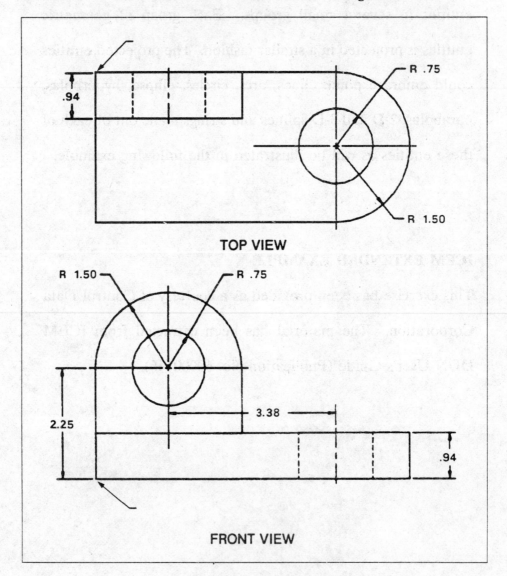

Figure 10-1. Three-Dimensional Bracket

Because you will be referring to figure 10-1 frequently throughout this practice session, you may want to remove the figure and place it next to you as you work through the session.

Getting Started

Log in using the procedures described in the Introduction to this manual.

Create a new part, using the following instructions:

Terminal Prompts	Comments
ENTER . . 1 . . 2 . . 3 . . PARTNAME SHEET NUMBER = 1	Enter the name BRACKET and accept the sheet number of 1.
NEW PART ASSUMED	
UNITS OF MEASURE 1.METRIC (MM) 2.ENGLISH (INCH) 3.ENGLISH (FOOT/INCH)	First, enter M to turn the menu display on. Next, select menu choice 2 to work in U.S. customary units.
DRAFTING STANDARD 1.ANSI 1982 2.ANSI 1973 3. 4. 5. 6. 7. 8. 9.	Select menu choice 1 to use 1982 ANSI standard dimensions.
ICEMDDN L=0 V=1 D=0.00 P=0 C=0	When the banner is displayed, you are ready to proceed.

Defining the Base Point

Define the base point of the bracket at (0,0,0) as follows:

Keyboard Selection

Select 9.POINT from the main menu.

Select 2.KEY-IN from the Point menu.

Select 1.TRANSFORM COORDINATES as the definition space mode.

Tablet Selection

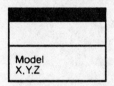

Model
X,Y,Z

Enter 0,0 to define the base point of the bracket:

```
1.XT =
2.YT =
3.ZT = 0.0000
```

Because the point you just created is located at the origin of the screen, part of it is off the screen. For this reason, the system displays the following prompt:

```
ENTITIES DEFINED OFF SCREEN
```

Enter] to return to the Definition Space menu.

Enter] again to return to the Point menu.

Changing the Screen Center

To make it easier to see your part on the screen as you create it, move the center of the screen to the approximate location of the point you just created as follows:

Keyboard Selection

Enter Z to go directly to the Zoom menu.

Select 2.NEW CENTER from the Zoom menu.

Tablet Selection

Zoom			
Auto Max-Min	Diag Position	**1/2 X**	**2X**
Save as Base		New Center Scale	Enter Scale
Return to Base	Retrieve Zoom	Name Zoom	Zoom from Hdcopy

You receive the following prompt asking for the position on the screen that will be the new screen center:

    INDICATE NEW SCREEN CENTER

Position the graphics cursor on or near the point you just created and select that position as the new center of the screen using the C key or the tablet pen.

The point now appears at the center of the screen.

Because you entered the Zoom menu using the Z key, you automatically return to the menu you were in before you used the Zoom function (in this case, the Point menu).

Defining the Front Drill Hole Center Point

Define the center point of the front drill hole as follows:

Keyboard Selection

Select 2.KEY-IN from the Point menu.

Select 1.TRANSFORM COORDINATES as the definition space mode.

Tablet Selection

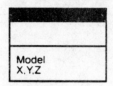

From figure 10-1, you can see that the xt- and yt-coordinate values of the front center point are 1.5 and 2.25, respectively. Enter these values in response to the following prompt:

```
1.XT =
2.YT =
3.ZT = 0.0000
```

Enter] to return to the Definition Space menu.

Enter] again to return to the Point menu.

Creating Two Arcs

Create two arcs around the point you just created as follows:

Keyboard Selection

Enter CTRL-A + RETURN to receive the Arc/Circle/Fillet menu.

Select 3.CENTER AND RADIUS from the Arc/Circle/Fillet menu.

Tablet Selection

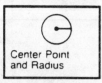

Position the graphics cursor on the point you just created and select it as the center of the circle using the P key or the tablet pen. An attention indicator appears on the point.

Enter .75 as the radius and accept 0 degrees and 360 degrees as the starting and ending angles, respectively, by entering]:

```
1.RADIUS         = 0.2500
2.STARTING ANGLE = 0.0000
3.ENDING ANGLE   = 360.0000
```

The system draws the first arc (a circle).

Select the same point again as the center point using the P key or the tablet pen.

Enter the following radius, starting angle, and ending angle values:

```
1.RADIUS         = 0.7500
2.STARTING ANGLE = 0.0000
3.ENDING ANGLE   = 360.0000
```

The system draws the second arc.

Enter] to return to the Arc/Circle/Fillet menu.

The display on your screen should now match the display in figure 10-2.

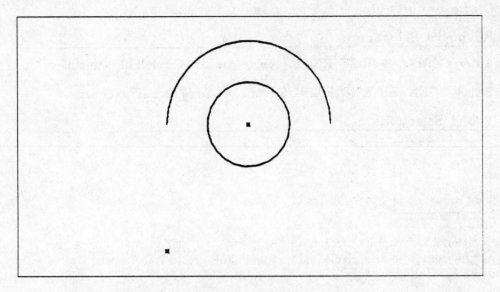

Figure 10-2. Creating Two Arcs

Completing the Front Plate

The next step is to create the sides of the front plate. These lines are highlighted in blue in figure 10-3.

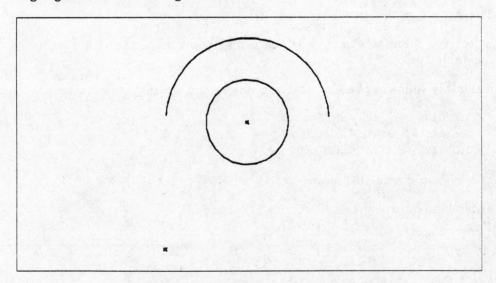

Figure 10-3. Sides of the Front Plate

Create the sides of the front plate as follows:

Keyboard Selection

Enter CTRL-L + RETURN to receive the Line menu.

Select 2.KEY-IN from the Line menu.

Select 1.TRANSFORM COORDINATES as the definition space mode.

Tablet Selection

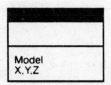

Model
X,Y,Z

Enter the following coordinate values between which the system will draw the lines. Look at figure 10-1 to see how these values were determined.

```
1.XT1 =
2.YT1 =
3.ZT1 = 0.0000
4.XT2 =
5.YT2 =
6.ZT2 = 0.0000
```

```
1.XT1 =
2.YT1 =
3.ZT1 = 0.0000
4.XT2 =
5.YT2 =
6.ZT2 = 0.0000
```

Enter] to return to the Definition Space menu.

Enter] again to return to the Line menu.

Join the two line segments you just created as follows:

Keyboard Selection

Select 14.JOIN 2 CURVES from the Line menu.

Tablet Selection

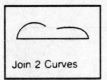

Join 2 Curves

Position the graphics cursor near the bottom of the left vertical line and select it using the L key or the tablet pen.

Position the graphics cursor near the bottom of the right vertical line and select it using the L key or the tablet pen.

NOTE

When joining two curves, it is very important that you select the entities you want to join near the ends that you want joined. Selecting the lines somewhere else produces unpredictable results.

Enter] to return to the Line menu.

Enter F to return to the main menu.

The display on your screen should now match the display in figure 10-4. (The line you added is highlighted in blue.)

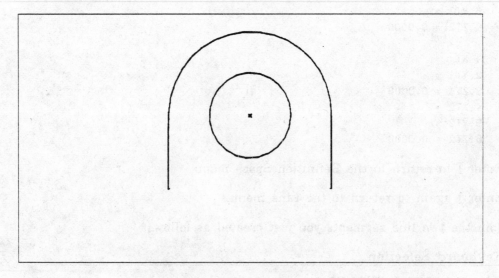

Figure 10-4. Completing the Plate

Projecting the Front Plate

Project the arcs and lines you just created as follows:

Keyboard Selection

Select 13.ENTITY MANIPULATION from the main menu.

Select 16.PROJECTED ENTITIES from the Entity Manipulation menu.

Tablet Selection

Entity Manipulation			
Mirror	Trans	Rotate	Rect Array
Dupl Mirror	Dupl Trans	Dupl Rotate	Circular Array
Stretch	Trans Rotate	Rotate Trans	Array Explode
Group	Dupl Trans Rotate	Dupl Rotate Trans	

In this example, the arcs and lines are projected towards you (positive zt direction) at a distance of .94 inches:

```
DELTA ZT = 0.0000
```

Position the graphics cursor on the full circle and select it using the A key or the tablet pen.

Enter CTRL-E to display the Entity Selection menu.

Select 2.CHAIN from the Entity Selection menu.

Position the graphics cursor on the right vertical line segment and select it using the L key or the tablet pen.

Move the graphics cursor a short distance along the outline of the plate and enter C or press down with the tablet pen to indicate the direction for chaining the contiguous curves.

Enter] to tell ICEM DDN that you have finished selecting entities.

Enter [to return to the Entity Manipulation menu.

Enter F to return to the main menu.

Displaying Four Views of the Projected Plate

Display the front plate in four views as follows:

Keyboard Selection

Select 8.DISPLAY CONTROL from the main menu.

Select 4.DISPLAY MULTIPLE VIEWS from the Display Control menu.

Select 9.VIEWS 6, 1, 3, 8 (TOP/FRONT/RIGHT/ISO1) to display the plate in the four standard views.

Tablet Selection

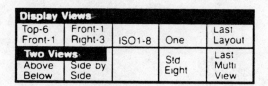

Next, you are asked to select the zoom scale for the display:

```
ZOOM SCALE FOR MULTIPLE VIEWS
1.LAST SCALE USED
2.BASE SCALE
3.SAVED SCALE
4.ENTER SCALE
5.AUTOMATICALLY MAXIMIZED
```

Select 5.AUTOMATICALLY MAXIMIZED as the zoom scale.

The display on your screen should now match the display in figure 10-5. The view names are not displayed, but are added here for your information.

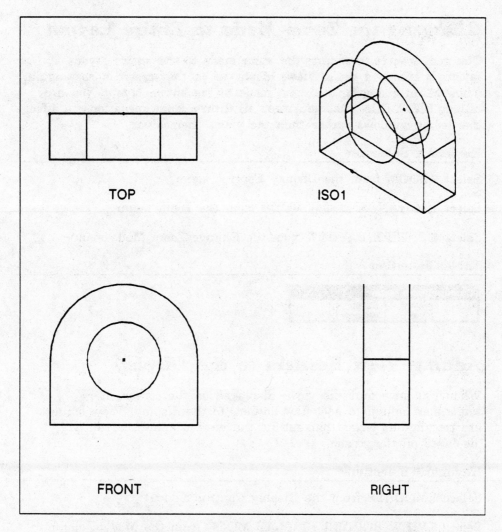

Figure 10-5. Four Views of the Projected Plate

Changing the Zoom Mode to Entire Layout

The next step is to change the zoom mode to the entire layout. A layout is simply a set of views displayed on the screen in rectangular windows. In changing the zoom mode to the entire layout, you are telling ICEM DDN that you want all future zoom operations to affect the layout windows rather than the views themselves.

Keyboard Selection

Select 6.ZOOM from the Display Control menu.

Select 17.CHANGE ZOOM MODE from the Zoom menu.

Select 1.ENTIRE LAYOUT from the Change Zoom Mode menu.

Tablet Selection

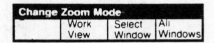

Change Zoom Mode		
Work View	Select Window	All Windows

Adding View Borders to the Display

When you have multiple views displayed on the screen, it is sometimes helpful to add view borders to the display. View borders are rectangular boxes that outline the view windows currently displayed on the screen.

Keyboard Selection

Select 1.MODALS from the Display Control menu.

Select 5.VIEW BORDER DISPLAY MODE from the Modals menu.

Tablet Selection

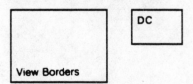

Select 3.DISPLAY IN ALL VIEWS from the View Border Display Mode menu. The system displays the view borders on the screen.

Enter] to return to the Display Control menu.

Zooming the Entire Layout

You can scale down the entire layout to 75 percent of its current size as follows:

Keyboard Selection

Select 6.ZOOM from the Display Control menu.

Select 8.ENTER SCALE from the Zoom menu.

Tablet Selection

Zoom			
Auto Max-Min	Diag Position	**1/2 X**	**2X**
Save as Base	New Center	New Center Scale	
Return to Base	Retrieve Zoom	Name Zoom	Zoom from Hdcopy

Next, you are asked to enter a new scale factor or ratio.

Accept 1.0 as the scale factor, but change the ratio to .75 as shown below. (You can modify only one of these values to determine the zoom scale.) The ratio is used to establish a new scale relative to the current scale. In this example, the display scale will be 75 percent of the current scale factor.

```
1.SCALE = 1.0000
2.RATIO = 1.0000
```

The entire layout is scaled down to 75 percent of the current scale factor.

The display on your screen should now match the display in figure 10-6.

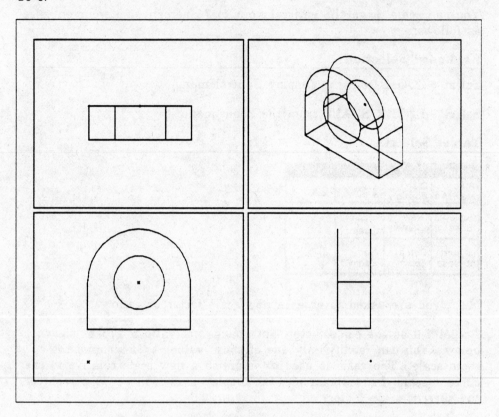

Figure 10-6. Multiple View Display at .75 Scale

Defining the Center Point of the Bottom Drill Hole

The next step is to define the center point of the bottom drill hole. But before you do that, it is important that you change the work view to view 6, which is the top view of the part.

The work view tells you how you are looking at your part. For example, when you change the work view from the front view to the top view, it is as if you are now looking down at the top of the part. If you have more than one view displayed on the screen, the display will not look any different than it did when the front view was the current work view.

If you have only one view of your part displayed on the screen, that view is always the work view. However, when there is more than one view displayed on the screen, as there is now, it is important that you know which of the displayed views is the current work view. If you are not sure, just go to the main menu heading and check the value of V. At this time, the work view is view 1, which is the front view:

```
ICEMDDN  L=0  V=1  D=0.00  P=0  C=0
```

Change the current work view to the top view as follows:

Keyboard Selection

Select 8.DISPLAY CONTROL from the main menu.

Select 5.CHANGE WORK VIEW from the Display Control menu.

Tablet Selection

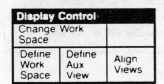

Enter 6 as the new work view:

```
WORK VIEW IS 1  SELECT ANOTHER
VIEW NUMBER =
```

Now define the center point of the bottom drill hole as follows:

Keyboard Selection

Enter CTRL-P + RETURN to receive the Point menu.

Select 2.KEY-IN from the Point menu.

Select 1.TRANSFORM COORDINATES as the definition space mode.

Tablet Selection

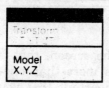

From figure 10-1, you can see that the xt- and yt-coordinate values of this point are 4.88 and -1.5, respectively. Enter these values in response to the following prompt:

```
1.XT = 4.88
2.YT = -1.5
3.ZT = 0.0000
```

Enter] to return to the Definition Space menu.

Enter] to return to the Point menu.

NOTE

Note that the point you just created is out of the view window in some of the views on the screen. Next, you will learn how to change the zoom mode in order to display all currently defined entities.

Enter F to return to the main menu.

Changing the Zoom Mode to Affect All Views

Change the zoom mode to display all of the currently defined entities as follows:

Keyboard Selection

Select 8.DISPLAY CONTROL from the main menu.

Select 6.ZOOM from the Display Control menu.

Select 17.CHANGE ZOOM MODE from the Zoom menu.

Select 3.ALL VIEWS from the Change Zoom Mode menu.

Tablet Selection

This tells ICEM DDN that you want all future zoom operations to affect all displayed views rather than the entire layout.

Now automatically maximize all of the views as follows:

Keyboard Selection

Select 6.ZOOM from the Display Control menu.

Select 11.AUTOMATIC MAX-MINS from the Zoom menu.

Tablet Selection

Zoom			
	Diag Position	1/2 X	2X
Save as Base	New Center	New Center Scale	Enter Scale
Return to Base	Retrieve Zoom	Name Zoom	Zoom from Hdcopy

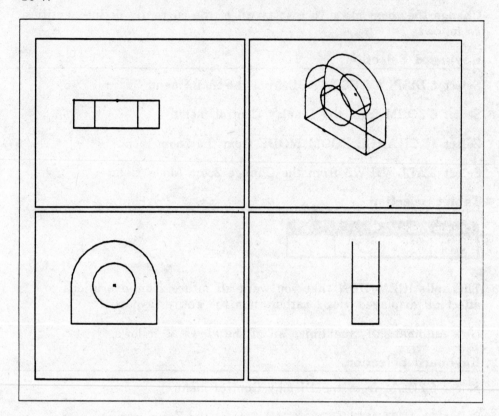

The display on your screen should now match the display in figure 10-7.

Figure 10-7. Automatically Maximized View Display

Creating the Remaining Arcs

Create two arcs around the point you just created as follows:

Keyboard Selection

Enter CTRL-A + RETURN to receive the Arc/Circle/Fillet menu.

Select 3.CENTER AND RADIUS from the Arc/Circle/Fillet menu.

Tablet Selection

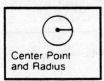

Center Point
and Radius

Position the graphics cursor on the point you just created and select it as the center of the circle using the P key or the tablet pen. An attention indicator appears on the point.

NOTE

It may be helpful to select these points in the isometric view. With ICEM DDN, you can select entities in any view you want—even if the view is not the current work view. When selecting entities in a view other than the work view, attention indicators appear in both the view you are selecting entities in *and* in the work view.

Enter .75 as the radius and accept 0 degrees and 360 degrees as the starting and ending angles, respectively, by entering]:

```
1.RADIUS          = 1.5000
2.STARTING ANGLE  = 0.0000
3.ENDING ANGLE    = 360.0000
```

The system draws the first arc (in this case, a circle).

Select the same point again as the center point using the P key or the tablet pen.

Enter the following radius, starting angle, and ending angle values:

```
1.RADIUS          = 0.7500
2.STARTING ANGLE  = 0.0000
3.ENDING ANGLE    = 360.0000
```

The system draws the second arc.

Enter] to return to the Arc/Circle/Fillet menu.

Note that the second arc is out of the view window in some of the views on the screen. Automatically maximize all of the views to display all of the entities as follows:

Keyboard Selection

Enter Z to go directly to the Zoom menu.

Select 11.AUTOMATIC MAX-MINS from the Zoom menu.

Tablet Selection

Zoom			
	Diag Position	1/2 X	2X
Save as Base	New Center	New Center Scale	Enter Scale
Return to Base	Retrieve Zoom	Name Zoom	Zoom from Hdcopy

The display on your screen should now match the display in figure
10-8.

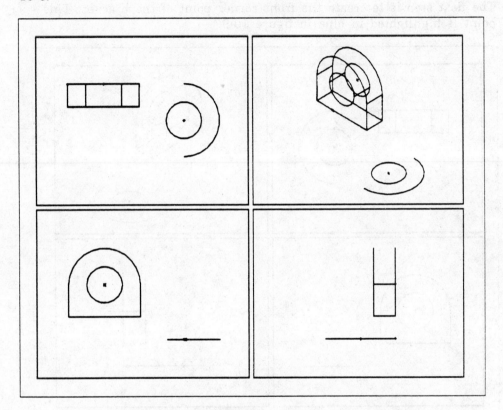

Figure 10-8. Creating the Remaining Two Arcs

Creating the Front Corner Point

The next step is to create the front corner point of the bracket. This point is highlighted in blue in figure 10-9.

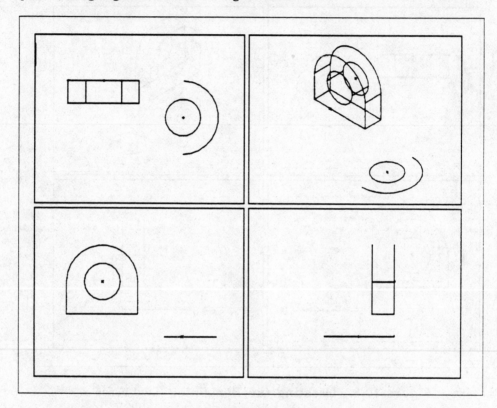

Figure 10-9. Creating the Right Front Corner Point

Create the front corner point as follows:

Keyboard Selection

Enter CTRL-P + RETURN to receive the Point menu.

Select 2.KEY-IN from the Point menu.

Select 1.TRANSFORM COORDINATES as the definition space mode.

Tablet Selection

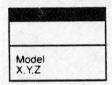

From figure 10-1, you can see that the xt- and yt-coordinate values of this point are 0 and -3, respectively. Enter these values in response to the following prompt:

```
1.XT =
2.YT =
3.ZT = 0.0000
```

Enter] to return to the Definition Space menu.

Joining the Base Point and the Front Corner Point

Join the base point and the front corner point as follows:

Keyboard Selection

Enter CTRL-L + RETURN to receive the Line menu.

Select 3.JOIN 2 POINTS from the Line menu.

Tablet Selection

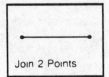

Position the graphics cursor on the base point called out in figure 10-10 and select it using the P key or the tablet pen.

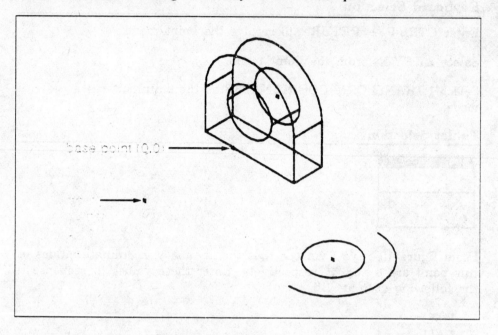

base point (0.0)

Figure 10-10. Joining the Base and Front Corner Points

Position the graphics cursor on the front corner point you just created (called out in figure 10-10) and select it using the P key or the tablet pen.

A line joining these points appears on the screen.

Enter] to return to the Line menu.

Completing the Base Outline

Complete the base outline of the bracket as follows:

Keyboard Selection

Enter CTRL-L + RETURN to receive the Line menu.

Select 14.JOIN 2 CURVES from the Line menu.

Tablet Selection

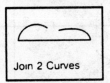

Join 2 Curves

Position the graphics cursor near the bottom end of the arc as shown in figure 10-11 and select it as the first curve using the A key or the tablet pen.

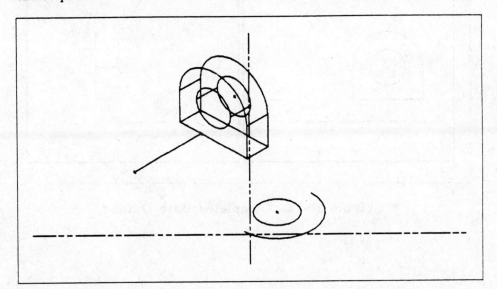

Figure 10-11. Graphics Cursor Position for Joining Two Curves

Position the graphics cursor on the front corner point and select it as the second curve using the P key or the tablet pen. Remember that a curve can be a point, line, or arc.

A line joining the point and arc you selected appears on your screen.

Using what you just learned, complete the base outline by creating the line opposite the line you just created.

The display on your screen should now match the display in figure 10-12.

Enter F to return to the main menu.

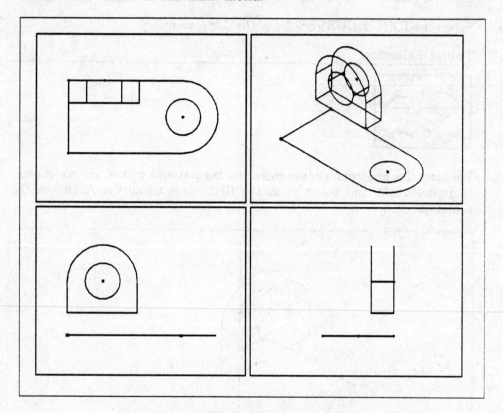

Figure 10-12. Completed Base Outline

Projecting the Base of the Bracket

Project the base outline of the bracket as follows:

Keyboard Selection

Select 13.ENTITY MANIPULATION from the main menu.

Select 16.PROJECTED ENTITIES from the Entity Manipulation menu.

Tablet Selection

Entity Manipulation			
Mirror	Trans	Rotate	Rect Array
Dupl Mirror	Dupl Trans	Dupl Rotate	Circular Array
Stretch	Trans Rotate	Rotate Trans	Array Explode
Group	Dupl Trans Rotate	Dupl Rotate Trans	

Enter RETURN to accept .94 as the delta zt value. (This value is preserved from the last time you projected entities.)

    DELTA ZT = 0.9400

Position the graphics cursor on the full circle and select it using the A key or the tablet pen.

Enter CTRL-E to display the Entity Selection menu.

Select 2.CHAIN from the Entity Selection menu.

Position the graphics cursor on the larger arc and select it using the A key or the tablet pen.

Move the graphics cursor a short distance along the outline of the bracket and enter C or press down with the tablet pen to indicate the direction for chaining the contiguous curves.

NOTE

It is important to remember that when you are using the chain selection method with multiple views displayed on the screen, you must select the first entity in the chain and indicate the direction of the chain selection in the current work view, which in this case is the top view.

Enter] to tell ICEM DDN that you have finished selecting entities.

Enter [to return to the Entity Manipulation menu.

Enter F to return to the main menu.

The display on your screen should now match the display in figure 10-13.

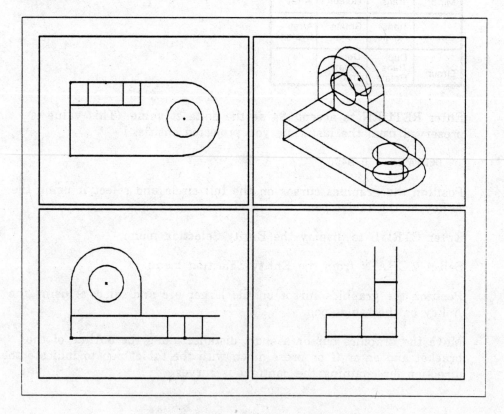

Figure 10-13. Completed Bracket

Filing and Exiting

This completes the exercise. Use the following steps to save your part:

Terminal Prompts	Comments
`ICEMDDN L=0 V=1 D=0.00 P=0 C=1`	If you are using the keyboard, enter 4 to select the File/Exit ICEM DDN menu.
	If you are using the tablet, you can file your part and exit from ICEM DDN in a single step by selecting the File/Quit square with your tablet pen.

`FILE CURRENT PART/EXIT ICEM DDN`
`1.FILE-CONTINUE CURRENT PART`
`2.    -GET DIFFERENT PART`
`3.    -QUIT SESSION`
`4.    -SUSPEND SESSION`
`5.DO NOT FILE-CONTINUE FROM LAST FILE`
`6.         -GET DIFFERENT PART`
`7.         -QUIT SESSION`
`8.         -SUSPEND SESSION`
	Select 3.FILE-QUIT SESSION to save your part and exit from ICEM DDN.

`ICEMDDN TERMINATED.`	
	Log out from the system as described in the Introduction to this manual.

CHAPTER 11

COMPUTER-GENERATED SECTIONS AND DETAILS: EXAMPLES

Introduction

So far, we have seen how it is possible to represent an object's shape and features by means of orthographic projections and pictorials. In the case of simple shapes, this is all you need. However, in devices and complicated parts it is necessary to show the interior details. As we discussed in Chapter 3, hidden lines provide us with an idea of the interior, but sometimes they tend to confuse the drawing. An unobstructed view of the interior of the object will clarify its description.

Sectional Drawings

Sectional drawings and views are utilized to provide the interior geometry of the object. To obtain a section, as it is commonly called, the object is imaginarily sliced by a cutting plane of projection. We pretend that the cutout portion between the cutting plane and the observer has been removed. The solid cut surface of the object is indicated by a pattern of diagonal lines (crosshatching) named section lining or cross sectioning, as shown in Figure 11.1

A full section is illustrated in Figure 11.2. Notice that the part (only

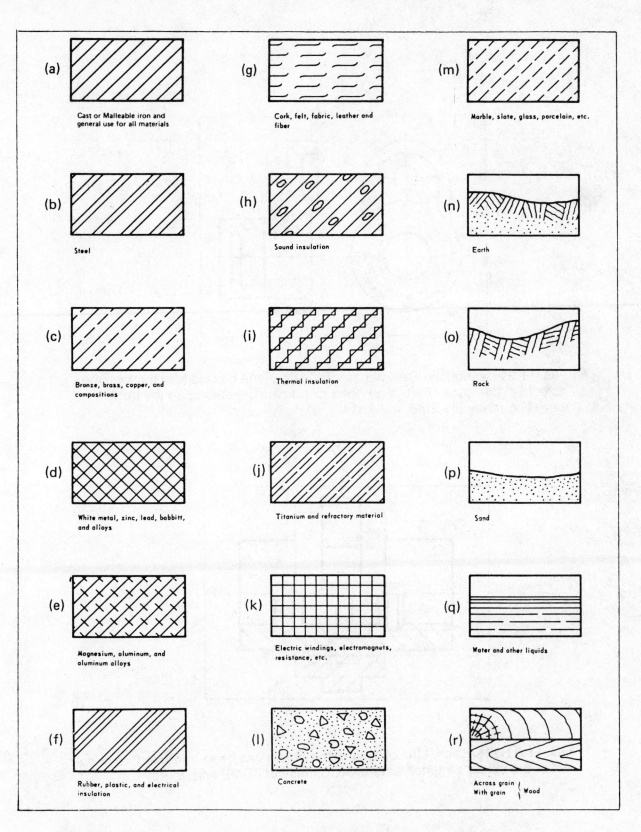

FIG. 11.1 Crosshatching, section lining or cross sectioning symbols. The general symbol is the pattern of diagonal lines on (a), other standard materials are on (b) through (r). (Courtesy of ASME and ANSI.)

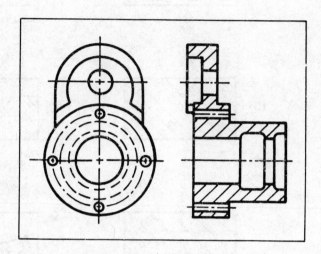

FIG. 11.2 Full section. The imaginary cutting plane passes fully through the object. In this case, there is no need to indicate the cutting on the front view. (Courtesy of ASME and ANSI.)

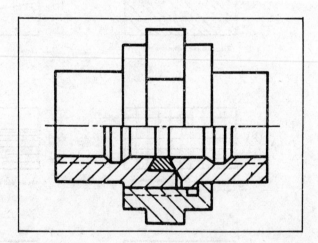

FIG. 11.3 Half section. One quarter of the object has been "removed" to show half of the object's interior features. (Courtesy of ASME and ANSI.)

the front view is shown) has been sliced in half. The imaginary cutting plane passes fully through the object along its center line of symmetry. Solid portions of the object are cross hatched and the exposed background features are indicated by visible lines. Since the cutting plane is evident there is no need to mark its position.

Figure 11.3 displays a half section assembly, in which one quarter of the object has been "removed" to show half of its interior features. The view is projected in two cutting planes passing at 90 degrees to each other, and folded along the axis of symmetry of the part. Again, the cutting plane line has been omitted since it coincides with the center line.

The position of a cutting plane is shown in Figure 11.4, by a dark, heavy line. Observe that the cutting plane line, D-D, indicates the edge view of an offset plane. Offset section, D-D, shows important features not positioned in a straight line. The cutting plane is usually stepped at right angles.

An aligned section is drawn when there are angular features, as shown in Figure 11.5. Section A-A is obtained by rotating the cutting plane into a plane of projection perpendicular to the lines-of-sight.

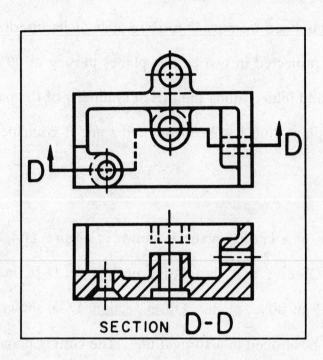

FIG. 11.4 Cutting plane D-D of an offset section. Shows important features not positioned in straight line. (Courtesy of ASME and ANSI.)

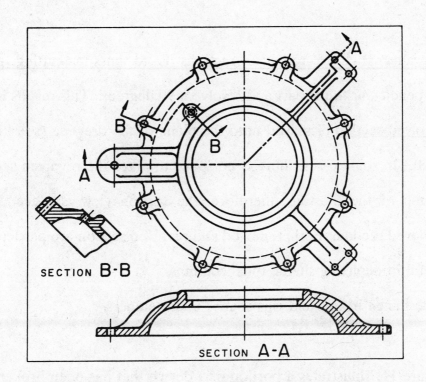

FIG. 11.5 Aligned section. Section A-A is obtained by rotating the cutting plane into a plane of projection perpendicular to the lines-of-sight. (Courtesy of ASME and ANSI.)

A series of <u>removed sections</u> are illustrated in Figures 11.6 and 11.7. ANSI defines a removed section as a section displaced from its normal projection position (i.e., not been in direct projection of the view comprising the cutting plane line). Some designers draw the removed sections at a different scale than the reference view.

An alternative to removed sections is to pass a cutting plane perpendicular to the part and revolve it 90 degrees. This results in the <u>revolved section</u> displayed onto the plane of the drawing (see Figure 11.8). In some cases, there is no space to place the revolved section in top of the drawing; therefore, the section view is placed as a removed section. Both, removed and revolved section are particularly useful in depicting shafts, rods, columns, wide flange beams and ribs shapes and members.

Figure 11.9 illustrates a portion of a device that has been broken-out to expose a portion of the object. These <u>broken-out sections</u> improve the representation of the device or object, without having to draw a complete section.

Examples of computer-generated sections and details
Figures 11.10 through 11.32 illustrate several examples of drawings created with the AutoCAD graphics package.

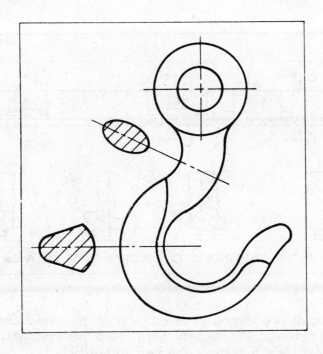

FIG. 11.6 Removed sections displaced from their normal projection position.
(Courtesy of ASME and ANSI.)

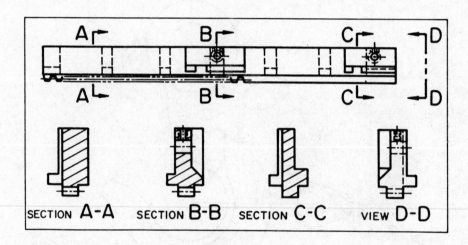

FIG. 11.7 Examples of enlarged removed sections and views. Sections A-A, B-B, C-C have been removed and magnify. View D-D provides additional details from a different point of view. (Courtesy of ASME and ANSI.)

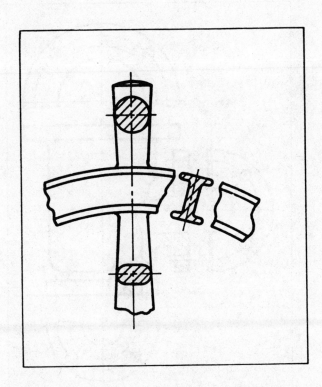

FIG. 11.8 Revolved section constructed by passing a cutting plane perpendicular to the part and revolving it 90 degrees. (Courtesy of ASME and ANSI.)

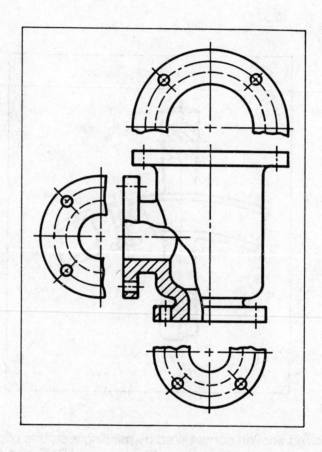

FIG. 11.9 Broken-out section. A portion of an object has been open to expose a piece of it. Partial top, left-side and bottom views of the object supplement its description. (Courtesy of ASME and ANSI.)

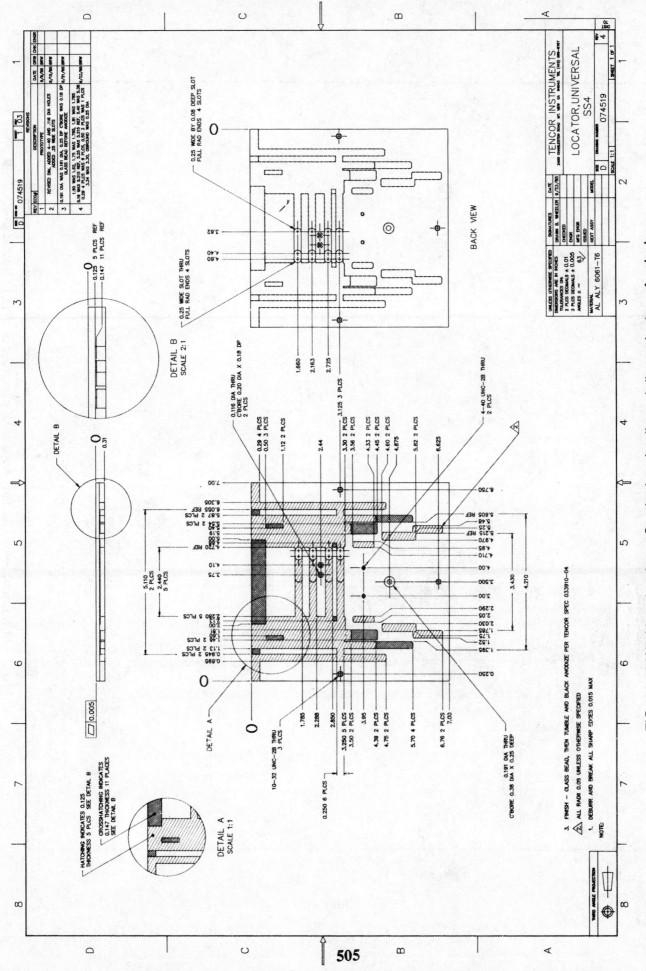

FIG. 11.10 Working drawings: Sectioning details and dimensioning of a device. (Courtesy of Tencor Instruments and Autodesk, Inc.)

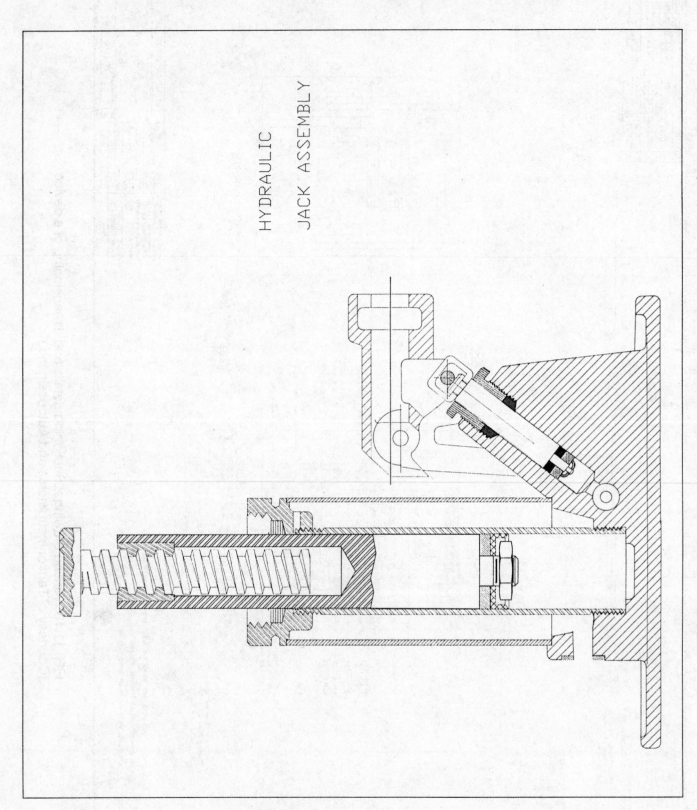

HYDRAULIC

JACK ASSEMBLY

FIG. 11.11 Section: Hydraulic Jack Assembly. (Courtesy of Univ. of Nebraska-Lincoln and Autodesk, Inc.)

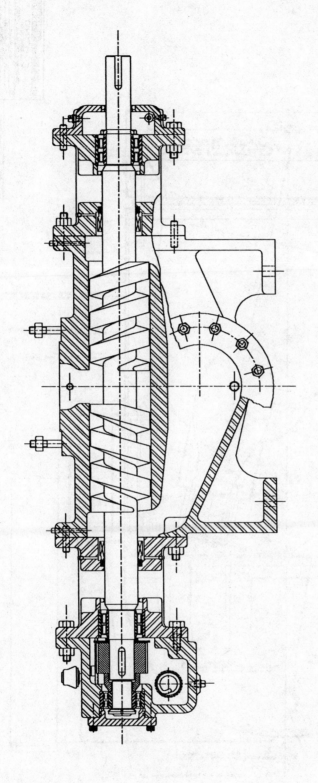

SECTIONAL – ROTARY SCREW PUMP

FIG. 11.12 Sectional drawing: Rotary Screw Pump. (Courtesy of Worthington Dresser and Autodesk, Inc.)

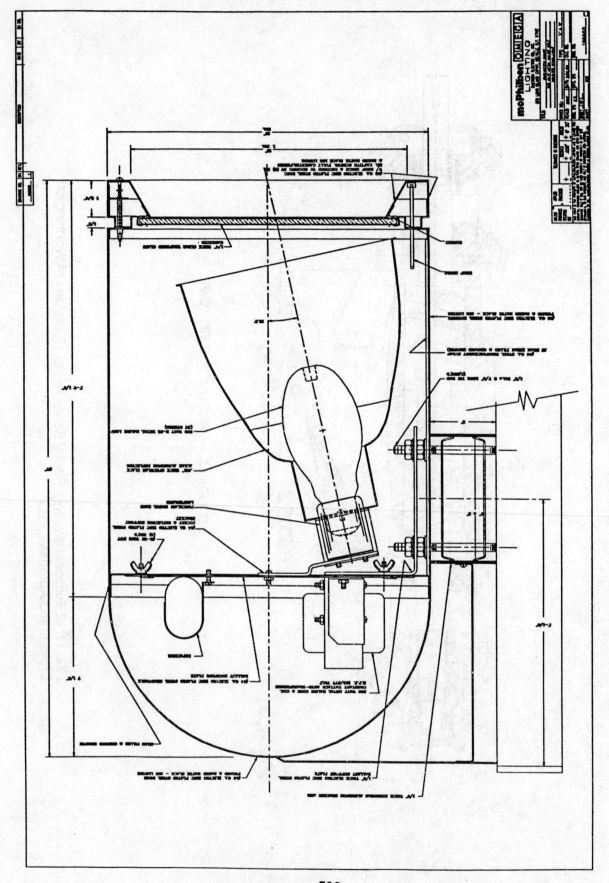

FIG. 11.13 Working drawing; lighting device. (Courtesy of McPhiben Lighting and Autodesk, Inc.)

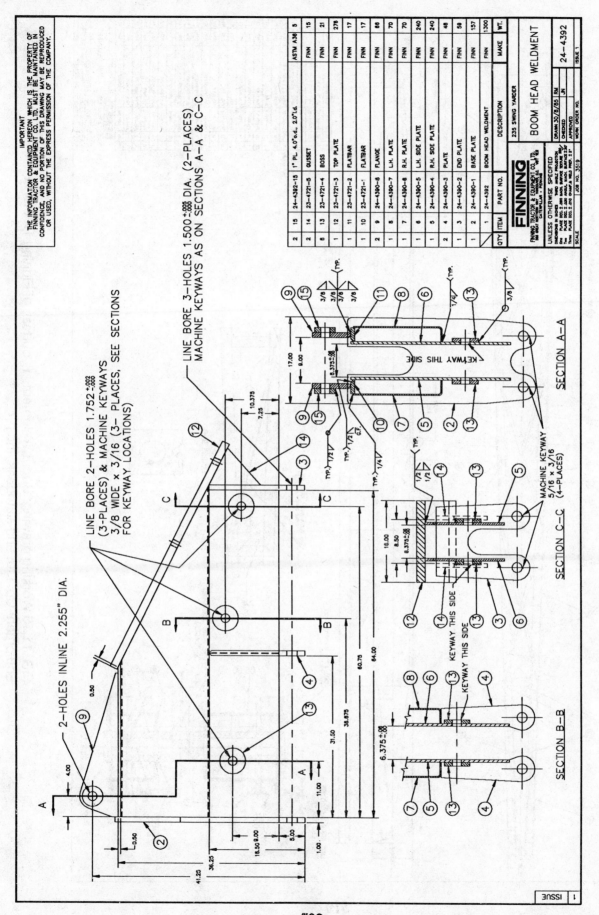

FIG. 11.14 Working drawing: Boom Head Weldment. (Courtesy of Finning Tractor & Equipment Co. Ltd. and Autodesk, Inc.)

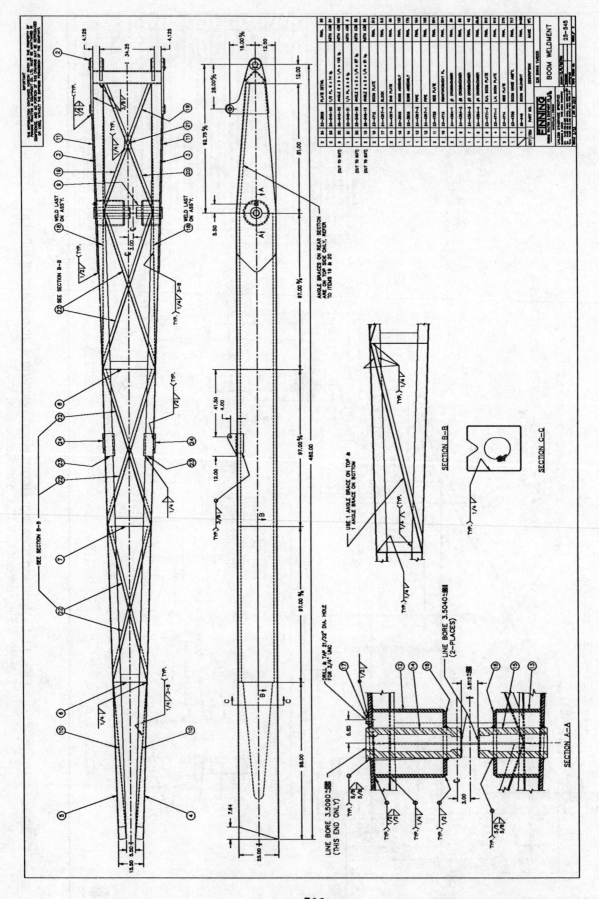

FIG. 11.15 Working drawing: Boom Weldment. (Courtesy of Finning Tractor & Equipment Co. Ltd. and Autodesk, Inc.)

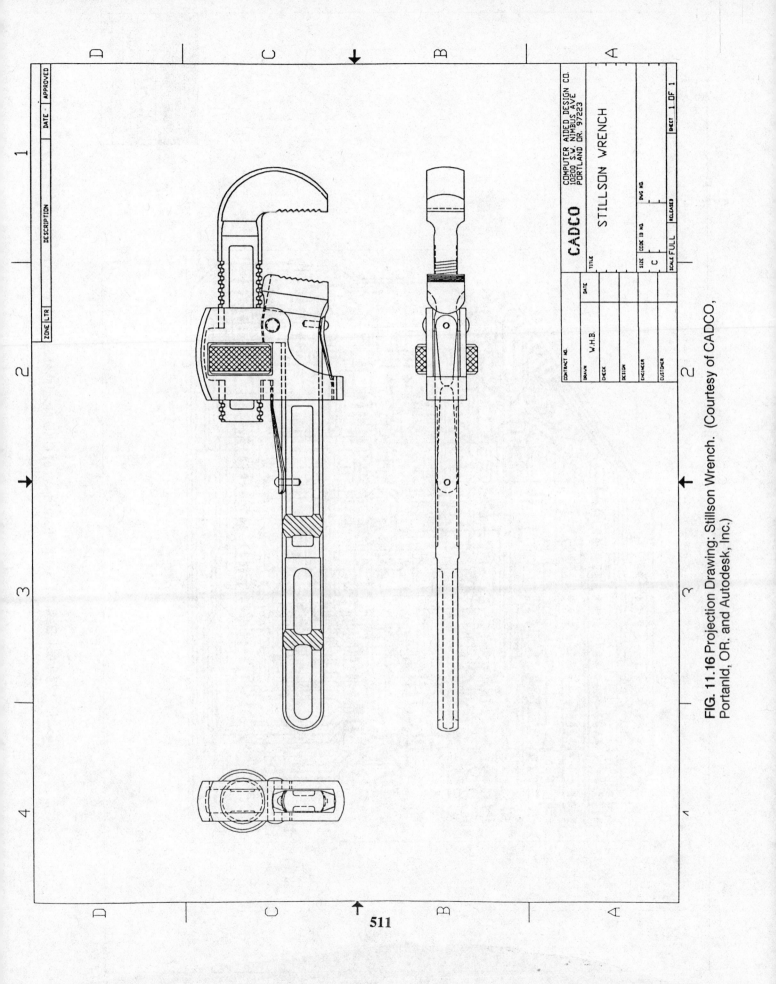

FIG. 11.16 Projection Drawing: Stillson Wrench. (Courtesy of CADCO, Portanld, OR. and Autodesk, Inc.)

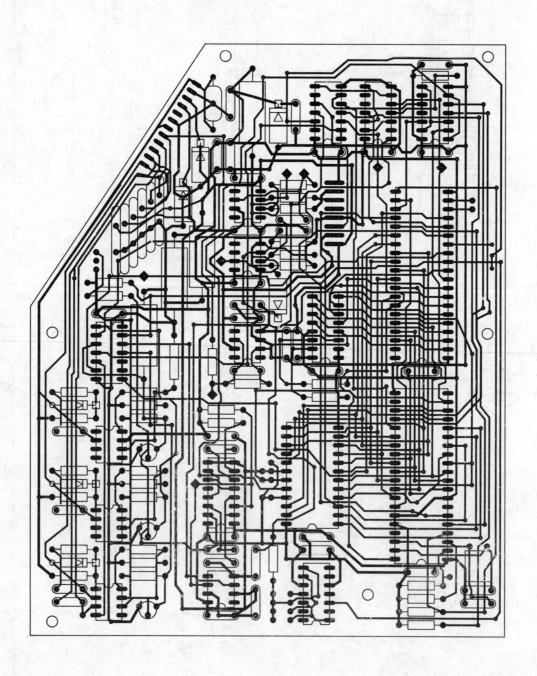

FIG. 11.17 Circuit Board Layout. (Courtesy of CAD Northwest, Inc. and Autodesk, Inc.)

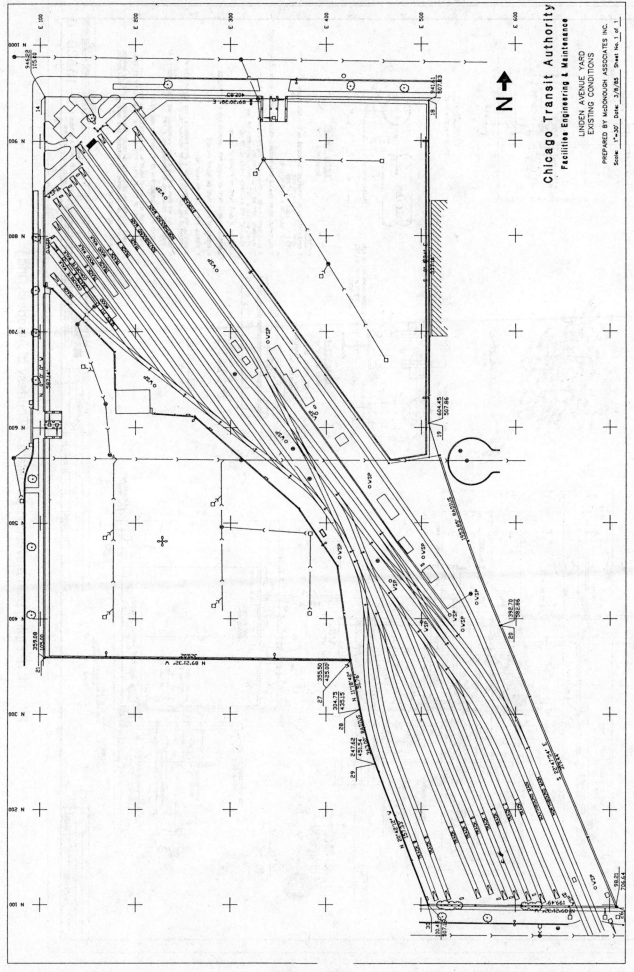

FIG. 11.18 "As-built" Drawing. (Courtesy of McDonough Associates, Inc., Chicago Transit Authority and Autodesk, Inc.)

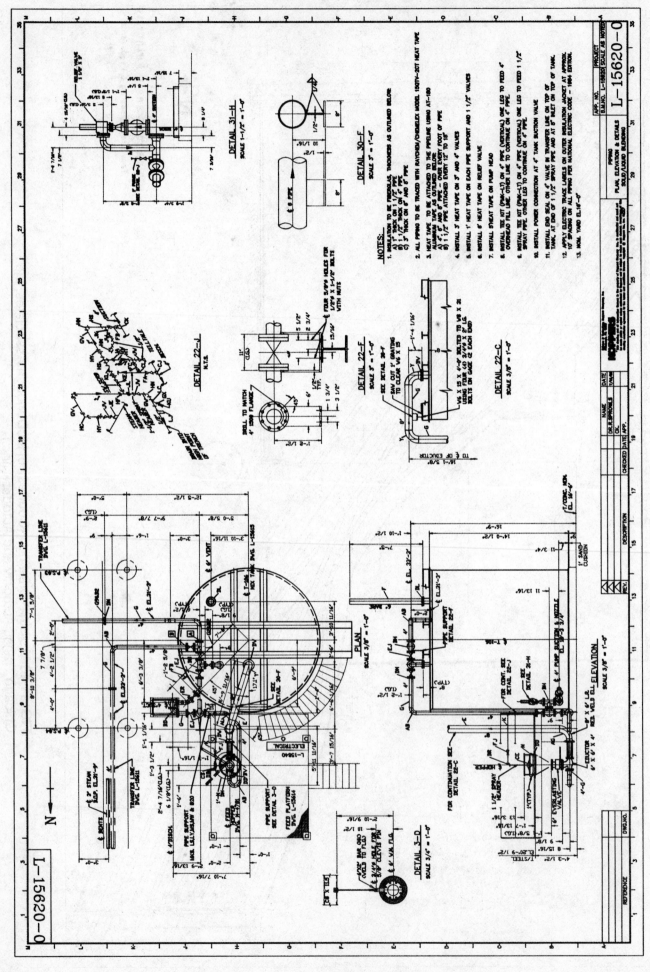

FIG. 11.19 Piping plan elevation and details. (Courtesy of Autodesk, Inc.)

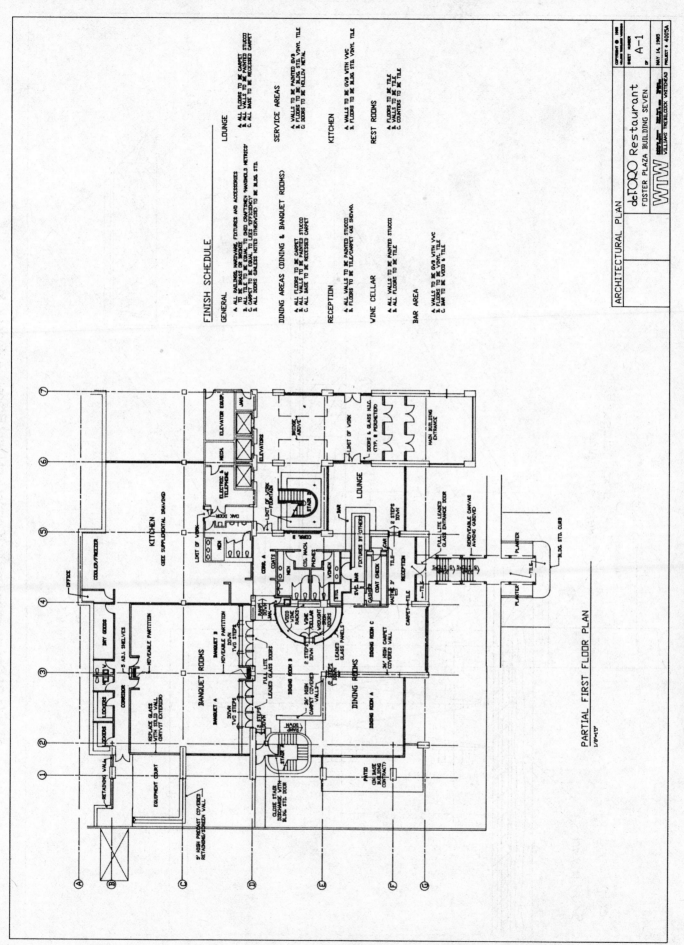

FIG. 11.20 Architectural Plan. (Courtesy of Williams, Trebilcock and Whitehead, Associates, Inc. and Autodesk, Inc.)

515

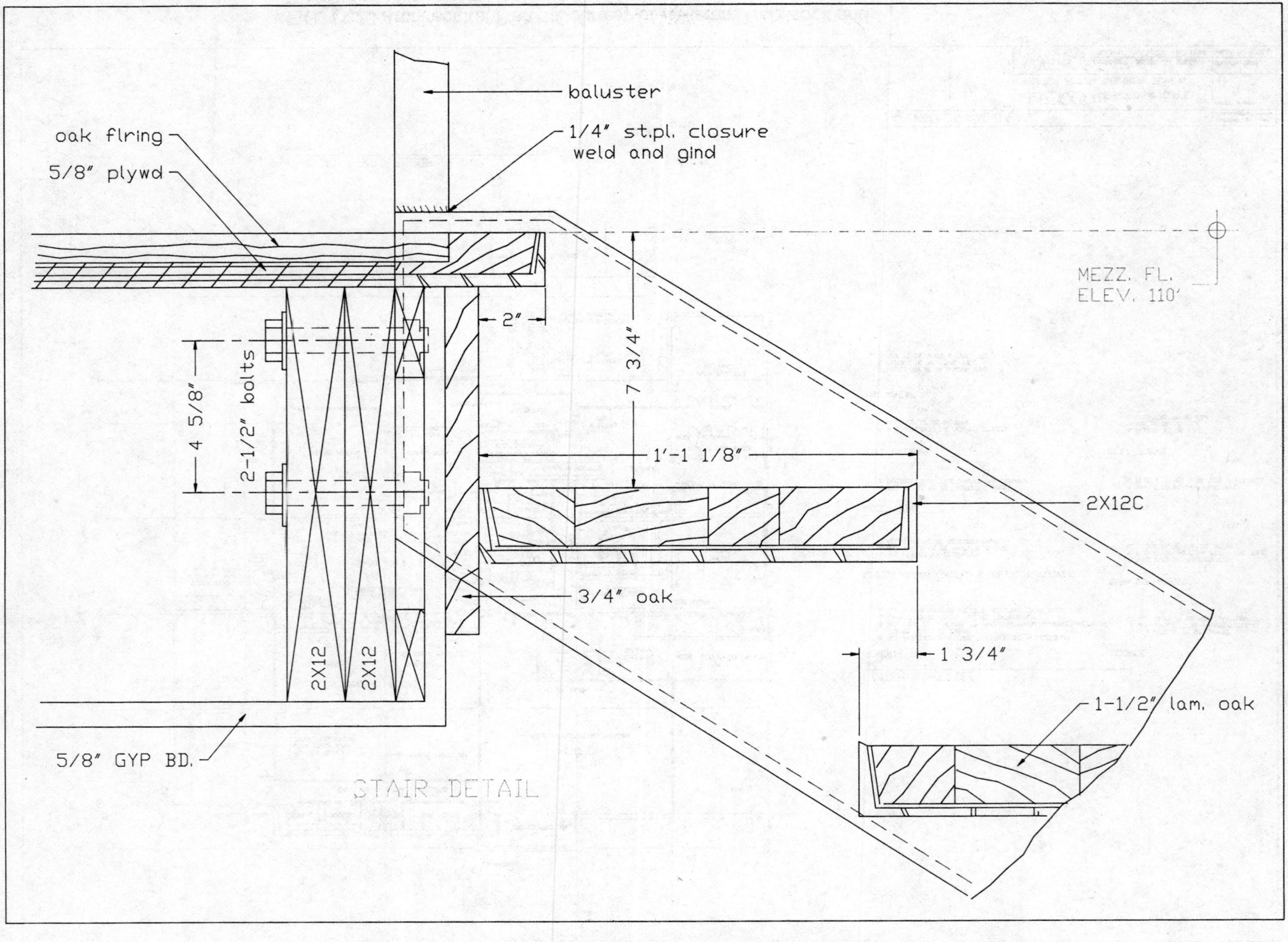

MEZZ. FL.
ELEV. 110'

baluster

1/4" st.pl. closure
weld and gind

2X12C

1'-1 1/8"

7 3/4"

1 3/4"

1-1 1/2" lam. oak

3/4" oak

2"

2X12

2X12

2-1/2" bolts

4 5/8"

oak flring
5/8" plywd

5/8" GYP BD.

STAIR DETAIL

FIG. 11.21 Construction Detail. (Courtesy of Peter Branett, Autodesk, Inc.)

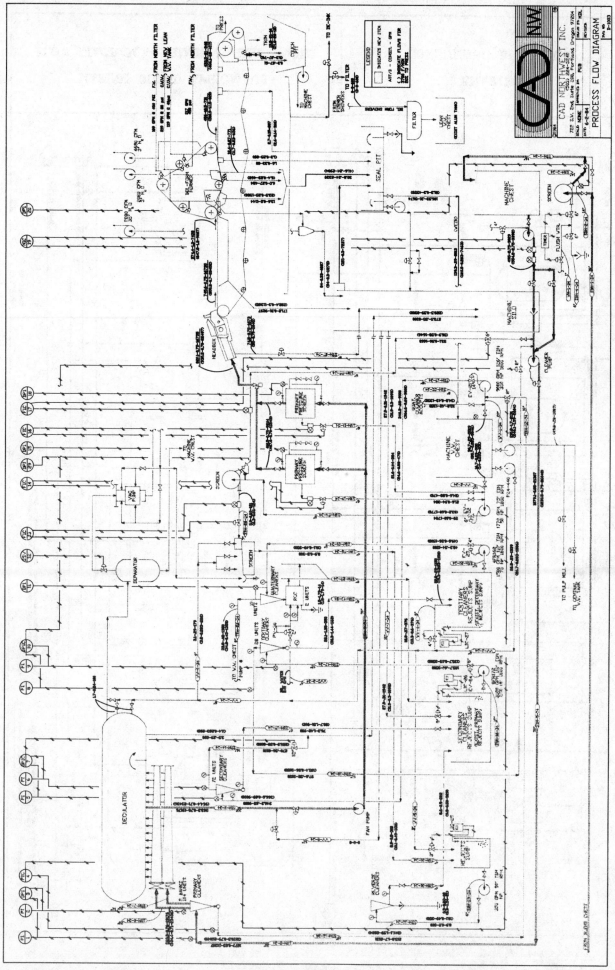

FIG. 11.22 Process Flow Diagram. (Courtesy of CAD Northwest, Inc. and Autodesk, Inc.)

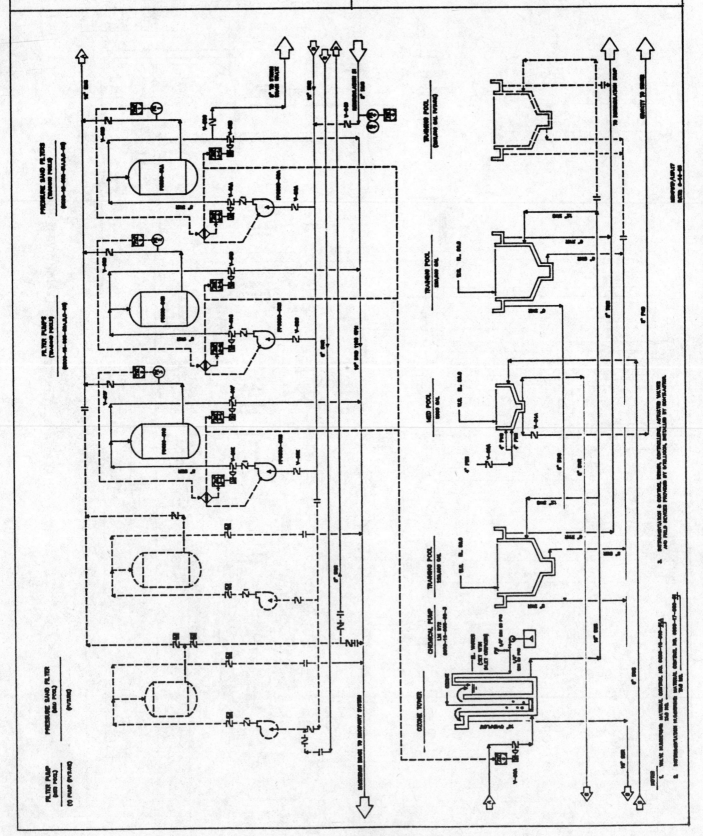

FIG. 11.23 Flow diagram. (Courtesy of ENARTEC Consulting Engineers and Autodesk, Inc.)

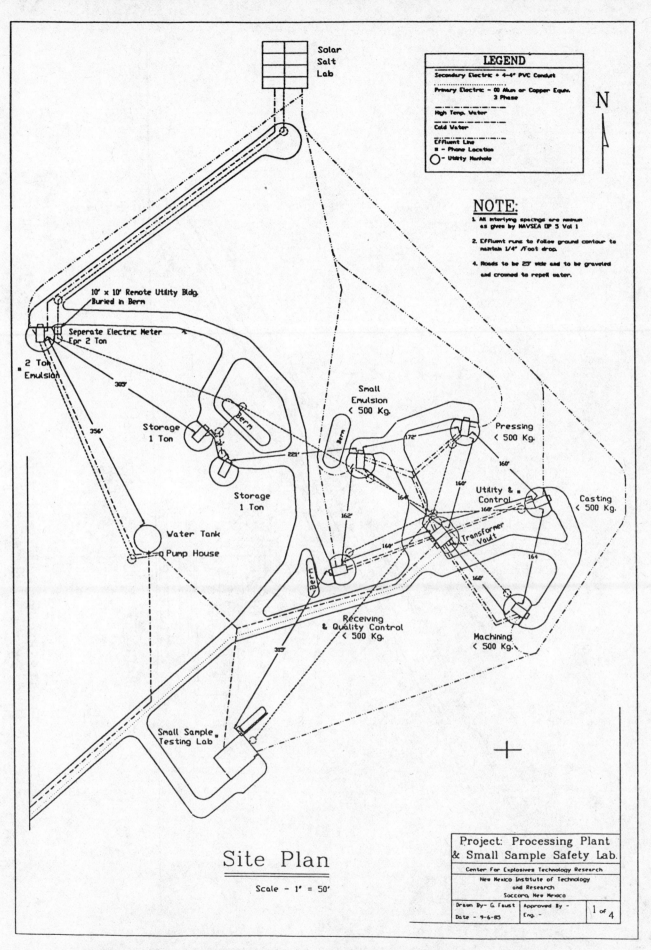

Site Plan

Scale - 1' = 50'

FIG. 11.24 Site Plan. (Courtesy of George Faust, Belen, NM and Autodesk, Inc.)

519

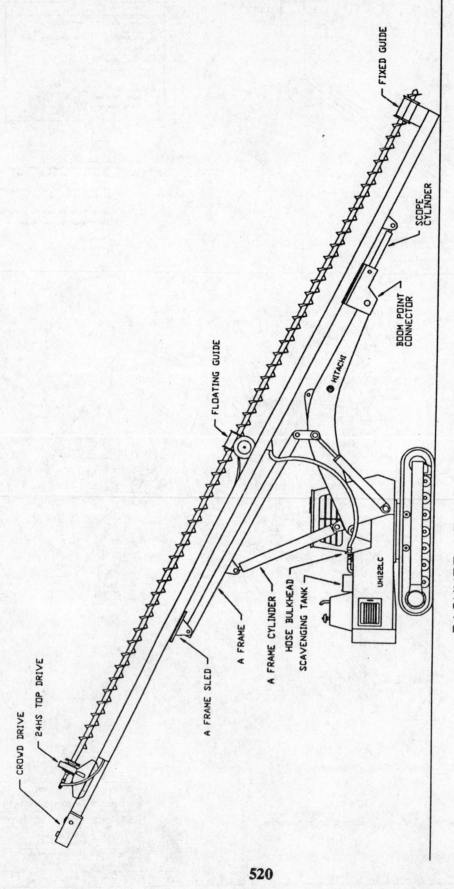

CROWD DRIVE

24HS TOP DRIVE

FLOATING GUIDE

FIXED GUIDE

SCOPE CYLINDER

A FRAME SLED

A FRAME

A FRAME CYLINDER

HOSE BULKHEAD

SCAVENGING TANK

HITACHI

UH122LC

BOOM POINT CONNECTOR

BACKHOE MOUNT TIEBACK MACHINE
GENERAL ASSEMBLY

FIG. 11.25 Backhoe Mount General Assembly Drawing. (Courtesy of Bay Shore
Drilling Systems, Inc. and Autodesk, Inc.)

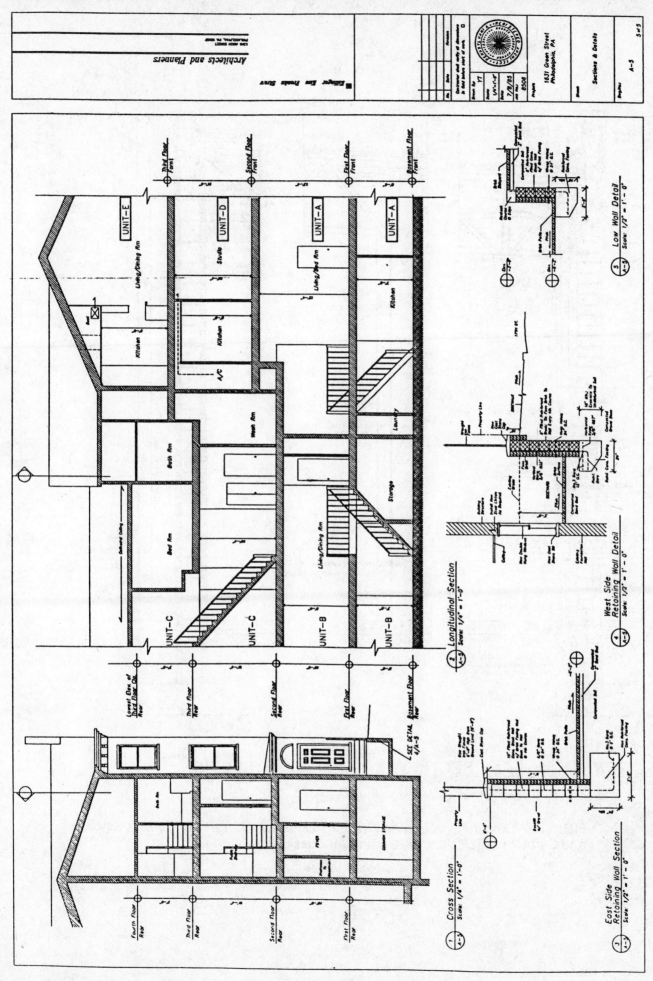

FIG. 11.26 Architectural Cross Sectional Drawing. (Courtesy of Kliger, Kise, Franks, Straw, Inc. and Autodesk, Inc.)

521

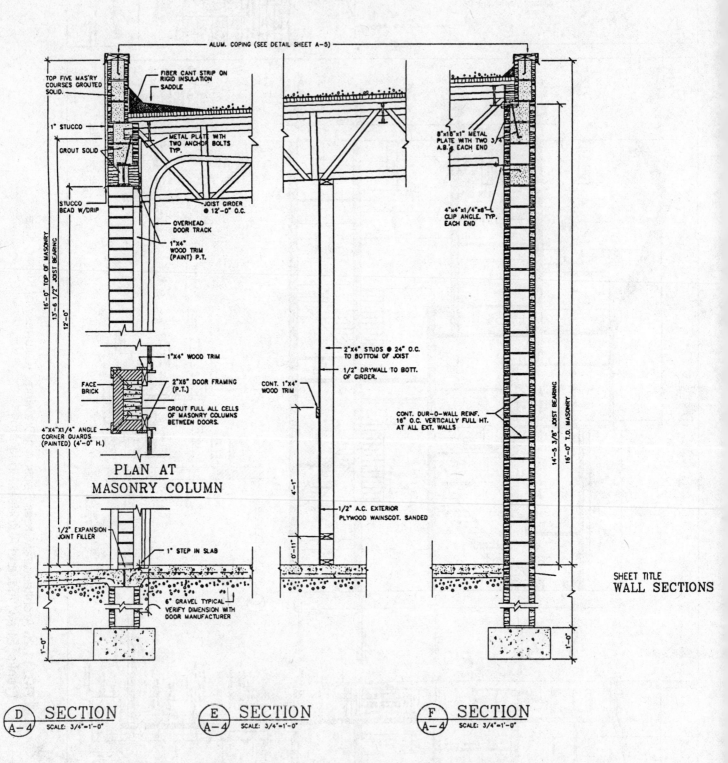

FIG. 11.27 Construction and Architectural Details. (Courtesy of Cynthia King and Carol Woodruff, Atlanta, GA and Autodesk, Inc.)

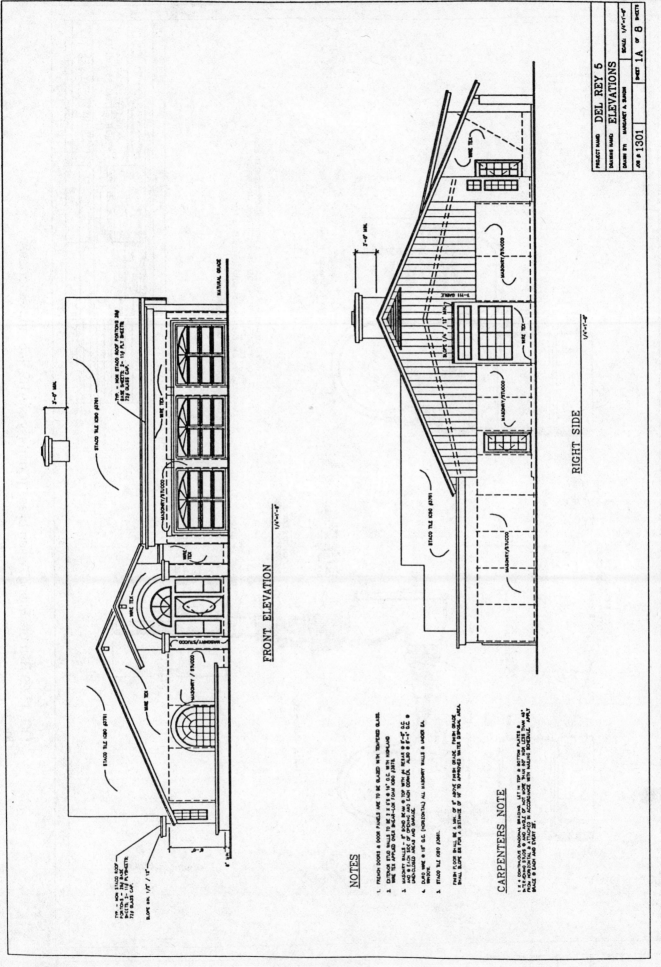

FIG. 11.28 Architectural Elevation Drawings. (Courtesy of Margaret A. Sundin, Phoenix, AZ and Autodesk, Inc.)

523

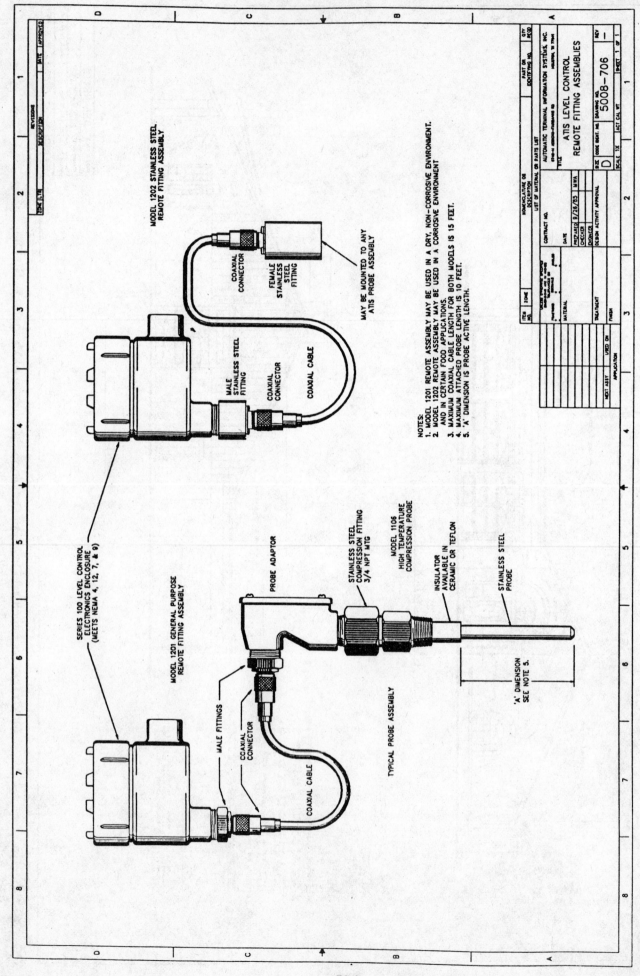

FIG. 11.29 Remote Fitting Assemblies. (Courtesy of ATIS, Inc. and Autodesk, Inc.)

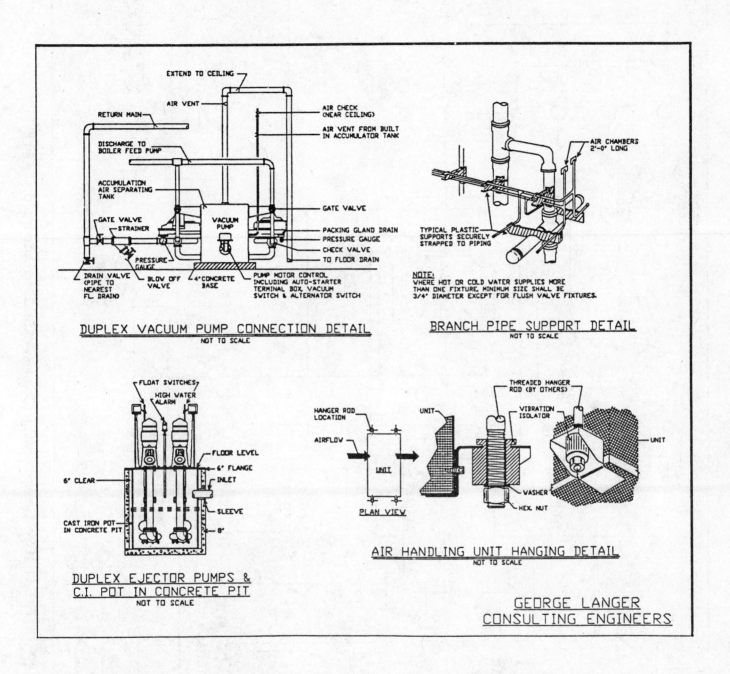

FIG. 11.30 Detail drawings. (Courtesy of George Langer, Consulting Engineer, New York, N.Y. and Autodesk, Inc.)

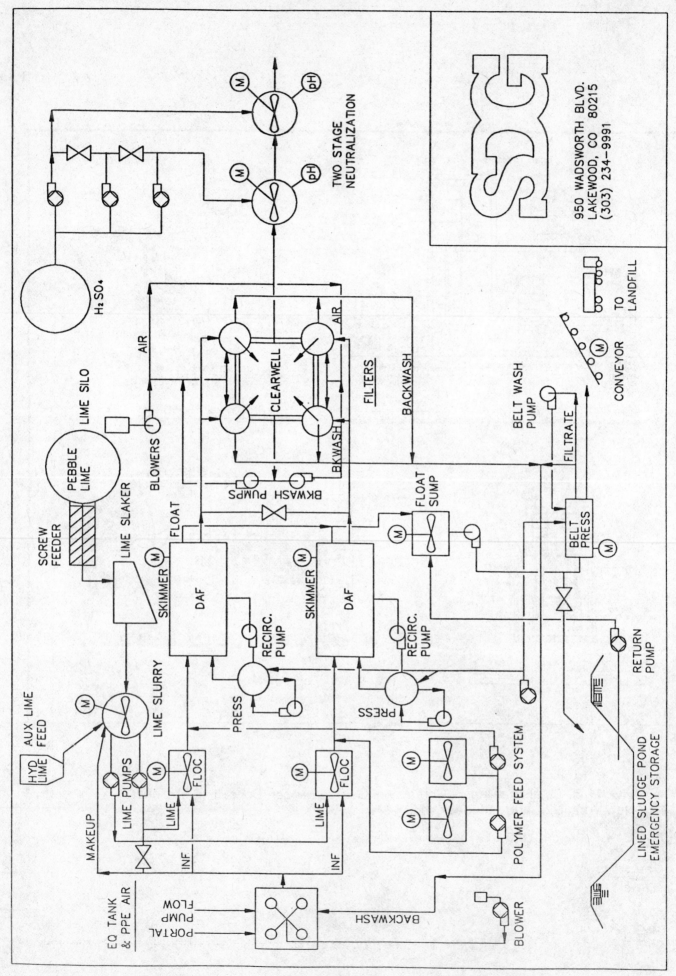

FIG. 11.31 Schematic Drawing. (Courtesy of SDG Inc., Lakewood, CO and Autodesk, Inc.)

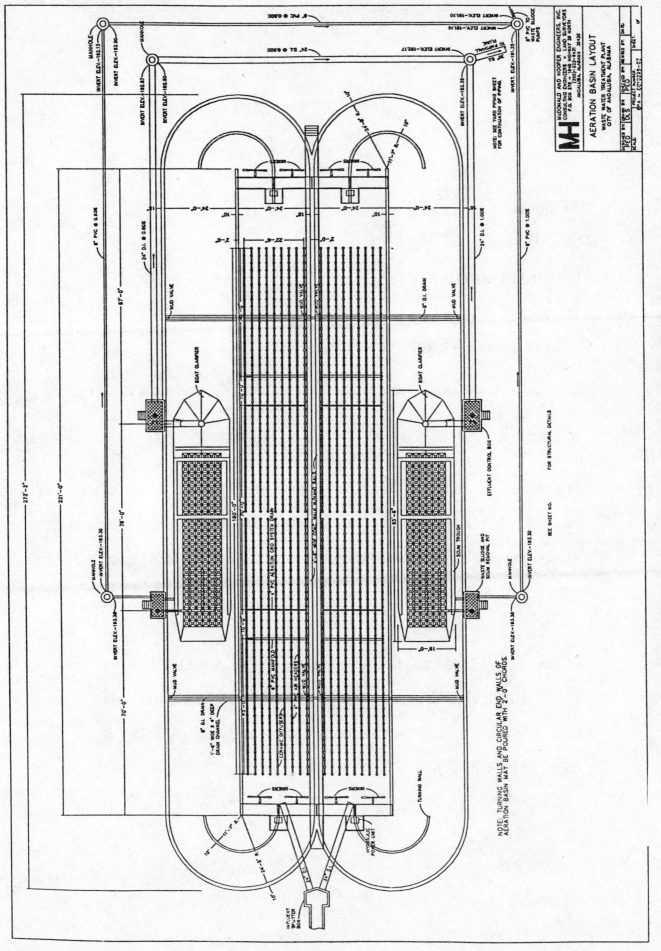

FIG. 11.32 Aeration Basin Layout. (Courtesy of McDonald and Hooper Engineers, Inc., Andalusia, AL and Autodesk, Inc.)

APPENDIX

DIMENSIONING,
TOLERANCING and
SCREW THREAD REPRESENTATION

The American National Standard Institute distributes a series of manuals published by the American Society of Mechanical Engineers. These manuals contain a wealth of information on accepted visual representation practices.

In this appendix, you will find selected portions of ANSI's Y 14.5M-1982 and ANSI Y14.6-1978 manuals. The information has been reproduced with permission of the publisher (ASME) in colaboration with ANSI.

FUNDAMENTAL RULES

Dimensioning and tolerancing shall clearly define engineering intent and shall conform to the following.

(*a*) Each dimension shall have a tolerance, except for those dimensions specifically identified as reference, maximum, minimum, or stock (commercial stock size). The tolerance may be applied directly to the dimension (or indirectly in the case of basic dimensions), indicated by a general note, or located in a supplementary block of the drawing format (see ANSI Y14.1).

(*b*) Dimensions for size, form, and location of features shall be complete to the extent that there is full understanding of the characteristics of each feature. Neither scaling (measuring the size of a feature directly from an engineering drawing) nor assumption of a distance or size is permitted.

NOTE: Undimensioned drawings – for example, loft, printed wiring, templates, master layouts, tooling layout – prepared on stable material are excluded, provided the necessary control dimensions are specified.

(*c*) Each necessary dimension of an end product shall be shown. No more dimensions than those necessary for complete definition shall be given. The use of reference dimensions on a drawing should be minimized.

(*d*) Dimensions shall be selected and arranged to suit the function and mating relationship of a part and shall not be subject to more than one interpretation.

(*e*) The drawing should define a part without specifying manufacturing methods. Thus, only the diameter of a hole is given without indicating whether it is to be drilled, reamed, punched, or made by any other operation. However, in those instances where manufacturing, processing, quality assurance, or environmental information is essential to the definition of engineering requirements, it shall be specified on the drawing or in a document referenced on the drawing.

(*f*) It is permissible to identify as nonmandatory certain processing dimensions that provide for finish allowance, shrink allowance, and other requirements, provided the final dimensions are given on the drawing. Nonmandatory processing dimensions shall be identified by an appropriate note, such as NONMANDATORY (MFG DATA).

(*g*) Dimensions should be arranged to provide required information for optimum readability. Dimensions should be shown in true profile views and refer to visible outlines.

(*h*) Wires, cables, sheets, rods, and other materials manufactured to gage or code numbers shall be specified by linear dimensions indicating the diameter or thickness. Gage or code numbers may be shown in parentheses following the dimension.

(*i*) A 90° angle is implied where center lines and lines depicting features are shown on a drawing at right angles and no angle is specified

(*j*) A 90° BASIC angle applies where center lines of features in a pattern or surfaces shown at right angles on the drawing are located or defined by basic dimensions and no angle is specified.

(*k*) Unless otherwise specified, all dimensions are applicable at 20°C (68°F). Compensation may be made for measurements made at other temperatures.

UNITS OF MEASUREMENT

For uniformity, all dimensions in this Standard are given in SI units. However, the unit of measurement selected should be in accordance with the policy of the user.

SI (Metric) Linear Units. The commonly used SI linear unit used on engineering drawings is the millimeter.

U.S. Customary Linear Units. The commonly used U.S. customary linear unit used on engineering drawings is the decimal inch.

Identification of Linear Units. On drawings where all dimensions are either in millimeters or inches, individual identification of linear units is not required. However, the drawing shall contain a note stating UNLESS OTHERWISE SPECIFIED, ALL DIMENSIONS ARE IN MILLIMETERS (or IN INCHES, as applicable).

Where some inch dimensions are shown on a millimeter-dimensioned drawing, the abbreviation IN. shall follow the inch values. Where some millimeter dimensions are shown on an inch-dimensioned drawing, the symbol mm shall follow the millimeter values.

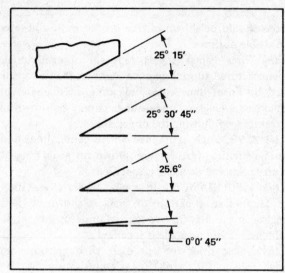

FIG. 1 ANGULAR UNITS

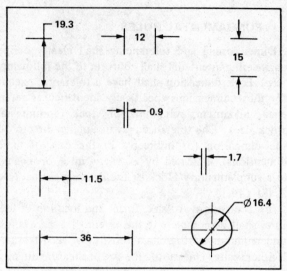

FIG. 2 MILLIMETER DIMENSIONS

Angular Units. Angular dimensions are expressed in either degrees and decimal parts of a degree or in degrees, minutes, and seconds. These latter dimensions are expressed by symbols: for degrees °, for minutes ', and for seconds ". Where degrees are indicated alone, the numerical value shall be followed by the symbol °. Where only minutes or seconds are specified, the number of minutes or seconds shall be preceded by 0° or 0°0', as applicable. See Fig. 1.

TYPES OF DIMENSIONING

Decimal dimensioning shall be used on drawings except where certain commercial commodities are identified by standardized nominal designations such as pipe and lumber sizes.

Millimeter Dimensioning. The following shall be observed when specifying millimeter dimensions on drawings.

(*a*) Where the dimension is less than one millimeter, a zero precedes the decimal point. See Fig. 2.

(*b*) Where the dimension is a whole number, neither the decimal point nor a zero is shown. See Fig. 2.

(*c*) Where the dimension exceeds a whole number by a decimal fraction of one millimeter, the last digit to the right of the decimal point is not followed by a zero. See Fig. 2.

NOTE: This practice differs for tolerances expressed bilaterally or as limits

(*d*) Neither commas nor spaces shall be used to separate digits into groups in specifying millimeter dimensions on drawings.

Decimal Inch Dimensioning. The decimal inch system is explained in ANSI B87.1. The following shall be observed when specifying decimal inch dimensions on drawings.

(*a*) A zero is not used before the decimal point for values less than one inch.

(*b*) A dimension is expressed to the same number of decimal places as its tolerance. Zeros are added to the right of the decimal point where necessary. See Fig. 3

Decimal Points. Decimal points must be uniform, dense, and large enough to be clearly visible and meet the reproduction requirements of ANSI Y14.2M. Decimal points are placed in line with the bottom of the associated digits.

Conversion and Rounding of Linear Units. For information on conversion and rounding of U.S. customary linear units, see ANSI Z210.1.

APPLICATION OF DIMENSIONS

Dimensions are applied by means of dimension lines, extension lines, chain lines, or a leader from a dimension, note, or specification directed to the appropriate feature. See Fig. 4. General notes are used to convey

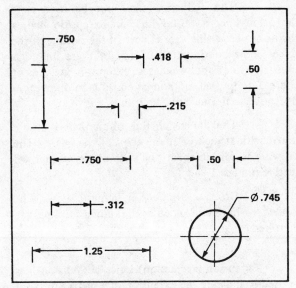

FIG. 3 DECIMAL INCH DIMENSIONS

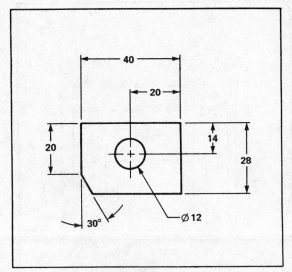

FIG. 4 APPLICATION OF DIMENSIONS

additional information. For further information on dimension lines, extension lines, chain lines, and leaders, see ANSI Y14.2M.

Dimension Lines. A dimension line, with its arrowheads, shows the direction and extent of a dimension. Numerals indicate the number of units of a measurement. Preferably, dimension lines should be broken for insertion of numerals as shown in Fig. 4. Where horizontal dimension lines are not broken, numerals are placed above and parallel to the dimension lines.

Dimension lines shall be aligned if practicable and grouped for uniform appearance. See Fig. 5.

Dimension lines are drawn parallel to the direction of measurement. The space between the first dimension line and the part outline should be not less than 10 mm; the space between succeeding parallel dimension lines should be not less than 6 mm. See Fig. 6.

NOTE: These spacings are intended as guides only. If the drawing meets the reproduction requirements of the accepted industry or military reproduction specification, nonconformance to these spacing requirements is not a basis for rejection of the drawing.

Where there are several parallel dimension lines, the numerals should be staggered for easier reading. See Fig. 7.

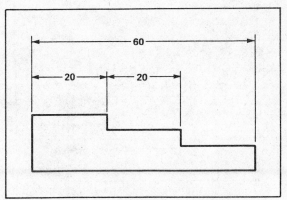

FIG. 5 GROUPING OF DIMENSIONS

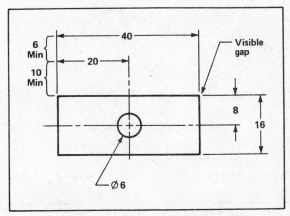

FIG. 6 SPACING OF DIMENSIONS

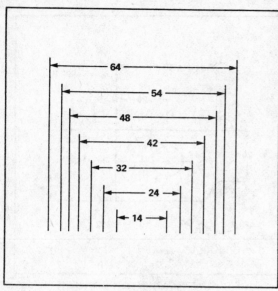

FIG. 7 STAGGERED DIMENSIONS

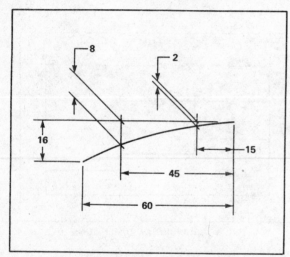

FIG. 8 OBLIQUE EXTENSION LINES

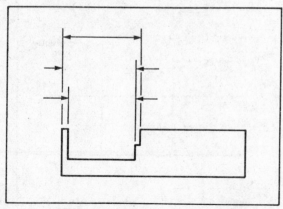

FIG. 9 BREAKS IN EXTENSION LINES

The following shall not be used as a dimension line: a center line, an extension line, a phantom line, a line that is part of the outline of the object, or a continuation of any of these lines. A dimension line is not used as an extension line, except where a simplified method of coordinate dimensioning is used to define curved outlines.

The dimension line of an angle is an arc drawn with its center at the apex of the angle. The arrowheads terminate at the extensions of the two sides. See Figs. 1 and 4.

Crossing dimension lines should be avoided. Where unavoidable, the dimension lines are unbroken.

Extension (Projection) Lines. Extension lines are used to indicate the extension of a surface or point to a location outside the part outline. Normally, extension lines start with a short visible gap from the outline of the part and extend beyond the outermost related dimension line. See Fig. 6. Extension lines are usually drawn perpendicular to dimension lines. Where space is limited, extension lines may be drawn at an oblique angle to clearly illustrate where they apply. Where oblique lines are used, the dimension lines are shown in the direction in which they apply. See Fig. 8.

Wherever practicable, extension lines should neither cross one another nor cross dimension lines. To minimize such crossings, the shortest dimension line is shown nearest the outline of the object. See Fig. 7. Where extension lines must cross other extension lines, dimension lines, or lines depicting features, they are not broken. Where extension lines cross arrowheads or dimension lines close to arrowheads, a break in the extension line is advisable. See Fig. 9.

Where a point is located by extension lines only, the extension lines from surfaces should pass through the point.

Limited Length or Area Indication. Where it is desired to indicate that a limited length or area of a surface is to receive additional treatment or consideration within limits specified on the drawing, the extent of these limits may be indicated by use of a chain line.

Symbology

GENERAL

This Section establishes the symbols for specifying geometric characteristics and other dimensional requirements on engineering drawings. Symbols should be of sufficient clarity to meet the legibility and reproducibility requirements of ANSI Y14.2M. Symbols are to be used only as described herein.

USE OF NOTES TO SUPPLEMENT SYMBOLS

Situations may arise where the desired geometric requirement cannot be completely conveyed by symbology. In such cases, a note may be used to describe the requirement, either separately or supplementing a geometric tolerance.

SYMBOL CONSTRUCTION

Information related to the construction, form, and proportion of individual symbols described herein is contained in Appendix C.

Geometric Characteristic Symbols. The symbols denoting geometric characteristics are shown in Fig. 68.

Datum Feature Symbol. The datum feature symbol consists of a frame containing the datum identifying letter preceded and followed by a dash. See Fig. 69. The symbol frame is related to the datum feature by one of the methods prescribed in 3.5.

Letters of the alphabet (except I, O, and Q) are used as datum identifying letters. Each datum feature requiring identification shall be assigned a different letter. When datum features requiring identification on a drawing are so numerous as to exhaust the single alpha series, the double alpha series shall be used — AA through AZ, BA through BZ, etc.

Where the same datum feature symbol is repeated to identify that same feature in other locations on a drawing, it need not be identified as reference.

Datum Target Symbol. The datum target symbol is a circle divided horizontally into two halves. See Fig. 70. The lower half contains a letter identifying the associated datum, followed by the target number assigned sequentially starting with 1 for each datum. Where the datum target is an area, the area size may be entered in the upper half of the symbol; otherwise, the upper half is left blank. A radial line attached to the symbol is directed to a target point (indicated by an "X"), target line, or target area, as applicable.

Basic Dimension Symbol. The symbol used to identify a basic dimension is shown in Fig. 71.

Material Condition Symbols. The symbols used to indicate "at maximum material condition," "regardless of feature size," and "at least material condition" are shown in Fig. 72. The use of these symbols in local and general notes is prohibited.

Projected Tolerance Zone Symbol. The symbol used to indicate a projected tolerance zone is shown in Fig. 72. The use of this symbol in local and general notes is prohibited.

Diameter and Radius Symbols. The symbols used to indicate diameter, spherical diameter, radius, and spherical radius are shown in Fig. 72. These symbols precede the value of a dimension or tolerance given as a diameter or radius, as applicable.

Reference Symbol. A reference dimension (or reference data) is identified by enclosing the dimension (or data) within parentheses. See Fig. 72.

TYPE OF TOLERANCE		CHARACTERISTIC	SYMBOL	SEE:
FOR INDIVIDUAL FEATURES	FORM	STRAIGHTNESS	—	6.4.1
		FLATNESS	▱	6.4.2
		CIRCULARITY (ROUNDNESS)	○	6.4.3
		CYLINDRICITY	⌭	6.4.4
FOR INDIVIDUAL OR RELATED FEATURES	PROFILE	PROFILE OF A LINE	⌒	6.5.2 (b)
		PROFILE OF A SURFACE	⌓	6.5.2 (a)
FOR RELATED FEATURES	ORIENTATION	ANGULARITY	∠	6.6.2
		PERPENDICULARITY	⊥	6.6.4
		PARALLELISM	//	6.6.3
	LOCATION	POSITION	⊕	5.2
		CONCENTRICITY	◎	5.11.3
	RUNOUT	CIRCULAR RUNOUT	↗ *	6.7.2.1
		TOTAL RUNOUT	⌰ *	6.7.2.2

* Arrowhead(s) may be filled in.

FIG. 68 GEOMETRIC CHARACTERISTIC SYMBOLS

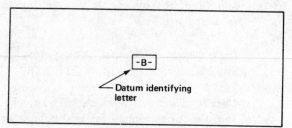

FIG. 69   DATUM FEATURE SYMBOL

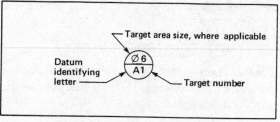

FIG. 70   DATUM TARGET SYMBOL

Arc Length Symbol. The symbol used to indicate that a linear dimension is an arc length measured on a curved outline is shown in Fig. 72. The symbol is placed above the dimension.

Counterbore or Spotface Symbol. The symbolic means of indicating a counterbore or spotface is shown in Fig. 73. The symbol precedes the dimension of the counterbore or spotface.

Countersink Symbol. The symbolic means of indicating a countersink is shown in Fig. 74. The symbol precedes the dimensions of the countersink.

Depth Symbol. The symbolic means of indicating where a dimension applies to the depth of a feature is to precede that dimension with the depth symbol, as shown in Fig. 75.

Square Symbol. The symbol used to indicate that a single dimension applies to a square shape is to precede that dimension with the symbol for a square, as shown in Fig. 76.

Dimension Origin Symbol. The symbol used to indicate that a toleranced dimension between two features originates from one of these features is shown in Fig. 77.

534

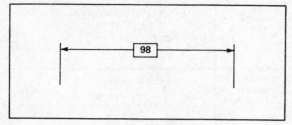

FIG. 71   BASIC DIMENSION SYMBOL

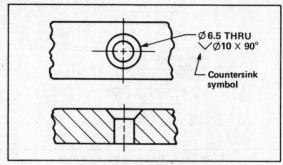

FIG. 74   COUNTERSINK SYMBOL

TERM	SYMBOL
AT MAXIMUM MATERIAL CONDITION	Ⓜ
REGARDLESS OF FEATURE SIZE	Ⓢ
AT LEAST MATERIAL CONDITION	Ⓛ
PROJECTED TOLERANCE ZONE	Ⓟ
DIAMETER	∅
SPHERICAL DIAMETER	S∅
RADIUS	R
SPHERICAL RADIUS	SR
REFERENCE	( )
ARC LENGTH	⌒

FIG. 72   MODIFYING SYMBOLS

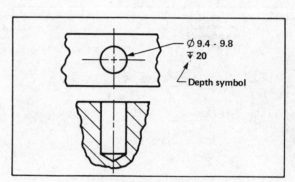

FIG. 75   DEPTH SYMBOL

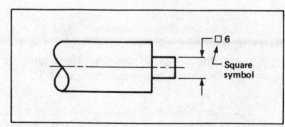

FIG. 76   SQUARE SYMBOL

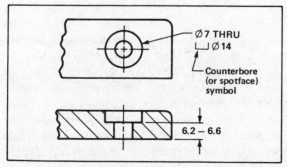

FIG. 73   COUNTERBORE OR SPOTFACE SYMBOL

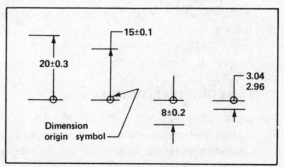

FIG. 77   DIMENSION ORIGIN SYMBOL

535

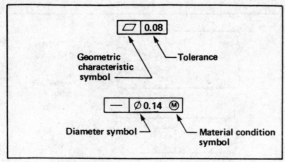

FIG. 78   FEATURE CONTROL FRAME

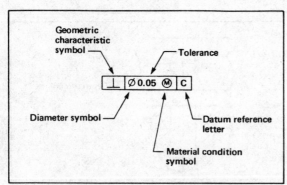

FIG. 79   FEATURE CONTROL FRAME
INCORPORATING A DATUM REFERENCE

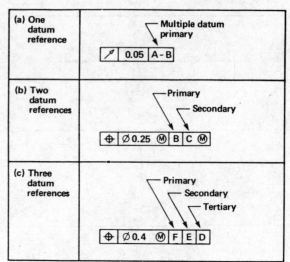

FIG. 80   ORDER OF PRECEDENCE
OF DATUM REFERENCES

Taper and Slope Symbols. Symbols used for specifying taper and slope for conical and flat tapers are shown in Figs. 64 and 66. These symbols are always shown with the vertical leg to the left.

Surface Texture Symbols. For information on surface texture symbol construction and application, see ANSI Y14.36.

Symbols for Limits and Fits. For information on the symbolic means of specifying metric limits and fits.

GEOMETRIC TOLERANCE SYMBOLS

Geometric characteristic symbols, the tolerance value, and datum reference letters, where applicable, are combined in a feature control frame to express a geometric tolerance.

Feature Control Frame. A geometric tolerance for an individual feature is specified by means of a feature control frame divided into compartments containing the geometric characteristic symbol followed by the tolerance. See Fig. 78. Where applicable, the tolerance is preceded by the diameter symbol and followed by a material condition symbol.

Feature Control Frame Incorporating Datum References. Where a geometric tolerance is related to a datum, this relationship is indicated by entering the datum reference letter in a compartment following the tolerance. See Fig. 79. Where applicable, the datum reference letter is followed by a material condition symbol.

Where a datum is established by two datum features — for example, an axis established by two datum diameters — both datum reference letters, separated by a dash, are entered in a single compartment. See Fig. 80, part (a). Where more than one datum is required, the datum reference letters (followed by a material condition symbol, where applicable) are entered in separate compartments in the desired order of precedence, from left to right. See Fig. 80, parts (b) and (c). Datum reference letters need not be in alphabetical order in the feature control frame.

A composite feature control frame is used where more than one tolerance is specified for the same geometric characteristic of a feature or features having different datum requirements. The composite frame contains a single entry of the geometric characteristic symbol followed by each tolerance and datum requirement, one above the other. See Fig. 81

The symbol used to indicate that a profile tolerance applies to surfaces all around the part is a circle located at the junction of the leader from the feature control frame. See Fig. 82.

Combined Feature Control Frame and Datum Feature Symbol. Where a feature or pattern of features controlled by a geometric tolerance also serves as a datum feature, the feature control frame and datum feature symbol are combined. See Fig. 83.

Wherever a feature control frame and datum feature symbol are combined, datums referenced in the feature control frame are not considered part of the datum feature symbol. In the positional tolerance example, Fig. 83, a feature is controlled for position in relation to datums A and B, and identified as datum C. Whenever datum C is referenced elsewhere on the drawing, the reference applies to datum C, not to datums A and B.

Feature Control Frame With a Projected Tolerance Zone. Where a positional or an orientation tolerance is specified as a projected tolerance zone, a frame containing the height dimension, followed by the projected tolerance zone symbol, is placed beneath the feature control frame. See Fig. 84. Where the projected tolerance zone is indicated with a chain line,   the height dimension is omitted from the frame.

FEATURE CONTROL FRAME PLACEMENT

The feature control frame is related to the considered feature by one of the following methods as depicted in Fig. 85:

(*a*) locating the feature control frame below or attached to a leader-directed callout or dimension pertaining to the feature;

(*b*) running a leader from the frame to the feature;

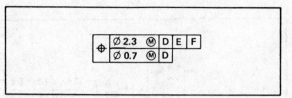

FIG. 81   COMPOSITE FEATURE CONTROL FRAME

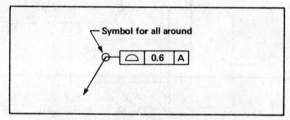

FIG. 82   SYMBOL FOR ALL AROUND

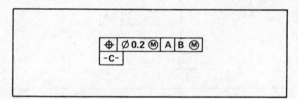

FIG. 83   COMBINED FEATURE CONTROL FRAME
AND DATUM FEATURE SYMBOL

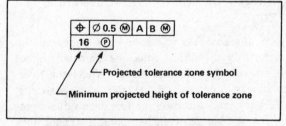

FIG. 84   FEATURE CONTROL FRAME WITH
A PROJECTED TOLERANCE ZONE

(*c*) attaching a side or an end of the frame to an extension line from the feature, provided it is a plane surface;

(*d*) attaching a side or an end of the frame to an extension of the dimension line pertaining to a feature of size.

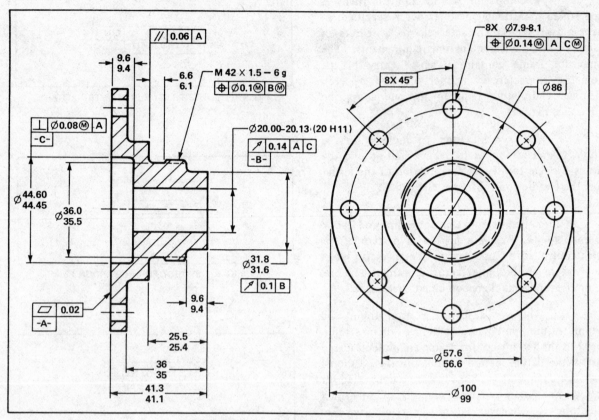

FIG. 85   FEATURE CONTROL FRAME PLACEMENT

IDENTIFICATION OF THE TOLERANCE ZONE

Where the specified tolerance value represents the diameter of a cylindrical zone, the diameter symbol shall precede the tolerance value. Where the tolerance zone is other than a diameter, identification is unnecessary, and the specified tolerance value represents the distance between two parallel straight lines or planes, or the distance between two uniform boundaries, as the specific case may be.

TABULATED TOLERANCES

Where the tolerance in a feature control frame is to be tabulated, a letter representing the tolerance, preceded by the abbreviation TOL, is entered as shown in Fig. 86.

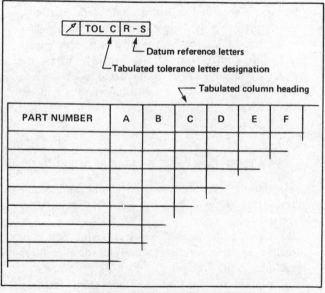

FIG. 86   TABULATED TOLERANCES

AMERICAN NATIONAL STANDARD
ENGINEERING DRAWING AND RELATED DOCUMENTATION PRACTICES
SCREW THREAD REPRESENTATION

SCOPE

This document establishes standards for pictorial representation, specification, and dimensioning of screw threads on drawings; it is not concerned with standards for dimensional control of screw threads. Information helpful in ...e design and selection of screw threads to meet specific requirements is included in the B1 and B2 series of the American National Standards for Screw Threads (see Appendix). Only certain metric thread references are shown in this standard.

APPLICATION

Straight unified screw threads are emphasized in this standard in consideration of their wide use and general purpose applications. The same drafting practices apply to straight and taper pipe threads, Acme, Stub Acme, Buttress, helical coil insert, and interference threads except for differences noted.

REFERENCE DOCUMENTS

Reference documents are listed throughout this standard and Appendix A. When American National Standards listed in Appendix A are superseded or revised and approved by the American National Standards Institute, Inc., the new or revised standard shall apply.

DEFINITIONS

Definitions of terms are in accordance with American National Standard for Nomenclature, Definitions, and Letter Symbols for Screw Threads, B1.7-1977, the applicable standard, and U.S. Department of Commerce, National Bureau of Standards, Handbook H28 (1969), Screw-Thread Standards for Federal Services.

GENERAL

Straight Threads. Straight screw thread drawing practices are based on the American National Standard for Unified Screw Threads, B1.1-1974.

Taper Threads. Taper screw thread drawing practices are based on the American National Standards for Pipe Threads (Except Dryseal), B2.1-1968,

and Dryseal Pipe Threads B1.20.3-1976 (Inch), and B1.20.4-1976 (Metric).

Note

Pipe threads are designated in established trade sizes which signify a nominal diameter only.

Taper Thread Features. Regular and aeronautical pipe thread forms allow crest and root interference or clearance when the flanks contact. When a clearance occurs, unless filled with a lute or sealer, a spiral passage will exist through which leakage can occur. The dryseal pipe thread form does not allow such clearance, but rather has crest and root metal to metal contact or interference when the flanks contact. It is this feature which eliminates the need for a lute or sealer to provide for leak-proof assemblies.

Taper Pipe (Screw) Thread Series (Except Dryseal). Aeronautical taper pipe thread requirements are specified in Military Specification MIL-P-7105 and are designated ANPT.

Dryseal Pipe Thread Series. Dryseal pipe threads are specified in ANSI B1.20.3-1976 (Inch) and ANSI B1.20.4-1976 (Metric).

The American National Standard dryseal taper pipe thread series, designated NPTF, include external and internal taper pipe threads for pipe joints in practically every type of service. See Figure 1. Gaging points shown in Figure 1 are not necessarily shown on a drawing.

The Society of Automotive Engineers J476 dryseal short taper pipe thread series, designated PTF-SAE SHORT, applies to external and internal taper pipe threads; it conforms in all respects to the dryseal NPTF pipe thread except that the length has been shortened by eliminating (A) one thread from the small end of the external thread, and (B) one thread from the large end of the internal thread. See Figure 2. Gaging points shown in Figure 2 are not necessarily shown on a drawing.

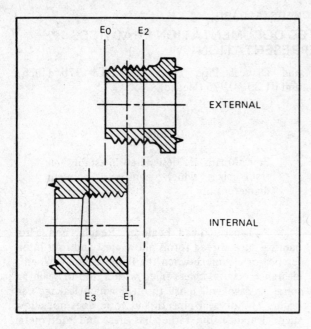

FIG. 1 NPTF DRYSEAL TAPER THREAD WITH GAGING POINTS E_0, E_1, E_2 And E_3

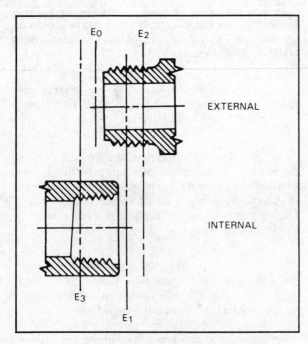

FIG. 2 PTF-SAE SHORT TAPER THREAD WITH GAGING POINTS E_0, E_1, E_2 And E_3

The dryseal PTF-SAE SHORT external thread is intended for assembly with dryseal NPTF or dryseal NPSI pipe threads, not for assembly with an internal dryseal PTF-SAE SHORT thread.

For pipe threads which conform to American National Standard except for shortening of the full thread length, the letter "N" is omitted from the designation and a description of the shortening added after the series symbol as shown in ANSI B1.20.3-1976 (Inch) and ANSI B1.20.4-1976 (Metric).

The dryseal internal fuel straight pipe thread series, designated NPSF, applies to internal straight pipe threads only and is primarily intended for assembly with external taper NPTF pipe threads.

The intermediate straight dryseal pipe thread series, NPSI, apply to internal straight pipe threads only and is primarily intended for assembly with dryseal PTF-SAE SHORT external taper pipe threads but will assemble with dryseal NPTF external taper pipe threads.

Limitations of design, clearances, or economy of material may require that full thread lengths shorter than dryseal PTF-SAE SHORT external and internal taper pipe threads be specified. Shorter series external and internal dryseal taper pipe threads with further shortening specifications and limitations are shown in ANSI B1.20.3-1976 (Inch) and ANSI B1.20.4-1976 (Metric).

Acme Threads. Acme screw thread drawing practices are based on American National Standard for Acme Screw Threads, B1.5-1977. See Table 1.

Acme Thread Series. Acme threads of the preferred series of diameters and pitches with limiting dimensions are listed in ANSI B1.5-1977. Where threads of the preferred series do not suit the application, tables are included.

Acme Thread Classes. There are four classes of general purpose Acme threads and five classes of centralizing Acme threads. The general purpose Acme threads have clearances on all diameters for free movement and may be used in assemblies where both internal and external members are supported to prevent movement.

540

The centralizing Acme threads have a limited clearance at major diameters of external and internal threads, so that the bearing at the major diameter maintains the approximate alignment of the thread axis and prevents wedging on the flanks of the thread. For any combination of these threads, some end play or backlash will result.

Stub Acme Threads. Stub Acme screw thread drawing practices are based on American National Standard for Stub Acme Screw Threads, B1.8-1977. See Table 1.

Stub Acme Series. Stub Acme threads of the preferred series of diameters and pitches with limiting dimensions are listed in ANSI B1.8-1977.

Stub Acme Class: There is only one class of Stub Acme thread established for general usage. It is the Class 2G (general purpose) thread using two threads with modified thread depths. It is included in ANSI B1.8.

Buttress Threads. Buttress screw thread drawing practices are based on American National Standard for Buttress Screw Threads, B1.9-1973. The Buttress thread is designated butt or push-butt. See Table 1.

Buttress Thread Series. Due to the special design of most components having Buttress threads, no diameter pitch series is recommended. However, the preferred diameter series and preferred pitch series are listed in ANSI B1.9-1973.

Buttress Thread Classes. There are two classes of Buttress threads: Class 2 (Standard Grade) and Class 3 (Precision Grade).

REQUIREMENTS

Representation, specification, and dimensioning of threads should be in accordance with the following paragraphs.

Thread Representation. There are three methods in general use for representing screw threads on drawings; the simplified representation in Figure 3, the schematic in Figure 4, and the detailed in Figure 5. One method is generally used within any one drawing. When required, however, all three methods may be used. See Figures 6 and 7.

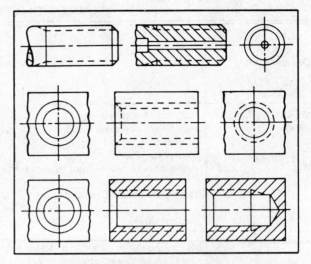

FIG. 3 SIMPLIFIED REPRESENTATION OF THREADS

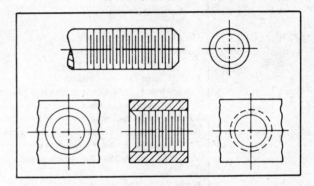

FIG. 4 SCHEMATIC REPRESENTATION OF THREADS

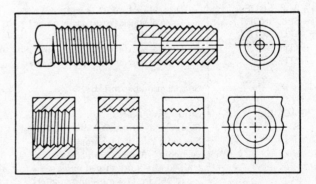

FIG. 5 DETAILED REPRESENTATION OF THREADS

TABLE 1 Thread Series Designations[1,2]

Designation (a)	Thread series	Reference ANSI	Reference H28
ACME-C	Acme threads, centralizing	B1.5	Part III
ACME-G	Acme threads, general purpose	B1.5	Part III
	(See also "Stub Acme")		
AMO	Microscope Objective threads	B1.1	Part III
ANPT	Aeronautical National form taper pipe threads	MIL-P-7105	
M	ISO metric threads-6mm and larger		Part III
PUSH-BUTT	Buttress threads	B1.9	Part III
N, NC, NF, NEF, NS . .	See table 2		
S	ISO metric thread - up to and including 5mm		
	Gas Cylinder Valve Outlet and Inlet Threads:	B57.1	Part II
NGO (b)	Gas outlet threads		
NGS	Gas straight threads		
NGT	Gas taper threads		
SGT	Special gas taper threads		
NH, NPSH	Hose coupling threads . . . . , . .	B1.22	Part II
NH	Fire-hose coupling threads		Part II
	Pipe Threads (except Dryseal):		
ANPT	Aeronautical National form taper pipe threads	MIL-P-7105	
NPSC	Straight pipe threads in pipe couplings		
NPSL	Straight pipe threads for loose-fitting mechanical joints with locknuts		
NPSM	Straight pipe threads for free-fitting mechanical joints for fixtures	B2.1	Part II
NPT	Taper pipe threads for general use		
NPTR	Taper pipe threads for railing joints		
	Dryseal Pipe Threads:		
F-PTF	Dryseal (fine) taper pipe threads		
NPSF	Dryseal fuel internal straight pipe threads		
NPSI	Dryseal intermediate internal straight pipe threads	B1.20.3	
NPTF	Dryseal taper pipe threads	B1.20.4	Part II
PTF—SAE, SHORT . .	Dryseal SAE short taper pipe threads		
PTF—SPL, SHORT . .	Dryseal special short taper pipe threads		
PTF—SPL, EXTRA			
SHORT	Dryseal special extra short taper pipe threads		
SPL—PTF	Dryseal special taper pipe threads		
SGT	Special gas taper threads	B57.1	Part II
STUB ACME	Stub Acme threads	B1.8	Part III
	Surveying instrument mounting threads		Part III
UN series	See table 2 (0.06 in. and larger)		
UNJ series	See table 2 (0.06 in. and larger)		
UNM	Unified Miniature thread series	B1.10	Section 5
	(0.055 in. (1.4 mm) and smaller)		
UNR	See Table 2	B1.1	

1 Methods of designating multiple threads are shown in ANSI B1.5, Acme screw threads, and Part III of NBS Handbook H28.
2 All threads, except NGO, are right hand unless otherwise designated. For NGO threads, designations "RH" or "LH" are required.

TABLE 2 Designations for UN, UNJ, UNR, And N Thread Series

Basic thread series	External thread root	Constant pitch	Coarse	Fine	Extra fine	Special diameters, pitches, or lengths of engagement	Reference	
							ANSI	H28
UN. . . .	With optional radius root on external thread.	UN	UNC	UNF	UNEF	UNS	B1.1 B1.1	Section 2 Section 3
UNJ . .	With 0.15011p to 0.18042p mandatory radius root on external thread	UNJ	UNJC	UNJF	UNJEF	UNJS	B1.1	Section 4
N[3]		N	NC	NF	NEF	NS		Appendix A1
UNR . .	With 0.10825p to 0.14434p radius root on external thread	UNR	UNRC	UNRF	UNREF	UNRS	B1.1	

[3] This series superseded by UN series

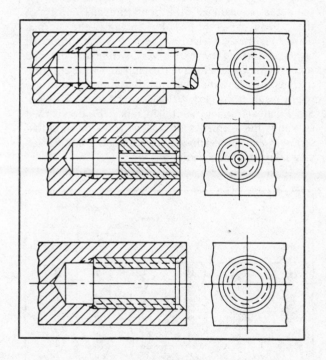

FIG. 6 SIMPLIFIED REPRESENTATION OF ASSEMBLED THREADS

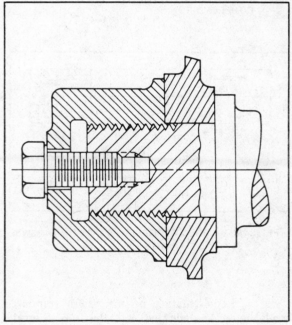

FIG. 7 MULTIPLE THREAD REPRESENTATIONS OF ASSEMBLED PARTS

Simplified Representation. The simplified drawing method is recommended for straight and tapered V-form, Acme, Stub Acme, Buttress, helical coil insert and other thread forms except where detailed representations are required. Figures 3, 8, 9 and 10.

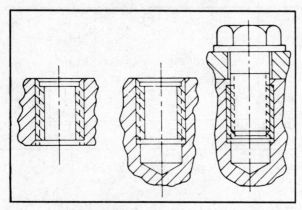

FIG. 8 SIMPLIFIED REPRESENTATION OF HELICAL COIL INSERTS

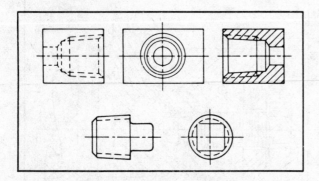

FIG. 9 SIMPLIFIED REPRESENTATION OF TAPER THREADED PARTS

Representation of the vanish (runout) thread should be indicated with the fully formed thread whether or not it is to be controlled. See Figure 3. When essential to design requirements, the vanish thread should be dimensioned.

The taper thread is shown in the same manner as the straight thread except that the lines form an angle of approximately 3° with the axis. See Figure 10.

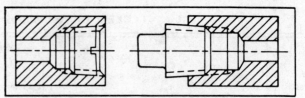

FIG. 10 SIMPLIFIED REPRESENTATION OF ASSEMBLED TAPERED PARTS

Schematic Representation. Schematic representation is nearly as effective as the detailed representation and is much easier to draw. The staggered lines, symbolic of the thread roots and crests, may be perpendicular to the axis of the thread or slanted to the approximate angle of the thread helix. This construction should not be used for hidden internal threads or sections of external threads. See Figure 4.

Detailed Representation. Detailed representation is a close approximation of a sectional view of the actual appearance of a screw thread. The form of the thread is simplified by showing the normal helices as straight slanting lines and the truncated crests and roots as sharp "V's". While the detailed rendering is comparatively difficult and time consuming, its use is sometimes justified where confusion might result from a less realistic thread representation. See Figures 5 and 11. Detailed representation is used to show the elements of a new form or modified screw thread, especially for dimensioning in enlarged views, layouts and assemblies.

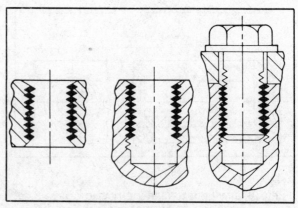

FIG. 11 DETAILED REPRESENTATION OF HELICAL COIL INSERTS

Thread Element Representation. Certain drawing practices may be used to define required thread elements as follows.

544

On end views of chamfered parts. where chamfer and minor diameter are very close to being the same, the minor diameter of a thread may be eliminated to improve clarity. See Figure 3.

On end views of countersunk threaded holes where countersunk diameters and the major diameters of threads are close to being the same, the major diameter may be eliminated for clarity. See Figures 3, 4 and 5.

Threads may be shown in more detail in enlarged views, checking layouts, and assemblies for clarity. See Figure 7.

6.1.5 Assembled Thread Representation. It is recommended that assembled straight and tapered thread components be shown by the simplified method. See Figure 6. However, where improved clarity in a representation is required all three conventions may be used on a single drawing. See Figure 7.

Thread Specification. In the United States the name and number of the controlling thread standard is frequently omitted from the drawing. Reference is made instead to the designation symbols of the standard, such as series symbols and class symbols. To avoid misunderstanding, it is recommended that the controlling organization and thread standard be specified or otherwise referenced on the drawing. Examples:

> .250-20 UNC-2A
> ANSI B1.1-1974
> .250-28 UNJF-3A
> MIL-S-8879

General Designation. On drawings with threaded parts, the designation of the screw thread is noted and optionally supplemented by the pitch diameter and its tolerance of pitch diameter limits for the standard series threads. See Table 3.

The thread designation should include in sequence, the nominal diameter, the number of threads per inch (or the pitch and lead), the letter symbol of the thread series, the number and letter of the thread class and any qualifying information. The nominal diameter should be in inches. The thread

length, the hole size and the chamfer or countersink may be included in the note or dimensioned on the drawing of the part.

In general practice the general designation and the pitch diameter limits are in note form and referenced to the drawing of the thread with a leader line. The following example illustrates and explains the elements of a designation of the screw thread.

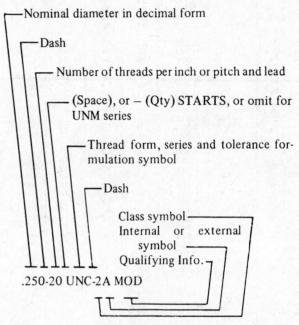

Nominal diameter in decimal form

Dash

Number of threads per inch or pitch and lead

(Space), or – (Qty) STARTS, or omit for UNM series

Thread form, series and tolerance formulation symbol

Dash

Class symbol
Internal or external symbol
Qualifying Info.

.250-20 UNC-2A MOD

PD.2127-.2164 (Specification of PD optional if uncoated)

Thread sizes should be shown as decimal size callouts except for fractional size. For decimal sizes a minimum of three or maximum of four decimal places, omitting any fourth place decimal zero, should be shown as the nominal size.
Examples:

> 1.000-8   UNC-2A
> .250-20   UNC-2A
> 1 ¾ -8   UN-2A

Numbered sizes may be shown because of established practices. The decimal equivalent should be in parentheses.
Example:

> No. 10 (.190)-32 UNF-2A

TABLE 3 — Unified Standard Screw Thread Series[4]

SIZES Primary	SIZES Secondary	BASIC MAJOR DIAMETER	Coarse UNC	Fine UNF	Extra fine UNEF	4UN	6UN	8UN	12UN	16UN	20UN	28UN	32UN	SIZES
0		0.060	—	80	—	—	—	—	—	—	—	—	—	0
	1	0.073	64	72	—	—	—	—	—	—	—	—	—	1
2		0.086	56	64	—	—	—	—	—	—	—	—	—	2
	3	0.099	48	56	—	—	—	—	—	—	—	—	—	3
4		0.112	40	48	—	—	—	—	—	—	—	—	—	4
5		0.125	40	44	—	—	—	—	—	—	—	—	—	5
6		0.138	32	40	—	—	—	—	—	—	—	—	UNC	6
8		0.164	32	36	—	—	—	—	—	—	—	—	UNC	8
10		0.190	24	32	—	—	—	—	—	—	—	UNF	UNF	10
	12	0.216	24	28	32	—	—	—	—	—	—	UNF	UNEF	12
1/4		0.250	20	28	32	—	—	—	—	—	UNC	UNF	UNEF	1/4
5/16		0.3125	18	24	32	—	—	—	—	—	20	28	UNEF	5/16
3/8		0.375	16	24	32	—	—	—	—	UNC	20	28	UNEF	3/8
7/16		0.4375	14	20	28	—	—	—	—	16	UNF	UNEF	32	7/16
1/2		0.500	13	20	28	—	—	—	—	16	UNF	UNEF	32	1/2
9/16		0.5265	12	18	24	—	—	—	UNC	16	20	28	32	9/16
5/8		0.625	11	18	24	—	—	—	12	16	20	28	32	5/8
	11/16	0.6875	—	—	24	—	—	—	12	16	20	28	32	11/16
3/4		0.750	10	16	20	—	—	—	12	UNF	UNEF	28	32	3/4
	13/16	0.8125	—	—	20	—	—	—	12	16	UNEF	28	32	13/16
7/8		0.875	9	14	20	—	—	—	12	16	UNEF	28	32	7/8
	15/16	0.9375	—	—	20	—	—	—	12	16	UNEF	28	32	15/16
1		1.000	8	12	20	—	—	UNC	UNF	16	UNEF	28	32	1
	1 1/16	1.0625	—	—	18	—	—	8	12	16	20	28	—	1 1/16
1 1/8		1.125	7	12	18	—	—	8	UNF	16	20	28	—	1 1/8
	1 3/16	1.1875	—	—	18	—	—	8	12	16	20	28	—	1 3/16
1 1/4		1.250	7	12	18	—	—	8	UNF	16	20	28	—	1 1/4
	1 5/16	1.3125	—	—	18	—	—	8	12	16	20	28	—	1 5/16
1 3/8		1.375	6	12	18	—	UNC	8	UNF	16	20	28	—	1 3/8
	1 7/16	1.4375	—	—	18	—	6	8	12	16	20	28	—	1 7/16
1 1/2		1.500	6	12	18	—	UNC	8	UNF	16	20	28	—	1 1/2
	1 9/16	1.5625	—	—	18	—	6	8	12	16	20	—	—	1 9/16
1 5/8		1.625	—	—	18	—	6	8	12	16	20	—	—	1 5/8
	1 11/16	1.6875	—	—	18	—	6	8	12	16	20	—	—	1 11/16
1 3/4		1.750	5	—	—	—	6	8	12	16	20	—	—	1 3/4
	1 13/16	1.8125	—	—	—	—	6	8	12	16	20	—	—	1 13/16
1 7/8		1.875	—	—	—	—	6	8	12	16	20	—	—	1 7/8
	1 15/16	1.9375	—	—	—	—	6	8	12	16	20	—	—	1 15/16
2		2.000	4 1/2	—	—	—	6	8	12	16	20	—	—	2
	2 1/8	2.125	—	—	—	—	6	8	12	16	20	—	—	2 1/8
2 1/4		2.250	4 1/2	—	—	—	6	8	12	16	20	—	—	2 1/4
	2 3/8	2.375	—	—	—	—	6	8	12	16	20	—	—	2 3/8
2 1/2		2.500	4	—	—	UNC	6	8	12	16	20	—	—	2 1/2
	2 5/8	2.625	—	—	—	4	6	8	12	16	20	—	—	2 5/8
2 3/4		2.750	4	—	—	UNC	6	8	12	16	20	—	—	2 3/4
	2 7/8	2.875	—	—	—	4	6	8	12	16	20	—	—	2 7/8
3		3.000	4	—	—	UNC	6	8	12	16	20	—	—	3
	3 1/8	3.125	—	—	—	4	6	8	12	16	—	—	—	3 1/8
3 1/4		3.250	4	—	—	UNC	6	8	12	16	—	—	—	3 1/4
	3 3/8	3.375	—	—	—	4	6	8	12	16	—	—	—	3 3/8
3 1/2		3.500	4	—	—	UNC	6	8	12	16	—	—	—	3 1/2
	3 5/8	3.625	—	—	—	4	6	8	12	16	—	—	—	3 5/8
3 3/4		3.750	4	—	—	UNC	6	8	12	16	—	—	—	3 3/4
	3 7/8	3.875	—	—	—	4	6	8	12	16	—	—	—	3 7/8
4		4.000	4	—	—	UNC	6	8	12	16	—	—	—	4
	4 1/8	4.125	—	—	—	4	6	8	12	16	—	—	—	4 1/8
4 1/4		4.250	—	—	—	4	6	8	12	16	—	—	—	4 1/4
	4 3/8	4.375	—	—	—	4	6	8	12	16	—	—	—	4 3/8
4 1/2		4.500	—	—	—	4	6	8	12	16	—	—	—	4 1/2
	4 5/8	4.625	—	—	—	4	6	8	12	16	—	—	—	4 5/8
4 3/4		4.750	—	—	—	4	6	8	12	16	—	—	—	4 3/4
	4 7/8	4.875	—	—	—	4	6	8	12	16	—	—	—	4 7/8
5		5.000	—	—	—	4	6	8	12	16	—	—	—	5
	5 1/8	5.125	—	—	—	4	6	8	12	16	—	—	—	5 1/8
5 1/4		5.250	—	—	—	4	6	8	12	16	—	—	—	5 1/4
	5 3/8	5.375	—	—	—	4	6	8	12	16	—	—	—	5 3/8
5 1/2		5.500	—	—	—	4	6	8	12	16	—	—	—	5 1/2
	5 5/8	5.625	—	—	—	4	6	8	12	16	—	—	—	5 5/8
5 3/4		5.750	—	—	—	4	6	8	12	16	—	—	—	5 3/4
	5 7/8	5.875	—	—	—	4	6	8	12	16	—	—	—	5 7/8
6		6.000	—	—	—	4	6	8	12	16	—	—	—	6

[4] Excerpt from ANSI B1.1-1974. Entries in column 'BASIC MAJOR DIAMETER' have been modified from the original by deletion of the fourth place decimal zero to emphasize the practice (described in para. 6.2.1.3 of this standard) of omitting any fourth place decimal zero on drawings. It is not intended to require conformance with this practice in the presentation of tabulated data.

The series symbols and the class symbols identify the controlling thread standard and define the details of thread design, dimensions and tolerances not specifically covered on the drawing. Series, class, and dimensional letters in a thread designation have the significance shown in Tables 1, 2, and 3 as follows:

A   – External, American, Aeronautical
B   – Internal
C   – Coupling, Coarse, or Centralizing
Cl – Chlorine
EXT – External
EF – Extra fine
F   – Fine, Fuel and Oil
G   – General purpose, gas, pitch allowance
H   – Hose
I   – Intermediate
INT – Internal
J   – Controlled Radius Root
L   – Lead, Locknut
LE – Length of Engagement
LH – Left Hand (absence of LH indicates RH)
M   – Metric, Mechanical, Microscope, Miniature
MOD – Modified
N   – National
O   – Outlet, Objective
P   – Pipe, Pitch
R   – Railing, Rounded Root, American National Class 1 allowance
RH – Right Hand
S   – Straight
SE – Special Engagement
SPL – Special
T   – Taper
UN – Unified

The method of thread fabrication is normally not stated on the drawing, but may be controlled by a specification referenced on a drawing. Otherwise, where a particular processing is required, it should be covered by a separate note.

If required, thread chamfers or countersinks should also be specified on the drawing. Further detail concerning hole size, chamfers, and countersinks is covered under dimensioning of screw threads. See 6.3.

In dimensioning a screw thread, dual dimensioning using decimal inch and metric units may be required in certain screw thread callouts. Rules for dual dimensioning are specified in the American National Standard for Drawing and Related

Documentation Practices – Dimensioning and Tolerancing, Y14.5-1973. Modifications should be in inches followed by millimeters in parentheses.

The hole size of internal threads before tapping is limited by the maximum and minimum minor diameters specified in the controlling thread standard. It is frequently advisable, however, for engineering or production reasons to restrict the hole size to a limited range of the tolerance afforded by the minor diameter limits. In such instances, the threads shall be considered as modified and the hole size limits should be specified on the drawing. For such cases it is not necessary to include "Modified" (MOD) after the designation.
Example:

.161-.164 DIA BEFORE THD
.190-32 UNF-2B

Note

Standard minor diameter is normally .156-.164

Designation of Left-Hand Threads. Unless otherwise specified, threads are right-hand. A left-hand thread shall be designated LH.
Example:

.250-20 UNC-2A-LH

Designation of Threads Having a Special Length of Engagement (LE). Where standard series and special threads have an increased length of engagement over that for which the standard pitch diameter tolerances are applicable, as indicated in ANSI B1.2-1974 Appendix B, the thread class symbol is qualified by the addition of the letters SE (Special Engagement) preceding the class symbol to indicate increased length of engagement and tolerance. The specification of the pitch diameter limits of size and the length of engagement (LE) are a requirement for guidance in selection of proper GO gage length.
Examples:

.500-13 UNC-SE2A
PD .4435-.4475
MINOR DIA .4041 MAX
LE 1.00

.250-24 UNS-SE2A
MAJOR DIA .2417-.2489
PD .2172-.2218
MINOR DIA .1978 MAX
LE .88

Designation of Threads Having Modified Crests. It is occasionally necessary to modify the limits of size of the major diameter of an external thread or the minor diameter of an internal thread. The modification is specified within the maximum material limits established for standard series and special threads in order to fit a specific purpose but without change in class of thread or pitch diameter limits. Such threads should be specified with the established thread designation and a statement of the modified diameter limits followed by the designation MOD. This practice applies to modifying the minor diameter limits of size of internal threads.
Examples:

    .375-24 UNF-3A MOD
    MAJOR DIA .3648-.3720 MOD

    1.500-10 UNS-2B MOD
    MINOR DIA 1.398-1.408 MOD
    PD 1.4350-1.4412
    MAJOR DIA 1.5000 MIN

Designation of Special UNS Threads (Unified Tolerance Formulation). UNS (special) threads have the basic designation except supplemented by the required special limits of size.
Examples:

    .250-24 UNS-2A
    MAJOR DIA 2417-.2489
    PD .2181-.2218
    MINOR DIA .1978 MAX

    .500-12 UNS-3A
    MAJOR DIA .4886-.5000
    PD.4419-.4459
    MINOR DIA .3978 MAX

    1.250-10 UNS-2B
    MINOR DIA 1.142-1.163
    PD 1.1850-1.1932
    MAJOR DIA 1.2500 MIN

Designation of Threads Otherwise Altered (Tolerances Not to Unified Formulation). Where standard series and special threads are altered in any respect other than a revised pitch diameter for a special length of engagement, the modification of crests, or the adjustment of the limits of size to accommodate a coating is designated.
Examples:

    .4375-24 UNIFIED FORM SPL-EXT[5]
    MAJOR DIA .4280-.4340
    PD .4025-.4065
    MINOR DIA .3853 MAX
    LE .38

    .500-13 UNIFIED FORM SPL-INT[5]
    MINOR DIA .4167-.4284
    PD .4500-.4580
    MAJOR DIA .5000 MIN
    LE .50

Designation of Multiple-Start Threads. If a thread is required with a multiple start, it is designated by specifying in sequence the nominal size, pitch (P) in decimals, the lead (L) in decimals, the number of starts in parentheses, and the series symbol.
Example:

    .750-.0625P-.1875L-(3START)-
    UNIFIED FORM SPL-EXT[5]
    MAJOR DIA .7391-.7485
    PD .7003-.7079
    MINOR DIA .6733 MAX
    LE .75

Designation of Special Form Threads. If a thread for design consideration required a deviation from Unified Standard thread contour such as when the detail of the root differs from that for the standard thread form, and is not covered by another recognized standard, the designation shall not include the letters UN nor the word UNIFIED.
Example:

    .875-18 SPL 60° FORM-EXT[5]
    MAJOR DIA .8668-.8750
    PD .8343-.8384
    MINOR DIA .8068 MAX
    LE .69

Designation of Unified Miniature Screw Threads (UNM). Dimensional data for Unified Miniature threads is tabulated in American National Standard for Unified Miniature Screw Threads, B1.10-1958 (ISO 68 and 261). Such threads shall be specified using the basic designation consisting of the nominal size expressed in hundredths of a millimeter followed by the thread series symbol and may include the decimal inch equivalent in parentheses.
Example:

    .80UNM (.0315 IN.)

---

[5] Where the thread designation is used in the text, or where it is shown on a drawing but the leader line does not clearly indicate the specific position, EXT or INT should be added to the designation.

INDEX